They Left Great Marks on Me

They Left Great Marks on Me

African American Testimonies of Racial Violence from Emancipation to World War I

Kidada E. Williams

NEW YORK UNIVERSITY PRESS
New York and London

NEW YORK UNIVERSITY PRESS
New York and London
www.nyupress.org

Library of Congress Cataloging-in-Publication Data

Williams, Kidada E.
They left great marks on me : African American testimonies of racial violence from emancipation to World War I / Kidada E. Williams.
p. cm.
Includes bibliographical references and index.
ISBN 978-0-8147-9535-4 (cl : alk. paper)
ISBN 978-0-8147-9536-1 (pb : alk. paper)
ISBN 978-0-8147-9537-8 (ebook)
ISBN 978-0-8147-8486-0 (ebook)
1. African Americans—History—1863-1877. 2. African Americans—History—1877-1964. 3. African Americans—Violence against—History—19th century. 4. African Americans—Violence against—History—20th century. 5. Lynching—United States—History. 6. Racism—United States—History—20th century I. Title.
E185.2.W67 2012
973'.0496073—dc23 2011039379

New York University Press books are printed on acid-free paper, and their binding materials are chosen for strength and durability. We strive to use environmentally responsible suppliers and materials to the greatest extent possible in publishing our books.

Manufactured in the United States of America

c 10 9 8 7 6 5 4 3 2 1
p 10 9 8 7 6 5 4 3 2 1

To my mother, my brother, and the memory of my father

Contents

Acknowledgments

In writing this book I have accumulated more debts than I can repay. I was privileged to receive a great deal of financial and moral support to write this book from family members, friends, colleagues, archivists, and institutions who sustained me throughout the process of researching and writing it. What is most interesting to me is that these people, institutions, and resources came into my life just when I needed them most. After more than a decade of conducting research and writing about this project, I am pleased to finally acknowledge their generous contributions.

I could not have conducted my research and written up my findings without incredible support from the start of my efforts to research this book through its completion. My research took me to the Library of Congress, the National Archives, the Harlan Hatcher Graduate Library at the University of Michigan, the Moorland Spingarn Research Center, and the Schomburg Center for Research on Black Culture. I owe a special debt to the archivists, librarians, and administrative staff members who helped me locate the materials that I needed. As a result of their help, I collected more data than I could possibly use in this book. I also had the good fortune to receive generous financial support from the King-Chavez-Parks Future Faculty Initiative (KCP), the University of Michigan, Wayne State University, and the Ford Foundation.

I received an astonishing amount of support throughout graduate school. I started this project as an M.A. student at Central Michigan University, where I received a two-year KCP fellowship. Being able to devote my energies to researching and writing was a luxury that only a few students in my program enjoyed. The lessons I learned about navigating the academy from Joyce A. Baugh, Susan Conner, Annette K. Davis, Mitchell K. Hall, Timothy D. Hall, Sterling Johnson, John R. Pfeiffer, Patricia Ranft, David Rutherford, Dennis Thavenet, the late Gabriel Chien, and the late Johnny D. Smith have guided me over the years. As a doctoral student in the History Department at the University of Michigan, earning a Rackham Merit Fellowship, the

Dean/Mellon Candidacy Fellowship, the Rackham Predoctoral Fellowship, and a Department of History summer research grant allowed me to travel to conduct my research and to write. I also had the great fortune to receive a one-year Ford Foundation Dissertation Fellowship, which not only financed a year of study but also introduced me to a whole new world of scholar-activism and fellowship with such scholars as Michelle Scott, Leslie Alexander, and Ula Taylor. While at Michigan, I had the amazing honor to work with Michele Mitchell, Matthew Countryman, Hannah Rosen, Sandra Gunning, Earl Lewis, Elsa Barkley Brown, and Julius Scott III. I can only hope that this book meets their expectations of my work and me. Finally, I am deeply appreciative of the immeasurable support I received from Lorna Altstettar, Chandra D. Bhimull, Pervis Brown, Sherri Harper Charleston, Sheila Coley, Gail J. Drakes, Kevin K. Gaines, Nsenga Lee Johansson, Martha Jones, Michelle Craig Mcdonald, Shani Mott, Moses Ochonu, Nicole Stanton, Penny Von Eschen, Tamara J. Walker, Stacy L. Washington, Shawan Worsely, and Tamara V. Young. Toward the end of my graduate education, I received a wonderful one-year position at the University of Oregon, where tremendous support and encouragement came from Martina Armstrong, Ellen Herman, Dayo N. Mitchell, Jeff Ostler, Martin Summers, Quintard Taylor, and the late Peggy Pascoe.

My good fortune continued after I completed my studies. I received a Ford Foundation Postdoctoral Fellowship, which gave me time to write and continued the support of the coterie of amazing Ford Fellows. I also earned a residency research fellowship from the University of Michigan's Eisenberg Institute for Historical Studies, which allowed me to develop my thinking and writing about violence and trauma by participating in the "Topographies of Violence" series, whose guests included Timothy Tyson, Nikhil Pal Singh, and Isabel Hull. Kathleen Canning, Shannon Rolston, the other fellows, and the graduate students and faculty from the University of Michigan provided a warm and supportive environment. Detroit's proximity to Ann Arbor has allowed me to maintain close relationships and broaden my intellectual development by participating in two of Michigan's vibrant working groups. The first is the Institute for Research on Women and Gender's Gender, Race, and History group. Hannah Rosen developed this group, which has furthered my thinking on gender-based violence. The second is the Department of Afroamerican and African Studies and the Department of History's Long Civil Rights Movement group. Angela Dillard, Matthew Countryman, and Matt Lassiter developed this group, which has enriched my thinking on social movements and civil rights.

My colleagues at Wayne State University have encouraged me and supported my efforts to complete this book. I owe special thanks to Marc W. Kruman, Lisa Ze Winters, Liette Gidlow, Elizabeth Faue, Fay Martin, Denver Brunsman, Danielle McGuire, Sandra Van Burkeleo, Hans Hummer, Jorge Chinea, Ginny Corbin, Gayle McCreedy, and Walter Edwards. Students in my lynching seminars helped me read deeper into the literature on racial violence and helped me work through theories related to violence and resistance to it. My undergraduates helped me think more specifically about making this book accessible to a diverse audience. Thanks as well to Beth Fowler, who has been patient and supportive as my work finishing this book has taken away from my advising and mentoring her. I owe an enormous debt of gratitude to two groups of writers at WSU. James Buccellato, Janine Lanza, Aaron Retish, and Carla Vecchiola helped me think through the book's revisions, write up my proposal, apply for grants, and start article-length projects. Indeed, our weekly writing boot camp sessions helped me learn to achieve a balance of writing while teaching. Lisa Ze Winters, Carla Vecchiola, and Lara L. Cohen provided writing support and daily accountability that helped me develop a habit for writing that I hope will sustain me over the span of my career.

While conducting my research and presenting my findings, I have had the pleasure to meet, speak to, and work with scholars whose work has informed and shaped mine. The 2002 "Lynching and Racial Violence in America" conference at Emory University gave me the opportunity to meet such specialists as W. Fitzhugh Brundage, Elsa Barkley Brown, and Leslie Harris, whose work on racial violence I had admired, and such rising scholars as William D. Carrigan, Koritha A. Mitchell, Crystal N. Feimster, and Bruce E. Baker, whose work is transforming knowledge about violence and resistance to it. On the conference circuit and the job market I also met scholars who took an interest in this book or in me. They include Sundiata Cha-Jua, Claude Clegg, Marcus S. Cox, Bobby J. Donaldson, Lisa Lindquist Dorr, Allison Dorsey, Jacquelyn Dowd Hall, Shannon King, Charles Lumpkin, Kate Masur, Gregory Mixon, Khalil G. Muhammad, Mark R. Shultz, Amy L. Wood, and Nan Woodruff. Bill, Gregory, Nan, and Koritha read earlier drafts of the manuscript and provided incisive critiques, while others shared insight at conferences.

I consider myself very fortunate to be publishing with NYU Press and to work with a group of people who were very enthusiastic about this project and who provided me with invaluable advice and support. Deborah Gershenowitz and Gabrielle Begue saw the promise of this book from the day I shared parts of it with them. Deborah provided insightful readings and encouraged me to bring out victims' and witnesses' testimonies of violence. Gabrielle and Constance Grady helped to calm my nerves by handling the minute details of publication while keeping me apprised of developments along the way. I also am deeply grateful to the anonymous readers for their careful readings of the manuscript and thoughtful and very specific comments on it. I believe that the book is stronger for their suggestions that I refine and clarify my arguments about African Americans' strategies for testifying to federal officials and that I sweat the big and the small stuff. Lastly, I am deeply appreciative of the time and energy that Despina Papazoglou Gimbel put into managing the editing and production of the manuscript and that Andrew Katz put into improving the manuscript by helping me to express my ideas in ways that I hope are more clear, elegant, and persuasive.

Finally, I wish to thank the members of my immediate and extended family, a combination of people who understand the challenges of the academy and those who do not but who stood by me and gave me the love, support, and the occasional "Come to Jesus" conversations that I needed to complete this project. Joann Anderson Johnson, one of my closest friends, has been a cheerleader. Sherry L. McKinley, the sister I never had, has helped me through difficult life moments by providing belly-aching laughter and inspiration when I needed it the most. Patricia Ranft has served as an inspiration and role model for developing a long and successful career. Tracy Collins, Koritha A. Mitchell, and Lisa Winters not only read parts of the project and provided precise and sharp feedback but also let me vent my frustrations before telling me to get back to work. Erinn Foley, Roderick Price, Pamela Taylor, Xanda D. Tonge, and Tamara V. Young provided vital moral support at critical points when my energy and enthusiasm for this project waned. Maxine Fitzpatrick and Ethan and Lois Dunbar opened their homes to me while I was conducting research and writing, while my aunts, uncles, and cousins monitored my progress and provided constant encouragement. Parker has taught me about being patient, living in the moment, and the importance of making time to play. My mother, Janet, and my brother, Danny, gave me an invaluable gift when they gave me unconditional love and supported a career path that was unfamiliar to them.

Introduction

"They broke me teetotally up. I left my things and they would not allow me to go back there, and I had to slip back and get my wife and children the best I could. They took everything I had, and all my wife had, and broke us teetotally up. I had to come away with nothing." This was the proclamation that James Hicks, a formerly enslaved man of Caledonia, Mississippi, made to the Joint Select Committee of the Forty-First Congress that was investigating the "Affairs of the Late Insurrectionary States" in 1871–1872.[1] Hicks was one of several million emancipated Americans living throughout the former slaveholding states who were working to establish authority and autonomy over their lives, which they believed was essential to their fate as a liberated people. For Hicks this meant reuniting family members separated by slave sales and the Civil War; establishing an independent household and acting as its head; negotiating a contract with a planter named Bill Darden that included land to farm, shelter, seeds, and farm equipment; voting in elections; harvesting his share of the crop; providing for his family's well being; and working with other blacks to establish institutions that were independent of white people's influence.

Hicks accomplished a number of the goals that African Americans had for life after slavery, until he ran afoul of Darden in a series of disputes in 1870. Hicks believed that Darden was trying to steal his crop by driving him from the land that he and his family worked before they harvested it. Hicks knew that he had produced the crop in accordance with the terms of his contract and that he was entitled to his share of its yield, so he had no reason to accede to Darden's efforts to steal the crop he produced. Besides, he knew that surrendering his crop and the property he rented would mean financial hardship for his family and undermine his hard-won advances beyond slavery. Therefore, instead of deferring to Darden's perceived authority over him, Hicks rebutted the man's claims to his crop. It was this defiance that prompted the white man to shoot at Hicks in an attempt to achieve what threats could not.[2]

Understanding that his life and that of his family would be in danger unless Darden possessed his crop or surrendered his demand for it, Hicks fled, believing that his absence might give the man time to calm down. In Hicks's absence, a gang of white men descended on his home, terrorized his family, destroyed his property, and threatened to kill him if he returned. Rather than remain on the land and endure continued threats to his life, Hicks returned to collect his wife and children and whatever belongings they could carry. Hicks and his family attempted to start anew in Lowndes County, Mississippi. Yet starting over without the money that Hicks might have gained had he been able to sell the crop he had produced was difficult. Moreover, a gang, presumably men who were angry over his defiance of Darden and their inability to punish Hicks, followed him to his new residence, donned disguises, and whipped him, which left Hicks incapacitated for several weeks. In the end, with the loss of the Hicks family's home, their belongings, their share of the crop, and James's injuries, there was little chance that they would recover from the losses that they sustained.[3]

James Hicks's experience of a degree of socioeconomic success, consequent violence, and resulting physical and psychological injury and dispossession was quite common for black southerners after slavery ended. What makes his experience stand out, however, is that he resisted the violence he and his family experienced by putting his account of what happened and his assessment of its impact on him and his family into the public record. Hicks did this in 1871, when he joined dozens of black people from across the South in testifying before members of the congressional committee about the violence they endured and witnessed. In these and other African Americans' efforts to advance beyond slavery, they collided with whites who insisted on maintaining the antebellum status quo of white supremacy and black subjugation. Southern whites used a variety of strategies for subjugating blacks, or bringing them under white people's control, that ranged from threats to murder. Black people who overtly resisted white supremacy risked the most violent repercussions.

As the testimonies of people like Hicks indicate, blacks wanted to strike back at their attackers; however, many of them understood the futility of such action given the monopoly of force enjoyed by white people and the limits of their power as a racially subjugated people. Indeed, African Americans' appreciation for the constraints on their agency comes through in the language victims and witnesses used to explain their action or inaction in the context of violent attacks.[4] For example, when a congressman asked Hicks why he did not defend himself and his crop against Darden's attack, Hicks explained, "I didn't do nothing. I didn't have nothing; I had my axe, too, but then I didn't want to—I knew I wouldn't—I oughtn't to hit him; at least I felt like if I hit him I would not be doing right, or, at least, I should not be protected in any way." With this statement, Hicks testified about his understanding of his positionality in the postbellum South—he wanted to defend himself and his property, but he knew that if he did, then Darden would be able to retaliate by killing him, driving his family off their land, and rendering the family destitute. Moreover, Hicks explained, "The majority of white people would punish me in some way or other, and for that reason I never hit him. I didn't want no fuss if I could get round him, and so I never did anything to him."[5]

The layers of African Americans' shared experiences of racial violence that had accumulated across slavery, the Civil War, and freedom had shown people like Hicks that if black people resisted white supremacy, then whites could use violence with probable immunity from prosecution. Until well into the twentieth century, white southerners who attacked or killed black people were rarely prosecuted because of the white community's tolerance of violence, in defiance of existing laws and procedures, to protect white power. As Christopher Waldrep argues, white southerners supported what he calls "popular constitutionalism," the idea that the Constitution supported local whites' right to decide what was right and wrong in their communities and which crimes could be punished outside the formal rule of law. Thus, violence to subjugate black people enjoyed support in many towns and cities across the country.[6] African Americans understood this, to be sure. In fact it is their conveyance of an intersubjectivity, a sense of themselves as subjugated people in relation to racial violence, to perpetrators, and to a nation that accepted white supremacy, that explains why blacks might have felt constrained during attacks by armed white men but, after the violence ended, also felt compelled to testify about it. These victims' and witnesses' subsequent refusal to endure violence silently constitutes an underappreciated form of resistance to white supremacy.

They Left Great Marks on Me weaves together the testimonies of people like James Hicks with a diverse selection of print culture to show how black people's sharing their experiences of racial violence informed their participation in and support of formal campaigns against racial subjugation. Many of the victims' and witnesses' stories explored herein are those of black folk, "ordinary people," who many scholars believed left few records detailing their experiences because many of them were illiterate. And into that void of black folks' seeming silence about the violence they endured have flown more assumptions about what it was like to experience violence or bear witness to someone experiencing violence than knowledge gained from scholarly examination. These people did create and leave records of racial violence. However, they produced these accounts of their experiences in ways that made sense to them, which was often in collaboration with family members, friends, neighbors, civil authorities, journalists, state and federal officials, and members of civil rights organizations. Consequently, this book presents a historical record of racial violence that victims and witnesses narrated from emancipation through the establishment of the NAACP's antilynching crusade.[7]

In highlighting African Americans' testimonies about violence, this book fashions an alternative to existing understandings of racial violence in the postemancipation era and of black people's mobilization to advance civil rights reforms. Though historians have explored records documenting African Americans' experiences of racial violence, their use of victims' and witnesses' testimonies to illustrate this violence leaves many unanswered questions about the effects of violence on blacks and about how some of them channeled the traumatic wounds they endured into orchestrated political action. Indeed, scholars who initially examined accounts of racial violence in the Freedmen's Bureau Records, the Joint Select Committee investigating the Klan, and ex-slave narratives often did so to correct Americans' historical amnesia on this violence, to prove that violence occurred, or to argue that black people resisted this violence.[8] Unlike those researchers who vigorously examine slave narratives and ex-slave narratives or the memoirs and public statements of civil rights crusaders of the 1950s and 1960s, scholars of racial violence and the earlier phases of African Americans' civil rights activism have not explored victims' and witnesses' testimonies of violence with the same verve.[9] Assuming silences where none existed, historians have missed opportunities to reveal who blacks thought they were as a people in direct relation to the violence that they and their family members, friends, and neighbors endured and how this aided African Americans' mobilization against violence.

This near silence in the scholarly literature on African Americans' specific representations of the impact of violence on them is unfortunate because blacks who testified about their experiences of racial violence were an exceptional class of people who had to overcome great odds to have their testimonies entered into the public record. These women, men, and children endured and witnessed some of the most violent desecrations of the social compact established by Reconstruction: that blacks and whites would coexist without slavery. They are exceptional because these people surmounted many victims' instinctive desires to banish memories of horrific events, which for black people in the postemancipation South ranged from the daily attacks on their bodies, psyches, and homes to the terrors of nightriding, lynching, massacring, and rioting. Regardless of the form violence took, it was a weapon that white Americans used to deny African Americans the opportunity to enjoy their citizenship rights. Violent whites achieved some success in their efforts to subjugate African Americans. Like survivors of other human atrocities, some black people subjected to racial violence were too traumatized and therefore psychologically incapable of bearing witness to what happened to them and relating it to others. In fact, scholarship on trauma suggests that even those who were able to relive traumatic events often did not want to relate their experiences to others for fear that they would be attacked or that listeners would not believe them. In this respect, suppressing memories or refusing to speak about violence is an understandable form of self-preservation and self-protection. Yet the existence of testimonies by people like James Hicks shows that some blacks either could not or would not suppress their memories and decided first to relive their experiences and then to find the words to explain to others what happened to them or to people they knew.[10]

Testifiers about racial violence faced additional challenges. They also had to prevail over environments made hostile by their unrepentant attackers running free in their communities, by unsympathetic law enforcement officers, by white patrons, and by state and federal officials who did not want to hear African Americans' stories of violent attacks. The actions of people who testified under these conditions suggest that some felt what Mary Prince described in her account of slavery as a "duty to relate" the horrors of their suffering to people who, to paraphrase Prince, did not know what victims and witnesses knew about this violence and who did not feel what victims and witnesses felt about it. Hence, black people's bold decisions to risk their lives and their credibility and to recover their agency and resist violence by proclaiming their trauma to strangers was essential to their mobilization against white supremacy.[11]

Testifying about racial violence was a crucial factor in African Americans' individual recovery and their collective resistance to white supremacy because whenever victims related their experiences of this violence, they created witnesses to their trauma. Family members, friends, and neighbors were the first people that victims made bear witness to suffering they endured or witnessed. A select few victims and witnesses took advantage of forums sponsored by federal officials, journalists, and civil rights organizations to report violence. For example, from 1865 to 1869, testifiers made thousands of complaints and gave hundreds of affidavits to U.S. Army officials and to Freedmen's Bureau agents stationed at federal satellites across the South. Officials recorded these statements word for word or offered their own perspectives on what transpired and shared their own observations and opinions of this violence in their reports to the military's and the Freedmen's Bureau's upper echelon. Additionally, progressive members of Congress joined the executive branch's efforts to record and suppress violence by calling for investigations into the Klan insurgency (1868–1871), political violence (1878), and the Exoduster movement (1879–1880). Dozens of victims and witnesses testified at these congressional hearings. These African Americans detailed the horror, shock, regret, and shame of enduring and witnessing this violence, the transcripts of which provide rich detail on their reflections on violence. Moreover, in the late 1880s, when federal officials stopped providing forums for black people to relate their suffering, some blacks made opportunities to provide evidence of their victimization at the hands of whites by writing letters, protesting public policies, publishing newspaper reports, and establishing and joining organizations to challenge violence.

When African Americans decided to testify about experiencing or witnessing racial violence, they were not merely giving statements; they were resisting violence discursively, engaging in what Shoshana Felman and Dori Laub describe as calculated "speech acts."[12] In fact, black people's proclaiming their traumatic experiences to family members, friends, neighbors, civil authorities, civil rights organizations, and state and federal officials represents an unappreciated form of their direct-action protests against racial violence.[13] When interpreted this way, Hicks's characterization of the white men breaking his family "teetotally up" suggests that he felt and wanted members of Congress and the American people to know that the life he and his family attempted to re-create after the raids on their home was not, and might never again be, as strong as it had been before the attacks. Accordingly, when testifiers made family members, friends, civil authorities, activists, or state and federal officials bear witness to their experiences of violence, they attempted to turn these people into witnesses or what Laub calls "co-owners of the traumatic event" they endured. Co-owners of trauma are people who, through their willingness to hear testimonies of violence, "partially experience" the fear, "bewilderment, injury, confusion, dread, and conflict" felt by actual victims. Thus, blacks who testified about racial violence hoped that they could make sure other people bore witness to their suffering and that understanding what had happened to them would motivate these people to identify with victims and support reforms to end violence and to punish known perpetrators. In that way, making white citizens and elected officials bear witness to black people's suffering from racial violence was a critical part of African Americans' efforts to recruit allies to their campaigns to end violence and advance civil rights reform.[14]

They Left Great Marks on Me recasts the history of African Americans' resistance to white supremacy by bringing back into view the women, men, and children who personally endured and witnessed racial violence and by highlighting the significance of their bold decisions to testify about the horrors of their experiences. African Americans' oral and written testimonies reveal victims' and witnesses' unique perspectives on having their lives transformed by violence and their desire to get justice by making other people hear and understand their suffering. For example, Mary Brown testified at the Joint Select Committee hearings that a gang of white men invaded her family's Georgia home and dragged them out into the yard, where they stripped and whipped them. In explaining, "they left great marks on me," Brown described the physical injuries she sustained when nightriders whipped her. However, when read against the testimonies of other victims and witnesses and through the lexicon of suffering and trauma that racial violence produced among black people, the larger implications of Brown's proclamations about what happened to her and to her family becomes clear.[15]

Juxtaposing African Americans' testimonies temporally and geographically reveals striking similarities in the language that victims and witnesses used to describe violent attacks. Though the contexts of racial violence varied by situation, these testimonies indicate that black people who endured or witnessed the extraordinary violence of rape, domestic captivity, attempted and successful lynchings, riots, or massacres went through what Michael Taussig calls the "space of death," experiences of terror-induced peril in which people face the uncertainty of surviving. Survivors of this violence conveyed that they were traumatized, *marked* physically, economically, socially, and psychologically by their experiences. In fact, many testifiers narrated their lives before, during, and after violence, suggesting that violent attacks became what Sasanka Perera labels critical "temporal markers" in the lives of victims and witnesses. In testifying to family members, friends, and neighbors, to law enforcement officers, Freedmen's Bureau agents, members of Congress, black northerners, elected and appointed officials, and to civil rights organizations, people like James Hicks and Mary Brown tried to explicate the traumatic marks they endured as part of their pursuit of justice for themselves and their loved ones.[16]

Testifiers' shared stories of traumatic injury cultivated intersubjectivity among African Americans and allowed them to create what Edward Baptist calls a "vernacular history" of racial violence. This vernacular history is "a narrative about the past constructed by laypeople in their everyday tongue . . . [that shows] who a people thought they were and how they got to be that way."[17] Testifying was the primary way that many black victims and witnesses resisted violence and thereby communicated who they thought they were in relation to the traumatic injuries they endured. Indeed, African Americans' experiences of racial violence informed their development of a rich, complex, and original public record of their lives after slavery. It is this narrative of triumph over the adversity of slavery and subsequent racial discrimination, violent suffering, and consequent survival that motivated blacks to mobilize against racial injustice and to demand that the country live up to its democratic principles by rejecting violence and advancing civil rights reform.

Testifiers generated this historical record of racial violence by providing oral and written testimonies of their experiences. African Americans continued to embrace a rich oral tradition after slavery, so more people spoke about their experiences than wrote about them. Many people who testified about violence often did so to familiars—family members, friends, and sympathetic whites—because they were worried about reprisals and because they did not trust strangers to believe, understand, or care what happened to them. There are only faint traces of these private discussions in the historical record. However, when victims and witnesses narrated their experiences and observations to outsiders—law enforcement officials, judges, legislators, state or federal officials, journalists, and civil rights activists—the grooves of black people's individual and collective experiences of violence are deeper and more easily traced historically. The decisions by some state and federal officials and civil rights activists to provide forums and opportunities for victims and witnesses to testify about violent attacks opened a discursive space for blacks to proclaim the violence they endured and witnessed. State and federal officials and these civil rights activists transcribed victims' and witnesses' testimonies or preserved them and then turned these records into the public transcripts of American history.[18] Additionally, black public figures contributed to this history by documenting violence and its impact on black people in private correspondence and newspaper reports, and they resisted this violence by writing editorials and speeches and by developing creative projects.[19] Likewise, literate black folk wrote about violence in their personal correspondence, and as literacy rates among blacks improved, more people authored their personal experiences, which they shared with federal officials and civil rights activists. Together these sources reveal African Americans' notions about who they were, as a people, in relation to the violence they endured and witnessed and the origins of their efforts to mobilize against violence.

Racial violence and the threat of it were key features in the postemancipation lives of black southerners, so it should come as no surprise that African Americans understood and discussed how it shaped them as a people.[20] Testifiers' accounts of lives breached by violence not only reveal that individuals endured violence; they also show that in the process of telling their stories some victims and witnesses often added the voices of others. These people supplemented their stories with those of others by layering stories of violence on other stories, authenticating their own narratives with the stories of others for skeptics and testifying on behalf of people who could not or would not testify. In listening to the stories of others and in sharing individual experiences, weaving the stories of family members, friends, and neighbors into their own, victims and witnesses created what Robert Stepto calls an "integrated narrative," a vernacular history of a people whose lives were transformed by violence.[21] What emerges from these testimonies is a transcript of violence, terror, and suffering that later campaigns against racial violence suggest became embedded into the social memory of black people. On the whole, the discursive processes by which blacks and their allies fashioned individual histories into one narrative fostered community and calcified African Americans' social and political links across time, space, and social status that formed the base of what became their collective effort to end racial violence.

When African Americans testified about this violence to Freedmen's Bureau agents and before members of Congress, when they wrote letters to federal officials and the NAACP, and when they published accounts of violence and used their creative talent to educate Americans about violence, they spoke as an afflicted community. Indeed, the language of African Americans' solidarity regarding racial violence and their eventual mobilization against it are testaments to the effectiveness of victims' and witnesses' efforts to make others experience violence vicariously through their testimonies. When testifiers spoke with a collective voice, they attempted to make sure that their fellow citizens as well as elected and appointed officials knew that the horrors black people endured were not limited to individualized physical pain. Victims and witnesses wanted listeners to know that what gave racial violence lasting meaning over African Americans' lives were the violent assaults on their bodies, psyches, dignities, families, homes, livelihoods, and communities. In other words, it was black people's understandings of the true costs of violence and their desire to achieve justice that made them testify and develop their own histories of the postemancipation era. Blacks carried these histories with them across time and space; they passed them on horizontally to their peers and relatives and vertically to subsequent generations. In this way, testifying helped black southerners and their northern and western counterparts understand what Dwight McBride calls their "collective corporeal condition" with respect to violence. Victims' and witnesses' finding their individual voices on violence allowed them to find "a voice in community with other voices" and to create a history of the "collective black body" as being under assault. This knowledge and shared traumatic history helped galvanize blacks and progressive whites to form a movement designed to end racial violence and other forms of racial discrimination.[22]

As this book shows, it was victims' and witnesses' stories about the traumatic impact of violence on individuals, families, and communities that, combined with the emergence of an environment that was receptive to reform, inspired African Americans to mobilize against the violence during the Progressive Era. In this manner, testifying about and against racial violence was a "consciousness-raising" process among blacks and their white allies that constituted what Lisa Gring-Pemble calls the "pre-genesis" phase of social movement formation. This activity, along with creating and making political opportunities to advance reform, ushered in the institutionalized activism of the early civil rights era that eventually yielded extensive legislative and judicial reforms.[23] Thus, black people's mobilization against racial violence started with testifying and congealed in the NAACP's antilynching crusade, which James Weldon Johnson described as the "first organized, systematic, persistent and financed effort" to end lynching.[24] This campaign helped move African Americans' suffering from closed conversations among black people back into the dominant public spheres where victims and witnesses stood a better chance of getting redress for their grievances as citizens from the federal government and from the American people. The reform movement against racial violence served as a political training ground for activists who went on to participate in civil rights reform. To illuminate one underappreciated dimension of black southerners' Sisyphean aspirations to rise above slavery and black northerners' and westerners' efforts to help them, this book explores the oral and written precursors to the establishment of an ambitious reform movement that helped activists to push for revolutionary reforms and to use African Americans' experiences of violence to achieve them.

The chapters that follow chart African Americans' testimonies about violence and their efforts to mobilize against it from emancipation through the establishment of the NAACP's antilynching campaign. The order is roughly chronological but becomes more thematic after 1900, when the chapters explore similar events in African Americans' mobilization during the First World War from different angles. Each chapter illuminates the historical contexts that informed white southerners' physical attacks on black people, victims' and witnesses' testimonies about their experiences, and the challenges blacks faced in advancing and eliciting political support to end violence. Through the prism of trauma theory and social movement theory, we see how blacks channeled the horrors they endured into a reform movement designed to end violence.[25]

After slavery, African Americans prioritized laying down the bricks and mortar of their freedom with the help of progressive Republicans who crafted policies to bestow sociopolitical power on black people so that they could protect their freedom. However, white southerners, who were outraged by Reconstruction policies that constrained their racial power over black people, responded by using violence to destroy the foundation of freedom. Using victims' and witnesses' complaints about violence to Freedmen's Bureau officials and their testimonies before Congress as a compass for charting the course toward the institutionalized crusade against racial violence, chapter 1 illuminates the violence blacks endured and presents the vernacular history victims and witnesses created about white southerners' violent insurgency against emancipation and Reconstruction and its impact on black people.

African Americans who survived Reconstruction lived through the purgatory of white people's experimentation with new frameworks for subjugating black people during the Gilded Age. Black people dealt with violence, segregation, and disfranchisement by testifying about ongoing racial violence, by migrating, and by attempting to retain the rights that they gained under Reconstruction. Chapter 2 shows how the absence of a sense of national urgency, the embryonic state of black institution building, the inexpert black national leadership, and federal officials' growing disinterest in providing forums for victims and witnesses to testify about violence all hindered African American activists' efforts to mount a reform movement that would inspire federal officials to intervene and halt the corrosion of black southerners' rights and the violence used to achieve that result.

African Americans' testimonies in the 1890s about racial violence indicate a growing appreciation for what W. E. B. Du Bois called a "descent to hell" regarding white supremacy and the ongoing deterioration of black people's rights. Chapter 3 shows how black public figures during this period used their political influence and their status, as representatives of black folk, to try to seize control of Americans' knowledge and understanding of racial violence and other forms of racial discrimination. They projected black folks' testimonies of their experiences of violence into the dominant public spheres. These activists wielded print culture to publish the vernacular history of black people's experiences of the changing dynamics of racial subjugation. Public figures represented African Americans' testimonies of violence, disfranchisement, and segregation as though they constituted a crisis that merited collective action. Their work illuminates the maturation of African Americans' efforts to build institutions to fight racial violence and to get support for civil rights reform from their fellow citizens and federal officials.[26]

Many blacks responded to the erosion of their civil rights by "turning inward" to regroup and address the needs of their local enclaves. Chapter 4 shows how reading reports of racial violence inspired a coterie of "organic intellectuals" from an archipelago of black community spheres to resist violence by penning letters to federal officials. In testifying about violence, these letter writers attempted to use the nation's principles of freedom, democracy, and citizenship to lobby federal officials to address violence. Working together across the nation, these activists constituted some of the foot soldiers in the mounting of a reform movement against violence in the 1910s.[27]

African Americans mobilized against racial violence by marshaling their resources and using all of their political might to launch an aggressive institutionalized campaign under the NAACP for federal legislation against lynching. Chapter 5 shows how testifiers worked with an interracial coalition of progressives to use racial violence to re-present the problems of black people and to elicit support for federal antilynching legislation. Victims and witnesses wrote letters to NAACP leaders in which they testified about the violence they endured and witnessed. In using written correspondence to testify about violence, these women and men helped turn nonsouthern activists into co-owners of the trauma of violence, which inspired the NAACP to develop an ambitious multiyear campaign to end violence.

They Left Great Marks on Me is not intended to be a definitive history of African Americans' experiences of racial violence or their campaigns against it. Instead, this book fits into a larger and longer conversation that scholars have been having about racial violence and civil rights campaigns. Indeed, I could not have developed this book without the remarkable research on violence and black resistance conducted by my predecessors. In attempting to provide more of what Nell Irvin Painter calls "a fully loaded cost accounting" of African Americans' testimonies about and against racial violence, this book seeks to shift the focus on racial violence from the physicality of the violence or the culture it produced, from the white perpetrators, or even from the well-known black and white activists and organizations that resisted violence, to the victims and witnesses and to their efforts to communicate their suffering as a way of resisting and ending violence.[28]

Understanding how victims and witnesses experienced and represented racial violence is important because in the collective memory of this violence, the white perpetrators, the individuals and institutions who aided their work, and the most prominent activists and organizations who crusaded against violence have taken the center stage of the academic and popular histories of this violence. As such, the actual victims of this violence, people like James Hicks and Mary Brown, have receded into the background. Victims' and witnesses' testimonies of lives transformed by violence and the aspects of violence that mattered the most to them rarely get the scholarly attention that they deserve. This has happened because scholars have inadvertently rendered all but a few victims anonymous, secondary subjects in larger narratives that prioritize understanding violence, the perpetrators of violence, and their apologists or institutionalized and armed resistance to it. Consciously or unconsciously, intentionally or not, historians and sociologists have not wanted to shift their attention away from the arguments they are trying to make about the motives of perpetrators and their apologists, the forms violence took, the rhetoric of violence, the roles of activists and institutions resisting this violence, or the imprint this violence left on American culture or collective social memory. Thus, many avoid victims' and witnesses' representations of suffering, moving back and forth between showing when, where, why, and how this violence occurred and the different people and institutions that resisted it. In the process of developing what have become the dominant narratives of racial violence in the United States, scholars have failed to expose what lay at the very heart of the violence for blacks, which was terror and trauma and black people's need for justice. In bringing the victims' and witnesses' stories of victimization and their efforts to achieve justice back into view, this book seeks to transform the historical narrative of racial violence and of African Americans' civil rights crusades.

Many decisions I made about this book were informed by my commitment to build on the existing scholarship and my dedication to excavating black victims' and witnesses' representations of this violence and to illuminating their efforts to share those experiences with others in their pursuit of justice and reform, while keeping the book accessible to a diverse audience. Rather than supply the traditional historiography section that would appeal to specialists but repel lay readers, I try to strike a balance by documenting the scholarship on which I have relied so heavily in the notes. I also try to use a few representative incidents and to resist the impulse of cramming in so many cases that they obscure more than they reveal. Moreover, I decided to make passing references to well-known activists and key historical events and to blend them into the larger narrative of racial violence and the institutionalization of responses to it, instead of elaborating extensively on specific antilynching crusaders or race riots that other scholars have covered so well.[29]

Additionally, my understanding of existing scholarship also informed the subjects on which I provide both cursory and lengthy analysis. Numerous scholars have provided comprehensive analyses of the public and legal aspects of the NAACP's formal campaigns to pass federal antilynching legislation and Progressive reform. What remains underexamined is how acts of resistance by black folk, women and men who were unknown to most of the nation and the world, fueled these formal campaigns.[30] I have therefore chosen to prioritize the mostly unpublished dimensions of the NAACP's efforts to learn more about this violence and to use print culture to transmit African Americans' experiences of violence to the nation and to frame their argument about the need for civil rights reform.[31] Lastly, in a book about black people's experiences of racial violence during an era when most whites believed they were racially superior to blacks and accepted violence as a way of maintaining white people's power, there lies the risk of painting all whites with the same brush. Thus, rather than unpack the dynamics of white supremacy, the diversity among white people's beliefs about blacks, or the use of violence to subjugate them, I use some clarifying language and defer to the scholars who have devoted ample time researching and writing about those subjects.[32]

I made the choices I did because I believe that James Hicks and Hannah and Samuel Tutson, who refused to surrender their livelihood; Alfred Blount and Randall McGowan, who insisted on participating in electoral politics; the formidable Mrs. M. Cravath Simpson, who read about racial violence and heard about it from family and friends; and Walter White, who helped spearhead the NAACP's antilynching crusade, were everyday people who did ordinary and extraordinary things to confront and stop this violence. As a result of reading their testimonies, I believe that one of the most important things they did was to testify about the violence they endured and witnessed.

In speaking their truths about what it meant to be a victim of or a witness to racial violence and in telling what only victims and witnesses knew, these women's and men's determination to defy the white power structure inspired them to tap into and pass on African Americans' tradition of resistance to try to remake the nation's legal and social structure. Without their stories, it is impossible to understand the real meaning of racial violence in American history and African Americans' formal campaigns against it. That is why their testimonies and efforts to end violence and advance civil rights reform fill the pages that follow.

1

"The Special Object of Hatred and Persecution"

The Terror of Emancipation

African Americans embraced freedom with hopes befitting centuries of enslavement. After the Civil War they were ready to make their ascent, to rise above the despair of slavery, and to soar with whites on the wings of American freedom and citizenship. Black people snatched opportunities to abandon rural farms and plantations or urban hotels and factories as federal officials adopted policies to institutionalize abolition. Blacks seized control of their lives by fortifying their families, acquiring work, and challenging restrictions on black people's landownership. Indeed, these people acted as such because they understood that secured families, land, satisfactory employment, education, and access to the political spheres were critical to their freedom. Free blacks already benefited from these opportunities, of course, but they were anxious to show their capacity for enjoying the benefits of citizenship that they believed accompanied freedom. Reuniting families, voting, receiving equal justice, testifying in courts, serving on juries, building sociopolitical institutions, and bearing arms ranked high on all African Americans' postemancipation priorities. Thus, with freedom and the promise of citizenship, land, education, and equal rights black people believed they could secure control over their lives and participate fully in American life.

African Americans were free, but their testimonies about emancipation show that freedom, as they envisioned it, was hard to grasp and harder to live in the former slaveholding states. Freedom presented ex-slaves with the mix of a promise of freedom and a daunting challenge: establishing and maintaining the integrity of their families and their communities and institutions. This was difficult because black southerners had to reunite and support their families and build their communities and institutions while they were surrounded by white people who believed and were determined to prove that ending slavery and reconstituting the nation in ways that included black people threatened white people's survival. However intense white people's opposition to freedom and citizenship rights for blacks might have been, it did not stop blacks from trying to enjoy their freedom. As an illustrative example of African Americans' hopes and dreams, black people in a mass meeting in Petersburg, Virginia, produced a resolution to the nation in which they spoke with one voice to make the following point: "We have no feeling of resentment toward our former owners, and we are willing to let the past be buried with the past, and in the future treat all persons with kindness and respect who shall treat us likewise."[1]

White southerners did not share the same feelings, so it is perhaps useful to say a few words about the changes in the white South. After slavery ended, white southerners faced significant challenges that shaped African Americans' ability to enjoy their freedom. For example, planters and industrialists had to work harder for their financial sustainability, and they even had to pay black workers for their labor while attempting to rebuild the wealth that the war and emancipation had destroyed. Additionally, white farmers and aspirant entrepreneurs before the war had to compete with a small free-black population for land, labor, power, and social position. Now, these whites faced the prospects of even greater competition from millions of free black people who were eager to enjoy and invest in the fruits of their labor. Neither the war's outcome nor the federal government's attempts to facilitate African Americans' transition to freedom extinguished what many whites believed was their natural and constitutional right to control black people. Indeed, the privileges of slaveholding, including the authorized use of violence to govern and to make black people submit to subjugation, were such essential features of racial subjugation during slavery that many whites—regardless of their antebellum social status—claimed them in the postemancipation era. These whites often demanded that blacks continue deferring to white people as they had during slavery. When black people refused to comply, the more pugnacious whites attacked. Over time, these whites used the nearly universal resistance of white Americans to equal rights for blacks and their shriveling support for Reconstruction to wrestle from northern and Republican progressives the gears of the policy machine that was restructuring the nation after the war. Rather than attack white progressives, white conservatives regained control of southern affairs via a war of attrition against black people, who became the "special object" of southern whites' fury over emancipation and Reconstruction.[2]

This chapter shows that blacks resisted racial violence by using a variety of strategies, including testifying about it. The history that victims and witnesses created when they testified to Freedmen's Bureau agents, to army officials, and to members of Congress highlights their attempts to realize their dreams for freedom. Testifiers proclaimed black people's social, economic, and political values. These African Americans also testified about the ways that whites, who were determined to protect their racial power, used violence to obliterate blacks' efforts to advance beyond slavery. Testifiers reported that violence started after emancipation and escalated as they started playing a more active role in southern life and politics. On the whole, victims' and witnesses' testimonies proclaim that emancipation violence left blacks sifting through the wreckage of violent attacks and trying to rebuild and to reconcile the differences in their lives before and after the violence. For some people, recovery meant narrating the horrors of racial violence by giving testimonial interviews to Freedmen's Bureau agents and to members of the Joint Select Committee of Congress that investigated the "Affairs of the Late Insurrectionary States." Many victims and witnesses made their stories known by testifying to family members and friends and by taking advantage of federally sponsored opportunities to testify about violent events and the resulting suffering.[3] The process of testifying allowed blacks to develop a vernacular history of racial violence and an intersubjectivity of its impact on black people, and that drove later efforts to end it.

The Ordinary Violence of Emancipation

The violence that white southerners had used to subjugate enslaved and free blacks before and during the Civil War continued and intensified after emancipation. Some federal officials' concerns for the well-being of freedpeople fostered the creation of new legal mechanisms and distinctively public forums that recognized victims' and witnesses' suffering from racial violence and allowed them to testify about it. Sympathetic army generals and progressive Republicans created spaces to investigate and establish a complete picture of postemancipation violence, its nature, causes, and violations of African Americans' rights as free people and as citizens. Among these spaces was the Freedmen's Bureau, which Congress created in 1865 to oversee emancipation and Reconstruction and to provide aid to freedpeople and refugees, and the hearings of the congressional committee investigating Klan violence. Bureau offices and the sites of the congressional hearings were where many victims and witnesses recalled for each other and for federal officials violent attacks and the conditions of lives that were transformed by violence. What is more, emancipation-era addresses, petitions, and memorials also point to black people's willingness to assert their citizenship rights by testifying about violence and by inserting their beliefs and opinions about it into the public spheres. Together these sources reveal the nature of violence that blacks endured and their assessments of its impact on them.[4]

The presence African Americans in Freedmen's Bureau offices and at the congressional hearings and their initiation of discussions about violence through their addresses, petitions, and memorials suggest their appreciation for public forums as opportunities for victims of and witnesses to violence to resume the acts of living by having some official acknowledgment of violence and its impact. This acknowledgment of racial violence and its impact on African Americans had two parts, relating to testifying victims and witnesses and to listening audiences. Veena Das and Arthur Kleinman have written that "the choke and sting of experience only becomes real—is heard—when it is narrativized." Acknowledgment of victims' and witnesses' pain and the role of perpetrators, Das and Kleinman argue, can also "give recognition to the injury or the deaths inflicted on a collective, and also legitimate that collective's quest for repair, revitalization, and healing."[5] Federal officials' willingness to provide spaces for black people to testify about violence served as a formal, albeit undeclared, acknowledgment of the wrongs that some southern whites committed against black people. The significance of having federal officials acknowledge their suffering was not lost on victims and witnesses.

African Americans' testimonies in these settings represented a collective effort on the part of victims and witnesses to create public knowledge about postemancipation violence, to make their audiences bear witness to their suffering, and to explain "who they thought they were" as a people in relation to the violence they endured.[6] Thus, their testimonies provide a ground's-eye view of white people's ordinary assaults on individual blacks and of their extraordinary attacks on families and communities. Their petitions and transcribed testimonies point to the dimensions of violence that mattered most to victims and witnesses—suffering—and form a vernacular history of emancipation that elucidates the way that whites looking to protect white supremacy laid waste to black people's efforts to live and to exercise their rights as free people. In fact, complaints to Freedmen's Bureau agents, testimonies before Congress, and some petitions and memorials highlight the everyday occurrence of violence and some contexts in which violence occurred. These testimonies show how violence created ruptures in African

Americans' paths to full participation in American life. Indeed, victims and witnesses testified about lives and homes torn asunder by violence, because they wanted white citizens and state and federal officials to acknowledge their suffering and to provide a degree of restorative justice.[7]

Slavery created a context for southern cross-racial exchanges in which African Americans' behavior in the interplay of the master-slave relationship was supposed to be deferential to white authority. Confederate defeat, emancipation, and the policies of Reconstruction were supposed to upset this dynamic. Nevertheless, violence often erupted across the former slaveholding states when blacks attempted to act on their freedom and their citizenship. The violence people endured during the first years of emancipation ensnared everyone. It often originated in quotidian disputes, from such matters as wages, land, and reputation to childrearing and such issues as the protection of girls and women from sexual coercion and rape. Political massacres such as those that occurred in 1866 in both Memphis and New Orleans are well known. However, African Americans' testimonies indicate that more common were acts of decentralized and spontaneous nonfatal violence committed by individual whites or small groups of whites who were seeking to punish blacks for failing to defer to their authority.[8]

The vernacular history of emancipation suggests that African Americans took aggressive steps to fortify their freedom by preserving the integrity of their families and by erecting cordons to insulate them from white people's influence and violence. Blacks established independent homes and "homeplaces" as the first line of defense. The family home provided physical space for shelter. Additionally, the homeplace, according to bell hooks, was the atmosphere that African Americans created inside their homes. It was a space where black people could achieve "a certain degree of autonomy and, by extension, power" over their lives and communities. The homeplace was the space where blacks constructed new identities and rebuilt their families and where they could "freely confront the issue of humanization" in the larger context of white supremacy. Therefore, homeplaces were spaces where blacks could "affirm one another, . . . heal many of the wounds inflicted by racist domination." Homes were places where blacks "could resist," reject the "social ideology of white supremacy and black inferiority," and prepare to live as citizens.[9] African Americans also established what Earl Lewis calls "home spheres," the "community, the streets, the neighborhood," the kinship groups of friends and family and shared institutions that surrounded and encompassed black people's homes. Within these enclaves, black people attempted to establish authority and autonomy over their lives and to limit the intrusion of white people's influence that they had had to endure under slavery.[10]

Reading African Americans' complaints to Freedmen's Bureau officials and to members of Congress, as well as ex-slaves' descriptions of the postemancipation era, it becomes clear that many of them modeled their homes, families, and communities on the mainstream white society and established male heads of households so they could claim the sociopolitical capital that infused the privileges of citizenship. Blacks recognized the ways that the challenges of finding satisfactory employment and reestablishing families presented certain obstacles to those who wished to establish homes that were similar to those of whites. Many families made the most out of their circumstances. They produced a wide swath of residences on the land of white farmers and plantation owners, on plots of land black people owned during slavery, and on land they purchased with money raised from sharecropping and wage work as domestics and farm and urban laborers.[11]

African American families worked to meet the demands of freedom by tailoring white people's family and communal dynamics to suit their specific goals and objectives and their distinct circumstances because of slavery. The responsibility of working steadily outside the home to provide economic security and shelter, as well as overseeing the lives of women and children, was seized by and fell primarily to black men, who often worked a series of jobs to provide for their families. For example, Alfred Richardson of Georgia and Joseph Nelson of Florida were carpenters. Skilled men such as these used their trades to generate wealth, while their unskilled counterparts likely took jobs performing field and farm work. Whether men were skilled laborers or not, many of them and their families balanced wage work with subsistence farming. People who generated enough produce, wheat, cotton, or poultry or livestock sold their overflow at the market. For instance, Richardson and his brother turned their skills and surplus cash into wealth and provided a service to their community when they collaborated to establish a grocery store. Charles Pearce was a minister for the African Methodist Episcopal church in Florida. Richard Pousser of Jackson County, Florida, was a constable who also testified that he would "hawk and peddle . . . chicken, eggs, butter, potatoes, beef, and pork" for his family. In all, free and freed black men worked hard to meet the needs of their families.[12]

The status of head of household—which was granted for the first time to emancipated men by Reconstruction—bestowed on all black men the cultural and legal right to control their families and to chart the destiny of their communities. Indeed, progressive proponents of Reconstruction believed that codifying black men's patriarchal authority to control their families' affairs and to make decisions about sexual partners, employment, and property, would help blacks establish self-sufficient families that could participate in American society. Black men acted out their gender roles by embracing the franchise, negotiating contracts and apprenticeships, and working their own land or that of another for profit. Yet, if black men controlled where, how, for whom, and under what circumstances they and their dependents worked, then what would happen to the authority that white men had enjoyed over black people before the war? If black men possessed this control over their lives and their communities, if they could decide where to work and determine the cost of land or crops, if they could control the formation of their families and the gender roles and sexual conventions to be carried out in them, then did that mean that they had the right to defend themselves against whites and to protect their interests? Many white southerners argued no. This authority in the hands of black men constituted a fundamental threat to whites who believed in the superiority of the white race and the need to subordinate blacks to whites in all matters of life.

Postbellum southern whites did not fail to observe and understand the power of African American families, institutions, and communities headed by black men. In fact, most postemancipation racial violence involved whites attacking and killing off the black veterans, politicians, contract negotiators, labor organizers, and aspiring entrepreneurs who insisted on asserting their authority over their own lives and those of their families. Accordingly, whites often attacked black men while they were performing the very gender roles and conventions designed to safeguard their own and their family's freedom. Indeed, conservative whites saw as threats black men who carried arms, lobbied for the right to vote, disputed labor arrangements, or protected women and children from harm. These whites thought the right to exercise these privileges should remain in the purview of white men. Preserving these activities for white men, they believed, was the best way for whites to retain their power. Black men's refusal to submit to white supremacy—as seen through their attempts to fulfill their roles as defenders and providers of their families—was the antithesis of white folks' ideas of acceptable behavior for black men. This clash of interpretations about freedom put African American men on a collision course with whites and drew violence down on them and their families.[13]

The case of Louisiana freedman Cuff Canara illustrates what happened when black men tried to defend their families against violent whites. Canara burst into the Freedmen's Bureau office at Sparta on August 1, 1866. Canara reported that he had confronted Dan Docking over the two sexual assaults the white man had committed on Canara's wife. The rape of enslaved women and girls had been recognized as in the purview of the slaveholding class. Although some enslaved men confronted white men about sexual assaults on their wives, daughters, mothers, or sisters, enslaved people had little legal recourse. Canara recognized that, as a free man, he no longer had to tolerate assaults on his wife, so he took his complaint to the bureau. When Canara ran for the bureau office, Docking, two other armed white men, and four dogs tracked him ten miles to prevent him from reporting the rapes. Canara arrived at the bureau office with one gunshot wound after slaying three of the dogs pursuing him. The Canaras, like other African Americans who endured or witnessed violence during this period, had committed the egregious offense of rejecting white people's continued presumptions of authority over them and their family members.[14]

Black women's testimonies of violent attacks to Freedmen's Bureau agents show that they joined black men in defending their interests and those of their dependents by resisting resubjugation and by testifying about the violence they endured. For example, Sylvia Parker of North Carolina reported to an agent that John Lawrence assaulted her in December 1866. When Parker confronted Lawrence publicly for his failure to pay her wages for picking cotton, he struck her with a stick. On February 3, 1867, Sylvia Henry of Bladen County, North Carolina, reported that Haywood Gailor "struck her a hundred times or more" and tried to shoot her. Sylvia's transgression was refusing to "live with him." Henry might have lived with Gailor at some point, but her refusal to continue to do so elicited his assault. Henry testified to a bureau agent that her white landlady's intervention spared her life. Later that year North Carolinian Lucy Smith reported that John D. Walker gave her "a severe and outrageous beating" for some unspecified transgression and then drove her off his plantation but detained her five children. These episodes are representative of the gender-based violence freedwomen across the South faced when they defended themselves against resubjugation.[15]

Attacks such as those committed on Mrs. Canara, Parker, Henry, and Smith indicate some white men's intent to retain their domination of black women. As a free woman, Sylvia Parker believed that she needed little reason to confront her employer over wages, beyond her belief that Lawrence still owed her money for work she performed. Parker's need to provide for herself and any dependents probably raised the stakes in her response to what she perceived as Lawrence's efforts to deprive her of earned wages. Lucy Smith's presumed offense against Walker was unreported, but Walker's decision to beat and run off Lucy while detaining her children reflects the ways that some whites tried to control freedwomen and their children. Rather than passively endure violent efforts to resubjugate them, these women and their loved ones took their complaints to army officials and then to Freedmen's Bureau agents, who conducted testimonial interviews that offered the formerly enslaved and previously free people a means of narrating their victimization with the hope of receiving some form of expiation or restitution.

These African Americans' decisions to report incidents of racial violence reflect their efforts to activate their citizenship and to bring their assailants to justice. Nevertheless, civil authorities prosecuted few whites accused of murdering or assaulting blacks because of the white majority's commitment to the principles of popular constitutionalism and to white conservatives' rule. Moreover, white juries rarely convicted whites for any crimes they committed against blacks. When civil authorities attempted to get a jury to convict the Docking party for its assault on Cuff Canara, Freedmen's Bureau officials reported that jurors believed Canara had "committed the greater crime by killing the dogs" than Docking had for his rapes of Mrs. Canara and even for shooting Cuff. The bureau's presence and its receptiveness to listening to black people's complaints enabled some blacks to assert their citizenship by reporting violence committed against them and their neighbors. The racially determined realities of the southern legal culture diminished the possibilities of black victims achieving financial and punitive amends. Unfortunately, the structural presence of the federal government in southern states was not enough to deter whites across lines of social position, political affiliation, and sex from using violence to subjugate blacks.[16]

Bureau agents' testimonies about racial violence they witnessed directly or learned secondhand from black victims and witnesses indicate that the violence of the peace became more potent and more deadly by 1866. For example, Texas Freedmen's Bureau agents used correspondence reports to their superiors to relate their assessment of local conditions and the motivations behind the violence and to explain the contexts in which it occurred. William N. Sanders, for example, reported that white planters and farmers in his district were "smarting under a lost sense of mastery" and were determined to prevent blacks from enjoying their freedom and newly acquired citizenship rights. Agent Albert Bevans observed that white men in his district organized to "thin the niggers out a little," a process that involved murdering black people who defied white people's authority and driving them from their homes with the promise of violence. According to bureau reports, violence intensified during the spring of 1867. Stationed in Galveston, Sanders and Bevans had a ground's-eye view of the emerging insurgency against Reconstruction. In addition, Louisiana agent E. W. Dewess testified that black Texans were rushing the border "trying to escape from Texas as if from death." Louisiana planters in Shreveport had formed armed gangs to stop the fleeing Texans from crossing the border. Dewess responded to this by begging bureau executives to send a cavalry to arrest the perpetrators. Sanders's assessment of southern conditions was precise: whites had begun coordinating to keep blacks "in perfect terror of their lives."[17]

Concerned about agents being inundated with black people's complaints about violence, some bureau executives issued directives instructing agents to relate the murders, riots, and "outrages," or "crimes against the community," in their reports on local conditions. Consequently, agents' reports enumerating the brazenness of white aggression poured into central bureau offices from 1865 to 1868. Many agents took detailed notes on black people's testimonies of violence despite the bureau's limited resources, the legal constraints on their authority, and the pervasive racial prejudices among white agents. Indeed, victims' and witnesses' testimonies of violence were the primary source of most of the bureau reports "relating to murders, riots, and outrages" and even suggest that testifiers turned some agents into co-owners of the traumas they endured.[18]

The assaults on individuals and families that African Americans reported to the bureau show how widespread recalcitrant whites' attempts to stop black people from enjoying their freedom were. While this individual violence was occurring locally, federal officials' efforts to bring blacks fully into the nation's body politic gained momentum. For example, congressional Republicans signaled to southern white Democrats their commitment to guaranteeing black people's status as free people and as citizens. However, these blacks confronted and defied whites at a time when white southerners started coordinating their attacks on black people and using violence that resulted in more fatalities. If emancipation unnerved whites looking to preserve the antebellum racial hierarchy, then African Americans' acquisition of political power through citizenship and the elective franchise, acquiring land and other forms of personal wealth, and adoption of the behavior of free people drove some whites to hysteria. African Americans' testimonies suggest that the everyday violence of emancipation that occurred from 1865 to 1867 was only a prelude to what was to come in response to progressive Reconstruction. Before explaining African Americans' testimonies about white resistance to Reconstruction, some explanation of progressive Reconstruction is necessary.

"Reign of Terror Set Up among Us"

Reconstruction was a complex federal policy initiative that involved, among other things, returning the seceded states to the Union, strengthening the federal government's relationship with and control over them, and restructuring the southern economic base around self-sufficient farmers. Initially, white southerners who were devastated by the war and its outcomes were receptive to Reconstruction and to many of the policies designed to integrate black people into American life. Andrew Johnson's commitment to a quick reconciliation between the white citizens and officials of the Union and the Confederacy permitted many former planters to reclaim their land by declaring their allegiance to the Union. Once returned to power, members of the former slaveholding apparatus worked to restore the South's antebellum hierarchy regarding race and class. Infuriated progressive Republicans responded by taking steps to ensure that emancipation was more than a nominal wartime measure. These proponents of progressive Reconstruction reasoned that without suffrage, African Americans were vulnerable to the whims of the white power brokers, who had already begun obstructing black people's social and material advancement.[19]

Progressives figured that African Americans could better secure their social and economic freedoms once they had some authority in local, state, and federal governance. Indeed, blacks themselves believed that they needed the authority of citizenship and the right to vote to protect their interests. For example, black North Carolinians assembled for a state convention in 1865 and issued an address. They explained, "[We know] we cannot long expect the presence of Government agents, or of the troops to secure us against evil treatment from unreasonable, prejudiced, and unjust men. . . . We know we must find both at home and among people of our own State, and merit them by our industry, sobriety and respectful demeanor, or suffer long and grievous evils."[20] To protect themselves blacks, along with their progressive white allies, argued that African Americans needed not only citizenship rights but also unobstructed access to the right to vote. In 1866, progressives began seizing the reins of Reconstruction from Johnson. They pushed through Congress the world's first civil rights bill and made passage of the Fourteenth Amendment, which overturned the *Dred Scott* decision's exclusion of blacks from the benefits of citizenship and guaranteed them due process and equal protection under the law, a condition for the Confederate states' readmission to the Union. Equally important, they stipulated that adult males in the former Confederate states, including black males but excluding some unrepentant Confederates and convicted felons, be allowed to vote in the new constitutional conventions in 1867.

By the time of black male enfranchisement, African Americans' testimonies before the Joint Select Committee suggests that black people had settled into what many hoped would be permanent locales. In fact, many blacks had married and created stable families. They had worked and saved money, purchased small plots of land, built homes, planted crops, and acquired other property and even formal education. Many African Americans were successful despite the former slaveholding apparatus's efforts to resubjugate them via violence, cheated wages, and campaigns to deny them access to land. In other words, testifiers believed that most blacks had eked out successful livings from sharecropping, farming, and hiring themselves out to farmers, planters, industrialists, and merchants. They had rebuilt their families and established communities and institutions to serve their economic, political, and social needs. Having acquired so much in such a short period, these people would do whatever they could to protect their interests.[21]

Although black men gained the legal right to vote and hold office, they did not enter the Reconstruction-era political arena alone. Blacks rushed to protect their collective interests by becoming active participants in the body politic by exercising authority in local governance. Men and women were active participants in the formal and informal political processes of convening conventions, establishing agendas, campaigning, electing delegates, and allowing black men to cast votes on behalf of the community. African Americans rejected the white mainstream's political framework for only allowing men to participate in the political process because they understood that their freedom was contingent on their collective authority and power. For this reason, both black men and women participated in their first election in 1868. The demographic contours of the Black Belt enabled some black men to govern by holding elected positions that ranged from police constable to state senator. These newly elected black officials and their supporters initiated campaigns to increase black people's education, civil rights, and economic development. What is more, activists designed plans to promote black landownership and enterprise. Black people's success and their desire to protect these sociopolitical gains, however, rendered them vulnerable to envious whites and those attempting to assert their authority over blacks.[22]

African Americans' inclusion in the body politic stoked some white southerners' hatred and prompted them to unite to relieve the South of what they saw as the burden of Reconstruction. Conservative white Democrats decried the progressive features of Reconstruction as an outrage against white southerners' innate right to self-governance. Their resolve to subvert progressive initiatives for advancing black people's civil and political rights generated organized violence against black people. By publicly terrorizing, killing off, and attacking blacks in the political arena, conservative whites fostered a culture of terror. In this political climate, poor and aspiring whites hitched their future to the planter class, whom they believed could harness and suppress the civil and political aspirations of African Americans, stabilize the economy, and reset the world thrown into disarray by war and emancipation. At the same time, the planter class collaborated with legislators and the burgeoning industrial class to restore the antebellum racial hierarchy.[23]

Before 1868, whites were prone to handle daily disputes with black people independently, just as they had during slavery. However, when individual threats and intimidation failed to elicit compliant and deferential black people, whites rallied their family members, friends, and neighbors to put defiant blacks in their place. After 1868, the numbers of white gangs and posses operating to resubjugate blacks increased, and these groups were more likely to administer fatal violence. They took advantage of white male social organizations' shift from social activities to campaigns of violence. What is more, these men donned robes and other forms of disguise and called on their family and neighbors to exact punishment for black people's refusals to accept racial subjugation and defer to white people's authority in all matters of southern life.[24]

The Ku Klux Klan was the perfect organization to service the southern Democratic Party's objectives for white southerners' economic, political, and social supremacy and to shield from prosecution whites who terrorized and attacked black people. With quasi-organized campaigns to dominate local and state elections and to force African Americans to accept a subjugated place in southern life, white conservative Democrats raised and planted banners of white supremacy across the South, scapegoating black men as the source of white southerners' social and economic problems. These whites identified suffrage as the nucleus of black people's power that needed to be broken. Thus, violence and intimidation became a feature of southern elections that restored white Democrats to power. Now, whites who had had run-ins with defiant blacks could use the cloak of political violence to exact revenge in what amounted to an insurgency against Reconstruction.[25]

This cabal of white insurgents vented their frustration at agents and symbols of the federal government, Unionists and Republicans, but African American men, women, and children were the primary outlets for their dissatisfaction with Reconstruction and the infringement on what they perceived as their right to rule. Accordingly, conservative white southerners began treating black people's attempts to live as citizens as aggressive political affronts that deserved violent responses. Since emancipation, these whites had formed loosely organized units to police black enclaves, to keep black laborers on plantations, to rob the prosperous, and to drive them from their homes, but they were rarely unified before 1867. White terror groups that operated under the rubric of the Klan often acted without official organization, yet they worked in concert toward the objective of white rule after 1868.

African Americans' testimonies and Freedmen's Bureau agents' reports suggest that the white-supremacist insurgency shifted into high gear in 1868. For example, Texas bureau agent B. G. Shields of Carolina, Falls County, wrote Governor E. M. Pease in June that "society is in a deplorable condition. If something is not done, a state of things will arise too horrible to contemplate." Shields called for a "general disarming" of everyone. Even without guns, white Texans and other white southerners inflicted debilitating and fatal wounds on black people, evidenced by reports of hangings, whippings, rapes, and assaults with knives and farm equipment. In July, Shields composed a letter to a commanding officer stationed at Austin testifying that his community "still bleeds under the hands of the assassin." This violence began when three white men invaded the home of a freedman named David Friar who still lived on the plantation of Labon Dodson, his former master. The men demanded money, and even though Friar relinquished between $100 and $200, the white men killed him and another male occupant of the home. This raid on Friar's home set off a chain of events in which black residents took defensive measures to protect themselves, and white residents responded by taking aggressive steps to assert their authority over black people once and for all.[26]

Shields explained to Captain William E. Oakes that the intensity and coordinated nature of white violence made black residents "very much alarmed and discouraged" about the prospects of surviving there. According to Shields, blacks declared "that they will leave the country as soon as they can get away." Shields also reported that African Americans in his district "had no protection under the law" because of predatory whites and terrified or indifferent civil authorities. Shields understood the condition of his society from that which he witnessed personally and from testifiers' reports about the violence they endured. In fact, Shields was one of many bureau agents who was inundated with victims' and witnesses' testimonies about violence and their efforts to turn agents into co-owners of the trauma they endured. From testifiers, agents such as Shields learned that organized bands of white men had attacked black people who appeared to be successful farmers or laborers who managed to save money. Some gangs killed for sport, anonymously and randomly. Other gangs sought retribution against blacks with whom they had some personal conflict. They worked together to make African Americans submit to white rule.[27]

The climate of racial terror intensified as the day of the 1868 election drew closer. Testifiers convinced agents such as Shields that federal officials needed to take action. Bureau agents reacted by begging federal officials for reinforcements. Joe Easely of Sulphur Springs, for example, complained that he was "situated like a mariner whose vessel is sinking, and he is dripping out slips of paper, hoping they may fall into some friendly hands, that the world may know what became of him." Easely explained that a "reign of terror" had been set up amid the peace in Texas.[28]

Reports of victims' and witnesses' testimonies about the violence they endured or witnessed in Georgia and Louisiana suggest that Easely's characterization of Texas was representative of conditions throughout the region. In an 1868 annual report of African Americans' complaints of violence for the division of Albany, Georgia, from January through October 31 there were twenty-five assaults on blacks—including hand-to-hand combat and incidents of whipping, beating, and stabbing. For much of the year, testifiers reported that the violence had occurred between individual whites and their black counterparts in disputes over such matters as land, labor, sex, racial etiquette, and politics. In Dougherty County, Georgia, for instance, Robert Bray delivered Henry Clay Carswell a scalp wound for reporting nonpayment of wages to the bureau. James Hall beat Ann Hampton over the head with a stick in a dispute about work.[29] Two reports of "Murders and Other Outrages" for the month of November 1868 reported to bureau headquarters from Louisiana illustrate the similarities of African Americans' assessments of intensifying violence throughout the region. Of the seventy-eight incidents from twenty-one Louisiana parishes, all but four involved formerly enslaved people attempting to make freedom real. Black residents reported about forty confirmed fatalities, four incidents of violent dispossession, one rape, twenty-three threats to kill, one riot with an estimated 101 fatalities, and twenty-eight reports of shootings, whippings, beatings, and assault and battery.[30]

Although black men represented the majority of the victims of this violence, some representative cases from Georgia, North Carolina, and Mississippi offer additional insight into some of the violence whites used to discipline and punish women after they were alleged to have threatened a white family's social standing in their community. In August 1868, five white men dragged Harriet King from her home in Calhoun County, Georgia. The men kicked and stomped King, laid her over a log, and gave her fifty lashes with a whip, setting their dog on her before forcing her to promise that she would not divulge what had transpired, or she would face death. King had allegedly called one of the men's children a "little mulatto," implying that the man's wife had conceived the child with a black man. A month later Fanny Gilmore, a resident of Dougherty County, was "severely beaten with a club and bruised considerably in different parts" by James Roby, a deputy marshal of Albany. Roby reportedly beat Gilmore because she was "suspected of having circulated slanderous reports about the assailant and his wife." In addition, Nelson Ladford of Pickens County assaulted Harriet Blackwell. Blackwell reported that Ladford "beat her at her own house and then fired at her as she was escaping" because "she accused him of being the father of her child." In each case, some defiance of whites' authority or some challenge to their superiority—whether real or imagined—occasioned the violent attack. In fact, the number of black women who testified about being whipped for impudence toward or slander against white women shows how what became the white-supremacist argument about protecting white women from sexual assault by black men also involved physical and rhetorical "assaults" by black women. In many of these cases, black women who were whipped or beaten fled to avoid further violence.[31]

One noticeable difference in the violence that testifiers reported to the bureau by the fall of 1868 was their observations of a surge in collective violence. For example, on October 31, someone reported that an unidentified freedwoman from Claiborne Parish, Louisiana, was "first ravished then nearly beaten to death" by four disguised white men. The agent noted that the men, in their trek to Minden, were "stopping at all cabins in their route committing violence and maltreating women." In addition, the local agent reported on November 10 that he had received information that blacks were "in complete subjection to the will of the whites by whom they were compelled to vote, subject to their dictation, under penalty of death from KKK &c."[32]

African Americans began testifying about white gangs in Louisiana riding the night, rampaging through black enclaves, and terrorizing residents. On the eve of the 1868 election, more of these whites were operating under the rubric of the Klan and other white terror organizations. Disguised men running through East Feliciana Parish, for example, identified themselves as Klansmen when they ordered blacks to vacate plantations. Blacks from Natchitoches, Sabine, and Winn parishes also complained of being forced to cast ballots for Democrats under the threat of violence. In sum, the Klan was a powerful umbrella under which white Democrats, working on a number of economic, political, and social levels, terrorized and policed black enclaves. The sanctuary offered by the Klan emboldened whites to terrorize black people at will and to kill them.[33]

African Americans' testimonies about violence in Bossier and Caddo show their observations of the white insurgents' increasingly bold and organized gestures to subjugate black people. Agents reported that black residents had complained of "constantly being taken from their homes by desperadoes and either being killed or forced to leave their homes, crops and everything they possess." For example, one unidentified freedman's body was discovered on November 9 with a warning of "death to any person who removes the body" pinned to him. The man's kin probably wanted to give him a proper burial, but whites wanted the body to remain where they left it to remind black people of the consequences of resisting their authority by fighting for civil and political rights. Additionally, white Louisianans rioted that September. On the twenty-ninth, an organized band of whites took nine freedmen to the Red River and ordered them to swim for their lives. Victims and witnesses testified that the white men slaughtered the desperate swimmers by firing on them whenever they surfaced for air. With the whites' thirst for blood still unquenched, witnesses testified that they even murdered three of the victims' friends as they constructed coffins for the burial.[34]

The concert with which these bands had started operating created such conditions that, as one agent reported, "freedpeople will not divulge anything even acts committed against themselves for fear of death." African Americans had reason to be worried about continuing to report violence to bureau officials. White bands had started slaughtering black people who reported violence to civil authorities and who testified against white men before grand jury investigations into violence. Thus, fear-induced silence and some local authorities' failure to prosecute violent perpetrators reported to them by the bureau and by victims and witnesses fueled the atmosphere of a war of attrition against blacks.[35]

Some congressional Republicans, mindful of the violence occurring under their watch, pressed on with progressive reforms. Over time, these men's efforts gained political momentum, national influence, and legitimacy as they promoted themselves as agents of the party of amity and advancement and cast Democrats as warmongers who threatened the fragile peace.

By 1870, progressive propaganda, lingering anger about the war, and conservative whites' recalcitrant responses to emancipation and Reconstruction forced some demoralized Democrats to move toward the political center and to agree to certain progressive aspects of Reconstruction. Accordingly, these Democrats endorsed select parts of Reconstruction with the hope that their acquiescence to such policies as black men's enfranchisement would cast them in a favorable light, subvert support for white Republicans, and attract newly enfranchised blacks to the Democratic Party. Members of the less conciliatory and more truculent faction of the Democratic Party, however, commenced a plan to return the South to what they believed were its natural white rulers.

According to Alexander K. Davis of Macon, Mississippi, squads of armed white men began military-style campaigns that terrorized black residents. Though some African Americans remained silent, others, such as Davis, testified as soon as they were given the opportunity. Davis testified that in Noxubee County white men drove five families off their land, whipped a woman named Betsey Lucas for having sexual relations with a white man, and killed a man named Sam Coger. The men also killed Dick Malone for "his threats to resist the visits of these killers." Davis reported that Malone had told his neighbors that he intended to give a "warm reception" to any white men arriving in their enclave and intending to harm black people. Malone had also encouraged black men to "arm themselves, and if [the white men] came around to give them a fight." Davis testified that when white men heard of Malone's defiant proclamations, they decided to teach the black man and his neighbors the price of challenging white supremacy.[36]

The nightrides, assassinations, aborted and successful lynchings, and other forms of violence that affected election outcomes finally prompted federal action. Congress passed the Enforcement Acts of 1870 and 1871. In federalizing some violations of southerners' civil and political rights, the Ku Klux Klan Act of 1871 was progressive Republicans' most measured step to suppress violence to date. Likewise, Congress created the Department of Justice (DOJ) to control crime and punish unlawful conduct while facilitating the executive branch's execution of the acts. One of the DOJ's first undertakings was an inquest into terrorist organizations. Congress commissioned to the DOJ a cadre of Secret Service agents from the Treasury Department to look into the terrorist clubs' interference with elections. By 1871, reports from the DOJ triggered the establishment of a congressional Joint Select Committee to investigate the "Condition of Affairs of the Late Insurrectionary States." The committee subpoenaed white and black people to southern towns and cities to testify about Klan activity in the region.[37]

"They Don't Allow Any Nigger to Rise That Way"

African Americans traveled across the South to testify at the hearings in such places as Atlanta, Jacksonville, and Macon. Their appearance before the committee underscores their desire to inform federal officials of what it was like to experience freedom and then have it shattered by violence. At the same time, the collective gathering of victims and witnesses presented blacks with an opportunity to create public knowledge about racial violence. In the waiting areas for the hearings, victims and witnesses no doubt shared their experiences of violence with each other. These exchanges of personal stories allowed individuals to understand how widespread and horrific the violence was across the region. The resulting intersubjectivity regarding violence fostered community among testifiers and helped them speak with one voice. Therefore, testifying before members of Congress also allowed blacks to develop the vernacular history about the pall cast over their lives by racial violence and to publicize their suffering.

Unlike the testimonies that African Americans shared within families or those they gave to bureau agents, which occurred in what were mostly private settings, the congressional hearings were more public events that were attended by citizens, elected and appointed local and state officials, and members of Congress and the press. This formal and public nature of the hearings educed strategic behavior on the part of victims and witnesses of racial violence, who did not miss the significance of these public hearings. In fact, the number of victims and witnesses who appeared and their candor about their experiences with violent whites suggest that African Americans appreciated the opportunity to explain racial violence and how it transformed their lives.

Many testifiers revealed their personal experiences of racial violence, but, like Alexander Davis, they also appended to their narratives what Robert Stepto calls "accompanying voices," the experiences of their family members, friends, and neighbors.[38] This suggests that they shared a "duty to relate" what black people felt and knew about the horrors of this violence and what they believed their fellow citizens, state and federal officials, and the press should know. In feeling a responsibility to relate their individual and collective experiences of violence, African Americans embraced what Dwight McBride calls the "politics of experience," whereby people who testified presented themselves not only as victims and witnesses but also as experts on violence and representatives of their people. McBride suggests that this "self-positioning" as victim, witness, and expert arose from black people's understanding that the intended white audiences of testimonies of violence were "ignorant of [the] particulars" of victims' and witnesses' experiences. Thus, the narrative these testifiers produced is more complex and sophisticated than individual stories and enables the testimonies to be read as a reliable historical record of violence that also speaks to the development of a sense of community surrounding violence.[39] Indeed, African Americans strategically used the settings of the hearings to develop and add their "collective voice" to the investigation into the "condition of the affairs" of the former slaveholding states. The "integrated narrative" that testifiers added to the hearings was twofold, reflecting the promises of freedom and the horrors of white resistance to emancipation and Reconstruction.[40]

African Americans' narrative of the terror of emancipation also opens a window onto black people's values and the lives they created after the Civil War. For example, it reveals that once blacks were given legitimate control over their families, homes, and labor, they made great strides in formalizing intimate unions, bringing together families separated by slavery and the war, establishing independent homes, acquiring employment, and wherever possible obtaining land. Creating lives as citizens, enduring violence, calculating the cost of violence, and attempting to get justice and to rebuild their lives are themes that coursed throughout the hearings. Moreover, victims' and witnesses' testimonies suggest that even though black men's participation in electoral politics and their acquisition of land served as two precursors to extraordinary violence, black people's enjoyment of any type of racial advancement under the reforms of progressive Reconstruction factored significantly into the violence they endured. For example, Floridian Robert Meacham explained that blacks were "poor, it is true; they work[ed] hard and ma[d]e very little," but they were "getting along" now that they could enjoy "the full fruits of their labor."[41] Most were doing this by working, purchasing land, managing their families, and exercising authority in local governance until they refused to accede to a white person's authority. Indeed, the people who testified at the hearings wanted officials to know what blacks had accomplished economically, politically, and socially in the short period of time since emancipation and what they lost to violence. Thus, many victims' and witnesses' testimonies explicate the acquisition and loss of homes, land, employment, suffrage, physical security, and loved ones to violence.

African Americans' testimonies suggest that they understood that land ownership would secure their self-sufficiency and bolster their freedom. Land allowed black people to grow food for their families as well as such commodities as cotton, sugar, and wheat to sell at market. Testifiers wanted members of Congress and the American people to know that acquiring land was a significant achievement for blacks because obtaining "good land" was difficult. Land was expensive, so people who had acquired plots of land while they were enslaved clung to it. Likewise, landless former slaves seized opportunities to own land. Many blacks were forced to live on white people's land in exchange for money or crops until they were ready to buy and maintain land. Congress provided black people with additional opportunities for land ownership by opening more than forty million acres of public land under the Southern Homestead Act. By setting the price at $1.25 per acre, Congress formulated conditions such that land ownership for black southerners became a more likely prospect. Floridian Emanuel Fortune complained that most of the land consisted of "generally swamp, or hommock, or lowlands."[42] The poor quality of some of the land did not hinder African Americans' determination to acquire and live off it.

African Americans testified that making it difficult for them to acquire land was a key part of white people's strategy to prevent blacks from achieving wealth by limiting them to subsistence farming. Fortune testified that whites had purchased massive amounts of the land and were holding land parcels "so that colored people cannot buy it." Specifically, white men only allowed black people to buy small, individual tracts of cultivatable land of "40 or 50 acres" but not the tracts of "100, 200, or 500 acres" that blacks preferred.[43] Robert Meacham, a state senator from Jefferson County, Florida, explained that "there is a thorough understanding among [whites] in the way of seeing that the colored people shall never have much; they are united one with another to see that that is done."[44] Likewise, Abram Colby of Greene County, Georgia, reported "there was an agreement among the white people not to sell or rent any land to negroes."[45] When whites did sell land to blacks, they inflated the prices, which made acquiring land more formidable.

Some African Americans who lived in the homesteading territories saved enough money to purchase land, even at inflated prices, and those who lived outside these areas joined caravans of migrants destined for these locales, where they established homes, homeplaces, and home spheres. Samuel Tutson of Florida, for instance, homesteaded 160 acres and bought three acres outright, on which he cultivated corn, potatoes, and cotton. Other scenarios involved men such as Doc Rountree, who held a composite of land holdings. In total, Rountree reported that he worked and lived on seven acres, some of which he homesteaded, four that he purchased outright, and some that he rented from his cousin.[46] Similarly, Alfred R. Blount of Natchitoches Parish, Louisiana, had land hop-scotched across the parish. By 1878, when he testified at the Teller Committee's investigation into election violence, Blount estimated his holdings at more than one hundred acres. In sum, land ownership was vital to African Americans' aspirations after the Civil War because it safeguarded their freedom and allowed them to make a living and to establish homes to secure their families.[47]

Some testifiers reported that the social mobility and independence that African Americans such as Rountree and Blount achieved is what triggered whites' orchestrated efforts to punish and wrest compliance with their racial authority from defiant and prosperous black people. In fact, southern whites shifted to extraordinary violence to acquire what ordinary violence did not: a subjugated black population. As the number of U.S. troops stationed throughout of the region declined, the number of white gangs and posses attacking blacks who enjoyed the fruits of their labor, who held political office, who acquired land, and who established independent homes increased. Thereafter, victims and witnesses testified that white men, whom many called "nightriders," terrorized black enclaves with violence that was both random and precise.[48]

Many testifiers attributed nightriding attacks to black people's participating in "politics" and ascribing to ideas of "radicalism." According to African Americans' testimonies, some Reconstruction-era whites defined radical or political conduct among black people as any activity or behavior that resembled that of white people. Thus, black "radicalism" or black people engaging in "politics" could include the obvious activities of pursuing or holding elected office and articulating an allegiance to the Republican Party. However, the violence that blacks endured for reporting violence, testifying against white men in grand jury inquiries, acquiring land and material wealth, refusing or challenging contracts, insulting or imitating white women, insisting on wages in exchange for work, demanding raises, reporting contract violations, and refusing to vacate land underscores the extent to which these seemingly apolitical activities were imbued with political meaning.[49] For example, William Coleman was a former slave turned sharecropper who testified that he had saved enough money to acquire land, eighteen hogs, twelve sheep, two cows, and two horses. Coleman and other black Mississippians were enjoying freedom, until violent whites swept through their communities. Eight disguised white men visited his home and ordered him out in 1870. Coleman declined. He later testified that he told them, "I am not going to open my door to nobody . . . that won't tell me who they are before I do it." He explained that the men took down his door and descended on him "like dogs string out a coon." Then, the white men dragged Coleman out to the road, where, he swore, "they . . . whipped me until I couldn't move or holler or do nothing, but just lay there like a log."[50]

Coleman offered several possible reasons for this attack that point to his defiance of white people's authority and their efforts to subjugate him. He explained that some of the white men paid him a visit because he had failed to lift his hat to a white man on the road. Additionally, he noted his public support of voting for the Republican Party. More specifically, Coleman cited what he described as "a little falling out" he had with a white man named Carlisle, on whose land he sharecropped. At the end of the season, as they were about to settle their wages and debts, Carlisle ordered Coleman to leave the crop unharvested. Coleman persisted, knowing that if Carlisle could get him to "run away there would be a chance for him to grab and steal all the crop." Then, Carlisle threatened to "blow [Coleman's] brains out" and to have him whipped unless he went away. Coleman explained that he went home thinking the matter was resolved, until nightriders appeared outside his home. Living as Coleman was, owning land and having the temerity to challenge a white man's authority, one of the white men commented that he was behaving too much like a white man. The man explained that they visited Coleman to remind him that he "was a nigger."[51]

After the attack, William Coleman and his family fled to Macon, where he later testified before Congress. When congressmen asked Coleman what he did about his abandoned property, Coleman testified, "Nothing; I have lost my year's crop, and my land, and everything else. I can't get nothing out of it, nor do anything about it." He swore, "I would not go back there if I had a gold piece of land there. My life is better than anything else. I would not go back there if there was gold there higher than one of these pines." In fact, when the committee asked if he knew any of his assailants, Coleman replied, "Of course I did. I ought to know them, [they were] my neighbors."[52] William Coleman's testimony, of the life he created after slavery, a violent attack, and feeling the need to leave everything behind, is representative of testifiers' accounts from across the region.

Once nightriding intensified after 1868, African Americans testified that they adopted preventive measures. Wherever possible, blacks formalized their relationships with whites and limited cross-racial interaction. Black people knew that nocturnal activities put them at risk for violent encounters with whites who, purportedly fearful of a black uprising, monitored black people's activities, just as they had during slavery. Blacks testified that they completed work and other sociopolitical activities before dusk. They stayed inside their homes after dark and did not open their doors to strangers.[53]

White men's arrival sent terror through black enclaves. Emanuel Fortune of Jackson County, Florida, explained that many black men were "called out of their doors and shot; some where shot through the cracks of their houses." Experience had shown blacks that, at the very least, those who offered themselves to white men would be stripped, whipped, and forced to apologize for some real or imagined offense. For example, Joseph Turner, a refugee from Caledonia, Mississippi, testified about his own whipping; he also provided a secondhand account of the assault of Dick Halliday, whom a white gang made run naked, pray, take sacrament, and eat bread. At worst, blacks who encountered nightriders were kidnapped, tortured, raped, run off, or murdered. According to Coleman, Klan activity in Winston County had made black families "afraid to stay in their houses at night." Black people began "laying out," sleeping underneath houses, in the woods, and in their barns and stables if conditions or events made them expect violence.[54]

When African Americans were called on by nightriders, some testifiers reported that they pretended they were not at home. If blacks could not hide, then they were forced to deal with the white men. Whites responded by attempting to draw their targets out of their homes, presumably to have black people perform antebellum rituals of subjugation by presenting themselves to the supposed white victims of their transgressions and then accepting whatever punishment those men or women delivered. However, Coleman's and Fortune's testimonies show that many black people were reluctant to reenact practices that had been common during slavery. They forced white gangs to break down their doors or to adopt ruses to gain access to their targets. For example, Joshua Hairston testified that a posse visited his home in November 1870. One of the men had attempted to gain access to Hairston's home by asking him for directions to Crawford, a locale some two miles from the Hairston place. In fact, requests for directions and assistance were a favored pretext of white men for attempting to gain access to black people or to enter their homes. Nightriders in Marianna, Florida, were craftier. When white men visited Henry Reed's home in October 1869, they claimed that a former bureau agent had requested his assistance at the courthouse. The men who raided Daniel Lane's home requested a "drink of water." White men looking for Bully Jack told his wife that their wagon had broken down and that they needed his help. Jack left to help and was stabbed to death near his home at Shuqualak, near Macon, Mississippi.[55]

African Americans who were visited by nightriders testified that they had limited options—they could submit, defend themselves, or flee. Many testifiers explained the split-second decisions that black people made. Some blacks who had advanced notice of violence fled to the woods, to the homes of neighbors, extended kin, or their white patrons. They ran because they hoped to save themselves and spare their families any harm. Many of these targets of violence reasoned that fleeing and returning home once tensions subsided was a safe strategy; yet flight had as many risks as staying. Flight meant living on the run and putting the lives of remaining family members at risk of violence or death.

Victims' and witnesses' testimonies suggest that during this violence African Americans felt that white men held them in a form of temporary "domestic captivity." Though there were no physical barriers blocking their escape, the threat of deadly violence posed by the men's presence trapped all family members inside or close to their homes. Indeed, when white men surrounded or invaded black people's home, they became the most powerful figures in the minds of the occupants. Communicating a willingness and ability to maim or kill everyone inside the home, white men exercised complete control over their hostages and demanded compliance with every request. Testifiers reported that the white men's presence presented black families with paradoxes of life verses personal dignity. Thus, any action a family member took could have devastating consequences for everyone. On the whole, African Americans' testimonies point to both premeditated and spontaneous strategizing to avoid violence or to deescalate the situation inside their homes during these raids.[56]

Several male testifiers revealed a diminished fear of violence meted out to family members who were not the white men's original targets. Specifically, William Coleman testified about telling his wife to remain in the family home, because "they don't hurt women unless some of the women is sassy to some of their wives, or speak like a white woman. . . . Then they go and whip them nearly to death." Coleman knew that his wife would "say nothing." He explained that she said "nothing, or only so little that you can't take no offense at it." Coleman's reasoning alludes to some families' strategies for dealing with nightriders by raising minimal objections to the invasion of their homes. Mrs. Coleman's deferential demeanor probably spared her from violence. However, the reports of women and children who endured violence, even when they were not angry whites' original targets, speaks to the capriciousness of whites during their assaults on black people's homes.[57]

Black men's flight could draw violence away from their families. However, the testimony of a schoolteacher in Tuscaloosa, Alabama, exemplifies the ways that black men's absence from their homes left their families unprotected. On September 8, 1871, several disguised white men visited Edward Carter's home and ordered him to leave because he had been living too much like a white man and because his work as a teacher was uplifting his people.

Carter sought refuge with a white patron, who counseled him to leave until the men dispersed. After Carter ran, two white men returned to his home. The men stormed into the home and subdued Mrs. Carter. Then, they collared the couple's daughter, carried her away from the home, and raped her. Afterward, one of the men bragged to Carter's employer about the sexual assault. Carter testified that when one of the perpetrators was asked about the assault on his family, he admitted "he had done that, and that he intended to do it again, and would do what he pleased with all of them, but 'lowed 'to kill the mother first.'"[58]

Men such as Carter, who were absent when the white men arrived, could not defend their families. However, as indicated by James Hicks's testimony about wanting to defend himself against the white Mississippians who attacked him but knowing that no white people would come to his defense, even if black men were present and armed when the nightriders came, there was no guarantee that they could have defended their families. Indeed, few of the witnesses testified to possessing or using firearms during raids on their homes. Carter's testimony suggests that his wife attempted to protect their children, but he provided no evidence of the family's possessing arms. Moreover, some local statutes prevented African Americans from carrying arms, drilling, and assembling in large groups, and civil authorities routinely disarmed black men. Additionally, the rise of collective violence in a black enclave could be sporadic and sudden, leaving many families and communities unprepared to take defensive action. Regardless of their preparedness for violence, Carter and others testifying at the hearings wanted members of Congress to know the difficult choices they faced when trying to protect themselves and their loved ones from violence.

Victims' and witnesses' testimonies from Georgia offer insight into some black families' efforts to communicate to the committee their inability to defend themselves against white gangs. Nightriders operating under the auspices of civil authorities participated in a raid on the Brown family in White County in May 1871. After a white man was murdered, someone informed the perpetrators that Mary Brown had evidence regarding the killing that she planned to share with authorities. The men stormed into the family's home and stated their purpose as being there to punish Brown for her temerity to participate in the legal system by offering testimony against white men. Joe Brown, Mary's husband, protested, but members of the gang pulled him into the family's yard and whipped him with large cane poles. With Joe incapacitated, the men turned their attention to Mary, whom they stripped and whipped. She testified, "They cut me all to pieces." Then, the white men strung a rope around her neck and choked her until she fainted. Mary Brown testified that while she lay barely conscious, the men debated whether they would kill her; they decided that because she had not gone to authorities, they would spare her life.[59]

With Mary and Joe incapacitated, the white men switched to other members of the Brown household. They dragged Mary's mother, Caroline Benson, and Mary Neal, a young woman living with the family, into the yard. Benson explained, "[The white men] had a show of us all there; they had us all lying in the road. . . . They had us all stripped there, and laughed and made great sport. Some of them just squealed the same as if they were stable horses just brought out." During the raid, one man claimed that they were punishing the Brown family for Joe's sexual relationship with a white woman, which Joe denied. Benson attributed the violence to what she thought was a more plausible reason: Joe Brown's newly acquired ability and decision to outbid a white man for the property on which he and his family resided.[60]

Black people throughout the region underwent treatment akin to that experienced by the Browns, and they testified that they also heard different justifications for the attacks on them. When purported Klansmen visited the home of Caroline Smith of Walton County, they ordered her outside, where they stripped and whipped her along with Sarah Ann Sturtevant. Caroline testified that although the men never specified why they were whipping her, they told her "not to have any big talk, or sass any white ladies." Smith or Sturtevant may have "sassed" white women, or their assailants may have felt the need to justify their action and offered a defense of white women as a pretext for terrorizing the women and making them defer to white women's authority. Two white men visited the home of Tilda and John Walthall. They snatched John from the couple's home and stripped and beat him, before finally shooting him to death. Walthall's relatives Hester Goggin and Rena and Letitia Little testified that several of the same men whipped them as well. The men explained to these women that John's sexual relationship with a woman whom John had described as a "low" white woman before his marriage to Tilda was the reason for the raid on the Walthall home that ended in John's death.[61]

As these people's testimonies show, African Americans understood that these assaults were intended to etch white people's presumed racial supremacy on black people's bodies, families, and communities. Thus, even if the assailants' explanation for their attacks—that they were punishing blacks for actual social or legal transgressions—is accepted, African Americans' understanding of white men's intent to show black people the penalties of engaging in activities that were offensive to whites or that challenged their authority remains clear. White men's practice of separating black men from their families and their stripping and whipping of black women was intended to signify black families' lack of protection in the context of domestic captivity. In fact, these types of attacks created conditions that were ripe for the rape of black women and girls. Although the violence inflicted on women in the Brown, Smith, and Walthall homes constituted gender-based violence, none of these witnesses identified rape as a part of the assaults on them. This may have been because some witnesses evaded specific descriptions of sexual assault to defend themselves against further harm, congressional representatives did not ask them, the transcriber simply omitted descriptions from the transcripts, or rape did not occur.[62]

The testimonies of Hannah and Samuel Tutson, however, show how easily African Americans' refusal to submit to white supremacy could result in raids in which sexual violence occurred and the extent of the devastation wrought by violent whites. In May 1871, nine white men working as a deputy sheriff's posse descended on the Tutson family home in Clay County, Florida. The men invaded the Tutson home and separated the adults. Hannah testified that then the men carried her to a pine tree and tied her arms around it. She explained, "They pulled off all my linen, tore it up so that I did not have a piece of rag on me as big as my hand." The men whipped Hannah several times, taking intermittent breaks. They also whipped Samuel and searched for the family's children, who had run into the fields at the beginning of the assault. Meanwhile, others searched for, confiscated, and destroyed some of the family's property. Hannah testified that when her other assailants left, George McCrea, the deputy sheriff, acted "scandalously and ridiculously" toward her and treated her "shamefully." McCrea's "scandalous" and "ridiculous" treatment of Hannah included sexual assault. Hannah reported that McCrea had her "stark naked" and "pulled [her] womb down so that sometimes [she] could hardly walk." In the end, the raid on the Tutson home left Samuel and Hannah whipped, their children terrorized, one child maimed, their home destroyed, and the family run off land they had rightfully purchased and successfully tilled.[63]

The Tutsons testified that the raid on their family originated with a dispute over land. Residents of Clay County for three years, Samuel and Hannah had saved enough money from sharecropping and washing clothes to purchase land on Number Eleven Pond near Waldo. Then, the couple purchased several acres of homestead land from a man named Free Thompson. After the Tutsons had built a home and planted cotton and other subsistence crops on the land, several white men made claims to the land. The men specifically demanded another payment for the property and ordered the Tutsons to leave if they could not pay.[64] Thereafter, when approached separately and on several occasions by white men with requests and then orders to vacate the land or face whipping and violent dispossession, both Hannah and Samuel refused. Whites rarely needed any specific reason to assault blacks, but Hannah testified that she believed her adamant refusal was more forceful than Samuel's, which might have insulted the men vying for the couple's land. In fact, Hannah testified that she spoke in a "very rash" way to the white men demanding her land. She explained that she was "sort of sorry" for having done so. The Tutsons testified that their employer believed the couple owned the land but knew the white men were determined to see the family dispossessed.[65]

The Tutsons survived the raid and took refuge with some of their neighbors. The couple reported the destruction of their home and the assaults on them to authorities, who apprehended the perpetrators. Shortly thereafter, Samuel retained a white lawyer named Buddington to shore up the family's claim and entitlement to the land. Buddington told Samuel to return to his land, to rebuild, and to kill anyone trespassing or trying to get him to leave. Mindful of the perpetrators' threats that accompanied the attack, specifically that they would tie the family up by thumbs, let them hang awhile, and then hang them by their necks before throwing their bodies into Number Eleven Pond, Samuel told Buddington that he was still afraid to return. Buddington then directed Samuel to work at his home during the daytime and to stay with his neighbors at night.[66]

Samuel testified that after considering these options and the quality of life that remaining under these conditions would subject his family to, he felt compelled to "quit there altogether." Tutson left his land and $150 worth of cotton on it. Samuel testified that he had the land and the title, "but nobody is living on it." Thus, at ages fifty-three and forty-two, respectively, Samuel and Hannah Tutson had lived most of their lives as slaves. In the six-year span since emancipation, the couple had worked, saved money, invested in property, and built a home to raise their children. The family was living the life to which they might have aspired during slavery. Violence, however, forced the Tutsons to abandon everything they owned after that night of terror. This allowed the white men who had vied for the Tutsons' land to claim the family's property without fear of their ever returning. The Tutsons and other survivors relocated within their counties, but many refugees from violence abandoned plantations, farms, and villages for such urban centers as

Jacksonville, New Orleans, and Macon. In fact, Georgian Thomas Allen, pastor of the Baptist church at Marietta, Jasper County, explained to members of Congress that African Americans enjoyed a degree of safety from whites "only in the cities."[67]

Victims' and witnesses' testimonies of white southerners' efforts to resubjugate them and drive them off their land illuminate the losses African Americans endured. Sharecropping, teaching, farming, and domestic work constituted advantageous work for free and freed blacks. Coleman's, Carter's, and the Tutsons' testimonies about the amount of land they acquired are indicators of the material wealth black people accumulated before white men attacked what they saw as threats to their power. Having seen black people pay as much as twenty dollars an acre for land, only to be driven from their property and the riches the land provided, Alfred Richardson of Clarke County, Georgia, testified that white folks did not allow "any nigger to rise that way" and that they used violence to drive people off their land.[68] Indeed, three days after the rape of Carter's daughter and with the white men's threats to repeat the raid on his home, Carter and his family left Tuscaloosa for Columbus, Mississippi. When congressmen asked whether he attempted to have the men who visited his home prosecuted, Carter testified, "I had not protection there at all; they threatened to kill me, because I told the neighborhood what they had done; we had no friends. Since I have left, they have taken everything I had, and sold it, and I have nothing to go upon—crop and all."[69]

These terror-driven migrations—from actual victims and those who expected to become victims—had an enormous effect on the economic fate of many African Americans. That many testifiers had acquired land and then lost the land and the financial security that land ownership provided is a testament to the ability of violence to transform black people's social and economic circumstances. Victims and witnesses testified that some blacks found themselves in the South's urban spaces not because they wished to relocate to benefit from social mobility but because they were in flight for their lives. In departing, such blacks as members of the Coleman and Carter families escaped further violence. However, African Americans testified that these departures also meant that some blacks abandoned ancestral connections and the land and property they had rightfully acquired and for which they would receive nothing. Thus, in leaving their land and homes, these victims became the South's "internally displaced," black people who were forced to flee their families, homes, and communities because their lives were in danger from persecution or from violence.[70]

This violence spared some African Americans' lives, but victims and witnesses testified that this displacement had left many victims materially destitute. A cycle of acquisition of modest wealth, violence and dispossession, and efforts to recover was a feature of many black southerners' experiences of emancipation. Richardson, for example, had worked as a house carpenter to support his family and to purchase 8.25 acres of land on three separate plots. After land-grabbing whitecappers ran him off, Richardson tried to sell his plots, but he explained, "I could not get anything for them." Richardson's white allies told him that he should let the land stand empty until tensions cooled enough for him to sell his property. Afterward, Richardson's neighbors—black men whom the white men had not targeted—bought several acres of his land and put homes on it, only to be driven off and replaced with white people. This displacement separated African Americans from their homeplaces or landholdings and from their home spheres. Dispersed across the regional and national terrain and forced to start over, to rebuild support structures, to acquire gainful employment and land, and to heal, some survivors might recover their losses, but many did not.[71]

Survivors also testified that they and their family members and friends carried with them physical reminders of their trauma. Scarred flesh, bullet wounds, amputated limbs, and sexually violated bodies constituted some of the physical injuries that blacks suffered in the terror of emancipation. Mary Brown explained, "I could not sit up for about three weeks after [my whipping]." A gang of white men asked Henry Lowther of Wilkinson County, Georgia, whether he would give up his "stones" to spare his life. Lowther testified that the Klansmen accused him and a group of other black men of conspiring to kill another black man, having too much influence in the Republican Party, and "seeing," or having sexual relations with, the white woman for whom he worked. Lowther testified, "I had a family, and I did not go to see this woman; I tended her land." To shore up his denial, Lowther explained that the white woman was "of bad character." Lowther consented to being castrated, or "altered," knowing that he would have significant physical wounds and not be the same man physically and emotionally as he had been before the assault. However, he would still be able to live with, protect, and provide for his family. Lowther sought medical treatment for the castration and departed the community. The injured man wrote to his wife, probably to advise her of his whereabouts so that she could join him. Lowther testified that his attackers intercepted the letter and followed him to his new place of residence, where they attacked him.[72]

Testifiers explained that these wounds reduced—temporarily and permanently—African Americans' ability to provide for their material needs and hindered their recovery from violence. In fact, both the Freedmen's Bureau records and the Klan hearing testimonies document a number of nonfatal assaults that left victims with debilitating and life-altering injuries. For example, Lowndes County, Mississippi, refugee Joseph Beckwith testified that when Klansmen visited him in the spring of 1871, they strung him up to elicit a confession of the whereabouts of buried money. Beckwith lost consciousness several times during the assault, only to be revived and strung up again. Because of the deprivation of oxygen to his brain, Beckwith was left with bloodshot eyes for months afterward. He testified, "I couldn't see at all hardly, and did no work for two or three weeks." Indeed, three months later, he reported that he was still suffering from his injuries.[73]

The violence of emancipation indicates that some whites were reluctant to give up the control over African Americans that they enjoyed before the war. The slaps, threats, and insults and their occurrence in broad daylight and during personal disputes made ordinary violence somewhat predictable and possibly easier for blacks to handle. Nightriders' premeditated and coordinated destruction presented a different horror. In fact, extraordinary violence resulted in torture, a greater loss of life, and the amplified likelihood of people sustaining traumatic injury. On the whole, African Americans' testimonies show how orchestrated, premeditated, and spectacular violence produced an overwhelming and more traumatic effect.

Congress held hearings to collect data on the insurrection against Reconstruction to restore peace and security to the region. This inquest allowed black folk—whose stories of violent resubjugation might have gone unheard or dismissed by some local authorities—to testify. Unfortunately, Congress's ability or interest in bringing legal or retributive justice to victims was unclear throughout the hearings. In fact, Republicans had limited capacity to act. In the U.S. political system, the Constitution elevates the powers of local and state governments over those of the federal government when it comes to prosecuting everyday crimes. Indeed, members of Congress had no power to resurrect the dead, to return victims' land, or to restore livelihoods affected by the violence. These officials could not even guarantee that local or state authorities would prosecute or punish known perpetrators of violence. What Congress did do was conduct the investigation and allow black people to participate and to explain what it was like to be a victim of or a witness to this violence. Thus, most investigators asked engaged questions; they listened to and recorded detailed and graphic descriptions of black people's suffering. Whether intended or not, this action was an acknowledgment of both victims' and witnesses' citizenship and the human pain they had endured.[74]

African Americans' testimonies suggest that many victims and witnesses were eager to communicate their values and their fitness for citizenship, to relate violent attacks, and to share their assessment of the ways racial violence changed them as a people. Indeed, testifying about intimate violations of their lives and bodies before strange officials in public proceedings that were observed by perpetrators, journalists, local authorities, and community members was a deeply personal and political act for women and men. Some blacks responded to the intensified violence of emancipation by engaging in a "collective silence" to avoid acknowledging what happened, as well as the shame, guilt, and humiliation they felt after enduring violence. Others remained silent to avoid reprisals. Some victims' and witnesses' silence, their refusal or inability to "give experience words," indicates a different type of agency born of deliberate decisions people made to move on from violent attacks by never reliving them. Nevertheless, people such as William Coleman, Mary Brown, and Samuel Tutson probably testified because they believed that testifying about the torture and injustice they endured was important for ending racial violence. Some victims believed that testifying would educe justice in the form of prosecution or financial compensation. For others, such as Alfred Richardson, Hannah Tutson, and Joseph Beckwith, narrating the violence they endured, identifying the perpetrators, and explaining the ways their lives were transformed by violence might have constituted strategic efforts to send a defiant message to their assailants and to persuade their fellow citizens and federal officials to help provide restitution for their suffering.[75]

Testifying before Congress, the press, and the nation, African Americans related the horrors of racial violence. These testimonies about and against violence also explicate some psychic costs of this violence. Although congressmen questioning witnesses did not ask specific questions about the emotional and psychological wounds of racial violence, and testifiers did not name "trauma" as a consequence of violence, their testimonies about night-riding violence allude to traumatic suffering. Indeed, from victims' and witnesses' testimonies we can see that blacks wanted members of Congress and the public to know that white men's arrival in the middle of the night—both with and without warning—engendered in black families raw feelings of fear, vulnerability, and loss of control. All of these feelings are indicators of the traumas that some families endured.

African Americans testified that this violence and its constraints on black people's agency upset the worlds of those who were specifically targeted, their immediate kin, and their communities. Victims' and witnesses' testimonies reveal that these attacks altered many people's sense of power and security. Survivors of extraordinary violence had to restore their links to each other and to work through feelings about their own conduct before, during, and after the violence. For example, those who were deferential might have wondered how self-defensive action might have spared them or their families pain, and those who were defiant could have wondered if they were to blame for what happened. Whatever their response, the decisions that they made in the context of this violence had short- and long-term implications for their individual and collective fates.[76]

In the end, the congressional inquiry into the white conservative insurgency against progressive Reconstruction created a public record of postbellum violence and yielded widespread arrests that drove the Klan and other white terror organizations underground. Nevertheless, the exhilaration that some victims and witnesses felt likely diminished when they realized that Congress had limited capacity to act beyond granting African Americans an audience for their grievances. The Justice Department took over prosecuting some insurgents and monitoring their activities, but many testifiers returned home to their devastated lives, where some perpetrators remained at large. Thus, Congress, while enabling black people to testify, did not offer witnesses protection for their testimony at the public hearings. Testifiers' accounts suggest that many African Americans understood the dangers of reporting violence to federal officials. For example, Alexander Davis was reluctant to give the names of victims who might testify because he knew "it would be dangerous to them." Davis also explained that he knew men who would not testify because doing so put "them in the position . . . [where they were] more liable to be killed," and they "didn't intend to be slaughtered." Indeed, people who testified at subsequent congressional hearings reported that some of these witnesses or their kin paid the price for testifying, with frequent threats to their livelihood or with their lives.[77]

The federal government's investment in remaking the South's social, economic, and political structure to include blacks presented African Americans with the promise of considerable advancement beyond slavery. Nevertheless, racial violence compromised those possibilities for blacks. On the whole, the Freedmen's Bureau, the DOJ campaign to suppress the Klan, and the hearings presented black people with the prospect of having a federal and public audience for their suffering. As African Americans watched whites intensify their campaign to restore the old southern order, their faith in increasingly indifferent local, state, and national officials began to erode.

The federal government's counterinsurgency stopped the Klan and other terror organizations, but African Americans' testimonies indicate that this was only after violent whites had laid waste to black people's lives. This federal campaign restored a degree of order to the South, but testifiers' accounts suggest that the violence had devastated victims and had disfranchised some black men who were afraid of enduring the potentially violent consequences of voting. What is more, whites rebelling against Reconstruction deprived many black southerners of newly acquired land and stripped them of their means for material self-sufficiency. These men also drove black people from their homeplaces and home spheres to towns and cities. However incapacitated black people might have felt during violent assaults, their behavior in the context of violence did not always stop them from trying to procure justice after the fact.

Testifying was some African Americans' only means of having a public record of the violence they endured and the losses they sustained. In fact, victims and witnesses who were not able to testify before Congress pressed their governors and legislators to prosecute violent whites; they also called on white citizens and federal officials to support their efforts to achieve justice. Failing to gain redress within Kentucky, a group of blacks from Frankfurt petitioned the Forty-Second Congress for relief. The petitioners depicted state legislators as being in denial about the terrorist organizations still operating throughout the state. These Kentuckians supplied federal legislators with more than one hundred incidents of violence as evidence of the need for federal intervention. Appealing to Congress specifically as citizens, the Kentuckians described themselves as "the special object of hatred and persecution" at the mercy of conservative white Democrats.[78] Shortly after the federal counterinsurgency ended, black petitioners from Alabama observed that recalcitrant whites had "a somewhat changed wardrobe and personal manifestation" but that the Klan still existed "in all its hideous and fearful proportions." These Alabamans determined that white Democrats, maintaining their purpose of nullifying the constitutional amendments through "secret war, violence and terror," had "only changed their tactics." The people saw the continued violence as the means to achieve what secession, ordinary violence, and the Klan insurgency had not, which was a resubjugated black population.[79]

Certain white southerners reacted to the federal government's counterinsurgency by disassociating themselves from the Klan, but violence continued, as more conservative Democrats joined the campaign to relieve the former slaveholding states of progressive Republican control. What is more, white folks' fears of competing with blacks for wages, sharing political power, and managing a liberated class of laborers prompted them to cross social lines to ensure white supremacy. Accordingly, in each election after 1870, the architects of white supremacy intensified their depiction of black people's culpability for the sociopolitical disorder throughout the region. As these Democrats returned to power in the legislatures and governorships, they formalized the political goals of restoring the old order by revising the new state constitutions to completely relieve the South of all political vestiges of progressive Reconstruction and to constrain the civil rights of blacks. Though Democrats faced intraparty resistance, growing ambivalence among white progressives over protecting African Americans' rights bolstered white-supremacist rule. Indeed, white northerners and Republicans, who were distant witnesses to violence and increasingly desirous of ending political corruption and addressing economic crises, became more conservative and passive after 1868. Thereafter, northerners' and Republications' retreat from Reconstruction advanced under Ulysses Grant's second administration. The white-supremacist campaign of Redemption and national ambivalence to continuing racial violence came to the fore in the 1876 election.[80]

Conclusion

By 1876, Republicans still controlled Florida, Louisiana, and South Carolina, after violence and Republicans' decreased political momentum had enabled the Democrats to reclaim their political power in the other states. White Democrats declared publicly that they would use every weapon in their arsenal to return the remaining former slaveholding states to the Democratic fold, including the use of violence and force. African Americans and white Republicans resolved to vote in the coming election and to defend their right to do so. Southerners on both sides of the political divide hunkered down for battle. Blacks and whites as well as Republicans and Democrats amassed arms, drilled, and clashed. White Mississippi Democrats upped the ante by launching a guerrilla campaign in what became known as the "shotgun policy" of restoring white rule. These Mississippians raided black and white Republicans' homes and killed men attempting to vote. The successful disfranchisement of Mississippi Republicans emboldened Democrats across the region to adopt a similar take-no-prisoners strategy with respect to voting in the election. In addition, whites massacred black residents of Hamburg, South Carolina. These Democrats overran black and Republican enclaves across the region and left injury, disfranchisement, destruction, and death in their wake.[81]

The Electoral College crisis of 1876 saw Rutherford B. Hayes assume the presidency, which escalated the formal conclusion of progressive Reconstruction. Democrats regained control of southern statehouses, and the last of the troops left the South. Moreover, in a string of decisions, the Supreme Court—an active participant in the federal government's retreat from progressive Reconstruction—constrained the federal government's authority to protect African Americans' civil rights. A decade-long campaign of violent white southern truculence and growing progressive indifference ended Reconstruction. After Reconstruction, many progressives in the Northeast and Midwest and in elected office in the South left black people to fend for themselves. Disinterest in fortifying and protecting black people's rights further undermined African Americans' efforts to transcend slavery. In fact, this indifference to southern affairs affecting blacks gave whites license to move beyond political domination.[82]

Many survivors of the terror of emancipation probably thought that the worst of their postemancipation nightmare was over. Although conservative Democrats had returned to power, many black men still enjoyed the right to vote and to hold office, as well as the Constitution's other legal protections. Indeed, some federal officials had intervened and vanquished the Klan and had shown their support for black people by providing spaces for them to testify about violence. Moreover, progressives secured equal access to public accommodations and facilities in the Civil Rights Act of 1875. Despite, and perhaps because of, Reconstruction's collapse, many black people refused to surrender their freedom and their newly acquired rights. Although many blacks remained determined to enjoy and exercise their rights as free people and as citizens, testifiers' accounts indicate that the violence of the peace was etched indelibly on their psyches, bodies, homeplaces, and home spheres and was embedded into their everyday experiences as a people.

Victims of violence salvaged what was left of their lives. Part of this recovery involved testifying about this violence and creating a public record of their suffering. Their collective memory of violence and federal officials' inability to do more than listen to their testimonies prompted African Americans to hunker down and attempt to retain authority over their lives and communities wherever possible. Violently disfranchised, dispossessed, and scarred and with their homes, crops, and livestock destroyed, some blacks living in rural areas departed to northern, western, and urban destinations to rebuild. However, the majority of victims remained rural dwellers who accommodated themselves to the violent conditions as they attempted to rebuild their lives. Some blacks continued to vote, to hold office, to acquire property, to build homes, churches, and schools, to create and maintain families, to pool their resources, and to participate in southern life. They also farmed independently, sharecropped, and toiled as agricultural and industrial laborers where racism was less blatant. Because of their testimonies, African Americans who lived through the terror of emancipation had a greater understanding of violence, its widespread nature, and its impact on them as a people; they had also put their experiences into the public record. In the coming years, blacks passed on the vernacular history of emancipation violence and a commitment to resisting subjugation and white southerners' efforts to strip away many of the remaining legal protections blacks enjoyed after Reconstruction ended.

2

"A Long Series of Oppression, Injustice, and Violence"

The Purgatory of Sectional Reconciliation

In January 1879, a small group of African Americans traveled to New Orleans. The procession moving about the Crescent City constituted a sociopolitical panorama of black life after slavery. The "reign of terror" that helped end Reconstruction notwithstanding, many blacks were still champions of the federal government and the Republican Party. In the fall of 1878, renascent whites in northern and central Louisiana attacked, leaving blacks traumatized and "charitably exiled," as one white man described the practice of giving African Americans the choice of leaving their homes or being killed. Black people scattered as white men overran their parishes. Some sought shelter in the woods and swamps or in the homes of neighbors and extended kin, but others ran farther, heading west to Texas, east to Mississippi, and south to New Orleans.[1] Victims' and witnesses' subsequent testimonies reveal that this violence left African Americans struggling to rebuild their lives and looking askance at the federal government's willingness to protect black people from racial violence. Mindful of earlier violence and observant of the violence in the election of Democrats, where they stood no chance of carrying an election legitimately, Congress summoned victims and witnesses to testify before the Senate committee charged with investigating "alleged frauds" and violence in the election of 1878.

Many Louisiana survivors recognized the importance of taking advantage of federally sponsored opportunities to share their experiences about violence. Thus, after they testified, a group of men who were displaced by violence appealed directly to President Rutherford B. Hayes for relief and protection under the nation's laws. In their letter, the men cited white men's threats of violence arising from their appearance before the committee. These men asked Hayes for federal assistance because they understood that returning to their homes was dangerous. "We cannot go home," they wrote, "yet our families are there in want. . . . We cannot ever hope to return to them for to return is to be *murdered* for daring to be free." The exile of these men from their communities left their land unattended, their contractual obligations violated, and their families at the mercy of violent whites. On the whole, these Louisianans' appearance as testifiers before the Teller Committee offers a partial vernacular history of black people's lives destroyed by violence after Reconstruction.[2]

To bellicose white southerners, the collapse of Reconstruction and the decline in the federal government's efforts to assert control over the states regarding the protection of African Americans' civil and political rights was a harbinger of the triumphant return of white rule. Subsequent conciliatory gestures by Hayes and his administration further intimated the opportunity for white conservatives to remake the South in their interests and to nullify the gains African Americans had made since the war. To accomplish this feat, these whites needed to arrest black southerners' feelings of their entitlement to enjoy citizenship and equality. This would be difficult to achieve because Reconstruction as well as progressive citizens' and federal officials' willingness to hear black people's testimonies of violations of their civil and political rights had crystallized African Americans' expectations for full and equal participation in American life. However, from the 1870s to the 1890s, white conservatives sabotaged black people's economic, political, and social advancement and amassed the political power ceded by white progressives, who were tired of attempting to transform the South. White southern conservatives used many white northern progressives' desire for sectional reconciliation in service of an aggressive but initially inchoate campaign of resubjugating blacks.

In the decade after Reconstruction, African Americans faced significant challenges in expressing and publicizing their suffering as they struggled to fight their way out of the purgatory of sectional reconciliation. Many white citizens and elected officials strove to set aside the ideological differences of the Civil War and lingering discord over Reconstruction to address such matters as the remaining effects of the Panic of 1873, subsequent economic crises, and the political corruption of the late nineteenth century. To do this and to finally put the Civil War and Reconstruction behind them, many white Americans believed that they needed to set aside the tensions still dividing them, namely, the integration of African Americans into American life. Achieving reconciliation was difficult because, for a time, whites still had different ideas about the war and Reconstruction and how to remember it. Indeed, most historians, when interpreting the discourse of whites and mainstream print culture, argue that the ideological reunion between the North and the South, when white northerners finally subscribed to white southerners' representation of the war and Reconstruction, did not occur until the early twentieth century. However, the vernacular history of sectional reconciliation that blacks produced through their testimonies at congressional hearings and through their print culture is one of experiencing increasing social, political, and economic marginalization and enduring and witnessing the violence used to achieve that end during the earlier period of the 1870s and 1880s.[3]

Some African Americans' testimonies suggest that they detected themes of a distinctly white social and political reunion occurring in the 1870s. In fact, black print culture identified the following as sources of black subjugation: declining progressivism, some threads of reconciliation discourse in Republicans' acquiescence to Democrats' demands for constraining black people's civil and political rights, the growing tolerance for racial violence, the revived rhetoric of the United States' being a "white man's country," and eventually the full retreat from Reconstruction. Expressing similar concerns, Frederick Douglass, in his 1875 speech "The Color Question," asked, "What will peace among the whites bring?" Douglass remembered the rhetoric of the Civil War, that it was a "white man's war," when he observed discussions about sectional reconciliation after Reconstruction. In sum, Douglass and other African Americans worried that the seeds of their resubjugation were being sown in the language of "fraternal feeling" between the North and the South during this period.[4]

Many white southern reconciliationists were blatant about the racial objectives of the "new [white] nationalism" of the post-Reconstruction era when they advocated violence, but white northern reconciliationists, who backed down from punishing perpetrators of violence and their apologists and who eventually subscribed to the southern point of view regarding Reconstruction, were complicit in black people's subjugation. Thus, even if reconciliationists were not explicit in their support for or tolerance of the violent subjugation of black people, then Frederick Douglass and other African Americans believed that southern Democrats' strategy for mingling states' rights, racism, and violence to relieve southern states of the burden of Republicans' purported misrule while rewriting the history of the Civil War and Reconstruction was in concert with northern Republicans' retreat from Reconstruction. These blacks experienced and bore witness to continuing southern violence in the 1880s. They also heard the amplified volume of white-supremacist discourse. White conservatives' political aggression and continuing racial violence coincided with the decision of some of the former lions of progressive Reconstruction to start running for political office on a reunionist platform and with more white northerners becoming less interested in providing forums for blacks to testify about violence and less open to providing some federal remedies. In all, black people had reason to be concerned about what they saw and heard among white conservatives from the South and white progressives from the North. African Americans started the post-Reconstruction era feeling very uncertain about their fate in the nation.[5]

Looking back on the 1880s from the 1910s, W. E. B. Du Bois likened this congealing of antiblack racism under the long process of sectional reconciliation to a "silent revolution," a series of tidal waves set in motion by cultural and political earthquakes. The consolidation of racism that started to occur in the late 1870s gave southern whites license to use violence to vanquish blacks who insisted on progressing beyond slavery. Thereafter, many African Americans felt that the nation crossed the threshold of their tolerance for racial violence and denial of black people's civil and political rights. White people's beliefs that blacks were biologically inferior to them had a long history, of course, but the federal government's commitment to protecting black people's rights during Reconstruction had constrained white southerners' ability to take legal action. Indeed, the successive waves that swept away black people's rights, which took the form of racial violence, disfranchisement, and segregation in the United States, did not hit African Americans with full force until the 1890s. Thomas Dixon and D. W. Griffith later dramatized these developments as the "[re]birth of a nation" united by white supremacy. It was with this "birth" of a united white America that blacks began their descent into what Du Bois and others described as "hell."[6]

Gilded Age blacks found themselves caught in a liminal state of racial consciousness, trapped between the jubilee of emancipation and progressive Reconstruction and what became the hell of the 1890s. These people were situated between the seismic plates of white Americans' opinions about African Americans' place in the reconstituted nation. One plate consisted of progressive white citizens and officials of the Northeast and Midwest who were concerned about protecting black people's rights and using some of the federal government's authority to do it. The other plate represented white citizens and authorities of the South who believed that federal officials should allow the South to handle its own affairs. After Reconstruction, evidence of conservative and progressive opinion and public policy straining against each other and the progressive side giving way to the other can be seen in federal officials' reactions to the 1878 election, to the Exoduster movement, and to white southerners' increasing use of extraordinary violence. Over time, progressive citizens and federal officials buckled under the cumulative stress of white conservatives' pressure to set aside sectional differences so they could reunite the nation. The effect of sectional reconciliation was that white Americans united to rewrite the collective memory of the Civil War and to reconfigure the relationship between race and public policy at the state and federal levels.

This chapter uses African Americans' testimonies before the congressional committees investigating the "Alleged Frauds in the Late Elections" and the "Removal of Negroes from Southern States" and their print culture to reveal black people's representations of the violence they endured after Reconstruction and their responses to the increasing challenges they faced in having their testimonies of violence heard. At the same time, the chapter shows the changing dynamics of white supremacy and how African Americans responded to these changes by creating their own discursive public spaces and by developing a leadership class to address their needs.This action of creating their own public and political spheres and fostering their own leaders continued the process by which black people found their collective voice on racial violence and started to develop institutionalized responses to white supremacy. Before turning to the challenges African Americans faced under the consolidation of racism, it is useful to examine the precursors to extraordinary violence, disfranchisement, and segregation by exploring the political climate of reconciliation.[7]

The Racial Ethos of Reconciliation

By 1877, most white Americans were anxious to put the war and Reconstruction behind them so that they could concentrate on addressing the economic crises and the climate of government corruption of the 1870s. Before they could tackle these new issues, Americans needed to resolve lingering sectional tensions. As the rhetoric of the sectional crisis and the early years of the Civil War revealed, many whites had seen the nation as a "white man's" country and the war as a "white man's" conflict. Although white southerners and northerners remained bitter about the war and its outcomes, they had similar ideas about the peace. These beliefs about the nation, the war, and the peace influenced white people's attitudes about African Americans' continuing fight for civil and political rights and about the policies coming from the White House after the contentious election of 1876. In response to these concerns, President Hayes made sectional reconciliation a priority of his administration. Reconciliation, or what Rayford Logan called Hayes's "let alone" policy, was the president's political scheme to salve the wounds between white northerners and white southerners over the war and Reconstruction. During his administration, more federal officials and white northern citizens agreed to tread lightly around white southerners' governance of race relations in the region.[8] Essentially, Hayes gave white southerners what they wanted: to be left alone to handle the region's economic, political, and social affairs. While white Americans were reconciling, black southerners' prospects for enjoying more than a nominal freedom and achieving social and political equality remained in doubt. After initially expressing outrage over violence in the 1878 election and investigating conditions producing black people's flight from the South, white progressive citizens and federal officials acquiesced to southern white supremacy in the late 1880s.

President Hayes commenced his campaign for reconciling sectional differences with a "good will" whistle-stop tour throughout the South in September 1877. The tour's promoters trumpeted the need for "peace and harmony" throughout the restored Union. By withdrawing federal troops, by ceding the remaining southern states to white Democrats, and by touting a laissez-faire policy toward southern governance, the president believed that he would heal the nation's wounds. Hayes framed sectional reconciliation in terms of submission to the Constitution's doctrine of dual federalism, wherein the national government has limited powers over local and state governments. Thus, when the president asked large crowds whether they would "obey the whole Constitution and [the Reconstruction] Amendments," cheers and applause persuaded him that a "fraternal union [between states] on the basis of the Constitution" was possible. Although a few mainstream northern-based progressive newspapers looked suspiciously at Hayes's tour, much of the expedition's press coverage alludes to general accord.[9]

African Americans, many of whom attended Hayes's speeches, reflected an anxious but hopeful constituency. Black public figures hosted the president's entourage in local meeting places. Hayes had assured such statesmen as Frederick Douglass and Virginia congressman John Mercer Langston that his plans for reconciliation would not translate into an abandonment of black people. Moreover, black print culture suggests that many public figures took the president at his word and communicated their optimism to black folk.[10] In contrast, blacks who had been caught in the vortex of racial violence and who understood that white southerners had their own interpretations of honoring the Constitution probably felt as though they were living in a parallel world. In the mainstream world, many whites hailed reunion, and black public figures constituted a sanguine cohort. However, in the world of survivors of earlier violence, different feelings raged about whites who used violence and intimidation to take control over local and state governments and who started to develop policies and practices that stripped away black people's authority in governance, which made them vulnerable to violence and other types of racial discrimination. A reporter from the New York *Tribune* observed that black folk in the audiences of Hayes's speeches appeared to be "less enthusiastic" than white folk. If these African Americans harbored questions or even resentment of Hayes's "let alone" policy, then it is doubtful that they voiced their misgivings or expressed their bitterness with whites watching them closely. Similarly, a reporter from the Nashville *American* observed a "great anxiety" among blacks. Because Hayes never solicited the opinion of his black constituents, the appearance of their consent allowed the president to believe that his "let [Reconstruction and the South] alone" approach enjoyed universal approval. In point of fact, had Hayes observed the black attendees, he might have seen the apparent absence of protest by black folk as a demonstration of loyalty and of fear rather than as an endorsement of Reconciliation.[11]

Hayes's assurances as well as the reporters' observations suggest that black folk were worried that the president, Republican members of Congress, and white progressive and moderate northerners were less concerned with black people's experiences of violence and their concerns about the threats to their civil and political rights than they were with appeasing white conservative southerners. Black southerners' fears were justified. Southern Democratic governors and legislators, on the condition that they be permitted to assume office in the disputed 1876 election, had assured the nation they would respect the spirit and letter of Reconstruction.[12] In fact, they did, except where they felt Reconstruction policies threatened white conservative rule. Legislators quickly undermined the future election of Republicans to local, state, and federal office by redrawing congressional districts and redistributing the polling places in preparation for the 1878 election.

White Democrats certainly had reason to worry. Black men viewed voting and holding political office through the same lens as white men did, which is to say that black people saw suffrage as the source of power and freedom just as white people did. Recognizing the ways that black people's political power threatened white rule, still-recalcitrant whites purged black officials from local and state offices and used threats to keep voters away from the polls. Southern Democrats' efforts to halt the election of Republicans became more ominous as the election neared. In fact, rather than permit Republicans to run for and assume office, Democrats launched preemptive strikes. Press statements informing readers of Democrats' intent to carry all of the elections, threats, arrest warrants, and rifle companies parading through Republican strongholds and black enclaves preceded the election. Having grown accustomed to threats, many black Republicans dismissed the political bulldozers' behavior as empty rhetoric. Most Democrats used tricks and threats, but some used force and violence during the election. In Louisiana, violence resulted in twenty-three fatalities, innumerable injuries, and violent dispossessions that sent African Americans running for their lives. The violence and election of white Democrats in locales where they were underdogs stunned Americans who believed that they had put the political violence of Reconstruction behind them. Some white northerners cried foul, the president promised to bring perpetrators to justice, and members of Congress decided to investigate by holding hearings.[13]

Alfred Blount, a former state senator of Natchitoches, was one of the victims who testified about political violence. On his way home from a Republican election meeting, neighbors alerted Blount that the "white men up town are arming themselves to breakup this meeting and kill you off." Blount initially dismissed the warning, but when the posse arrived, he barricaded himself in his home with two shotguns, a borrowed gun, a Winchester rifle, and a "couple of pistols." The gang, acting under the guise of law enforcement, demanded Blount's surrender for allegedly plotting to attack Democrats. Blount, however, stood in his galley with the determination, he said, "that any man put violent hands on me, I would shoot him." Explaining that he "wouldn't surrender to any such mob coming as they did," Blount swore that he had "done nothing." The vernacular history of the violence of Reconstruction had taught him that "to surrender to such a mob, who were whooping and hollering, would be death." Authorities promised Blount that no harm would come to him, prompting his surrender.[14]

Like a number of men testifying at the hearings, Blount subscribed to the masculinist doctrine of a manly defense of one's family, property, and community even at his own expense. Thus, he testified that fear for the safety of his wife and daughter made him lay down his arms. Blount explained what would have happened if he had been alone: "I could never have been taken alive." Upon learning of Blount's arrest, a group of black men armed themselves and descended on the jail to protect him from harm. The authorities ordered the men to disband and even sent word from Blount, but only the pleas of his wife, Alice, convinced the black men to disperse. Authorities eventually released Blount on the condition that he left Natchitoches. Though the Blounts and the men who came to their assistance escaped physical violence, many African Americans in neighboring parishes did not.[15]

Randall McGowan, a sharecropper from Pointe Coupée Parish, Louisiana, shared a story of political violence that was similar to that of Blount. Interracial political cooperation had permitted men such as McGowan to hold the office of police juror and constable during Reconstruction. McGowan explained that, by 1878, black men from Pointe Coupée stood little chance of occupying any political offices once white Republicans withdrew from the election because they were fearful of being "strung up" by Democrats. McGowan, however, was a member of a frustrated but determined cohort of blacks who refused to cow to political bullying. Believing that nominating, voting, and holding office were their rights as citizens, these men decided to proceed without white Republicans. McGowan testified that black people's defiance and their insistence on exercising their political rights primed the pump of white Democrats' resentment and activated a decision to use violence.[16]

McGowan testified that white men roused his family from their sleep with a blast of gunfire. Randall scrambled under the bed to retrieve his gun, but the white men grabbed Mrs. McGowan, eliciting his surrender. Then, the bulldozers dragged the couple out of their home, where only Randall's pleas and those of a white neighbor to show mercy to his wife and not force her to see her husband murdered spared the black man's life. The white men carried McGowan on their spree of terror, during which, he reported, the men paraded through the parish "raiding, whipping, and scaring women and men." Afterward, the Democrats released McGowan, informing him that he "would have been a dead man" were his wife not able to identify them. After his release, Randall McGowan attempted to bring his kidnappers to justice, but the white men's repeated attempts to kill him thwarted his mission and forced him to leave his home, land, crops, and Pointe Coupée. Leaving the parish was difficult because McGowan owned seventy-four acres of land on which he had unharvested crops. The violence and McGowan's "charitable exile" prevented him from gathering and selling his thirty-five acres of cotton and twenty acres of corn. Like Blount, McGowan testified that he did not dare return to the life he had built for himself and his family.[17]

Louisiana testifiers indicated that they doubted white Democrats' intent to carry the election violently. In fact, these blacks might have believed the crowds attending Hayes's speeches, but the armed white men's arrival in their communities likely dissipated any lingering uncertainty among African Americans about the white men's intentions to subjugate them politically and violently. As black people fled, many used the natural landscape to hide because they understood that white men "were taking out colored men and hanging and shooting them." Alice Blount testified that victims' and witnesses' flight to the woods and swamps near Natchitoches activated a support network among African Americans throughout the region. These refugees from the violence worked together, Mrs. Blount testified, because they knew that "if they catched one they would catch the whole lot." They listened for conversations and announcements indicating the intentions and whereabouts of the white men, the extent of the violence, and when they could return home safely or make a run for New Orleans or across the state's borders. Residents of the locales where violence occurred were aware of the fact that escapees were hiding nearby, and they provided whatever assistance they could. Mrs. Blount described the people of these locales as being "in dread of their lives." She and others reported that several escapees died from exposure, physical injury, and disease, but most survived, which Blount believed was a testament to their ability to rely on their collective relationships for security.[18]

Testifiers reported that there was some defensive action among black Louisianans. For example, a group of blacks sought sanctuary on the Bass and Gillespie plantations in Tensas Parish, where, according to one witness, those at Gillespie reportedly declared, "If any body came up there they would defend themselves." They knew that if they did not take action to defend themselves, then "they would be killed like dogs." A gunfight ensued between these men and white gangs, resulting in injury and death on both sides. Anticipating violence, blacks in Caledonia Parish stored arms at the home of a wealthy black farmer named Madison Reams. When authorities tried to seize the stockpile, reports indicate that the black men fired on them. Whereas these people fought back, many testified that black folk were isolated, outnumbered, and outgunned and therefore unable to launch an effective opposition to the bulldozers. Moreover, witness Washington Williams explained that some blacks were simply "skert almost to death" of mobilizing a strong defense against the white men.[19]

Many testified that survivors fled their homes and communities because they anticipated future violence, but others decamped because they had received specific threats. Rebecca Ross, for example, was the domestic servant of a murdered black man named Alfred Fairfax, whose home Democrats had invaded and then attacked the occupants and killed two men. Ross testified that she left Natchitoches because she heard that "all that were there at Fairfax's that night were going to be killed." Likewise, when Arthur Fairfax was asked by the Teller Committee whether he wished to return to Tensas, he testified, "If I thought I could go back there in safety, I would go there as anywhere else." Arthur cited having heard threats that the survivors of the assault on his brother Alfred's home "should never go there again." Accepting the white men's word, Ross, Fairfax, and other black Louisianans testified that they abandoned their homes, land, and sometimes their families to avoid violence.[20]

The raids, deaths, and injuries, combined with the unrepentant attitude of white Democrats and the apparent indifference of local and state officials, further traumatized survivors. In fact, victims and witnesses testified that the violence they endured and witnessed forced African Americans to desert their rural homes for more urban ones, with New Orleans being a primary destination. Their counterparts in other states sought shelter in such urban locales as Atlanta, Charleston, and Little Rock. In fact, when members of the committee asked uprooted blacks about their flight from their homes and their refusal to return, they spoke with one voice to explain that they did not feel safe. Most refugees testified that they wanted to continue enjoying the lives that they had created since the war. Threats of future violence in places where black people had built homeplaces and home spheres, however, stopped many victims and witnesses from achieving this goal.

White Democrats' orders that African Americans who refused to accept political subjugation leave their homes or face death were assumed in some cases, but in other cases, the orders were direct and specific. Natchitoches authorities released Blount on the condition that he, and a cohort of political actors, first tell "niggers to desist from politics at once" before vacating the parish, never to return. Blount asked for permission to settle his social and economic affairs and to tend to his family, but local officials only permitted him to return to his home and say goodbye to his wife and daughter. Blount testified that, in the end, he was "glad to get away." However, in leaving—like many of those displaced by violence—Blount had to abandon two houses and several lots of land amounting to some 120 acres, altogether valued at $7,386. With Alice Blount possibly unable to manage the family's land and the odds against Alfred that whites would allow him to return to sell his property for a decent profit, the Blounts would have to relocate and start anew. The refugees' kin, friends, or neighbors might have aimed to take ownership of their property, but whitecappers, those white people who acquired black people's land through violent dispossession, were more likely to settle there.[21] The Blounts were not alone, of course.[22]

Testifiers at the 1878 hearings wanted members of Congress and the public to know that the terror these whites wrought on them, although political in nature, had social and material consequences. Driven from their long-term residences, the Blounts and McGowans joined other refugees displaced by racial violence. If starting over was daunting to prosperous blacks such as the Blounts, then restarting lives would be more difficult for those who were struggling financially, such as the McGowans. Blacks of the McGowans' social status had labored under less-than-desirable conditions to achieve even modest gains after slavery. Thus, many victims and witnesses testified about the difficulties of having their lives destroyed by violence, which was an overwhelming experience that was magnified by the prospects of starting from scratch or, worse, in debt.[23]

African Americans' testimonies before the Teller Committee suggest that many had grown accustomed to white southerners' trickery and harassment whenever black men attempted to vote; however, the scale of the violence in Louisiana horrified many victims and witnesses. For example, Robert J. Walker testified to having heard "wild talk" by Democrats. Walker explained that residents felt the language was "not much more than usual just before election day." These blacks hoped that white people's animosity toward black male suffrage had subsided after Reconstruction and that, in the first election under Reconciliation, they could exercise the franchise without fear of physical harm. Even those individuals who were targeted specifically, such as Blount—who testified that whites had warned him during the 1876 election to abstain from trying to vote or to hold elected office—initially dismissed the 1878 threats. Overall, these people cited the regularity of white people's threats and use of ordinary violence during previous elections, the improbability of a daytime attack, and the general goodwill throughout the parishes after Reconstruction as reasons they did not anticipate extraordinary violence.[24]

These testimonies indicate that emancipation's reign of terror might have dulled some African Americans' sensitivity to the possibility of violence. However, the white men's menacing words inspired other blacks to consider additional options for protecting their interests. Washington Williams, a sharecropper and former coroner of Tensas, explained that he had "got so bitter" about the prospects of electing a Republican ticket that he and others began negotiating an independent fusion ticket with moderate Democrats. Even this concession was not enough to make bulldozers and whitecappers stand down. Williams testified that an armed gang went to his father-in-law's home issuing threats that they would "blow the head off" Williams if he made any public, political statements. Some residents were apprehensive enough about the threats and notices of arrest warrants that they became anxious about convening any political meetings. Black Louisianans' collective will to exercise authority in local governance and skepticism that they would be harmed saw a large number of them continue to meet. The raids, however, shattered African Americans' remaining illusions about the white Democrats' resolve to stop black men from voting and holding office.[25]

Victims and witnesses testified that they expected violence from avowed racists, but some survivors' testimonies suggest that betrayals from acquaintances compounded the horror they experienced. Given the past relationships and the close proximity in which blacks and whites lived, many people testified that they knew their attackers. Indeed, testifiers' accounts indicate that the long-term intimacy between these residents permitted some blacks to believe they had no reason to fear violence from their white neighbors. For example, Fleming Branch of Tensas Parish testified that he had no reason to believe that J. S. Peck, the white man whom his mother had nursed at birth, would lead the invasion of the Fairfax home, kill two men, and cripple him. Similarly, A. J. Bryant testified to knowing some of the people who congregated outside his home with a prepared noose, including a man whom he identified as a "friend." Moreover, violence in the 1876 and 1878 elections had shown Louisianan Henry Adams that if white men were determined to carry an election, "there is nothing too mean for them to do to prevent it." Adams provided an assessment of the changes in white people's attitudes toward black people when it came to voting in elections. Adams testified, "If I am working on his place, and he has been laughing and talking with me, and I do everything he tells me to, yet in times of election he will crush me down, and even kill me, or do anything to me to carry his point."[26] Some African Americans' testimonies about their assessment of their safety before the election suggest that it was impossible for black people to determine which white men might defend them against a mob and which men might be a part of it.

African Americans certainly felt betrayed by their white acquaintances, but their testimonies reveal that they also felt let down by state and federal officials. David Young of Vidalia, Louisiana, summarized many black southerners' interpretations about what the violence during the 1878 election revealed about Reconciliation. Young testified, "I lost all confidence in the ability of the [Hayes] administration to protect the lives of my people down here." So he came to a decision: "to leave the place or leave out politics, . . . to make friends with the worst bulldozers and lay [Republicans] aside because they can't protect us." Similarly, Blount described the Republican Party as the one that "sold out this state and gave it away [to the Democratic Party]." Young, Blount, and other blacks knew that suffrage helped them to protect all of their rights, to buttress their demands for protection from violence, and to achieve their goals for racial progress. However, they wanted members of Congress and the American people to know that their experiences of violence and of white state and federal officials' failure to stop or prosecute it after the 1878 election portended doom.[27]

African Americans' testimonies about violence indicate their beliefs that Reconciliation amounted to an abandonment of Reconstruction's principles of bringing black people into the national polity. Their arguments were persuasive to some members of the committee but not to all. Although some Republican members of the Teller Committee were sympathetic to African Americans' reports of political violence, the committee, which was dominated by Democrats, concluded that, while white southern Democrats' use of violence and political maneuvers to win the election had violated Republican voters' political rights, the national government could not intervene on the victims' behalf. Some Republicans were convinced that the federal government should do more to protect black people's political rights, at least in the election of members of Congress. However, members of the committee conceded that the Constitution constrained Congress by limiting its power over elections to prescribing the "times, places, and manner" in which they occurred. Progressives knew that the federal government could not rely on state officials to prosecute political irregularities. Members of Congress, as they had during Reconstruction, investigated the violence and provided a forum for black people to testify about their experiences, but they offered victims no justice or restitution.[28]

White southern Democrats carried the 1878 election violently, but many African Americans learned from the violence and from their participation in the Teller hearings that the federal government would do nothing to reverse the election's outcomes or to punish the perpetrators. They also knew that many state officials were largely indifferent to violations of black people's rights. Democratic Governor Francis T. Nicholls of Louisiana, having conducted his own internal investigation presumably because of the negative attention that the violence had shone on his state, offered bromides of repentance. He apologized for the violence that he thought occurred "practically beyond the reach of the constituted authorities" and was committed by men who "substitute[d] their own ideas of justice and methods of remedy." Barely acknowledging the political motives behind the violence—possibly because similar actions and attitudes permitted his own assumption of office—Nicholls denounced the attacks as "wrong" and "without justification" but took no action to prosecute even known perpetrators.[29]

In many African Americans' minds, the 1878 midterm election was the first test of Reconciliation, and state and federal officials had failed to uphold the spirit of Reconstruction. White Democrats had promised that they would respect black people's political rights. Yet they exhibited their willingness to continue employing violence and political chicanery to reestablish white conservative hegemony over southern politics and life. Some white congressional Republicans, such as Senator William E. Chandler of New Hampshire, expressed outrage at Hayes's failure to protect black southerners' rights. Chandler warned the nation that black people would start defending themselves, setting off a "war of races" unless "you give to the negroes the rights which are secured to them by the Constitution." Honoring the spirit of Reconciliation, many white Republicans ignored Chandler and ceded control of southern politics to white Democrats.[30]

The fact that the political violence that shaped the outcome of some national elections did not beget any federal action, beyond investigation, represented the political ground moving under African Americans' feet as the resolve of white northern progressives to uphold the principles of Reconstruction yielded to the determination of white southern conservatives to limit the federal government's influence on their affairs. The 1878 election forced black people to consider abandoning all undertakings in southern political life, leaving rural and southern locales, or joining the Democratic Party. Some blacks started to eschew politics and to prioritize institution building in their communities. As these people soon learned, quitting politics would not pacify whites who demanded economic, political, and social control over southern life. What is more, some white progressives' disengaged reaction to the violence was a portent of the buckling of their support for any additional federal remedies to address racial violence and to protect black people's civil and political rights.

The "Subtler, Darker Deeds" of Reconciliation

As long as white progressives threw up their hands about southern violence, white conservatives felt little need to exercise restraint in using their interpretation of popular constitutionalism to resubjugate African Americans. Indeed, conservatives did not have the power to change black people's legal status as citizens; they simply used the logic of white supremacy and black inferiority to control the future meaning of freedom and black people's citizenship rights. The belief that whites were superior to nonwhites and that their superiority entitled them to dominate society informed the doctrine of white supremacy that guided the social norms and the political policies regulating southern life. Initially, some blacks dismissed these claims of white supremacy coming from ex-Confederates and their supporters as the dogma of the defeated. What they probably did not realize was that the new white nationalism of Reconciliation was part of larger global revolution tied to what Du Bois, in "The Souls of White Folk," called the "discovery of personal whiteness among the world's peoples." The "new religion of whiteness" advocated white control of the earth and dominion over nonwhite peoples. Du Bois explained, "After the more comic manifestations [of white supremacy] and the chilling of generous enthusiasm come subtler, darker deeds." In the 1880s, African Americans saw the "subtler, darker deeds" of Reconciliation in the institutions that became administers of white supremacy and the white folk who became its agents on the ground. The resulting cognizance of what was unfolding economically, politically, and socially in the South eventually prompted many blacks to take action by leaving the region and developing vehicles of communication to testify about violence and to combat the deterioration of their rights.[31]

Many African Americans who wanted to believe in Reconciliation and who had downplayed white-supremacist rhetoric probably did not appreciate the global context of what was occurring in the postbellum South. Against the backdrop of Reconciliation was the cataclysm of Europe's rush for natural and manmade goods, exploitable labor, and profitable markets in Africa, Asia, and Latin America. White Europeans saw it as their duty to "divide up the darker world and administer it" for the global good, and they did, by using the logic of white people's superiority and black and brown people's inferiority to seize control of resources and to subjugate peoples they deemed primitive, uncivilized, and therefore incapable of managing themselves or their resources. White Americans joined Europeans in expanding the scope of white supremacy in the 1880s in domestic and imperial campaigns. In the United States, whites manipulated the levers of power to completely resubjugate black people. They proceeded at so slow and so subtle a pace that African Americans' unstructured response to escalating violence, the increasing violations of their rights, and the failure of federal officials to take action in the early 1880s suggests that they did not fully appreciate the civil and political catastrophe unfolding or that they did not have the vehicles to publicize their concerns widely until later in the decade. Indeed, Du Bois, in "The Souls of White Folk," argued that the earthquakes of a consolidated white supremacy occurred underwater, which probably blunted black people's ability to appreciate their implications and develop a successful response. What is more, it was not until middecade that whites moved to resubjugate blacks aggressively and publicly and did so without much interference from blacks, from white progressives, or from federal officials.[32]

Although the "darker deeds" of Reconciliation did not become obvious to everyone until the 1880s, they started to take form after the war. White southern industrialists and planters introduced labor conditions that resembled slavery and used their financial and political might to persuade like-minded legislators to rewrite statutes to accommodate their need to control black people's labor. These men used legally binding agreements to extract underpaid and unpaid work from blacks. At the same time, planters and landlords used minor infractions to claim that a laborer or tenant had violated a contract, which often landed black laborers and tenants in the convict-lease system because white juries typically accepted the white employer's or land owner's word over that of the black laborer or tenant. In the 1870s and the early 1880s, southern lawmakers enacted laws that stripped black people of their ability to enjoy the fruits of their labor, and they criminalized many elements of black people's behavior. Thus, when blacks disputed wages, prices, or contracts, these challenges provoked both individual and institutional responses that advanced white people's interests over those of black people. As such, force, violence, and a vast system of fines, taxes, and property restrictions, as well as changes to the penal codes and the expansion of convict leasing, became the tools by which the white power brokers restored financial stability to the southern economy and exacted from black laborers what amounted to informal compensation for emancipation.[33]

Black people who testified in congressional hearings, in speeches, at conventions, and in newspapers explained that their goals for transcending slavery remained unchanged. They still wanted fertile land, freedom from fraudulent and debt-compounding labor practices, the right to secure and enjoy the fruits of their labor, control over their families, and some authority in local governance. In fact, many African Americans seemed to understand that state and federal governments would not protect their right to enjoy what they believed were the privileges of freedom and citizenship. These blacks had limited options: accept the terms of southern life as white people dictated or defy them. Any response short of deference impelled whites to spontaneous or premeditated violence. Thus, even if whites did not use overt violence to resubjugate blacks, the changes that they made to public policies gave them the authority to manage defiant blacks.[34]

As the nation permitted the white South to make these small, deliberate steps toward violent white majority rule, African Americans took flight. Blacks were already moving from the region's farms and plantations to its towns and villages, but some people sought to escape violence by leaving the region. Indeed, Henry Adams testified that once Democrats took control over state houses, many southern blacks had "lost all hopes" in their state governments. African Americans had found themselves "in such a condition" in the region: "we looked around and we seed that there was no way on earth, it seemed that we could better our condition."[35] Although during the war many blacks had rebuffed Lincoln's plans for resettling free African Americans in the Caribbean and Central America, migration and emigration gained currency among black folk during Reconciliation as the nation's tolerance for the violent resubjugation of African Americans grew. [36]

Migration to Liberia remained popular among black people who were looking to break the grip of southern whites, but such places as Kansas, Indiana, and Missouri became the key destinations for migrants because of the reputed availability of land. The postemancipation trickle of individual migrations to the Northeast and Midwest morphed into a flood as several thousand blacks decamped from North and South Carolina, Mississippi, Louisiana, Tennessee, and Texas in 1879. As black people started departing the region in large numbers, the white southerners who were dependent on black people's labor reacted by trying to stop the migrations. These efforts to coerce migrants to remain only emboldened black people's determination to leave. The migrations, the arrival of desperate blacks in northern and western territories, and the reports of violence received extensive media coverage and invoked comparisons with the Israelites' departure from Egypt.[37]

Congress responded to the reports of the migrations by investigating the causes of the "removal of southern Negroes." Although black women constituted a large portion of the migrants, black men from Texas, Mississippi, North Carolina, and Alabama represented the majority of those who testified at these hearings. Testimonies about the Exoduster movement reveal black people's endurance of violence, a void of national black leadership, and rifts among African Americans about their quality of life after Reconstruction. Indeed, although the migrations were popular among some farmers, farm workers, and domestics, they did not enjoy the support of some prosperous southern blacks, some people in locales where the migrants settled, and some public figures. What is more, some prominent black landowners, newspaper editors, politicians, and lawyers rejected and downplayed migrants' complaints of horrible living conditions in the South. Whether these affluent blacks adopted what the sociologist Juan Corradi has called a "passion for ignorance"—a collective denial about reports and rumors of violence followed by a rationalization of its occurrence (for example, that the victimized were deserving)—or they testified as they did for personal or political gain is unclear.[38] What is clear is that, if prosperous southern testifiers were "passionately ignorant" of violence, then the migrants, the migration's coordinators, and some of the northern and western first responders to the crisis the migrations caused were not. When refugees flooded their towns, northerners and midwesterners established relief organizations to alleviate the suffering of those who were destitute upon their arrival. These people put the suffering they endured or witnessed among the migrants into the public record.[39]

The accounts of migrants, of the migration's coordinators, of some returnees, and of some of the people who received them and heard their testimonies about what made them leave the South provide evidence of some early consequences of Reconciliation for African Americans. For example, John H. Johnson, a St. Louis attorney and secretary of that city's refugee board, testified that migrants described to him and others conditions in the South in which black people enjoyed no security in "life, limb, or property." Some migrants complained that black men were "shot down for political purposes." These conditions prompted many black men to pack up their families and their belongings and to leave the region. Other migrants testified to men such as Johnson that violence during Reconstruction left many black families without male heads of household who might have provided for their families and protected them from violence. The men's surviving family members coped for as long as they could before they decided to improve their plight by migrating. Many St. Louis arrivals were single, widowed, and married black women against whom white men had used physical and sexual violence in their efforts to resubjugate these women and their families. Specifically, Johnson explained that a number of the Mississippians and Louisianans to whom he spoke objected to "all the impositions practiced on colored women." Johnson re-presented female migrants' stories of husbands, fathers, and brothers slain by whites for political activism or defying a white person's authority as well as women's stories of sexual harassment and violence. As an illustrative example of the violence directed at women, Johnson testified to learning from two female migrants leaving Louisiana about a pregnant woman whom white men shot when she conveyed that she was leaving the state to join her husband in Kansas. The shots killed the woman and triggered the premature birth of her child, which, Johnson testified, "came to life" and which one of the men reportedly "took . . . and mashed its brains out."[40]

Some St. Louisans sought to convince the migrants to return to their homes. Outraged refugees responded by testifying about violence and explaining that they would rather "go into the open prairie and starve there than go to the South to stand the impositions that were put on them down there." Johnson reported that some Missourians even tried to test the migrants' sincerity by offering to pay for their return passage. Johnson testified that one man threatened to assault him for suggesting that he return south. Missourian J. W. Wheeler also testified that the consensus of the migrants he interviewed was that "they said they had only one death to die, and they might as well die in the North as in the South." Thus, neither the cold weather conditions nor the very clear indications that northerners and westerners wanted the migrants to return to the South could convince them to turn back.[41]

The testimony of Henry Ruby, a migrant from Texas, exemplifies the role of violence and its impact on black politics and families as a factor in the exodus. Ruby testified that he attended a "colored men's convention" in Houston in May 1879 before he left. Ruby shared with the committee the convention attendees' complaints about racist policies regarding juries, education, land, and convict labor. A more specific incentive for blacks to leave Texas was the violence used to break African Americans' operations to establish black settlements in the state's panhandle. Bulldozers and whitecappers had killed the leaders of these settlements and used a scorched-earth campaign to drive blacks from the settlements. In addition to reporting this violence, Ruby testified that the treatment of black women and girls was one of the "main grievances" and "causes" of some migrants' desire to leave the South. Black southern men, he explained, knew that their wives, daughters, and mothers were "not safe," that they were "liable to be insulted at any time." Ruby testified that these men understood that if they attempted to defend black females or to avenge white men's assaults on them, they were likely to be "shot or taken out at night and bushwhacked or killed."[42]

Henry Adams compiled an inventory of first- and secondhand accounts of violence committed against black southerners that the committee allowed him to enter into evidence. Hundreds of black people testified to him about the violence they endured and witnessed. These people shared their experiences because they hoped that Adams would relate their stories to others and that hearing victims' and witnesses' stories of suffering would educate listeners and inspire them to take action. This catalog, which Adams supplied as evidence of the migration's causative factors, included nearly seven hundred reports of black Louisianans harassed, beaten, and slaughtered by whites. For example, one account came from Washington Douglas of Bossier Parish, who reported that a white man by the name of "Bloody" John Gage beat him over the head with a six-shooter. Douglas testified to Adams that he told Gage that he could not enter his house without an invitation and that the white man could not "keep" his daughter. Douglas's daughter was possibly under an apprenticeship or a convict-lease arrangement or was simply the object of Gage's lust, but Douglas's defiance of the white man sparked the pistol whipping he received. In sum, victims and witnesses testified to Adams that whites working to deprive blacks of wages, land, education, franchise, separate institutions, and the sanctity of their families was not their only problem. The larger underlying issue was that white people used violence to accomplish those ends, leaving death and physical and psychological injuries in their wake. Having endured, witnessed, or expected victimization from this violence, migrants testified that they decided to leave the South rather than subject themselves to more of it.[43]

Congressional investigators at the Klan hearings were empathetic to testimonies about violence, but many members of the Exoduster committee were not, which prompted some African Americans testifiers to try to set the record straight. In fact, some Democratic congressmen openly expressed their skepticism about some first- and secondhand accounts of racial violence. An appalled Benjamin Singleton responded to some committee members' hostility toward the migrants by castigating them for summoning black men from "good circumstances and [who] own their own homes, not the poor ones." Singleton's evaluation of the witnesses called to testify before the committee was well informed. Many of the black southern witnesses who were given the most respectful treatment by the committee's Democratic majority were born into wealth or able to attain a higher social status that separated them from the poor black masses. Many of the black southern witnesses whose testimonies the committee's majority often dismissed were people of lesser financial means who were more vulnerable to racial violence. Singleton, who was an undertaker in Nashville, testified that he personally witnessed the devastating aftermath of violence for slain black men's families. Singleton reported that the consequences of racial violence left black families "coming down, instead of going up."[44] Singleton's testimony, along with that of Adams, Johnson, Ruby, and Wheeler, shows that victims and witnesses cited violence as a significant factor in some black people's decision to leave the South.

Although thousands of African Americans migrated, the majority remained in the South. Indeed, when asked by the committee how blacks felt about the South, testifiers responded that many of the migrants and the people who spoke on their behalf expressed an affinity for the region. According to Johnson, one migrant explained that the South was "the home of the colored man." Testifying on behalf of this migrant, Johnson explained that blacks have "improved that part of the country, and done more to advance the material interests of the South than any other race or nation." Benjamin Singleton testified that "confidence [in the South as a safe and secure place for blacks to live] is perished and faded away." Black people "don't want to leave the South," he explained. When African Americans had confidence in their ability to live their lives freely, Singleton offered to "be an instrument in the hands of God to persuade every man to go back because that it is the best country." Short of improved social and economic conditions, an end to violence, and a reversal in what appeared to be white southerners' refusal to respect black people's civil and political rights, there seemed to be little to convince migrants and their supporters that they had erred in migrating or that blacks should return south or even that those who were still there should continue to reside in the region.[45]

The vernacular history of the Exoduster movement echoed the sentiments of African Americans victimized during Reconstruction and the 1878 election. These testifiers reported that blacks had been coping with life under Reconciliation. The economic, political, and social gains that some black people had achieved, combined with any specific defiance of white people's authority, made them vulnerable to violent attacks. It is difficult to know how many migrants experienced violence. Nevertheless, many of the migrants' testimonies to Adams and Singleton, to first responders in the North and Midwest, and to members of the committee point to African Americans enduring or witnessing racial violence and being familiar with the vernacular history of racial violence. What is more, both Johnson's and Singleton's testimonies suggest that the attacks on black men took their toll and heightened women's and children's vulnerability to whites attempting to subjugate them. The local and state governments' failure to offer victims relief and security from violence powered some of the migrations. That the displaced people embraced taking up new residences—facing the challenges of starting over, acquiring employment, finding homes, and doing these things away from any existing support structures, as well as relating their reasons for migrating—speaks to the magnitude of desperation in some families and communities. Black migration during this period was a more oblique style of resistance to white supremacy than was confronting violent whites directly. However, these testimonies suggest that migrants and their supporters saw the migration as a form of resistance to violence.

As Exodusters explained their reasons for leaving the South to their receivers in the North and Midwest and to members of Congress in the hearings, they also had to account for the opposition to the migration by some prominent black public figures, whose critiques commanded the attention of white citizens, officials, and the dominant public spheres. The migration's organizers voiced disdain for self-proclaimed and white-appointed black public figures. Both Henry Adams and Benjamin Singleton distanced themselves from black politicians, landlords, ministers, and merchants, citing their penchant for self-interest. When questioned by the committee on black public figures' role in the migration, Adams asserted, "We was afraid that if we allowed the colored politicianer to belong [to our organization] he would tell it to Republican[s]," and white Democrats would discover their plot to migrate en masse and "get after us." Explaining some local politicians' request that organizers "don't stir up the people to go away; [to] wait until next year and we'll elect somebody that'll give us our rights," Adams testified, "we didn't trust any of them."[46]

Many black southerners had expressed support for such organic intellectuals as Adams and Singleton and contempt for public figures. One black Nashvillian proclaimed, "The colored people have no national leaders." In this man's assessment, most "leaders" or public figures were "all the defeated colored Congressmen and all other office seekers who are disappointed." The annual meetings of groups such as the Colored Men's Conventions were nothing but forums for the deposed black men to "give vent and expression, as they were the leaders of the colored people and could control their votes." This man claimed that the only individuals whom black folk could look to for guidance were "those whom they personally know and live and associate with." Louisianan Alfred Blount echoed his Nashville counterpart by describing black public figures as "false leaders." Migrants' distrust of black public figures was justified. Such prominent black public figures as Frederick Douglass, P. B. S. Pinchback, and Blanche K. Bruce were among the migration's loudest critics. Douglass condemned the Exoduster movement as a titanic capitulation to white supremacy, and Pinchback belittled the migration's organizers as "small-fry politicians."[47]

Some black public figures' criticism of the exodus notwithstanding, the migrations were an impressive feat for black folk to carry out, and they were a testament to African Americans' growing frustration with resubjugation. Nonetheless, some public figures' patronizing critiques of the migrations reflect the ideological distance between the people in enclave communities and some national figures. Both black public figures and black folk believed that it was important for African Americans to resist resubjugation, but they had different opinions on the best approach. Both groups favored what I call the politics of defiance, an insistence on resisting white supremacy, but they saw the migrations in different ways.[48] This discord between public figures and black folk complicated African Americans' efforts to combat northern and Republican indifference to intensified violence.

Though federal officials allowed African Americans to testify publicly about violence and to insert their beliefs and opinions about it into the public spheres, the investigation into the "removal of negroes from southern states" marks a turning point in Reconciliation. Unlike the U.S. Army and Freedmen's Bureau and the two previous hearings, where officials were largely receptive to black people's testimonies of violence and contemplative of extending some of the federal government's authority to provide them with some protection, the increasing marginalization of blacks created a different atmosphere for the investigation into the migrations. Southern Democrats—who had regained congressional power and therefore constituted the majority of the committee investigating the migrations—rejected violence as a factor in black people's flight from the region. Democrats argued that the migrations were a politically motivated affair that "could not have arisen from any deprivation of [African Americans'] political rights or any hardship in their condition." The condition of black people in the South, the committee's majority claimed, "is not only as good as could have been reasonably expected [after slavery], but is better than if large communities transferred." The Democrats dismissed black people's complaints of violence, claiming they found "nothing or almost nothing new" on that matter. The Republican minority objected, charging that a "long series of oppression, injustice, and violence" was the catalyst for the migrations. These Republicans believed that the migrants had acted "in utter despair, fled panic-stricken from their homes and sought protection among strangers in a strange land." They believed that federal officials should provide African Americans with some protection from violence and discrimination at the local and state level, but they were overruled.[49]

The Democrats' interpretation of the migrations reflected the way that racial violence had become something that the nation would tolerate in exchange for sectional reconciliation. Damning evidence of violence was not enough to persuade Democrats that it played a role in black southerners' flight or that black people needed federal officials to intervene on their behalf. The Republican minority's observation that there had been a "long series of oppression, injustice, and violence" was astute, but it obscured the systemic and systematic evolution of southern white supremacy in the late 1870s. The committee's tacit decision that this violence was acceptable and that what was not acceptable remained in the purview of the states was part of a sequence of federal policy statements that signaled the way that violence during the presumed peace of Reconciliation had lost its power to shock and appall Americans. Subsequent Supreme Court decisions, economic crises, and African Americans' continued efforts to transcend slavery and to fight for civil and political rights became the springboards for intensified racial violence. What is more, increasing numbers of northern whites and federal officials refused to acknowledge that new policies governing black southerners' lives bore a striking resemblance to slavery.

The investigation into the Exoduster movement was one of last instances when federal officials provided public forums for black folk to testify about violence and its effects in the nineteenth century. After this period, there is a near official state silence on racial violence as many white citizens and agents of the state and federal governments embraced Reconciliation and white southerners' brand of popular constitutionalism. When some white progressive holdouts attempted to address these new policies and practices that undermined the letter and spirit of Reconstruction, their loss of political power and influence in the South hindered their efforts to stop white citizens and local and state officials from violating black people's rights. White southern officials knew that as long as their policies and practices were no overt violation of the Constitution, then white progressive citizens and federal officials would continue to leave them alone. The nation's growing indifference toward racial violence and to white conservatives' triumphant return to power broke the political chains that had been restraining the white opponents of emancipation and Reconstruction from chipping away at black people's civil and political rights. Although violence was not a subtle method of resubjugation, ongoing racial violence during Reconciliation made it easy for white progressives to ignore.

During the 1880s, relying on empathetic citizens and federal officials was no longer a viable option for African Americans. Black southerners were increasingly excluded from participating in state and federal politics and in the dominant public spheres, as many citizens and elected officials and some newspapers refused to acknowledge racial violence or to provide spaces for black people to share their suffering. Blacks coped with these changes in the nation by testifying about violence to each other, and those records have been lost to historians except where they exist as part of occasional public forums and black folk traditions and family histories.[50] However, evidence of black people's efforts to testify about violence and to challenge white supremacy exists in the form of speeches by black public figures and reports and editorials in black print culture, records that bear the signs of victims' and witnesses' accounts of violence.

The speeches of black public figures and the work of journalists and newspaper editors, who took up the mantle of relating black people's reports of violence and other types of subjugation, indicate that ordinary violence remained a key feature of black southern life during the 1880s. This violence failed to evoke action from federal officials and white progressives in part because it was smaller in scale. Unlike the insurgency against Reconstruction and the lynchings of the 1890s, the violence in the interim, although devastating, was less extraordinary. Racial violence became commonplace, which made ignoring the less obvious depredations of white supremacy easier. Reconciliation gave southern whites greater authority to resubjugate blacks. Southern whites embraced this new authority, and over time they molded it into the region's institutions. Ordinary white folk and many newly arrived immigrants from Europe became invested in maintaining white people's racial supremacy in their daily interactions with black folk.[51]

One difference between Reconstruction and the Reconciliationist sentiment of the 1880s is that some Republican federal officials tried to use their constitutional powers to combat resubjugation in the earlier period and ignored it in the latter. Freedmen's Bureau and army officials had captured the testimonies of victims and witnesses, and many progressive Americans wanted to hear them and to have violent whites brought to justice. As the DOJ's bureaucracy grew, U.S. marshals replaced bureau agents as federal law enforcement officers. African Americans reported violence to these officers, who, in adherence to the ethos of Reconciliation, deferred to local and state authorities, many of whom the region's Democratic white power brokers put into office. The DOJ became a repository for complaints about violence, but the agency neglected to offer victims shelter, to command local and state authorities to prosecute crimes against black people, or to take the lead in prosecuting whites when these authorities failed to uphold their states' basic laws on crime and murder. The DOJ's policy regarding southern racial violence epitomized the position of many sectional reconciliationists who did not care about violence as long as it was contained in the South. Racism, combined with repeated exposure to violence, dulled many white progressives' sensitivity to racial violence against African Americans. If news about the riots and massacres at places such as Memphis, New Orleans, and Colfax, as well as the Klan raids during Reconstruction, had attacked white progressives' sense of peace, then the reports and complaints about ordinary violence during the early 1880s must have seemed less shocking and more mundane.[52]

To African Americans who experienced and witnessed the violence of Reconciliation, the unending reports of violence and the nation's apparent indifference to it, as shown by the reaction to the Exoduster movement, signaled a tragic end of the possibilities of Reconstruction's promise of citizenship to black people. Knowing how many black people whites dispossessed, maimed, raped, exiled, and killed during Reconciliation is impossible. Victims testified about violence to largely unsympathetic local officials and some journalists, but many of their personal reflections are lost. With fewer federally sponsored public forums, progressive white and black newspaper reports on massacres, riots, and lynchings are the best indicators of African Americans' experiences of and responses to violence and the evolution of white supremacy. Underneath the klieg lights of newspapers headlining reports of racial violence that rose from what became the daily disputes in the postbellum South are details about the causes of the violence. Indeed, African Americans' development of their own print culture and their efforts to fill the void of national leadership provide the most compelling evidence of violence, black people's individual resistance, and their collective efforts to confront white supremacy. Where even cursory details exist, black people's earlier testimonies about violence provide insight into the seemingly monotonous and distant details of newspaper reports.

Victims' and witnesses' testimonies illuminate the quotidian nature of racial violence, but most mainstream newspapers rarely reported daily contests for white supremacy and black survival unless they rose to the surface of southern life in the form of a lynching or a riot. Black newspapers, however, were more likely to publish black people's accounts of violence and to cover violations of their civil and political rights. In both black and white progressive newspapers, the extraordinary violence that merited headlines often obscured the violence of the everyday. Nonetheless, details in reports of attacks and critiques of white southern "lawlessness" and the "perils of southern democracy" in black and white progressive print culture lend evidence to the continuing violence, while increasing the obstacles to exploring it.[53] For example, newspapers reported in late 1881 that black South Carolinians started fleeing the state. Migrants testified that their departure was motivated by the state's "tinkering with our freedom" and the ways that blacks were "ostracized, hunted down, plundered, tortured, and killed for presuming to vote as they wished, . . . at the mercy of Ku-Klux and red-shirted midnight riders." Racial violence was enough to drive some black folk "to Arkansas or somewhere, it doesn't matter much where," so long as "the laws were just and those who administer them humane." One migrant testified that blacks were "worse off now" than when they were slaves, because the value of black people's lives had decreased in the minds of whites. The labor force's departure prompted some South Carolina state executives to ask white residents to respect black people's rights. The Chicago *Tribune* responded by admonishing white civilians and elected officials in the state. Now that blacks had "taken the only redress in their hands," the editors explained, "the [white] people of South Carolina suddenly discover that they are indispensable to the cultivation of the soil, and that the productiveness of the State might languish if they are allowed to go."[54]

That some issues surrounding labor were at the center of the South Carolina exodus illuminates a key factor in many interracial clashes that ended in violence. African Americans' earlier testimonies about racial violence indicate that most incidents of southern violence originated in places where and on occasions when black people were most likely to interact with whites, especially those surrounding labor. Disputes between white employers and black workers were always subject to violence, but black people's increasingly orchestrated resistance to deplorable and exploitative working conditions evoked collective aggression from the white power structure. Black laborers worked to earn shares and wages while improving working conditions by negotiating and even arguing with their employers. They also organized cooperatives and work stoppages and joined unions that admitted them. For instance, Louisiana sugar workers chafed under the enduring gang-labor protocol, planters' withholding of pay until year's end, and wage cuts amid merchants' inflated prices; they responded by striking in 1880. The state responded by commissioning militias to the parishes to arrest the strike's organizers. In 1881, Atlanta police broke an orchestrated strike of black washerwomen by arresting and fining participants. White civilians' use of violence to control and exploit black people's labor and the willingness of state officials to intervene on behalf of employers when African Americans resisted made black southerners feel that they had to leave the region.[55]

The practice of using violence to manage African American labor was repeated throughout the decade, often with more violent results. In August 1883, white gangs went on a terror spree in Georgia. The posses, presumably agents of Georgia's white power brokers, invaded African Americans' homes, flogged them, and drove tenants and sharecroppers off the land after they had planted crops. Driving these people off the land allowed white landowners to harvest and profit from the crop without having to share the bounty with black laborers. A gang beat one woman because she had not yet planted her cotton. Another chased a boy and shot him. In Eastman in 1883, C. W. Skelton, of the blacksmith firm Skelton & Son, reportedly attacked a seven-year-old black girl inside the store. The merchants called on the girl's mother to get her; the mother, accompanied by a local doctor, recovered her child and discovered that Skelton, who had absconded, had sexually assaulted her daughter. The Arkansas *Weekly Mansion* declared that Skelton should be captured and "lynched to the first tree as they do colored men." Because of the social and political climate of Reconciliation, white men who attacked African Americans in the 1880s had no reason to fear arrest or prosecution. Indeed, newspaper reports from this period show little evidence that authorities attempted to bring to justice white men who attacked black people.[56]

African Americans experiencing and witnessing this violence probably thought that conditions were already bad, but in 1883 the Supreme Court delivered another dose of resubjugation when it determined that the 1875 Civil Rights Act was unconstitutional.[57] In the *Civil Rights Cases*, the Court decided that the equal protection clause of the Fourteenth Amendment only protected blacks from the states' infringement of their rights regarding public accommodations and facilities, not the discriminatory actions of private citizens or businesses. In sum, the Court prohibited states from segregating by race but upheld the right of private businesses and some civil service providers to draw the color line in their restaurants, hotels, and trains and streetcars. At a convention of African Americans that September in Washington, D.C., delegates discussed the decision and offered their assessment of conditions for blacks. They concluded, "Our civil rights are still infringed upon all over the country. . . . Our political rights are now almost wholly ignored, and the voice of six and one half millions of people with peculiar interests at stake lost from the legislative halls of government."[58]

Black newspaper reports from across the nation suggest that African Americans were divided over the implications of the decision, underscoring the ideological rifts among blacks. For some conservative black public figures, the decision was inconsequential, but to such progressive public figures as Henry McNeal Turner, the Court's ruling harbingered an urgent constitutional crisis. Turner condemned the decision as one that "makes the American flag to [the Negro] a rag of contempt instead of a symbol of liberty." Turner believed that the decision "absolves the Negro's allegiance to the general government, . . . opens all of the issues of the late war, sets the country wrangling again, puts the negro back in politics, revives the ku-klux klan and white leaguers." The Arkansas *Weekly Mansion*'s conservative editors disagreed. They saw the decision as "of little significance" because the Court had "only nullified the manner of redress commencing in the United States courts." From their viewpoint, all aggrieved blacks had to do was "commence their efforts for redress at the state level." In other words, instead of African Americans appealing directly to the federal government for relief from what they argued were violations of their civil rights, they should initiate their lawsuits in state courts. The *Weekly Mansion* was not alone in its characterization of the decision, as the white, conservative Arkansas *Gazette* agreed with the paper's characterization of the decision. Black and white conservatives argued that the civil rights bill's nullification lacked significance because the Court had upheld black people's rights. As long as state governments did not violate black people's civil rights, then the fact that they were allowing white citizens and businesses to deprive blacks of their rights on a racial basis did not matter.[59]

Some progressive newspapers, such as the New York *Globe* and the New Orleans *American Citizen*, likened the *Civil Rights Cases* decision to the Court's decision in the *Dred Scott* case. The *Globe*, for example evoked Justice Roger B. Taney's exhortation that black people had no rights that white men needed to honor. The *Citizen* decried the more recent decision as "inhuman, intolerant and dastardly." "Prejudice, bigotry and hate," the paper railed, "has consummated the greatest crime of the century, and to-day seven millions of intelligent law abiding people are by virtue of the court's illiberal opinion relegated back to the dark days of Taney." The Boston *Hub* disparaged the Court for having "deliberately refused the sanction of their authority to the security of the civil rights of the colored people." The Chicago *Conservator*'s assessment was perhaps the most sobering. "For eighteen years," the editors declared, "the colored people of this country have been hugging a delusion. The dream may have been pleasant, while it lasted, the awakening is rude and sudden."[60] Public figures' speeches and writings and black print culture indicate that blacks increasingly understood that the economic and social tentacles of white supremacy could reach into all areas of their lives and that federal officials would take no action to protect their rights.

The rude awakening presented by the Court's decision outraged African Americans who believed that the federal government had not only the constitutional authority but also the responsibility to protect black people from civil rights violations at the hands of white citizens, business owners, or local and state officials. These African Americans believed that estimations such as those of the *Weekly Mansion* ignored the southern states' failure to uphold their responsibilities to preserve black people's rights to due process and to equal protection under the law. With the Court's decision, blacks felt white progressives' resolve for preserving black people's rights slip against white conservatives' determination to achieve full black resubjugation. Blacks across the nation held "indignation" meetings to express their outrage over the decision. They drafted resolutions to President Chester A. Arthur in which they testified about their suffering and asked the president to apply the authority of his office to execute the existing laws. These people also asked the president to encourage members of Congress to add additional amendments to the Constitution to provide more African Americans with federal protection from civil rights abuses by private citizens and by businesses. Black citizens of Louisville, Kentucky, called for a "systematic national organization" of blacks that would monitor such civil rights abuses and boycott the businesses of whites who abused or who discriminated against black people.[61]

Black southerners knew that matters of accommodation and equal access were not the only ones at stake during Reconciliation. If the federal government was unwilling to intervene when white citizens violated black people's rights, then it was not reasonable to presume that southern states would be any more aggressive. Timothy Thomas Fortune offered his assessment of the decision. On the Court's decision to refer blacks to the state courts, Fortune complained, "as if they would have appealed to the one had the other given him that protection which sovereign citizenship entitles them!" The Supreme Court decision, combined with violence and the decline of white progressive support for protecting black people's rights, put black citizens at the mercy of ambivalent state officials and of their hostile white employers and neighbors.[62]

Southern whites did not miss the significance of the Court's decision. They interpreted it as giving them full license to handle their own affairs and to resubjugate blacks. Where no specific legislation existed, conservative whites added new customs that redefined the terms of interracial interaction and demanded that blacks defer to white people's authority. Private companies and small business establishments drew the color line by providing segregated accommodations and workplaces or simply excluding black people altogether. Any form of individual, and especially collective, resistance by black people—or even the appearance of recalcitrance—was met with violence by whites.[63]

In this social and political climate, whites violently ejected black people from railroad cars, restaurants, and hospitals, and they attacked them in polling places, on plantations, and in their homes and did so with impunity and with no fear of prosecution. Du Bois observed that when blacks defended themselves and injured or killed whites, agents of white supremacy advanced in the "van of human hatred—making bonfires of human flesh and laughing at them hideously, and making the insulting of millions more than a matter of dislike,—rather a great religion, a world war-cry: Up white, down black." The ground moved underneath African America. Black people's descent to their postemancipation hell quickened as the determination of white southern bulldozers, bushwhackers, whitecappers, segregationists, and lynchers to resubjugate blacks crumbled any residual white progressive resolve to make white folk and elected officials safeguard black people's rights and protect their lives.[64] With these developments, African Americans crossed the threshold from the purgatory of Reconciliation to the hell of the consolidation of racism.

Crossing the Threshold

Du Bois noted that after whites united in their beliefs in white supremacy, "the descent to hell"—marked by a "great mass of hatred, in wilder, fiercer violence" and the "orgy of cruelty, barbarism, and murder done to men and women of Negro descent"—was "easy."[65] Lynching or violence that occurred outside the law but was sanctioned by a communal majority was the "fiercer violence" that Du Bois described. Extralegal violence had been a key part of American life and culture, and the practice knew few racial distinctions until the postbellum era, when whites used it to resubjugate blacks.[66]

In the 1880s, the thin line dividing legal and extralegal violence collapsed under the consolidation of racism. Americans were enthusiastic witnesses to public executions, but midcentury reformers lobbied for formalizing and privatizing capital punishment. White southerners resented the authority of the legal system and the Constitution's mandate for due process when formal justice interfered with their desire for administering their own brand of punishment to blacks. Denied access to lawful proceedings that had fascinated the national public, southern whites' frustration with what they claimed was black people's regression toward savagery after slavery fed their appetite for what Michael Pfeifer calls "rough justice." Pfeifer argues that rough justice was a style of extralegal justice that favored speedy, personal retribution and, in the South, emphasized white supremacy. Much of racial violence was persistent and diverse in scope and remained private and personal, lacking public ceremony until violent whites' actions took on a more consistent, deliberate, public, and racialized form. Beginning in the mid-1880s, these killings ranged from individual murders in retaliation for real and supposed crimes to organized killings by mobs and massacres as the nation tolerated the violent resubjugation of blacks.[67]

From 1877 through 1888, more than one hundred successful and aborted lynchings of black people were reported in the New York *Times*.[68] Whereas rape became white southerners' primary public justification for extralegal racial violence in the 1890s, more than eighty of the men lynched were charged with, accused of, or implicated in the death of whites. These killings emerged from scenarios in which black men had clashed with whites over land, labor, politics, or white people's expectations for black people's deference to their authority. The white people's family members, friends, and neighbors retaliated by lynching African Americans. Although white progressives were increasingly disengaged from ordinary violence, many remained concerned about lynching and its impact on standards for behavior in a civilized society. As Pfeifer shows, "due process campaigns" spread across much of the nation to end this violence. However, adherents to rough justice retained a stronghold in the South generally and in real and alleged transgressions of societal norms involving African Americans particularly. Blacks who transgressed white people's authority in the home, on the farm or a plantation, and in the town square or the marketplace constituted a threat to white supremacy that needed to be nullified. Relying on the legal system to punish defiant blacks was too slow and too impersonal a process for whites who insisted on swift and personal vengeance to crush black people's defiance. Reflecting this racial thinking and behavior, newspaper reports of the extralegal killings of black men increased between 1882 and 1892.[69]

For victims and witnesses of racial violence, attacks on black people in the 1880s were nothing new. However, the increasingly spectacular nature of the killings, the reports of sadistic ritual in some murders of black men, and the apparent indifference of white progressives and federal officials were new. Some white gangs, posses, and mobs killed African Americans under the cover of darkness, only to leave their bodies on public display in trees; others killed black people in broad daylight without fear of prosecution. Some bystanders and participants posed for pictures that preserved the memory of these killings and shared the images with people in their communities. African Americans saw the danger in the increasingly audacious and spectacular nature of the murders of black men, which had begun to include torture, castration, burning, and souvenir collection.[70]

Black public figures felt compelled to speak for the black men who were accused of crimes and who became victims of lynching because mobs had deprived them of their right to due process of law and to nineteenth-century ideas of a natural, "good death." These people knew that mobs had killed men from other racial groups, but they saw and suspected that antiblack racism informed the macabre aspects of these killings of black men. Black southerners marked the rise of the lynching of African Americans with protest parades condemning violence and with newspaper reports of the failure of authorities to punish perpetrators. Lynching apologists' claims to be suppressing black crime notwithstanding, African Americans knew that black people were being killed because of whites' "tyranny in the administration of the law." They charged white southerners with using "oppressive laws governing the relations of employer and employee, and by the inauguration and maintenance of a penitentiary system" to subjugate blacks. When these policies did not work, African Americans claimed that white folk used violence and refused to follow basic criminal procedures that would uphold black people's constitutional rights and bring white perpetrators to justice. Black people across the nation saw the threat and reality of mob violence as the engine behind the continuing deterioration of their rights.[71]

African Americans who endured violence or who expected it testified to state executives and called on them to offer their protection, but their petitions were rarely acknowledged. Although white southerners' efforts to legally disfranchise black men were only beginning to gain traction by the 1890s, white men's use of force and violence in local and state elections continued to disfranchise thousands across the region. Thus, many Democratic governors could ignore complaints by black people, who voted overwhelmingly for Republicans, without penalty. By middecade the editorial board of the New York *Freeman* had seen enough reports on white southerners' reliance on mob violence and the state militia to stop black people from protecting their interests and organizing their labor that it and other black newspaper editors felt compelled to take a stand. It is remarkable, the board commented,

> how a Southern white grows blue in the face in the presence of a real or expected Negro uprising, and how frantically he appeals to lawful authorities for protection! . . . But when the same white rascals arm themselves with rifles and shoot down inoffending blacks by the score in the very temple of justice . . . the Negro appeals in vain to lawful authority, of county or of state. His cries are unheard!

The *Freeman* condemned the failure of the mainstream press to acknowledge, in its coverage of these incidents of violence, the "propensity of the

Southern whites to rise above the law when they feel in a mobocratic humor, and their reliance upon and frantic appeal to the protection of the law whenever the Negro feels like taking the law in his hands." The *Freeman* surmised, "what is sauce for the goose is not sauce for the gander in the South." Other newspapers joined the *Freeman* in its fight against racial violence and the nation's tolerance of it.[72]

In March 1886, fifty white men rode horses to the courthouse in Carrollton, Mississippi, and fired on black men who were waiting for their trial. The gang killed thirteen men and wounded seven in what the New York *Times* described as a "terrible and inexcusable massacre." The *Times* reported that black men were seen jumping from the courthouse windows, attempting to escape the men who were seeking reprisal against one black man who had fatally struck a white lawyer named Liddle in a labor dispute. Between 1886 and 1887, in Yazoo County, Mississippi, white planters had warned labor agents away from their black laborers. They warned a preacher named Elder Green, who evidently tried to educate black cotton pickers about their labor rights despite injustices perpetrated on them by their employers. Kidnapping and killing the preacher, his slayers reportedly sent a notice to his friends with the message, "If you want Elder Green you had better send a box for him."[73]

African Americans struggled to resist violence and violations of their civil and political rights. Many white law enforcement officers, agents of the mainstream press, and people in the citizenry interpreted black people's efforts to defend themselves from white threats and attacks as justifying racial violence. Thus, white men could defend themselves from the abuse of other white men and from black people. Yet black men's entitlement to protect themselves and their families, homes, and interests from a white person's intrusion contradicted the logic of white supremacy. In this social and political climate, nearly any violent action that a white person took against a black person was justified. White citizens could even appeal to state authorities for assistance, and governors would respond by dispatching state militias to protect whites from blacks who dared to defend themselves or to organize into collectives to advance their economic interests. Any cooperative action—organizing voters, creating cooperatives, staging work stoppages, forming unions, or resisting lynching—among blacks or between black and white laborers could merit state intervention under the pretext of quelling a rebellion or protecting white life or property. It was under this pretense that southern locales came to rely heavily on state authorities to suppress black people's ability to defend their rights and to attack and kill black people with impunity.

African Americans shared reports of violence within and across their communities, and black and sympathetic white newspapers responded by providing extensive reporting on the violence to the public at large. For example, the New York *Freeman* reported that in late November 1887, one hundred whites invaded the jail at Frederick City, Maryland, and abducted twenty-three-year-old John Bigus for his alleged sexual assault of a white woman named Mrs. Yeagle. The mob carried Bigus from the jail, hanged him from a tree, and riddled his body with bullets. Bigus's body, reportedly "with every vestige of clothes torn off and his body covered with blood frozen, from the bullet holes," remained in public view until ten o'clock the next day. White men drove any black witnesses from the town. Incensed by what newspapers described as "the most appalling murder that has ever taken place in this community," the local Brotherhood of Liberty offered a reward for informants and sought to bring members of the mob to justice.[74] Readers of this and other newspapers learned that whites had seized African Americans from jails or the custody of civil authorities and summarily executed them, but the torture and public spectacle of the killing of John Bigus was particularly gruesome, albeit not without precedent. The obvious difference is that white Marylanders and their counterparts across the South usurped the state's authority in acting outside the bounds of law. Readers of these newspaper reports also learned that white southerners were also resorting to more spectacular and modern forms of extralegal killing and were doing so more frequently.

Bigus's alleged transgression was raping a white woman, and African Americans who endured and witnessed violence began to understand that raping white women was one excuse for which the nation would tolerate such treatment of black men. Of the 120 attempted and actual lynchings of black men from 1877 through 1888, there were approximately 45 instances of white men's attacks on black men for assaulting, soliciting sex from, and raping white females. Countering the mainstream press's frequent association of spectacle lynching and rape, the New York *Freeman* reasoned, "The real cause of the matter is to be found in the desire of lynchers for some sort of excuse for their rascality, and we venture to say that three fourths of the accusations of this character are pure fictions, set up by the mob and its apologists as an excuse for the exceeding infamy of their deviltry." "The real cause of the matter," reported the *Freeman*, was circumventing the Constitution to resubjugate black people. The number of extralegal killings for black people's alleged murder, arson, and nonsexual assault of whites outweighed allegations of rape. However, black men's real and alleged sexual violence against white women was the one crime that most whites believed justified "rough justice." From incidents of labor strikes and arson to murder, the specter of rape overshadowed discussions, rumors, and newspaper reports on crime involving black men. African Americans had seen whites use violence to resubjugate black people, but in listening to victims' and witnesses' testimonies and in reading print culture, they noticed the shift toward a more spectacularly brutal form of violence. These blacks saw southern whites' comfort in rationalizing their action and northern whites' silence about it as the continuing erosion of their citizenship rights.[75]

After reading reports and listening to victims' and witnesses' testimonies about this violence, many black public figures who had believed Reconciliation would not amount to an abandonment of African Americans' rights, who had told the southern black majority that they were unjustifiably alarmed by the *Civil Rights Cases* decision, who had ridiculed the migrations, and who had longed for interracial cooperation began understanding Reconciliation's consequences. Appealing for relief, showing loyalty to the Republican Party, hoping that southern state authorities could be trusted to uphold and protect black people's rights, and providing examples of black people's industriousness, respectability, and fitness for citizenship had come to naught. In 1888, the Jacksonville *Southern Leader* observed that the lynching of black people had become "a fixed southern regulation and pastime."[76]

The New York *Freeman* observed that Reconciliation had allowed white conservatives to control "all the machinery of lawmaking and enforcing power; having revived slavery by odious and oppressive laws governing the relations of employer and employee, and by inauguration and maintenance of a penal system." Responding to the lynching of five black South Carolinians who were charged with "braining a white lad," the *Freeman* noted that the whites of the state held "all reigns of government in their hands." As long as they held the reins of power, lynching would continue. More contemptible than "Judge Lynch" himself, the paper railed, was his apologists' effrontery to rationalize his "lengthy defense of his usurpation of the laws to the newspapers of South Carolina," saying that he "boldly proclaims that in defiance of law and of outraged personal rights he shall continue his infamous proceedings as long as men commit crimes and the processes of the courts continue to move as slowly as they have done." White southern impudence—evinced through the brazen and brutal nature of the violence, the unapologetic coverage in the mainstream print culture, and its tacit sanctioning by state and federal authorities—started to impel black people to action.[77]

The rise in the extraordinary violence of lynching in the late 1880s illuminated reunion's "darker deeds" for African Americans. Mob violence served as the most chilling example of the new racial order in the United States. The penalties that black people would pay would be high for transgressing white-determined southern mores by attempting to defend their material and familial interest, to acquire wealth or property, and to assert authority over their own lives. Local law enforcement officers rarely protected blacks marked for death by mobs, and they failed to prosecute even known perpetrators. Observing the changing trends, Mansfield E. Bryant testified, "We are robbed, swindled, cheated, assassinated, falsely imprisoned, lynched, told to stand back and have every indignity heaped upon us. The future will tell a sad story if this is continued."[78]

What exasperated African Americans the most was not just the fact that this violence occurred. The apathy expressed in the silences or the endorsements of racial violence by white citizens and elected officials raised the choler of black people across the nation. Absolute antiblack racism played a significant role in white people's tolerance of extraordinary violence. Certain whites thought that black people deserved the violence. Some claimed that black people exaggerated the level violence, and others offered platitudes lamenting the ways that lynching reflected negatively on Americans' ideas about the rule of law and national character. African Americans testified that, in failing to challenge perpetrators of racial violence, the majority of whites constituted a coalition of collaborators in the violence of white supremacy and the violation of black people's citizenship rights.

Black activists, feeling the sociopolitical ground shift beneath their feet, rushed to shore up support for black southerners' rights. They believed that black people's fate lay in their ability to put aside old intraracial differences for the collective weal and to exert pressure on white citizens and on federal officials to honor black people's citizenship rights. Achieving these feats would be easier said than done. The tensions over the Exoduster movement exposed one of many rifts in African America. Indeed, emancipation and Reconstruction had given blacks the opportunity to establish their own institutions and organizations. From the socially inclined schools, lodges, fraternal orders, and churches to the more politically and economically inclined Union Leagues, business leagues, and alliances, blacks had developed institutions and organizations reflecting their diverse interests and needs as a people. None of these institutions or organizations could topple white supremacy and reverse the consequences of Reconciliation individually, and there had been little indication that these people were ready to work collectively.[79]

The debates surrounding the establishment of the Afro-American League provide an example of the challenges that African Americans faced in forming organizations, selecting leaders, and choosing the best agenda for challenging white supremacy. In a 1887 speech before a Chicago audience, T. Thomas Fortune pitched the establishment of an Afro-American League, an organization intended to inaugurate "the promise of addressing and solving the problems of the race." Fortune imagined that the league would fold existing organizations into "one grand body for the uplifting and upbuilding of the fortunes and the rights of the race." Blacks in northern and midwestern states, who were unrestrained by racial disfranchisement and the oppressive threat of extraordinary violence, would "create public opinion in those sections and coerce politicians into taking a broader view of our grievances and compel them to pay more respect to our representations and requests than they have ever done before." Together they would pressure federal officials to extend the federal government's constitutional authority over the states to protect black people's civil rights.[80] Fortune's call for the league was a jeremiad on the problems facing black southerners, including what he called "the universal and lamentable reign of lynch and mob law, of which we are made the victims in the South, all the more aggravating because all the machinery of the lawmaking and enforcing authority is in the hands of those who resort to such outrageous, heinous and murderous violations if the law." There was no "dodging the issue," Fortune wrote. "We have got to take a hold of these problems ourselves." Indeed, many blacks saw their worst fears about sectional reconciliation coming true in the rise of lynching, segregation, and disfranchisement.[81]

The revelation of Reconciliation's "darker deeds" was not enough to dissolve the ideological disputes among African Americans. Opponents to the league expressed their concerns that "bloodshed may follow in the wake of the work," if white southerners saw the league as a direct threat to their power and decided to make a preemptive strike. Fortune addressed this concern by explaining that whites "profited by [black people's political] disorganization." He asked his audience, "Are we to remain forever inactive, the victims of extortion and duplicity on this account?" Fortune's answer to this question was a resounding no. The league's leadership proposed to accomplish its goals by peaceful means—"through the ballot and the courts." Yet as Fortune explained, "if [whites] use the weapons of violence to combat our peaceful arguments it is not for us to run away from violence." Invoking the bravery of such black heroes as Crispus Attucks, Nat Turner, and Toussaint Louverture, Fortune demanded that African Americans begin to fight resubjugation "at once." "And if there come violence let those who oppose our just cause," Fortune declared, "throw the first stone!"[82]

Most African Americans agreed that they needed to confront white supremacy aggressively, but they debated the merits of the league vigorously. The tensions over class and ideology reflect the divisions. Some activists agreed about the need for such an organization. The St. Louis *Western Appeal* condemned existing institutions, namely, black churches that "look more toward the disposition of our bodies after death than toward our welfare while living." The paper's editorial board agreed with Fortune's argument that "something must be done to improve our condition and it will only be better if it assumes a national character." Critical of the southern criminal justice system, in which "every Negro is guilty until he has proven himself innocent," and observing that "the list of murdered Negroes is annually on the increase," the Halifax *Enterprise* of South Boston, Virginia, declared, "If the law be powerless to protect its most humble citizen, let the tribunals be kicked to pieces and so-called justice be scattered to the earth's four winds." African Americans had cautiously observed the ethos of Reconciliation policy and the federal government's decisions to defer to the authority of the states in most matters of violence and their civil rights. These public figures reasoned that if, as some southern state officials claimed, they could not stop their white citizens from carrying out the will of their communities, then the responsibility for intervening belonged to the federal government.[83]

Some African Americans were concerned that mobilizing politically would only further antagonize white southerners. The Jacksonville *Southern Leader* feared that the league and Fortune's radical rhetoric might "intensify rather than allay the race troubles in the South." The New Orleans *Standard* echoed this opinion, cautioning, "If Mr. Fortune desires to see a redivivus of the white league, [Ku Klux Klan], and all sorts of things, let him proceed with his league." The Boston *Advocate* warned against "politics" infecting the movement toward establishing the league. The paper's editors knew that even though de facto disfranchisement existed throughout the South, many African American men still enjoyed the franchise. This authority in governance gave black men power that enraged whites. These cautious editors worried that organizing to remove from power whites attempting to deny blacks their citizenship rights might evoke extraordinary violence in the form of a massacre on the scale of the riots and massacres in Memphis, New Orleans, or Colfax. Nonetheless, using the ballot box to elect officials to protect black people's interests was exactly what league advocates had in mind. The league's supporters reasoned that whites attacked black people because they had no fear of prosecution, but if African Americans played a greater role in electing law enforcement officers and the people who appointed prosecutors, they could ensure that whites who attacked blacks would be punished. They also argued that the key to stopping the rise of legalized racial segregation and disfranchisement was electing officials who would enact legislation to protect African Americans' civil and political rights.[84]

As Fortune predicted, whites "profited" from the volatile debates among black public figures and from African Americans' political disorganization. The league eventually faltered under the weight of the inability of public figures and existing institutions to agree on the means to confront the increasingly menacing nature of white supremacy. Conservative southern whites turned toward the full redemption of the white South as many progressive and moderate northern whites came to share their ideas about racial subjugation. By the late 1880s, white southerners' murdering of black people was still in the process of becoming more spectacular, and legalized disfranchisement and segregation remained in their infancy. Therefore, blacks who opposed the league's bold scheme to confront white supremacy by pressuring federal officials to intervene when local and state governments failed to protect black people's rights probably did not feel the need to take aggressive action. However, some of those who were observant enough to recognize the changes in white supremacy believed that focusing on internal matters of racial uplift and matters of gender identities and conventions, suffrage, and economic development would ameliorate conditions or at least stop the downward spiral. African Americans did not start to unite around ideas like Fortune's until after lynching increased and became more spectacular and after southern legislators started to disfranchise black men and to enact legal segregation.[85]

As racial violence continued, more black journalists and newspaper editors related violence that they had experienced or had witnessed secondhand from reports of victims and firsthand witnesses. They also decried the failure of local, state, and federal authorities to punish known perpetrators. Editors regularly advocated self-defensive action and prophesied the consequences of continued unchecked violence. In a piece titled "The Logic of Force," the New York *Freeman*'s editors wrote that southern blacks had "bent their necks to the heel of whites," hoping that a "policy of peace and servile submission" would make "the unjust condition of things . . . pass away." The editors argued that incessant violence and white southerners' new efforts to disfranchise African Americans and to segregate them in areas of public life revealed that black people's failure to resist racial violence and discrimination aggressively, with the hope that inaction would reduce white southerners' belief in the need to resubjugate black people, had achieved nothing. The editors believed that the time for a more direct course of aggressive political action was upon African Americans. The editorial continued, "We have no objection to peace, . . . [but] there has been no peace since the war. Lynch and mob law and gross injustice in the administration of the law have marked every stage of the history of the Southern States since the war." This editorial reflects a growing sentiment among some black newspaper editors that it was time for African Americans to confront racial violence.[86]

Although black public figures sympathized with the victims of this violence, they were often critical of what they saw as the inability of black folk to strike back in more collective and effective ways. In 1888, during black people's continued flight from the South, some southern papers such as the Huntsville *Gazette* and the Chattanooga *Free Lance* and midwestern ones such as the Chicago *Conservator* condemned the renewed migrations. The *Gazette* counseled southern blacks to "have grit and stick" it out in the region, while the Columbus *Messenger* of Georgia refused to endorse migration over what its editors dismissed as "little grievances." "We think that the Negro can have all his rights in this country if he will contend and fight righteously for them," wrote the *Free Lance*. The *Conservator* asked, "How much better could the Negro prove his inferiority than by abandoning the land of his birth, where the laws are equal if the execution is not, and cowardly tuck tail and run away?" In the minds of these black newspapers' editors, African Americans needed to defend their interests by resisting racial subjugation where they lived.[87]

Some black southerners were running away from violence, but many of these people had calculated their responses to racial violence. Testifying about violence and migrating away from farms and plantations to southern towns and then to northern and midwestern cities also represented black people's defiance of racial violence. Newspaper articles and reports from this period show that more black folk were, in fact, yawing toward defensive action. For example, portions of a note sent purportedly from a group of black laborers to Governor Thomas Seay in 1887, reprinted in the Montgomery *Advertiser*, offers an illustrative example. "We have made up our minds to go down fighting for the race," they wrote: "We expect to [carry] down a goodly [number of whites] with us. . . . Fires will burn and that you know and this town can be sent down to ashes very soon. . . . It don't make any [difference whether] its the man that did the killing or not just so it's a white man between the ages of 16 and 150 years old. . . . We don't care who get killed."[88] Writings such as these appeared in black and white progressive newspapers. They suggest that even though black folk were often outgunned and outnumbered, they were attempting to "take hold of the problem" of white supremacy themselves.[89]

Shifts in black southerners' responses to a reinvigorated white supremacy became clear by the late 1880s. In Lowndes, Alabama, black farmers and farm workers dared to discuss and try to bring to justice the lynchers of one of their neighbors via a clandestine grand jury. Upon discovering the plot, local authorities arrested the conspirators. White men sent a notice to a man named Merriweather, informing him of their intentions to strike. They warned him to be silent or "be done up." Merriweather gathered more witnesses to the lynching, which elicited another menacing notice from the perpetrators. An undeterred Merriweather then assembled a group of his neighbors for shelter. A firefight commenced at his home, resulting in several injuries and Merriweather's escape. The local sheriff telegraphed Governor Seay requesting troops to suppress what whites characterized as a black rebellion. Seay sent the militia, but it found no evidence of trouble and returned to the capital. Despite all of the complaints by Alabama Democrats about government waste and about its inability to marshal resources to educate African Americans or protect black prisoners from mobs, the Birmingham *Negro-American* was certain that the "patriotic taxpayers of Alabama would not say a word if every dollar in the treasury was spent to 'keep the Negroes down.'"[90]

In August 1888, African Americans near Palatka, Florida, assembled to prevent the lynching of James Austin, a prisoner who scuffled with Lowring, the deputy sheriff, over his using offensive language to white people. Lowring died of a gunshot wound to the stomach, which triggered the assembling of a posse to kill Austin. Black residents informed the sheriff that they "were determined not to submit quietly to lynch law." If whites tried to lynch Austin, then his supporters were ready to "resist [the white men] to the bitter end." The sheriff responded with threats: if the prisoner's defenders did not disassemble, he would have "every militia company in the State summoned here and kill every one of them." The sheriff believed that the threat of state intervention on his behalf was enough to persuade Austin's protectors to disperse, but it did not.[91] African Americans remained on watch, determined to prevent a lynching. These southerners had every reason to fear that whites would lynch James Austin. They had listened to and added to the vernacular of racial violence, and they had observed the changes in white supremacy throughout Reconciliation. If granted the opportunity, whites would probably have done more than subdue Austin for his assault on the law enforcement officer. In all probability, they would have killed Austin and made a spectacle of the killing. Austin's defenders saw the possibility of the lynching of one of their own as constituting a need for direct action.

Lynching was not the only form of extraordinary violence that African Americans had to fear. White rioting in black communities increased during the 1880s. The failure of one black and one white man to yield on a Mississippi road activated a riot when black men ambushed a lynching party later that year. As the *Age* reported, when "they went to catch the colored man, they caught a dose of hot lead instead." The black men fled to the woods, and the white men burned the property and the stock of the refugees. Faced with the option of resisting violence and risking a riot and sensing the need for more direct action, more southern blacks left for the North and the Midwest, while others renewed their appeals to federal officials for relief.[92]

Conclusion

In 1888, black Louisianans gathered again in the Crescent City. These activists had joined forces across lines of class, vocation, and ideology, and they petitioned the state and federal government for relief from racial violence. No longer invited to testify before state-sponsored public forums, African Americans had created their own alternative spaces for sharing experiences of racial violence and broadcasting into the public spheres the vernacular history of racial violence, segregation, and disfranchisement. These victims and witnesses testified about violence, declared that a "reign of terror" existed throughout the state, and identified black citizens as the principal victims. The petitioners related that they were tired of being "robbed of [their] political rights, . . . executed by armed bodies of men styling themselves as regulators." They also noted the governor's readiness to "hasten his mercenaries or militia to the scene with cannon and rifles ostensibly to preserve the peace but actually to re-enforce the already too well fortified Negro murderers falsely assuming to be lawful posses." "We have exhausted all means in our power to have our wrongs redressed," they wrote, "all in vain." Now, "because of our murdered fellow-citizens and [because we are] apprehensive for our own safety, we appeal to the awakened conscience, the sense of justice and sympathy of the civilized world, and of the American people in particular."[93]

The protests of these Louisianans, as well as those of black public figures, were ignored. By the decade's end, white progressives had capitulated to white conservatives. As sectional reconciliation gave way to a renewed white supremacy, African American intellectuals and politicians thought they understood the lengths to which whites would go to resubjugate blacks. A decade later, they realized that what they had imagined could not get worse did. With the rise in lynching and legalized disfranchisement and segregation, African Americans descended into the hell of their postemancipation experience. Blacks testified about and against the rise of lynching and the further deterioration of their rights, but they also started to mend intraracial rifts, to harness their collective power, to broadcast the vernacular history of the consolidation of racism, and to crusade more aggressively against it.

3

"Lynched, Burned Alive, Jim-Crowed . . . in My Country"

Shaping Responses to the Descent to Hell

On the morning of December 28, 1889, a black female cook was strolling to work along the road heading into Barnwell, South Carolina, before she saw something that probably stopped her dead in her tracks. On one side of the road, the woman saw one black man's body tied to a post and another tied to a nearby tree. Tied to several trees, on the other side of the road, were the corpses of six more men. Horrified, she turned back toward her neighborhood to share her discovery with family and friends. Soon, a crowd of African Americans gathered at the execution site to make sense of what happened: Several hundred white men had overrun the county jail in the predawn hours. They abducted eight black men from police custody and dragged the prisoners to the outskirts of town, where they tied the men to trees and to a post before shooting them. When white residents of Barnwell came across the kill site, newspaper accounts indicate that they found a sullen, whispering crowd of black folk who were brimming with anger as they mourned the loss of beloved community members—including a deacon at the Baptist church.[1]

National newspapers printed different narratives of what some called the Barnwell "massacre." The New York *Times* provided a superficial report noting that the lynchings were the culmination of several months of local interracial strife, in response to "repeated acts of violence on the part of negroes against white men of the best character." Black journalists compiled reports from the testimonies of local victims and witnesses and ran a detailed counterstory, which reported that authorities had arrested the eight men for murdering two white men.[2] Authorities charged Harrison Johnson and Mitchell Adams with killing J. J. Hefferman. Witnesses claimed that Peter Bell, Rafe Morrell, Hugh Furz, Ripley Johnson, Robert Phoenix, and Judge

Jones had murdered Robert Martin. While the men awaited trial, their family members and friends raised money for bail and for court costs, but the mob exacted rough justice before authorities could prosecute the men. Black papers also reported the devastating impact this violence had on Barnwell's black community. It is from these publications that readers learned that eight black families lost fathers, sons, and brothers. Seven women lost their husbands and their contributions to the family's social and financial well-being. Twenty-five girls and boys who lost their fathers faced an uncertain future. The larger community lost friends, co-workers, and fellow worshipers.[3]

While the coroner conducted his inquest, what started as a local affair gained state and national attention. Rumors circulated throughout the county that some of the victims' families had requested assistance from kin in the neighboring locale of Blackville. Local whites were so fearful that African Americans would "rise up and avenge the lynching" that they called on Governor John Richardson to send the state militia to Barnwell to preserve the "peace." Barnwell's white citizens had reason to fear reprisal. African Americans had shown their willingness and ability to retaliate in the wake of such acts of violence. With the actual and imagined uprisings that occurred throughout the South since the colonial period, many whites worried about African Americans striking back. Whenever black people showed signs of retaliating against racial violence, white southerners raised the specter of a violent black uprising to counter black people's resistance to subjugation. The possibility that blacks would strike and kill whites was perhaps too real for civil authorities to ignore, especially in places where black people constituted the racial majority, as they did in parts of South Carolina. Governor Richardson, a Democrat, understood the possibility that black people would exact revenge and that this would set in motion a massacre of whites or, worse, a devastating race riot. The governor commissioned an infantry to Barnwell to stop African Americans from avenging the killings. Alarmed but armed and surrounded by the state militia, the white citizens of Barnwell probably slept well, knowing that they enjoyed their state-sanctioned monopoly on violence and that their black neighbors could do them no harm. Neither the black citizens of Barnwell County nor those blacks living throughout much of the South during the turn of the century faced dusk with the same assurance. With the refinement and institutionalization of racial violence, as seen through the rise in lynching, southern blacks lived under the threat that any encounter with a white person could morph into a fatal one. They also knew that state authorities would not intervene on their behalf.[4]

The bloodletting in Barnwell marked the reported rise in the lynching of black people that eventually helped African Americans to mobilize against racial violence. The historian Rayford W. Logan, in *The Negro in American Life and Thought*, described the consolidation of racism in the 1890s, reflected in the appearance of the rise of lynching and the legalization of disfranchisement and segregation, as the "nadir" of postemancipation race relations. W. E. B. Du Bois, who lived through this period and who recounted the changes he observed in white supremacy in "The Souls of White Folk," described it as the "descent to Hell." Du Bois reported seeing among white Americans new "curious acts" that revealed the self-conscious ways that they thought about themselves, as a race of superior people, and how their views shaped the ways that they thought about and acted toward African Americans. He observed the effects of the new racial identify in the "strut of the [white] Southerner[s]," when they were in the presence of black people. He also saw a white person's assumption of this new posture while watching "a quiet, peaceful man curl back in a tigerish snarl of rage," in response to black people's attempts to enjoy some of the same rights and privileges assumed by whites. While traveling by train, Du Bois saw a white man "grow livid with anger" over seeing a black woman sitting alone in a Pullman car. Du Bois explained that white people's anger about black people defying a white person's authority, threatening white people's power, or expecting a degree of racial equality could give way to violence, ranging from an insult to an attack on the level of the Barnwell killings. Du Bois likened what he called the development of white people's "personal discovery" of their whiteness to a "great mass of hatred" that descended over the United States. The coalescence of antiblack racism evolved slowly as the quakes of sectional reconciliation triggered a swell and the swell evolved into tsunami-like waves, with devastating effects for black southerners.[5]

Because of African Americans' testimonies about and against racial violence, more blacks developed a shared understanding of the costs associated with the consolidation of white supremacy. This chapter shows how this insight prompted black people to start developing new political spheres that fostered among African Americans a tone and attitude of what Komatra Chuengsatiansup calls "deliberate citizenship." According to Chuengsatiansup, a "sphere of deliberate citizenship" is created when people whose voices and stories have been marginalized decide to organize into political spheres and to challenge the paradigms informing their oppression by making sure that people in positions of power hear their voices and stories.[6] Black public figures and black folk were linked umbilically, but they operated along separate tracts in their opposition to violence, forming these new political spheres and institutions in different ways, both of which were critical to the eventual shift in equilibrium of white supremacy and black resubjugation. Private citizens developed "enclave public spheres" in their local communities, a topic that is addressed in the next chapter. Public figures formed a black "counterpublic sphere" that this chapter addresses. According to Catherine Squires, the "black counterpublic sphere" "is signified by increased public communication between the marginal and dominant public spheres, both in face-to-face and mediated forms."[7]

The African Americans who developed the black counterpublic sphere consisted of activists in the public eye, namely, journalists, editors, authors, intellectuals, and politicians, as well as clubwomen and convention men. They resisted white supremacy discursively by using the power of their celebrity and their mastery of black print culture to challenge racial violence, disfranchisement, and segregation in the turn-of-the-century period. Specifically, having experienced and witnessed the new convulsion of white supremacy through the wire services, newspaper reports, and speeches, as well as having listened to victims' and witnesses' testimonies, these African Americans stampeded into the dominant public spheres and created an alternative discourse on white supremacy and the violence used to achieve it. Carrying forth the legacy of such antebellum activists as John Russworm, Frederick Douglass, Henry Highland Garnett, David Walker, and Maria Stewart, these turn-of-the-century activists publicized the vernacular history of the consolidation to educate Americans, to guide black people's resistance, and to break down the apathy of white citizens and state and federal officials who they did not believe understood this violence and its impact on African Americans and on the nation. Using the counterpublic sphere, black public figures tried to create what sociologists call an "oppositional consciousness" regarding the consolidation of white supremacy.[8] These people broadcast the vernacular history of racial violence, tried to mobilize black people to action, and tried to make African Americans' concerns about violence understandable to white citizens and elected officials.

Re-presenting the Violence of Resubjugation

The black press's reporting of the killings in Barnwell signaled a shift in African Americans' responses to racial violence. After the consolidation, black public figures started to gain, in the fight against resubjugation, the same authority that their antebellum counterparts had enjoyed in the fight against slavery. As the public face of an increasingly marginalized and resubjugated people, black public figures felt the "duty to relate" victims' and witnesses' experiences of violence. Reflecting a mission to report developments happening in black communities, to advocate racial pride, to inform readers of policies and practices affecting blacks, and to protest violations of African Americans' rights, these avatars of African America, "race men" and "race women," sought to end violence by publishing the accounts of people who were shut out of public forums and whose testimonies of violence were ignored by federal officials and the mainstream media. These public figures sought to shape black people's knowledge about the legal, political, and social developments of the consolidation. To get this knowledge, activists often interacted directly with victims, witnesses, or their proxies. When they did not interact with victims or witnesses, participants in the counterpublic sphere relied on newspapers or on other activists to understand and to convey the changes in American life and culture.

With activists, intellectuals, journalists, and newspapers dispersed across the nation, producers of black print culture spread knowledge about white supremacy and the violence used to achieve it. Public figures publicized African Americans' accounts and experiences of racial violence and related developments regarding white supremacy. These men and women had several objectives in developing the black counterpublic sphere. They hoped to motivate blacks to defend themselves against violence and to resist segregation and disfranchisement. Public figures wanted to challenge the dominant public sphere's representations of white supremacy and black inferiority. In presenting black people's accounts and views of violence and racial discrimination, these African Americans wanted to wrest from whites the meaning of lynching, disfranchisement, and segregation and its implications for blacks.

The new racial posture of white Americans reflected white southerners' renewed enthusiasm to solve the "problem" of African Americans' insistence on resisting white supremacy and enjoying the benefits of citizenship. Turn-of-the-century whites pursued several strategies in their campaign to subjugate black southerners. The architects of white supremacy—namely, the planters, industrialists, governors, legislators, and judges—developed the legal mechanisms for denying African Americans their civil and political rights. White public figures fueled ordinary white people's hatred of blacks by trumpeting pseudoscientific theories of race and by circulating caricatures of African Americans. One the one hand, these leaders and members of the press depicted African Americans as a race of ignorant and childlike people who were not fit govern themselves or who were not deserving of civil and political rights. On the other hand, they cast African Americans as a race of uncivilized and savage people whose insistence on civil and political rights warranted violent subjugation to protect white people's interests. Additionally, artists and entertainers produced new racist caricatures of blacks, which circulated across the globe via photographs, advertisements, and live and cinematic performances. White folk could not help but believe that they had a stake in supporting white supremacy. They broadcast their racial superiority in their individual interactions with blacks, maintained the color line, and used violence to assert their authority over black people. Lastly, agents of the state and federal governments turned deaf ears and blind eyes to black people's complaints about racial discrimination and their testimonies of racial violence. This new program of white supremacy was united in politics and conviction. White people's reliance on the state to achieve resubjugation through disfranchisement, segregation, and the penal system smoothed the process for violence and its occurrence both inside and outside the authority of law. The spasm of white southerners' frustration over black people's resistance to resubjugation and their resolution to end it created a social and political climate for the rise in extraordinary violence.[9]

African Americans experienced and witnessed the gathering wave of renewed white supremacy and the threat to their lives and their rights as free people and as citizens in slow motion. After Reconstruction, most blacks saw each act of violence, each screeching headline, each piece of legislation disfranchising black men, or each racist political speech as individual events, whose aggregated meaning they struggled to comprehend. Many blacks probably shared their feelings about their individualized experiences of violence and the violations of their rights. However, most of them probably did not understand that each event involved what Du Bois later described as the tidal wave of white supremacy drawing back from the shores and gathering force out at sea. Public figures used the black press, which expanded in scope throughout the 1880s and became a representative institution in African America, to help blacks bear witness to the cauldron of southern life. These men and women used the counterpublic sphere to bring home to African Americans the prospect and reality of violent resubjugation. Thus, in the 1890s, when the tidal waves of racial violence and new pieces of legislation restricting black people's access to public accommodations and black men's access to the franchise struck the South, the horrors of white supremacy took on greater shape and meaning in the minds of African Americans. It was this insight that inspired blacks to mobilize.

Public figures documented the social and political developments of white supremacy occurring in the 1880s and 1890s. Specifically, they explained to readers the ways that the Supreme Court's decision in the *Civil Rights Cases* empowered individual businesses to deny services to blacks or to segregate them from whites. These figures' intervention into the growing problem of disfranchisement serves as another example of policies and practices they broadcast to their audiences. In 1888, when the Florida legislature disfranchised black men, public figures characterized the vote as a juggernaut, with implications that extended far beyond that state's borders. Often focused on the priorities of survival, many black folk might have seen these developments as unrelated. However, public figures triangulated the data they saw represented in mainstream press reports. Then, they situated these separate incidents in the larger social and political context of American life to help blacks make sense of the changes in white supremacy so that they could resist resubjugation.

In addition to representing the problems that African Americans faced regarding violence, segregation, and disfranchisement, public figures wanted to challenge the dominant public sphere's representations of hegemonic white male power. Claims that white men were the most biologically evolved and civilized of the world's peoples pervaded both white-supremacist discourse and mainstream print culture. According to this logic, white men's innate racial superiority entitled them to govern themselves and people they deemed to be their inferiors. When it suited their claims to their entitlement to rule, whites characterized as weak or feminine any people who were not white and male. Thus, declarations that the United States was a "white man's country" and that black men were inferior, savage, and, therefore, unfit for civil and political rights filled the discourse of mainstream print culture in the 1890s. This language explained white people's need to resubjugate black people with the triple threat of disfranchisement, segregation, and violence.[10] Public figures used the counterpublic sphere to offer their own re-presentations of black male superiority and their assessments that black men were fully capable of self-governance. Through representations of racial violence in black print culture, members of the black press also exposed the contradictions of the white men's claims of being civilized, racially superior, and qualified to govern and enjoy the benefits of citizenship by publishing reports of what they depicted as white men's savagery and their willingness to lie, cheat, steal, rape, and murder to subjugate black southerners. Black newspaper editors and journalists spread knowledge of the ways white supremacy affected all black people and tried to use this information to inspire more African Americans to resist.

The Washington *Bee*'s report on the rape of a black woman provides an illustrative example of the ways public figures used the counterpublic sphere to shape knowledge about a feature of the consolidation of white supremacy that received little attention in the dominant public spheres: white men's rape and sexual coercion of black girls and women. White southerners' distortion of black female sexuality via characterizations of black women and girls as sexually loose filled the discourse of the dominant public spheres and was part of a larger pattern of widespread systematic sexual violence. Public figures believed that these representations of black girlhood and womanhood and the mainstream print culture's silence on white men's sexual predation toward black females rendered girls and women vulnerable to rape. In January 1890, readers of a *Bee* report titled "Raped" learned of an attack on Victoria Day. The report allowed readers to envision Day as an upstanding schoolteacher visiting her pupils in Newton County, Georgia. A white man interrupted the schoolteacher's day and life by grabbing her from the road and taking her into the woods, where he raped her. Then, the man ordered the injured woman into his buggy and took her to meet a friend of his, and the two men assaulted her before dropping her off at a black man's home. Afterward, Day, her kin, or the man at whose house her assailant delivered her reported the attack to local authorities, who made no effort to bring the men to justice. It was authorities' failure to take action that likely resulted in Day or her kin relating her story to the print media.[11]

The *Bee*'s description of Victoria Day's harrowing experience suggests that the editors wanted to teach readers about the vulnerability of black womanhood in light of the consolidation. They attempted to show readers that the teacher was not just any woman; she was a lady who both embodied Victorian womanhood and interrupted the mainstream society's representation of black women and girls as sexually loose. "Raped" sought to drive home to readers the ways that female respectability did not shield black females from racial violence. Indeed, industrialization and urbanization had produced conditions in which more black females worked outside and away from their homes. Consequently, women and girls traveled greater distances to work, to visit kin, or to patronize business establishments. This mobility presented white men, who, because of the social and political climate of renewed white supremacy, were already predisposed to subjugating African Americans, with more opportunities to exploit and rape them. "Raped" tried to show that even the most honorable black females had little protection from and means of retribution against white men who propositioned and attacked them, in the context of the general failure of white southern customs to recognize their right to decline sex. Black communities adapted to females' vulnerability by counseling women and girls to avoid situations in which they were isolated or alone with white men. The attacks on such women as Day, however, showed readers some consequences for females when these safety mechanisms failed.[12]

Black activists, such as the editors of the *Bee*, who were challenging sexual violence were pushing against the tide. Although mainstream newspapers blazed with reports of allegations of black men's sexual assaults against white females, they rarely documented white men's sexual violence against black females. Essays such as Rebecca Latimer Felton's "Needs of the Farmers' Wives and Daughters" filled the literature and the discourse of the dominant public spheres and fortified the rape justification for the lynching of black men. When print culture covered the rape of black females, it was black activists who represented rape as one of white men's many instruments of resubjugation. Black newspapers reported assaults on black females and the failure of authorities to prosecute the perpetrators, situating the incidents within the framework of racial violence.[13]

Black activists reported this violence and the context in which it occurred for several reasons. First, they recognized that black women and girls suffered a range of violence that often went unappreciated vis-à-vis the rape of white females and the lynching of black males. Second, public figures wanted readers to understand that the authorities' failure to prosecute white men for raping black females and the mainstream newspapers' silence on white-on-black rape fed stereotypes that black females welcomed sexual encounters with white men. Black rape survivors, with little formal recourse for their suffering, found themselves in difficult situations. The families and community institutions of black females would have offered the most natural resources to help them heal the physical and psychological wounds of rape. However, testifying about rape might activate a desire to seek reprisal in the girls' or women's fathers, brothers, and sons. Black men attacking white men—even while avenging sexual violence—could have lethal consequences for these men and their families.[14]

In fact, public figures were typically cautious about publicly addressing any aspect of black female sexuality, lest they cast a media spotlight on women and girls unable to defend themselves against sexual violence and discursive assaults on their sex. However, concern about southern white men's rape of black females amid the dominant public sphere's growing association of lynching with black-on-white rape resulted in the black press's discursive intervention. These activists felt that they had a responsibility to relate sexual violence as a way of protecting black females and encouraging African Americans' resistance to white supremacy. For example, in 1893, the

Richmond *Planet* published an account, titled "White Men's Crimes," that informed readers that two white men overran a black family's home near Charlotte, Tennessee. When Joseph Vanter returned home, his wife, his daughter, and a family friend reported that the men had "outraged" them, a term used to describe rape and sexual harassment. Afterward, the Vanters reported the invasion to authorities, who arrested the men. The women's male defenders knew, from understanding the vernacular history of racial violence and from reading newspaper reports, that even when some authorities arrested white men for raping black females, their cases rarely made it to trial. This is because when civil authorities tried to bring white men to justice, they often presented their cases to all-white, male jurors who, often embracing the white-supremacist claims that black women and girls never refused sex and were always available to satisfy white men's needs, were unlikely to convict these men of raping black females. Knowing this, Vanter and his supporters threatened to take the two men from jail and to administer their own brand of justice. Local authorities took seriously the black men's threat to exact extralegal justice. So, they arranged for white civilians to reinforce security at the jail holding the two men. Had the black men stormed the jail, reports such as those on Barnwell portended a likely deadly outcome.[15]

Though some women reported assaults against them, or had family members report for them, the milieu of violence against black men who defied the logic of white supremacy by retaliating against attacks on their loved ones intensified black females' tradition of silence about sexual violence by white men. To be sure, most women and girls did not report rape. However, certain black females who would not be silent—or who because of severe physical and psychological trauma could not deny or ignore attacks—testified about rape to their families and even to local authorities. These victims and their families demanded responses from local authorities and ensured that even if authorities failed to bring rapists to justice, members of the larger community knew what transpired. Thus, even if female victims' families could not secure justice for them, the women's and girls' victimization, as well as their readiness to subject themselves to scrutiny by testifying about sexual violence, fueled the efforts of black public figures to defend black female honor by ensuring that their experiences were heard.[16]

Editors such as the *Bee*'s W. Calvin Chase and the *Planet*'s John Mitchell, Jr., as well as activist-authors such as Ida B. Wells and Pauline Hopkins, used newspaper articles and reports, pamphlets, and essays to re-present incidents of sexual violence and to rail against the rape of black women and girls. These public figures aimed to level the playing field by making

Americans understand black females' vulnerability to rape by white males. What is more, they also wanted to shame white people in the communities where sexual violence against black women occurred. These activists wanted white journalists and authors to report and depict incidents involving black females with the same vigor as they did for white females who claimed black men assaulted them. Similarly, public figures also demanded that authorities prosecute alleged white rapists of black women with the same enthusiasm as they did alleged black rapists of white women. Activists hoped that their reports and commentaries on sexual violence might facilitate its end by encouraging African American families to adopt measures to protect black females and pressuring authorities to bring the assailants to justice. Overall, the vulnerability of black women and girls was one of several dimensions of the counterpublic sphere's larger re-presentation of racial violence from this era, when other developments made many African Americans think that the promise of freedom and full citizenship rights had collapsed.[17]

The social, economic, and political upheavals that marked the nineteenth century's last decade hit black southerners especially hard. Laws disfranchising black men spread across the region, a development that motivated more black public figures to take aggressive action. In the minds of many public figures, disfranchisement served as a midwife of racial resubjugation that delivered segregation and extraordinary violence. White southerners' targeting of African Americans with violence to enforce disfranchisement and segregation and to skirt the legal system amplified already-heavy impediments to black southerners' efforts to enjoy their freedom and their civil and political rights. Thus, by the century's end, readers of black newspapers would have understood the epic scale of the "great mass of hatred" that Du Bois later described. They would have also participated in and witnessed earlier public debates about how to undo the damage.

Public figures intensified their arguments against any further subjugation of blacks. For example, in 1890, black men held conventions to discuss and attempt to address the institutionalization of white supremacy. In fact, having witnessed debates embracing disfranchisement at state constitutional conventions across the South, these activists understood that with black men's right to vote blocked, most African Americans' authority in local governance would be eliminated. Stripped of this power, black men would not be able to protect themselves and their families from violent assault, further disfranchisement, or legalized segregation. Therefore, J. W. Thompson, the editor of the *People's Journal* (Jacksonville, Florida), appealed to southern delegates from the National Convention Movement to attend a southern conference in Atlanta to discuss racial violence. Likewise, T. Thomas Fortune continued to call on black people to join the Afro-American League, while others petitioned President Benjamin Harrison, Congress, and their fellow citizens for relief.[18] In sum, men such as Thompson and Fortune had reason to be concerned: some blacks began hearing and seeing in reports on rape, lynching, and the shifting social and political context of segregation and disfranchisement a need to pursue more assertive responses to white supremacy.[19]

John Edward Bruce's response to reports of violence provides an example of some public figures' attempts to re-present violence as a way to mobilize blacks to defend themselves. As a black southerner and a journalist, Bruce understood the situational contexts involving white men's attacks on black people. However, as a man who witnessed the rise of extraordinary violence and who understood the new dynamics of white supremacy, Bruce argued that if whites continued to demand black people's blood to assert white racial superiority, black men should "exchange [violence] with them, until they are satiated." In a 1899 speech, Bruce vented his frustration over what he saw as African Americans' disorganized and reactive responses to violence throughout the period. Like Fortune, whose Afro-American League Bruce joined, he argued that self-defense and retaliation were the "best remedy" for dealing with violent whites. Moreover, Bruce believed that blacks were confronting aggressive whites on a case-by-case basis, without ending the violence and confronting the logic of black inferiority behind it. Individual acts of resistance, petitions, memorials, and speeches by activists were beneficial, he posited, but blacks would only find security in collective defense and retaliation.[20] John Bruce argued, "If they burn our houses, burn theirs, if they kill our wives and children kill theirs, pursue them relentlessly, meet force with force everywhere it is offered."[21] Bruce believed that communicating with white men in a language that they understood and a method they respected was the best way to dissuade white men from believing that they could kill and terrorize black people without penalty. Bruce was not alone in his conviction. Statements from other public figures hint at a belief that southern blacks had the power to confront the effects of the consolidation of racism. The increase in reports and commentaries on African Americans' armed self-defense and collective defiance of white supremacy suggest that blacks did not dismiss these calls to arms.

Public figures wielded print culture to re-present African Americans' resistance to the consolidation and to encourage more black people to act. Newspapers from across the country reported black people's defiance of white supremacy. In reports from across the region, readers would have seen regular illustrations of white supremacy's diverse contours and black people's resistance. For example, in 1895, white residents of Alvin, Texas, had initially refused to allow blacks to settle inside Alvin, but a number of black families resided there eventually. Black women responded to discrimination they faced in employment and while conducting business in Alvin's commercial spaces by staging a boycott and then organizing a mass meeting to generate more support for their cause and to address the problem. People who attended the meeting shared their stories and adopted resolutions to continue boycotting the businesses of white people who mistreated African Americans. The black residents also drafted a proposal to "organize a Negro stock company to operate a grocery store to cater to Negro trade alone."[22] Incensed white storekeepers, who relied on black people's business and who did not want to face the competition of a black-owned grocery store, "commanded [the black organizers] to leave town . . . or be prepared to meet death." Some African Americans refused to leave; others, mindful of reports of massacres, packed their belongings and decamped to more welcoming communities. Few white business leaders and newspaper editors explained white people's running black people off their land and from their communities in explicitly economic terms, that they feared they could not withstand the economic competition. White communities, through their sheriffs and sympathetic newspapers, justified the exile of blacks through charges of African Americans' supposed criminality and their "disposition to shield Negro criminals."[23]

Agents of the black press aimed to make sure that their readers understood the harassment that African Americans faced, black people's defiance of white supremacy, and white people's consequent efforts to use violence to preserve their social and economic power. Thus, through reports such as those on the Alvin affair, producers of black print culture showed black readers the ways that some blacks worked to sidestep white power. Activists highlighted the difficult choices that black people faced and the decisions they made. African Americans who read newspaper articles and reports on black people's experiences of and responses to racial subjugation would learn that although some blacks always deferred to white people's authority, others refused. Accordingly, readers would understand that African Americans had limited choices when whites assumed postures of racial superiority in disputes over land, labor, or commerce and in the punishment of black children, sexual access to and exploitation of black women, and encounters with law enforcement officers. Either blacks would use the politics of deference and abdicate their rights and humanity in their submission to white supremacy, or they would deploy the politics of defiance and take up the cudgels to make a stand using a large and diversified arsenal. Many blacks, who were tenacious and dogged in their determination to exist as independently of whites as possible and to live as citizens and who were emboldened by militant public figures, started embracing the politics of defiance.

Black newspapers in the 1890s blazed with such headlines as "With a Rifle in His Hand" and "Burned at the Stake." In these articles, public figures reported the instances when black southerners who asserted their dignity and who challenged white supremacy were lynched for their defiance. Activists used reports of white violence and black resistance to drive home the point that many incidents of violence resulted not from rape or murder but from occasions when blacks violated the white-supremacist-determined social decorum. Indeed, many of the people who endured violence had aggressively resisted racial subjugation; they showed tangible evidence of material progress, advocated civil and political rights, resisted arrest, or even demonstrated confident personal carriage. Like Bruce, other militant public figures wanted to demonstrate to readers the importance of fighting back, even in the face of death. In advocating a vigorous self-defense, some activists were articulating to the larger black community the feelings and opinions of those subjugated; they also tried to convince other blacks of the need for concerted action against violent whites. The circulation and consumption of black print culture in homes, schools, churches, barbershops, and other public and private settings educated African Americans about the widespread nature of violence and connected previously remote black communities. On the whole, southern blacks' reading about violent assaults on black people in newspapers or hearing about them in their home spheres brought violence and the possibility for their own victimization home to them in ways that engendered anxiety, discontent, and a greater willingness to fight back.

The ways that African Americans' collective stress over the potential for racial violence stirred more people to action is illustrated in an interracial fight near Texarkana, Arkansas. In August 1896, readers of the *Planet* learned that a fight broke out between white-immigrant and black laborers of the Kansas City, Pittsburgh and Gulf Railway. Black and white industrial laborers were locked in a constant battle for wages because race shaped the ways that industrial wages were structured, so employers paid black workers less money than they paid white workers. To provide for themselves and for their families, black men accepted smaller wages than did white men, which often forced white men to lower their wages or starve. When white men were faced with these challenges during the consolidation, they decided that eliminating the competition was the best strategy for preserving their social and economic power. White laborers in Polk County, Arkansas, who wanted to drive black laborers from the town and from their jobs on the railroad, ambushed the black campers in the middle of the night. The black men, either alerted to the white men's intentions or armed because they knew the economic threat their presence posed to white laborers, fought back. A reinforced mob gathered and injured eight black men and killed three more before driving the remaining black laborers from the work camp. The *Planet* described the violence as "a horrible butchery," to drive home the ways that the frustrated white laboring classes used black people's willingness to compete with whites for jobs to wipe out any real or perceived threats to white supremacy.[24]

While producers of black print culture showed the ways that interracial tensions surrounding labor and commerce were ripe for violence, they also revealed that conflicts that threatened the sanctity of black families produced equally explosive results. In a report titled "A Brave Defender," the *Planet* illustrated to readers how some conditions of southern life presented challenges for black parents seeking to guard their children against racial violence. An interracial dispute between two adolescent boys erupted into a fight in Palmetto, Florida, in 1896. Trice, the fourteen-year-old black boy, emerged victorious, having defeated Hughes, the son of a local police officer. After the elder Hughes learned of his son's defeat, he commissioned a posse of fourteen white men to "regulate" the Trice boy. The posse surrounded the Trice cabin and ordered the family to surrender the boy. Jack Trice, the boy's father, refused. The white men fired into the family's home, trying to draw them out. Jack, rather than relinquish his son, returned fire, killing three of the white men. The "regulators," sensing the futility of their cause, retreated for reinforcements.[25]

Readers of some black papers would have read accounts explaining that Trice and his son departed for the swamps in an attempt to evade the mob likely to assemble and pursue them after Trice had killed the white men. When a mob returned, issuing vows that they would burn the father and son at the stake, the two had vanished. The men reacted by driving Trice's elderly mother out of the family's home and burning it to the ground. Then the mob, accompanied by bloodhounds, tore through the countryside. The men fired into the cabins of the Trices' neighbors, hoping to wound the father and son or anyone attempting to provide them sanctuary. When they could not apprehend Jack Trice and his son, the men burned African Americans' homes, ordered an exodus of the black population, and threatened to boycott the businesses of those whites who failed to dismiss their black employees.

This scene, in which a seemingly quotidian interracial encounter ended in violence, had become a staple of modern southern life.[26] As the reporting of the Trice incident showed readers, the prospect of black men using guns against whites, regardless of the circumstances, enraged whites and resulted in more violence and the intervention of the state. Thus, blacks' self-defense might result in the deaths of whites and blacks, but the reporting on the Trice episode also highlighted the ways that resistance allowed certain blacks to avoid being lynched and showed white men some consequences for their use of violence.

By the mid-1890s, activists had used the counterpublic sphere to document significant changes in American life. Re-presenting the surge in the number of black lynch sufferers, the move of southern legislatures to disfranchise black men and whites who would form political coalitions with them, and the extension of the color line, these activists helped readers make sense of the changes as African Americans lost the social and political gains of Reconstruction. The black press published accounts and testimonies of violence and helped readers bear witness to the consolidation of racism. Their reports brought violence into readers' homes and allowed African Americans to consider how their own lives and potential reactions to white supremacy might be similar to or different from those of the sufferers about whom they read. In projecting information about this violence across the nation, public figures strengthened the sense of intersubjectivity and oppositional consciousness among blacks. At the same time, they also made more readers "co-owners" of the trauma endured by those who experienced the wave of violence directly.[27]

Readers of the *Afro-American Sentinel* in Omaha would have understood the editors' question, "Can't lynching be stopped?" The editors believed "the only way those barbarians can be made to desist from engaging in such brutal butchers is to assure them that they will run a great risk of being compelled to bite the dust on every occasion of their entering upon such a devilish pastime."[28] Readers of black print culture conceivably shared Joseph Wiley's prediction that future historians would document the 1890s as "the reign of mob violence, when law was handicapped and liberty oppressed, when caste and prejudice had full and unchecked sway."[29] Using newspaper articles and reports, speeches, and literature, public figures began seizing control of the reporting on racial violence. Their discursive intervention into turn-of-the century print culture showed African Americans that this violence was neither isolated nor harmless to black people. Controlling the meaning of the consolidation also allowed public figures to try to adjust African Americans' responses to it.

"Re-training the Race"

Activists used the counterpublic sphere to publish the vernacular history of racial violence and to create a collective sense of urgency about violence to empower African Americans to challenge white supremacy. They did this, in part, by constructing a "New Negro," an identity informed by the education of black people to the realities of the consolidation of racism and about the need for aggressive action. The response of John Mitchell, Jr., the editor of the Richmond *Planet*, to a violent attack on a pregnant black woman illuminates public figures' efforts to instruct black people on how to respond to racial violence. In September 1896, when a white overseer named Smith criticized the gardening techniques of Jim Beavers of Montgomery, Alabama, Beavers reportedly complained about the white man's cursing and abuse. The infuriated overseer responded by lunging at Beavers with a pitchfork and inflicting an arm wound. The injured man went home, believing that the dispute was resolved. Beavers soon learned from friends that a posse was amassing to punish him for his recalcitrance, and he was advised to flee with his pregnant wife. The couple left, but upon their return, the white men came. Beavers left his home again; this time he left his wife behind.[30]

In a piece titled "Horrible Treatment," the *Planet* reported the events that occurred after Jim Beavers took flight. The journalist reporting the events that unfolded did not interview the couple, who might have been in hiding or been too traumatized to be interviewed. According to an interview with a physician whom Beavers consulted to treat his wife, the distraught man had explained, "The [white men] were mad because they couldn't get me." The men found Mrs. Beavers to be a fitting surrogate for them to vent their rage over Beavers's defiance of white supremacy. Beavers testified to the doctor that the white men dragged his "poor wife out of bed, made her get in a buggy in her night clothes, and took her two or three miles down the river." When the fifteen white men arrived at another plantation, they "beat [Mrs. Beavers] over the head in making her get up, and then while carrying her down the road, one after the other jabbed her in the side with their guns, and cursed her for everything they could think of." The doctor described Mrs. Beavers as "the worst whipped creature" he ever saw. The white men had laid the expectant mother over a log and whipped her so badly that "great welts formed and the fingers could be laid in the furrows of the flesh." Afterward, the men instructed Mrs. Beavers to remain at the site of her assault until dawn.[31]

Rather than simply report the violence, Mitchell decided to use this incident as an opportunity to critique and to instruct black men on the proper response to racial violence. Mitchell probably learned about the assault on Mrs. Beavers through the newswire and decided to use the report as a call to arms for protecting black women. Reports that a pregnant woman had faced a white gang incensed Mitchell. Thus, he used the editorial page to protest Mrs. Beavers's assault and Jim Beavers's absence. Mitchell directed his attack at the white perpetrators and at black men who failed to defend their families from violence. The September 12 edition roared,

> [Black] womanhood must be protected, and the men who would take out in the dead of night his wife . . . should be sent to their long home. We feel like assisting [Beavers] in this matter although he is no kin to us. When black men determine to die in defense of their homes, then these outrages will cease. . . . Colored men, make up your minds to die in defense of yourself and your families.[32]

If black men were not equipped to defend their homes, then how could they demonstrate their manliness and masculinity? If they could not do this, then how could they convey African Americans' entitlement to full citizenship rights? Though Mitchell never asked these questions directly, the tenor of his editorial implied that he thought there was a link between black men's willingness and ability to defend themselves against violence and African Americans' efforts to make their case for civil and political equality.

The editors of black newspapers routinely denounced black men who did not defend themselves and their families and communities, because they were worried about the dominant public sphere's representation of black manliness in the context of escalating racial violence and its implications for women and children left alone to face violent whites. The *Planet*'s commentary on the Beavers affair did not speculate on why Jim Beavers left his wife at home the second time he fled. Readers might have considered that Beavers believed that the white men would pursue him and leave his wife alone. They might have imagined that Beavers wanted to take his wife along but feared harming her or their unborn child if they both took flight again. Besides, had Beavers been at home he might have defended himself and his wife, but only if he had the resources to purchase a gun or if he was not overwhelmed by white men invading his home. Beavers was not home when violence arrived, and according to several newspaper reports, his absence made his wife vulnerable to the white men's assault. In the opinion of such militant public figures as Bruce, Fortune, and Mitchell, there was no excuse for black men not having the means or the resolve to protect their families. This sentiment was embraced widely by some public figures operating in the counterpublic sphere.[33]

Many activists who criticized black men did so because they saw the consolidation of racism through the prism of gender and African Americans' fight for civil and political rights. They called on black men to defend their social, political, and economic interests. The current of calling on black men to practice self-defense ran through speeches, editorials, political pamphlets, novels, and short stories. Recognizing that slavery had stripped many black men of the right to be the arbiters of their destinies and that the two decades following emancipation had yielded what Anna Julia Cooper surmised was a "ruddy manhood," unable to protect their deteriorating rights, public figures saw "the re-training of the race" as their responsibility. Immersed in the culture of manhood and masculinity and concerned about racial violence and other forms of discrimination, these activists used print culture to try to construct a new identity in light of the consolidation of racism.[34]

Though the phrase "New Negro" did not enter the official lexicon of African America until the 1920s, activists such as Fortune, Wells, Cooper, and Bruce were guided by a belief in the need to construct a new identity and a new class of black people to battle the forces of the consolidation in the 1890s. With respect to fighting racial violence, they reasoned that if black men fulfilled their roles as protectors, then they might spare their families harm. Some public figures argued that if black folk harnessed their power, by having men assert their manliness and masculinity to protect their families and their interests, then southern whites and the nation would respect and take seriously black people's demand for civil and political rights. These women and men argued that with white men's passion for using violence to subjugate blacks, there was little doubt that when armed white men visited black people's homes, violence ensued. Feeling that nothing less than the race's future was at stake, journalists and editors such as Mitchell, Bruce, and Ida Wells called into question the manhood and masculinity of black men who failed to protect their families and to defend their homes.[35]

With the rise in the number of black people being lynched, public figures used black print culture to instruct black men on the best ways to defend themselves and their families. A common feature in the *Planet*'s editorial pages during the 1890s was directives and edicts such as "it should be as much a duty to have a repeating rifle and a revolver as it is to carry an insurance policy" to protect one's homeplace and home sphere. Newspaper articles and reports used headlines to describe black men who defended themselves as "Brave Defender[s]" who "Resist[ed] Lynchers." These activists placed the responsibility for defending African Americans squarely on black men. Activists wielded the print culture to commend and to condemn. In doing so, black public figures were attempting to adjust black people's responses to racial violence. Thus, black men who resisted white supremacy by possessing and brandishing guns to defend their homes and communities were praised as brave, manly, and quintessentially masculine. Activists brooked few excuses regarding the protection of black families and censured black men who failed to defend their interests. Some of them cast as weak and cowardly the black men who failed to defend themselves and their families.[36]

Public figures also provided African Americans, who were shut out of American life, with a safe space to report violence and to express their determination to defend themselves and their community. For example, R. B. Garret of Greensboro, North Carolina, wrote a letter to the *Planet* in which he expressed pride about how he and several hundred men protected a black male prisoner named Tuttle from would-be lynchers. Although some local firms refused to sell ammunition to the men, they managed to have their "Winchester rifles and revolvers in readiness." Moreover, they also reported that they had "enough [ammunition] to shoot one thousands times" to guarantee Tuttle's safety. The editorial pages of the *Planet* and other newspapers were filled with black people's written testimonies about white violence and black resistance.[37]

In publishing reports of violence and their prescriptions for resisting it, black public figures positioned racial violence and the need for manly and masculine responses to white supremacy firmly within the context of larger social, economic, and political developments of the 1890s. Other state legislatures followed Florida's lead, disfranchising black men. As white southerners intensified their efforts to subjugate African Americans legally, more black newspapers reported and challenged every white-supremacist speech justifying disfranchisement and every vote by elected officials to use legislation to subjugate African Americans. Public figures argued that legislators had to take legal action because, despite the violence African Americans endured when they tried to vote, they remained committed to having authority in governance. Legally restricting black men's ability to vote and to hold office, public figures argued, was the only way that white southerners could deny African Americans their civil and political rights. They protested disfranchisement to no avail. By the century's end, most southern states had used legal or extralegal methods to strip thousands of black men of their authority in local governance and their ability to protect themselves from any further violations of their rights. For example, in the *Civil Rights Cases* decision, the Supreme Court had barred states from segregating based on race but upheld the right of private businesses and some civil service providers to draw the color line in restaurants, hotels, and trains and streetcars. Public figures detailed and decried the drawing of the color line and unpunished attacks on blacks who crossed it, but their protests were ignored. The Court in *Plessy v. Ferguson* opened the doors for states to segregate public services and the workforce as long they provided "equal" service and accommodations. Within a decade of the 1896 decision, white southern legislators had segregated or shut African Americans out of many areas of public life and denied them access to public accommodations that ranged from education, employment, and transportation to housing, finance, and medical care. Once basic practices of white supremacy became public policy, white citizens and civil authorities saw it as their duty to uphold the law. What is more, whites did not hesitate to use violence and the threat of it to police cross-racial interactions and to enforce Jim Crow and disfranchisement.[38]

The sense of calamity among African Americans seemed to intensify as newspaper reports and victims' and witnesses' accounts of the consolidation cast a denser cloud over black southerners' civil and political rights and their lives. It also activated debates over the best responses to these developments. Consumers of black print culture appreciated the ways that the hydra-headed problem of a consolidated white supremacy constituted an unprecedented crisis. Therefore, most blacks understood that segregation, disfranchisement, and extraordinary violence were now entrenched features of black southern life and that they needed to develop appropriate responses to resist. However, members of the counterpublic sphere often differed in their interpretation of events. They seesawed over the responses they wanted from people inside and outside the black community and used the counterpublic sphere to exchange ideas about the best strategies for resisting racial violence. These exchanges were consumed by the masses of black people.

The action of the Afro-American Council in 1899 and the op-eds in several black newspapers with national circulation, illustrate some of the debates and recommendations coursing throughout the counterpublic sphere. The council, which emerged as a replacement for the defunct Afro-American League, called on black citizens to fast in protest of lynching. What is more, some African Americans revisited the options of migration and emigration. In an 1899 op-ed in the Indianapolis *Freeman*, Emery D. Williams declared,

"The Caucasian and the Negro cannot exist side by side, equal, and yet apart, a separate and distinct people, and yet together." Williams was one of many blacks who feared black people's extermination by way of continued violence. He therefore proposed that African Americans "save themselves" by establishing a black American state in Liberia or somewhere in the territories of the trans-Mississippi West. On the other hand, the *Freeman*'s editorial board was more buoyant. The *Freeman* reprinted lynching statistics compiled and reported by the Boston *Courant* from 1885 to 1899, which reflected a peak of reported lynchings in 1892, with 235, which was followed by a gradual decline. Seizing on the apparent decline in lynching, the editors, led by George C. Knox, declared that the "evil is dying out from the weight of public opinion." Knox expressed confidence that the "mellowing influences of time and right endeavor [of African Americans]" would "soften the racial asperities" that had plagued the nation.[39] A report from the *Freeman*, declaring that the combined developments of the preceding decade amounted to "the first step into a new slavery," appeared later that year, however.[40] A month later, in a survey of conditions black people faced, the paper published more optimistic essays about the difficulties facing blacks. For example, in "What of the Twentieth Century?" the *Freeman*—reflecting the conservatism of Knox—predicted that the problems associated with black people's violent exclusion from American life would eventually "pass away with the other encumbrances." Such highly selective interpretations of the changes in white supremacy at the local and national level likely delayed African Americans' initiation of collective reform efforts.[41]

Industrialization, urbanization, some advances in education, unionization, increased black landownership, and mature civic, social, and economic institutions found African Americans such as Knox using segregation to make racial progress. For example, Booker T. Washington advocated agricultural and technical training to improve black people's socioeconomic status in the nation. Washingtonians did this because they appreciated the crisis blacks were facing. However, they also believed that a successful industrial middle class could establish businesses and provide the public services that African Americans needed. This class, Washingtonians reasoned, could serve each other's needs as well as educate and employ poor black people, who, over time, would rise socially and in turn "uplift" those who were struggling. Advocates of this philosophy argued that this process of racial uplift would allow blacks to avoid situations in which whites attempted to subjugate them. Moreover, many proponents of accommodating white supremacy believed that establishing black organizations and service industries would create an intraracial and intergenerational cycle of wealth and respectability that would challenge some of the claims whites made about black people's racial inferiority as the primary justification for racial subjugation. Many blacks subscribed to Washington's program of uplifting the masses to combat the hydra of white supremacy instead of confronting whites directly.[42]

John Bruce, W. E. B. Du Bois, and Ida Wells-Barnett saw things differently. They interpreted the recent developments as putting a vast abyss between blacks and their rights as citizens and their ability to protect themselves from violence. Assessing the cumulative weight of lynching, disfranchisement, and segregation, these writers argued that legalized white supremacy, as it stood by 1900, had already begun to sabotage many African Americans' ability to carry out Washington's plan for racial uplift. These activists argued that the only way for blacks to achieve economic, political, and social progress was for them to demand their rights as citizens and to make the nation uphold the principles of its founding. These people understood that blacks bore some responsibility for challenging white supremacy, but they had borne witness to a decade of individual suffering and resistance with little relief. They decided to take to the entire nation the case for reform. Public figures seized on lynching and other forms of violence as one of the most egregious violations of black people's lives and their rights. Bruce explained in "The Blood Red Record" that "justice [was] apparently slumbering; a public sentiment seems apathetic." Bruce remained confident, however, that blacks would help justice "shake off her lethargy" by defending themselves against violence.[43]

In the nascent phases of the rise of Jim Crow, there were two more developments relating to public figures' efforts to coordinate African Americans' responses to racial violence. The criminal justice system became more formalized as uniformed officers patrolled communities to preserve order and to protect the white power structure. Simultaneously, newspaper reports point to more blacks having weapons and using them to defend themselves against racial violence by citizens and by law enforcement officers. A white and often-antiblack police presence and the availability of guns came together with reverberations for black people living throughout the South.[44] Having endured and borne witness to the consolidation and the seesawing debates over the appropriate responses to it, more blacks who encountered these new developments seem to have returned fire against whites using violence to preserve white supremacy. For example, in March 1893, the *Planet* reported that black Mississippians in Purvis set fire to the town in retaliation for the arrest of a preacher. According to news reports, fires started simultaneously across town, destroying five residential and commercial buildings. Rumors that some of the town's black residents had burned the town "in revenge" spread on the northbound New Orleans Northeastern train that passed through the decimated town. The Richmond *Planet* reported that "a posse of [white] citizens" left the town of Meridian for Purvis to put down what they saw as a black uprising against whites. Similar reports of black resistance after the turn of the century commanded the nation's attention about the problems of white supremacy.[45]

Public figures used the counterpublic sphere to argue that the formalization of criminal justice procedures that reinforced white supremacy and accommodated lynching by allowing perpetrators to go unpunished made the South a more dangerous place for black people who were attempting to assert their right to live as free citizens. They also disseminated information about instances when law enforcement officers failed to protect blacks from white citizens who were attempting to lynch them and from authorities who failed to prosecute even known perpetrators. The formalization of criminal justice procedures did not produce a more violent South for black people. However, activists argued that the cronyism and the enforcement of social customs and laws favoring white supremacy did. They argued that lynching and the formalization of a racist legal system worked in tandem to enforce white supremacy. Public figures argued that white southerners used the law and custom to persecute blacks who defied white people's authority or threatened their interests. Accounts of black people being arrested for real and bogus crimes and of authorities who turned black prisoners over to mobs or who failed to protect prisoners filled black print culture. Public figures detailed civil authorities' violations of African Americans legal rights and connected them to the larger context of the consolidation. Moreover, they informed readers of the best ways to get redress for their grievances and demanded that civil authorities help blacks get justice.[46]

Black southerners who learned through experience or through the press about the biased administration of justice and the gruesome penitentiary system, with its high inmate mortality rate, became more suspicious of the states' peacekeeping forces. Distrust of the system bred contempt and a greater resistance toward entering it. Surrendering to police or to those who purported to work on their behalf, according to John Mitchell, meant deliberately placing oneself "in the hands of a howling mob" for mutilation and burning. Some black men started to violently resist peace officers who attempted to arrest them, especially when officials and others posing as officials lacked warrants. Some defiant black folks' possession of guns resulted in the deaths of white civil authorities and their subordinates, which incited white civilians to lynch and engage in other types of extraordinary violence against the perpetrators or their family or community on a routine basis.[47]

Activists working in the counterpublic sphere also documented the conditions in southern penitentiaries, where black convicts were beaten and killed, disappeared, and often attempted to escape even knowing the risk of death.[48] Newspaper reports brought conditions in the penitentiary and in the convict-leasing system into the open and likely intensified African Americans' reluctance to comply with law enforcement officers. For example, readers of the *Planet* learned in August 1898 that when armed authorities from Atoka, Tennessee, tried to levy the household goods of Mike Hill, they found not Hill but his wife and two sons at home. According to the report, titled "Murdered Them: A Frivolous Excuse for Taking Human Life," when the officers approached the family's residence, Mrs. Hill, who was armed with a shotgun, went outside and "attempted to shoot the officers." In the gunfight that ensued, Hill's sons joined the melee. By the end, authorities had killed the Hill boys and injured Mrs. Hill. If Mike Hill returned, he likely found his wife devastated by the raid, nursing her injuries and mourning the loss of their sons. As these incidents of African Americans resisting arrest or firing on law enforcement officers occurred throughout the region, public figures used print culture to broadcast these new developments in racial violence and black people's resistance to it.[49]

Reading black public figures' reports of racism within the criminal justice system gave African Americans greater reason to distrust law enforcement officers. Perhaps the most notorious aborted arrest was that of Robert Charles, a Mississippian living in New Orleans in 1900. Charles, who had borne witness to and was infuriated by the 1899 spectacle killing of Sam Hose, resisted two attempts of authorities to arrest him. In the first arrest attempt, when officers confronted Charles for engaging in some presumably suspicious activity while he was sitting on a doorstep of a friend, Charles resisted, wounding and killing several patrolmen before he escaped. Charles's flight activated a mob of civilians and angry police officers that tore through the city in pursuit. Some newspapers reported that the mob, acting with the sanction of civil authorities, "hunted" black people and "shot [them] down in cold blood." In fact, the search for Charles resulted in casualties among the city's black population. The mobs pursuing Charles killed two black men, wounded several others, and destroyed African Americans' property. African Americans in New Orleans helped Charles to evade arrest until police cornered him in a building. Rather than surrender, Charles exchanged fire with police, wounding and killing more officers and other whites until they managed to kill him. Black public figures re-presented the mainstream print culture's depiction of Charles as a brute by writing reports of Charles's bravery and the savagery of the white mob. The *Planet* ran with headlines announcing, "The Butchery at New Orleans" and "With a Rifle in His Hand," but Ida B. Wells-Barnett's pamphlet "Mob Rule in New Orleans" narrated the mob's slaughter of black residents and destruction of black people's property while they searched for Charles.[50]

The Hill family's actions and Robert Charles's stand against the mob dramatize the lengths to which some African Americans were willing to go to prevent arrest or to avoid being taken into police custody. According to the *Planet*, Charles and other black people "knew what to expect if [they were] taken alive." If black people committed these crimes, then their knowledge of the corrupt nature of southern justice might have left them feeling that they had no choice but to resist violently. Either way, few African Americans—in spite of their responses to what they believed were dubious arrest attempts—escaped the mob's will. As Brundage posits, some whites saw attacks on and murders of peace officers as "unmistakable attacks" on their communities, which justified "elaborate, ritualized, and unambiguously public mob violence." White mobs hunted African Americans and attacked not only the intended targets but also any blacks they encountered. Although black people who violently resisted arrest often suffered the most brutal consequences of the white mob's wrath, as the hunts for defiant men such as Charles illustrate, all African Americans were vulnerable to mob violence.[51]

African Americans' ability to acquire guns made some efforts to avoid arrest possible. By the late nineteenth century, newspaper reports on black people using guns to defend themselves or to resist arrest suggest that guns were easier for black people to acquire, despite routine efforts by some white citizens and authorities to prevent them from possessing arms. Thus, gun possession held currency among black southerners who wanted to defend themselves against whites; it also increased the likelihood that black people might settle their disputes with whites with weapons. In sum, the availability of guns and some African Americans' willingness to use arms to contest or preserve the administration of justice or to protect their lives and livelihood equalized their ability to defend themselves against the violence of a crystallized white supremacy.[52]

Believing that certain arrest attempts were bogus and knowing from experience and reading reports of blacks in police custody who never made it to trial, some African Americans joined forces to prevent arrests, and some members of the press cheered them on. Newspapers reported that black activists also guarded jails housing black prisoners to allow legal justice to take its course. For example, the *Planet* reported on the case of Ben Heed, which exemplifies the steps that black people started taking to defend members of their communities. In July 1892, several hundred black Floridians attempted to protect Heed from a mob that was amassing in Jacksonville. Authorities charged Heed with murdering a white man named Frank Burrows. On the first night of the siege, black men waited in the bushes near the jail and fired on five whites to prevent them from disarming the lone man guarding the Duval County jail. The black men, worried that their presence outside the jail and their firing on the white men might activate a mob, called on their family members and friends to join them in protecting Heed. The gathering of armed black men and the possibility of a white mob forming impelled local authorities to call in state troops, who got the men to disperse by promising that a mob would not lynch Heed. The black men—evidently organized in squads and reportedly outnumbering the troops—left the immediate vicinity of the jail as instructed. However, sentries remained within close proximity so they could assemble the black men on any sign of a mob forming.[53] Publishing reports such as this one, black public figures offered readers of black print culture an opportunity to glean insight into incidents of communal self-defense.

Public figures' debates about the best strategies for challenging racial violence open a window onto some interesting gender dynamics of the counterpublic sphere. Subscribing to the gender norms of the times, many male activists probably believed that black men were responsible for challenging racial violence and that the dominant public sphere and counterpublic sphere were spaces that were reserved for men. Black female activists, however, were very active and vocal participants in campaigns against white supremacy. Following a trail blazed by such public figures as Ida Wells-Barnett, Anna Julia Cooper, and Mary Church Terrell, members of the Michigan State Federation of Colored Women stepped boldly into the public spheres and the political arena in 1900. These clubwomen attempted to flip the script by articulating a belief that the burden for ending racial violence rested not with African Americans but with elected and appointed agents of the state. They authored a memorial to Congress asking for legislation so that if "any State be found guilty of [allowing] mob laws and lynching it be expelled from the Union." The "negro haters," they continued, could be evacuated to their own state, "wherein they need not see a black face." This statement reflects some black women's opposition to emigration as a means of avoiding violence. Some white people's readiness to act on their desire to be rid of blacks led them to describe African Americans' criminal behavior as the primary source of cross-racial tensions and white people's use of extraordinary violence. These clubwomen believed that most black people modeled the best practices of citizenship and were constitutionally entitled to remain in the United States if they chose. If some white citizens and local and state politicians had problems with black people's claiming their citizenship rights and they were willing to violate the nation's laws to do it, then, the clubwomen argued, the federal government should make suitable arrangements for *them* to relocate.[54]

George Knox denounced the clubwomen's memorial as "incendiary" and unrealistic. If federal officials granted the clubwomen's request, he wrote, then "there would be little or nothing left of the Union," given many white people's hatred for blacks. Knox's complaints notwithstanding, the clubwomen's petition reflected their commitment to determine, as Anna Julia Cooper put it, "when and where [black women] enter[ed]" the public spheres and the political arenas to do their part to end lynching. The petition also shows black women's belief that the states and the federal government bore responsibility for protecting blacks from racial violence. The clubwomen were not alone in their beliefs about the role of state governments in ending violence. Frustrated by the ways that lynching undermined the constitutional guarantees of due process and equal protection under the law, Indiana and Ohio sought to legislate against mob violence. However, this legislation did nothing to protect the majority of black people who still lived south of the Mason-Dixon line. With southern legislatures continuing to institutionalize white supremacy via segregation, disfranchisement, and violence, the clubwomen's appeal to Congress for federal relief made sense to legislators in these states, even if not to conservative black men such as Knox.[55]

While black men convened discussions of the problems of Jim Crow, black women increasingly asserted their voices into the counterpublic sphere and the dominant public spheres. The National Association of Colored Women (NACW) used its 1901 annual meeting in Buffalo, New York, to issue a public statement against lynching. The association adopted resolutions that addressed this "barbarous method of punishment" and the women and children "who suffer[ed] from its operation to an alarming and painful degree." The clubwomen interpreted the violence they witnessed directly or indirectly through the testimonies of victims and the larger vernacular history of racial violence. From the clubwomen's perspective, mob violence was not a practice that would simply die out; it had to be driven out. Their resolutions underscored their understanding that whites were showing little indication of stopping their use of violence to subjugate black people. As long as lawlessness continued and state and federal officials refused to protect black people or bring known perpetrators to justice, the clubwomen reasoned, then white men would continue to slaughter black men, whose families would have to live with the emotional and material costs of their deaths.

Pointing out those "who suffer from its operation to an alarming and painful degree," the clubwomen's public statement reflects their appreciation for the vernacular history of racial violence and the ways that violence affected women disproportionately as the actual victims of violence and as the female survivors of assaulted and slain men. In this way, clubwomen tried to re-present the chronic costs of mob violence for the lynch sufferers' surviving family members. The killing of family members and friends was tragic, but the murders of black men devastated African Americans' family dynamics and compromised their ability to survive. Female public figures, such as Ida B. Wells-Barnett and dramatist Angelina Weld Grimké, used their investigative and creative talent to illuminate black women's suffering, as victims of violence and as survivors of violence directed at black men. Wells-Barnett, in her pamphlets "The Red Record" and "Southern Horrors," illuminated the sexual violence these women endured at the hands of white men. Grimké, in her play *Rachel*, tried to show that even after family members worked through their grief, they still had to confront the matter of adjusting their lives and their lifestyles to the loss of income and male protection. Clubwomen wanted Americans to know that behind every lynch victim was a devastated family. These surviving family members would have had to turn to their extended kin and sometimes to the state for survival. This violence, female activists argued, had wider implications for women than was often understood. In organizing and airing their grievances publicly, clubwomen tried to re-present black women's unique experiences of racial violence and its costs.[56]

Black women even developed their own campaigns to fight violence. For example, in the 1920s, Mary Talbert's Anti-Lynching Crusaders devised campaigns that supplied women with pamphlets detailing accounts of women lynched by mobs and asking them to donate one dollar to the cause of ending the violence. The nation's failure to recognize these women as full citizens was not enough to deter them from charging into the dominant public sphere and the counterpublic sphere and calling attention to women's experiences and needs. Black male activists' reactions to the clubwomen's work was mixed, but this lukewarm response to women's intervention into these debates did not dissuade these "donations" in their belief that black women needed to do their part to defend African Americans' interest in the face of white supremacy.[57]

The reporting on the lynching of an elderly black man named Berry Washington shows black public figures' efforts to highlight black people's acts of self-defense and to illustrate the potentially fatal consequences of such action. With the title "Negro Dies Defending His Race," the Indianapolis *Freeman* wanted to spotlight what the paper believed was an appropriate response to racial violence, even though it resulted in a man's death. Seventy-two-year-old Milan, Georgia, resident Berry Washington was murdered for his attempt to protect a widow and her two daughters from two white men. On the morning of May 24, 1919, John Dandy and another white man went into the black residential district and demanded entrance into the home of Mrs. Emma McCollers. When McCollers refused, Dandy fired into her home, forcing her to run to a nearby well and her daughters to flee under the porch of a neighbor, with the white men in pursuit. Washington, upon hearing the females' screams, ran outside with his gun. When Washington confronted Dandy, the white man questioned his interference. Washington responded that he came "to see what is the matter with the women and children." When Dandy threatened to kill Washington for his interference, Washington shot Dandy and drove away his accomplice. Afterward, Washington turned himself in to local authorities for killing Dandy. That night a mob of between seventy-five and one hundred whites stormed the jail. Then, the men dragged Washington back to the site of Dandy's death and hanged him from a post before riddling his body with bullets.[58]

As a witness to the new era of white supremacy, Washington likely knew that, in the minds of many white civilians and civil authorities, his killing of the white man would probably trump Dandy's prowling in the black enclave for female sexual quarry. Either Washington felt no regret about defending the McCollers females from certain rape and possible murder, or he hoped that by surrendering, the authorities would protect him and white civilians might spare his life for defending a woman and her daughters. In the end, Washington's death and the display of his body reinforced for black southerners the reality that crimes for which white men typically went free would be punished severely for black men. For members of Washington's family, his death was a torturous loss with consequences that extended horizontally across his family and vertically to subsequent generations. For members of the counterpublic sphere, Washington's action and his lynching gave them the opportunity to spotlight a black man's brave and manly "defense" of his race and the ways that his willingness to surrender to authorities was not enough to spare him from the mob's wrath.

As the reporting around Washington's killing shows, people who engaged in armed self-defense against whites often did so with the disdain and fear of whites but with the consent of some public figures, who advocated self-defense in gendered terms. Papers such as the *Planet* and the Omaha *Afro-American Sentinel* not only advocated gun possession and self-defense among African Americans; they also congratulated black men who engaged in armed self-defense and exalted them as the epitome of manhood and masculinity. For example, in June 1897, when the well-armed black residents of Key West, Florida, refused to allow a mob to lynch Sylvanus Johnson, whom authorities charged with assault, some black newspaper editors lauded their work. The *Planet* wrote, "A few more mounds on the hill-side with the relatives of lynchers beside them will settle this great question. When lynching becomes a deadly pastime [for whites], thoughtless murderers will abandon the habit." The *Sentinel* expressed a similar opinion, writing, "It was a wise precaution on the part of our Florida brethren to have provided themselves with guns and ammunition. It was a glorious thing that they possessed sufficient courage to use them so well. Let colored men everywhere imitate the brave example of those in Key West, and lynching will soon become rare." The *Planet* similarly hailed the work of black Floridians in the defense of Ben Heed, as a "manly stand" against lynch law. Such sentiments helped encourage African American men to protect their homes and their loved ones from whites.[59]

As the rhetoric surrounding the incidents involving Berry Washington, Ben Heed, Jack Trice, and Sylvanus Johnson shows, gender conventions in the context of the consolidation dictated that black men defend their families and communities against whites. However, as the action of Mrs. Hill illustrates, black women also brandished firearms to challenge violent whites. African American women had endured violence with limited means of individual self-defense, but the availability of guns offered these women some measures to defend themselves and their families in the absence of black men. The counterpublic sphere celebrated black men's defense of their homes. Masculinist doctrine infused white-supremacist discourse, so black public figures' focus on black men's defense of their families makes sense and perhaps explains their failure to give black women's "womanly" acts of armed self-defense equal coverage. Nonetheless, incidents of black women bearing arms to defend their families punctuate the ways that these women resisted racial violence.[60]

Whether it was black women or men who took up arms, the presence of guns in African Americans' homes and black people's willingness to use them heightened the chance for armed confrontations with groups of white civilians and authorities. Public figures distributed examples of black resistance and its potential effectiveness for compelling some violent whites to think twice before attacking blacks. Black people's growing resistance to racial violence induced whites to launch even greater offensive assaults after the turn of the century. Public figures' re-presentation of the consolidation crystallized in black people the need to defend themselves. In response to reports on riots and massacres, the publicized rhetoric of the black counterpublic sphere became more radical.

Public figures reported that racial massacres and race riots in such places as Wilmington (1898), Atlanta (1906), and Springfield, Illinois (1908) often emerged from African Americans' clashes with law enforcement officers and whites' attempts to assert authority over blacks. Besieged but determined to enjoy their rights as citizens, blacks continued to resist white supremacy in ways that fit into a pattern that emerged in riots. In each case, black people either fought back immediately or launched a counterattack, which unified white communities. United and sometimes accompanied by police and state militias, whites sacked black residential and business districts through campaigns of looting, arson, and lynching. Some of these attacks were indiscriminant, but white rioters used these occasions to settle scores against their enemies as well as prosperous black people. Concern for further violence prompted state and federal authorities to intervene by sending in militia or guardsmen, some of whom participated in the violent assaults on black communities, ignored these attacks, or performed their tasks in a racially biased manner. Interracial clashes and African Americans' forceful resistance to racial violence were not unique to the Jim Crow era. Part of what changed in the turn-of-the-century decades, was the growing concentration of these incidents throughout the South, state-sponsored missions to prevent and suppress them, their occurrence in northern, urban spaces, and finally, black public figures' efforts to shape Americans' understandings of them.[61]

Riots in the twentieth century's first decade paled in comparison to the ones that occurred, in such places as East St. Louis, during the second decade. In fact, during the First World War, the signs of pending racial conflagrations became apparent to consumers of the print culture's coverage of race relations. As incidents in places such as Barnwell and Robert Charles's New Orleans made clear, white citizens and elected officials were aware of the threat of retributive justice on the part of blacks. This threat became more real as African Americans, galvanized by their frustrated efforts to combat racial violence and their increasing commitment to organized resistance, asserted their right to full citizenship. Public figures cheered on defiant blacks, citing ongoing violence and black people's contributions to the war as their entitlement to defend themselves against violence.[62] These activists' full-throated support for blacks who defended themselves during the riots was part of black people's political mobilization against racial violence. Indeed, "re-training the race" and the construction of a "New Negro" identity came to the fore in the mobilization for the First World War.

Public figures wanted their constituents to understand the aspects of racial violence that people discussed in their communities but that mainstream newspapers did not cover. Whereas newspapers often reported the actual event of violence, some investigators provided contextual evidence of community relations before, during, and after the violence. In-depth coverage provided readers of black print culture with some details of violence that were often missing from mainstream newspaper reports. Using journalists who collected first- and second-person narratives of violence from black and white witnesses, black newspaper articles and reports offered candid interpretations of the behavior of those involved. Armed with this evidence, black activists illuminated some of the noxious manifestations of white supremacy.

Black public figures' efforts to re-present racial violence and to adjust black people's responses to it had mixed results. Indeed, they helped black Americans appreciate the new dynamics of white supremacy. Although black folk clearly had their own opinions about responding to violent whites, public figures' salvos about and against violence and their celebration of self-defense against violence kindled a growing opposition to white supremacy, which African Americans eventually channeled into a full frontal assault on racial violence. Other developments in the consolidation came to the fore during and after the First World War and induced in activists operating in the counterpublic sphere a need to further adjust black people's responses, to challenge white Americans' behavior, and to explain to the nation African Americans' actions.

"Tone of Menace and the Threat of Violent Resistance"

By the spring of 1918, African Americans' more public and increasingly organized resistance to white supremacy became more apparent to white civilians, the mainstream media, and federal officials. Although blacks remained the primary audience of the counterpublic sphere, activists also "project[ed] the hidden transcripts" of black people's endurance of white supremacy to "the dominant public sphere." In fact, black public figures were mindful of the fact that white citizens, officials, and journalists consumed and monitored black publications and speeches. These activists wanted to make the case for the need to challenge violence, as Charles W. Chesnutt explained to Du Bois, to "thinking whites," those people "who are after all the arbiters of our destiny." Specifically, they hoped that making moderate and progressive whites bear witness to the social and legal horrors of racial violence would help them develop a greater "oppositional consciousness" to white supremacy that would be the linchpin that African Americans needed to transform the nation's legal and social structure.[63]

As effective as reading reports of the consolidation might have been for beginning to mobilize African Americans, public figures' efforts to change the minds of white citizens and federal officials had gained little traction. After 1900, black journalists, authors, and artists continued to re-present to Americans the different dimensions of racial violence and the contexts in which it occurred. Although public figures used print culture to educate blacks, they shifted some of their efforts toward whites. They flooded the national discourse with their critiques of white supremacy and attempted to seize control of the representation of white supremacy from those who operated in the dominant public spheres. These activists wanted not to goad and shame the perpetrators of violence, many of whom because their use and endorsement of violence would have been indifferent to the suffering they inflicted on blacks. Instead, black public figures focused their energy on the vocal and silent bystanders to this violence in communities across the nation. They focused on using reports of violence and juxtaposing them with the nation's democratic principles and citizens' claims of their support for the Constitution to evoke moderate and progressive white folks' disgust with violent whites. Activists hoped that some white Americans' empathy for victims of violence and their commitment to the ideas of due process and equal protection under the law might inspire them to support black people's fight against extralegal violence. As black people took steps to defend themselves against violence and some white civilians and federal officials became more alarmed about the impact of the unchecked violence on the nation, public figures defended black people's resistance, published the vernacular history of the consolidation, and warned the nation to take action.[64]

Most white Americans accepted lynchers' claims that they only lynched black men who committed the terrible crimes of raping white women or killing law enforcement officers and that when lynchers stepped outside the law, they exacted rough justice in an orderly and civilized manner. Black and progressive white newspapers routinely wrote about the chaos of turn-of-the-century mobs that killed black men and the macabre aspects of some spectacle killings. The lynching of a black woman in 1915, however, gave black public figures a unique opportunity to challenge the dominant public sphere's representation of lynching and to change white people's opinions about this violence and the people who committed it. In December 1915, the Chicago *Defender* reported that a gang of white Mississippians kidnapped Cordella Stevenson from her home at gunpoint, dragged her through the streets "without any resistance," and hanged her from a tree in a public space. The *Defender* reported that railway passengers, who saw Stevenson's remains as they came through town, reported that there was evidence that the men had sexually assaulted Stevenson before they killed her. Afterward, local people informed investigators that Stevenson was an upstanding woman in her community and a good tenant and laborer. However, when Gabe Frank's barn burned down, whites suspected Stevenson's son of setting the blaze. Stevenson informed local authorities that her child could not have committed the crime because he left town months before the fire. Cordella and her husband, Arch, believed the matter was resolved, until the white men invaded their home. Press reports are not clear about why the younger Stevenson departed or about why they lynched Cordella and did not harm Arch.[65] Nonetheless, the lynching of a black woman contradicted the dominant public sphere's reporting on lynching as a crime whites committed against black men for raping white females or killing law enforcement officers, which opened a discursive space for public figures to address many Americans' assumptions about lynching.

The *Defender* and other papers re-presented the lynchings of women with great care because they wanted readers to know that all African Americans were vulnerable to lynching if they or their loved ones violated the law or social norms. These activists also used the sexual aspects of lynchings such as Stevenson's to expose the white men's behavior and to cast them as uncivilized beasts who not only killed a black woman but also made a sexual spectacle of her killing. Public figures hoped they could shame white Americans for tolerating this violence. In publishing reports of this nature in black newspapers, public figures also wanted to change the ways that the mainstream press covered these killings. Believing that many white newspaper editors were complicit in cultivating a tolerance for lynching, Charles W. Chesnutt derided their publications as "noosepapers" in his fiction. When mainstream newspapers failed to report incidents of racial violence or refused to report them in a way that did not presume the guilt of a black person, black public figures published their own accounts, wherein they highlighted violence and the contexts in which it occurred. They used print culture to draw attention to the aspects of the violence that they believed the mainstream press ignored but were important for understanding the dynamics of lynching.[66]

Even if public figures' publication of reports of violence and testimonies of African Americans' experiences of it did not persuade whites to end racial violence or to stop tolerating it, their work did not escape notice. In fact, the increasingly confrontational tone of public figures and their support for black people's defending themselves against violence attracted the attention of white citizens and contributors to the dominant public spheres as well as elected and appointed federal officials. For example, U.S. Postmaster Robert Adger Bowen wrote a report on what he deemed to be the increasingly overt expressions of radical commentary in black and progressive white New York City publications once black troops went to France during the First World War. Bowen surmised from editorials in the New York *News* and New Jersey *Informer News* in April 1918 that "the Negro, having gone abroad to fight for Democracy, would upon his return know how to use his rifle and bayonet to fight for Democracy (the Negro's Democracy) at home." The postmaster's investigation of black print culture led him to the opinion that before wholesale black enlistment in the war cause, black newspapers were replete with "bombast and nonsense." Afterward, and particularly when public figures discussed lynching and racial discrimination in the army, he found that it revealed that blacks were "in a mood different from bombast and nonsense. And the Negro himself knows it!! He means business, and it would be well to take him at his word." Bowen was concerned that the cumulative effect of these publications indicated a "sense of resentment and race antagonism" among blacks, who, since the war started, had "increasingly employed the tone of menace and the threat of violent resistance." Before the war, Bowen, white citizens, and elected officials had dismissed black people's complaints about racial violence. The war and the shift in the tone of public figures and the behavior of black folk meant that all Americans needed to take seriously African Americans' responses to white supremacy.[67]

Other newspapers during the First World War also signaled their understanding of the emergence of the New Negro and the effort by public figures to communicate directly to whites the circumstances behind this transformation in African Americans' mentality and posture. For example, in an editorial titled "How the Negro Feels," the Hannibal *Record*, of Missouri, reckoned that "the more we talk Democracy, the more outraged [the Negro] feels. He sits down disconsolately and soliloquizes: 'Lynched, burned alive, Jim-crowed, discriminated against, boycotted industrially, robbed of the ballot in my country.'" The editor believed that African Americans had rightfully claimed the nation as their own. Racial violence was bad enough, but the fact that the victims were citizens of this country and had helped the nation achieve its greatness engendered anger and despair among black people. The July 1918 editorial predicted that "black men are going to fight for human rights and they will give no country in which they live after the war any peace until they are accorded these rights just as other men are accorded them." Other publications warned Americans of the consequences of continued racial violence.[68]

Public figures represented black people's self-defensive action against white people who were attempting to subjugate them as a justifiable response to violence. The federal government's fear of Bolshevism allowed some of its agents to assume that this sentiment was merely the "bombast and nonsense" of pesky radical activists. Close attention to black print culture, however, might have illustrated the extent to which these public figures were not simply attempting to inject extremist sentiment into black southern communities but were trying to use the counterpublic sphere and print culture to articulate the frustration of people pushed to the edge by violence.[69]

Black folk needed little convincing that their participation in the war should ameliorate conditions caused by the new era of white supremacy. When these expectations failed to come to fruition, black people's resistance to whites intensified. Re-presenting the violence faced by blacks throughout the South, activists working in the counterpublic sphere documented resistance at the local level. For example, the wartime threat of black people's retaliation against whites was real enough for authorities in Richmond, Virginia, to attempt to convince gun sellers not to sell guns and ammunition to black men in late 1918. In early November, a riot occurred in Hopewell, Virginia, following a white steward's slapping of a black cook. Ensuing violence forced the governor to send soldiers from Camp Lee to quell the fighting. Within weeks, state officials convened a special summit of the State Council of Defense and summoned black activists to attend, in response to reported large numbers of blacks purchasing weapons and ammunition in anticipation of more fighting.[70]

Rumors circulated throughout the mainstream and black print cultures that black residents of Richmond had made threats that "once their soldiers returned from Europe they intended to force the white man to give them equal rights." Indeed, talk of blacks retaliating against whites made some whites apprehensive enough to call for meetings and to discourage gun dealers from selling guns to blacks. The potential for black people to carry out these threats with the assistance of returned veterans fueled white southern animosity toward black soldiers upon their return from the war. White residents of Vicksburg, Mississippi, harbored similar fears following several local lynchings. Officials claimed to have received credible threats that blacks "intended to start riots here to kill white people in retaliation" for the recent violence. Authorities reacted by doubling the on-duty police force, preventing the sale of firearms, and converting the jail into an arsenal. Whether blacks made the threats in Richmond and Vicksburg because of the war or took seriously the recommendations of radical public figures that they fight back is not clear. Nevertheless, the potential for violence, represented in white Americans' fears about black people's capacity to carry out the threats of retaliation, suggests a growing resistance to white supremacy.[71]

In February 1919, returned soldiers from the all-black New York Old Fifteenth National Regiment marched up Manhattan's Fifth Avenue in demonstration of their proud service. For African Americans, the parade of soldiers personified black citizenship and masculinity. Black people attending the event reveled in the soldiers' contribution to the war effort and the promise of improved conditions at home that their return suggested. To white Americans—either indifferent to black women's and men's suffering or a direct party to it—this parade of black soldiers had to be an awesome sight. Having become more attuned to black people's growing desire to overturn legalized white supremacy via the public sphere and their own encounters with black people who were determined to resist racial subjugation, some whites braced themselves and bolstered their defenses against the potential that African Americans were ready to start fighting back.

White Americans' concerns about black resistance signified their awareness that their efforts to subjugate blacks had engendered a sense of vengeance in their victims, which made some of them rightfully afraid. The war and black military service constituted an opportune moment for black retribution; to reduce the possibilities of being attacked, some white southerners took precautions. In communities across the South, whites moved to prevent the sale of ammunition and firearms to blacks, to confiscate African Americans' weapons, and to strengthen police forces, activities that dramatize some white southerners' belief that blacks might be ready to strike back at their oppressors. African Americans' military involvement in the war and increasing racial discord made the threat of black retributive action more credible, as Red Summer dawned and Americans saw the predictions of newspaper editors realized and the venting of local people's indignation.

The twenty-five racial disturbances that occurred in 1919 were among the first collective efforts of blacks to forcefully assert their resistance to the hydra of white supremacy. Indeed, the events of Red Summer illustrate black people's punctuated and magnified responses to racial violence. In the context of the war and the resurgence of the Ku Klux Klan, every cross-racial encounter in which a black woman or man defied whites who were attempting to assert their authority over them carried the potential for a formal and violent challenge to white supremacy. A black person's refusal to defer to a white person who was attempting to assert authority over him or her was the match that ignited each of the riots. In such cities as Charleston, Chicago, Longview, Omaha, and Norfolk, white people's rage over black people's defiance accelerated the cycle of violence that often ended in death and destruction. When whites united to put down what they deemed was black people's attempt to overthrow the existing racial order, blacks fought back by injuring and killing whites. Black people's collective resistance helped to mobilize white communities and agents of the state, who pushed back against African Americans with devastating force. Public figures reported the many dimensions of the violence and its implications for black people and the nation.[72]

The violence of Red Summer also inspired Claude McKay to write his poem "If We Must Die," which was published by the liberal periodical the *Liberator*. In the poem, McKay's speaker underscores black people's determination to "return fighting" against white supremacy. The speaker notes that even if blacks were doomed to live under oppressive conditions, then "let it be not like hogs / Hunted and penned in an inglorious spot." If black people must die, then it was better that they "face the murderous, cowardly pack / Pressed to the wall, dying, but fighting back!" McKay, a Jamaican-born resident of Harlem, had read about racial violence in print culture and had discussed the matter with southern transplants to Harlem and with black public figures based throughout Manhattan. McKay, like other Caribbean immigrants, had borne witness to the violence meted out to African Americans and saw himself included in the persecution of those who were descended from people enslaved in this country. He envisioned a black racial consciousness irrespective of nationality, an African America united by past and present white racial repression. Like other activists, McKay had also witnessed and experienced enough of black life in America to capture the drift in a collective, transnational black sentiment toward the nation's continued tolerance of racial violence. The violence he witnessed inspired him to join other public figures in their calls for and celebration of black self-defense. Thus, language such as "return fighting," "know the reason why," "dying, but fighting back" published in the counterpublic sphere accentuated beliefs coursing throughout African America that self-defense was the only way for black people to survive. Indeed, the threads of defiance emanating from black print culture and in the behavior of black people during and after the war were some of the earliest indicators of the lid blowing off African America's restraint in simply coping with the consolidation of racism.[73]

The riot in Longview, Texas, in July 1919 reflects ongoing violence and public figures' roles in reporting it. State authorities sent Rangers to Longview to suppress a riot in the aftermath of white men's attempt to lynch a black man named Samuel L. Jones. Jones was a schoolteacher, a local correspondent for the Chicago *Defender*, and an active member of a black cooperative named the Negro Business Men's League. He had defied whites by allegedly informing the *Defender* of the June 16 lynching of Lemuel Walters, a man reportedly discovered in the bedroom of a white woman. Few national newspapers provided coverage of the Walters lynching, so Jones decided to share what he knew, which was that authorities arrested Walters and turned him over to the mob that killed him. Black community leaders responded to the killing by calling on local authorities to find and prosecute the perpetrators. However, when authorities took no action, Jones submitted a report to the *Defender* that illuminated the context behind Walters's killing, including his reported consensual relationship with the white woman that white men believed he raped, local authorities' role in Walters's killing, and their failure to arrest the perpetrators. When Jones's report in the *Defender* arrived in Longview, white residents' sense of outrage flared over having the spotlight shone on them and on their town. A fifteen-man posse descended on Jones's home in Longview's black residential district. Jones escaped, and armed black men fired on the posse, wounding four white men, which prompted the rest of the men to retreat for reinforcements. When the mob that formed returned, they found the district vacant. Because they could not attack Jones or the men who fired on the posse, the white men settled on burning black people's homes. Afterward, Governor William P. Hobby sent troops, who restored order by arresting blacks and whites for participating in the riot. In the end, the Longview riot was one of the first of more than twenty such incidents that year.[74]

A larger, bloodier riot started in Washington, D.C., days after the one in Longview ended. On July 19, responding to newspaper reports from the Washington *Post* on a black "crime wave," two hundred white sailors, marines, and civilians descended on the southwestern section of the District, following reports that authorities had released a black man suspected of assaulting the wife of a white sailor. Some black men struck back rather than allow the white men to wreak havoc on their neighborhood, which incited greater numbers of white men to join the effort to subjugate defiant blacks. District and military police tried to suppress the violence by arresting black and white rioters. The fighting intensified when soldiers marched the streets, ignoring the military's calls for the cessation of fighting. Many black residents fled the immediate scene of the violence, but returned veterans remained. These men, who had been "soldiers of democracy" in the war, fired at their white assailants and attempted to prevent the arrest of black men who were defending their community. Reports indicate that the black men boarded streetcars and piled into automobiles, from which they staged drive-by shootings of white rioters. The men beat and fired on whites who were approaching their neighborhoods. Reportedly, "eight or ten automobiles were manned by armed Negroes and were used as armored cavalry in lightning attacks on white residential districts, randomly firing at houses and people."[75]

When President Woodrow Wilson commanded the secretaries of war and the navy to intervene, the District's black residents retreated, and the Washington riot ended after four days. The New York *Commoner* declared that the police's inability or refusal to protect blacks from white attacks left black residents with no choice but to resort to self-defense. The paper affirmed, "Let every Negro arm himself and swear to die fighting in defense of his home, his rights, and his person. In every place where the law will not protect their lives, Negroes should buy and hoard guns." The *Commoner* used language urging all African Americans to defend their communities. Public figures, such as the editors of the *Commoner*, mourned the loss of life, but they also published celebratory reports on black men's armed defense against violent whites. They also wanted to insert into the dominant public spheres an assertion of black people's readiness and ability to defend themselves.[76]

Press reports on the riots startled the entire country, making clear, possibly for the first time, the extent to which some African Americans were willing to go to defend themselves from violence. So credible became the threat of rioting and of black people fighting back, killing white people, and destroying public property that state authorities dispatched militias and National Guard units to forestall race conflicts. On July 23, 1919, a Dublin, Georgia, posse—in pursuit of Hubert Cummings—surrounded and fired on the home of Bob Ashley. Ashley returned fire, killing Gregory Green, a white farmer, wounding another man, and forcing the posse to retreat. Authorities eventually apprehended Ashley and took him into custody. When local black residents learned of his arrest, they reportedly "made all kinds of preparations for any eventualities," making whites so concerned about black people rioting that they got in touch with Governor Hugh Dorsey. Dorsey authorized the National Guard to protect the jail holding Ashley. He went further and ordered the Home Guard and troops of Savannah to prepare for out-of-town service. Chambers of commerce, which were charged with protecting the business interests of the South, also applied pressure to local and state authorities to curb violence.[77]

Some southern governors' willingness to authorize state forces to suppress black people's participation in riots, rather than to protect blacks who were being sought and apprehended by vengeful whites, illustrates less their desire to check racial violence in their states than their commitment to preventing the riots. Some southern authorities were so afraid of the loss of life, of the cost of rebuilding destroyed property, of the embarrassment that riots brought, and of the threat of federal intervention that they made a more concerted attempt to avert mob violence by protecting imprisoned African Americans and by offering rewards for crimes committed against them. For example, in response to newspaper reports and complaints about the state's failure to protect black citizens and their rights, Governor Dorsey offered a reward of $750 for information that led to the arrest of the lynchers of a black man named Eli Cooper and for related church burnings in Caldwell. No such protection had existed for the imprisoned black citizens of Barnwell, South Carolina, and other southern locales thirty years earlier.[78]

The counterpublic sphere's re-presentation of racial violence enjoyed some positive results. Public figures' salvos about and against racial violence helped to offset and alter some of the dominant public sphere's reporting of the consolidation. Mainstream papers such as the New York *Times* eventually went from publishing white southerners' justifications for racial violence in their communities to producing more critical analyses of violence.[79] This work also forced some white people who were reading reports about mob violence to question the violence and to consider its reflection of the nation's character.

Conclusion

The race conflagrations during and following the First World War were signs of the enduring significance of the vernacular history of racial violence and African Americans' increasing political mobilization. Public figures publicized racial violence. They advised blacks to defend themselves and counseled white citizens and federal officials to play a role in ending violence. Though public figures' entreaties to white people may have fallen on deaf ears, their directives to black people did not.

The intensity of black people's responses to racial violence in 1919 stunned Americans who had previously dismissed and ignored black public figures' efforts to publicize victims' and witnesses' testimonies of violence and to educate Americans on the impact of violence on black people and its potential implications for the nation. These riots exposed Americans' anxieties about race, sex, labor, and politics, anxieties that the conditions of the war had exacerbated. Ordinary racial violence, legal disfranchisement, and segregation had not been enough to quell black people's defiance of white supremacy, so whites resorted to greater attempts to demonstrate their racial superiority in response to black people's insistence on protecting their civil and political rights. Black public figures contextualized the riots in terms of African Americans' suffering from the hydra of white supremacy. For black people's long-term pain and for their wartime patriotism, black public figures reported that black people expected an end to the violence and to white people's efforts to resubjugate them. When black women and men returned violence with violence, some public figures celebrated it. These people expressed the cumulative weight of racial violence, the limits of African Americans' endurance of it, and the federal government's apathy toward their plight. Black public figures even started to enjoy more support from such white progressives as James E. Gregg, who was principal of the Hampton Institute and penned an essay describing the "alarming, ominous" riots and offering suggestions to "prevent such horrors from ever happening again." Gregg argued, "These race riots of 1919 ought to be *the last* that disgrace the United States; and it is the duty of us all to see that this ideal is made fact." Gregg attributed the riots to a history of neglected opportunities to cultivate mutual respect and understanding between blacks and whites. Gregg argued that black and white rioters should be brought to justice.[80]

Black people's actions during the riots brought public figures' predictions about the consequences of the hydra of white supremacy to fruition. African Americans' resistance during the riots sent ripples throughout a shocked nation as white citizens and local, state, and federal officials pondered the possibility of a black rebellion. Black people's willingness to defend themselves precipitated white-supremacist retribution that was more violent and government action that was intended to suppress "Negro radicalism." What the nation learned from the public figures during the Great War was that when blacks returned fighting, they would do so with every weapon in their arsenal, including self-defense. As black people's defensive stance during the riots showed, public figures were not the only blacks who resisted racial violence. Some black rioters and their supporters were organic intellectuals, people who, until the riots, did not enjoy the same national audience as avatars of the counterpublic sphere. These African Americans had been resisting white supremacy all along, but in more covert ways.

4

"If You Can, the Colored Needs Help"

Reaching Out from Local Communities

"If you can, the colored needs help in Mississippi," a group of black soldiers claiming to be from the 378th Illinois Company A testified, in a letter they wrote to the War Department in 1919.[1] African American soldiers in the Great War had reveled in the Allied victory over the Central Powers. However, returning home to a nation where a consolidated white supremacy hemmed black people in their homes and communities and circumscribed black people's enjoyment of the freedoms that soldiers went to war to protect dampened these celebrations. The Hattiesburg soldiers were part of a cohort of blacks that had borne witness to the hydra of white supremacy. Indeed, these men had joined thousands of black men in answering Woodrow Wilson's call for "soldiers of democracy." Many of them wanted to help "make the world safe for democracy" because they believed that military service would prove black people's loyalty to the nation and demonstrate their suitability for civil and political rights. After the war, the veterans returned home to their family members and friends, many of whom had learned of soldiers' accomplishments in the war. These African Americans expected that black soldiers would apply the fervor with which they fought the enemies abroad against the whites attempting to subjugate black people at home. When the soldiers returned home, they found a nation full of white people who feared the very things for which their black family members and friends ached.

As veterans gleaned insight into developments on the home front through conversations with kin, newspaper reports on attacks on black soldiers and civilians dashed African Americans' expectations that whites would look at blacks differently after the war. Nonetheless, these letter writers believed that they could use their influence as soldiers to help black civilians confront racial violence, so they gathered and composed a letter to the War Department. The veterans explained to federal officials that they had observed black citizens being "treated like dogs" by white southerners. The men also cited the lynchings of a black man named Will Moore in Ten Mile and four black youth in Shubuta as reasons why black Mississippians needed the "help" of federal officials. Black soldiers had "sheded blood for this country," the men explained. It "look like [black people] ou[gh]t to have alittle rights" in return for this service. In writing this letter, the men formed a chorus of African Americans who wrote frank testimonies to federal authorities expressing their frustration with the failure of local and state authorities to protect black people from racial violence.[2]

In typed and handwritten letters, these organic intellectuals explained to federal officials the difficulties that African Americans faced after the consolidation of racism. These testifiers demonstrated their deliberate citizenship when they reported racial violence and explained its impact on black people's lives. Dr. James S. Lennon, of Philadelphia, wrote, "I humbly beg protection under the flag which we have alway[s] supported with the best within us," in his to appeal to President William H. Taft to provide southern blacks with relief from violence. Lennon seemed to suspect that his request that the president intervene and take action against violent whites might fall of deaf ears, so he wrote, "For God's Sake—Help Us. We *have helped you.*" Indeed, in writing, "we have helped you," Lennon aimed to remind the president of the support that enfranchised black men had given him during his campaign for the White House.[3]

John F. Monroe, a resident of Newburgh, New York, explained to President Woodrow Wilson, "We are disfranchised, We are segregated, We are having our properties destroyed and taken from us without due process of law, We are having the lives of our loved ones taken in the most brutal forms before our eyes and we are helpless in the defense of our selves or our own."[4] Neither Lennon nor Monroe described violence they endured personally. However, like the Mississippi veterans, they used their letters to testify about witnessing the horrors of racial violence meted on their family members, friends, neighbors, and even other folk whom they did not know but with whom they identified. These letter writers communicated shared racial aims and experiences of violence in the language they used to describe the plight of African Americans. They also spoke with one voice about black people's collective vulnerability to racial violence. Records do not indicate that the White House responded to all letters. However, the Department of Justice's Assistant Attorney General W. R. Harr sent typed form letters to these men in which he acknowledged the administration's receipt of their letters and explained that the federal government had "no power under the Constitution" to intervene into state matters. These African Americans' entreaties to federal officials reveal their efforts to share with federal officials the vernacular history of the consolidation and their judgment that it represented a breach of the Fourteenth Amendment's assurance of citizenship, due process, and equal protection under the law. Federal officials' responses to these letters suggest that they were not yet ready to bear witness to African Americans' testimonies and to take action to end white southerners' violations of black people's civil and political rights.[5]

Historians of the turn of the century have argued that the consolidation of racism forced many black people to "turn inward" as they struggled to make sense of the loss of their civil and political rights. White people's claims that the United States was a "white man's country" notwithstanding, many black people believed that it was their country too and that they were entitled to enjoy all the benefits of American citizenship. Nonetheless, they had experienced whites' shutting blacks out of the most valuable aspects of American life and doing so with the assistance of the state and federal governments. Black people assessed the damage, relied on their own communal resources, and attempted to develop strategies to surmount the new forces of white supremacy. Public figures devoted themselves to racial uplift. They strove to defend themselves and black folk against white people's depictions of black people's supposed racial inferiority, which southern racists argued justified resubjugation.[6]

Largely shut out of public life because of race and class, ridiculed by whites in the dominant public spheres, terrorized in their homes and communities, and denied access to mainstream legal and public forums, many black folk were forced into enclaves. People in enclave communities, however, did not close themselves off from the mainstream society entirely. This chapter shows how black folk took advantage of their political and social marginalization to discuss white supremacy's changing dynamics and to develop strategies of resistance by constituting "enclave public spheres." According to Catherine Squires, enclave public spheres represent an oppressed group's "utilization of spaces and discourses that are hidden from the view of the dominant public [sphere] and the state." These people use the security of their marginalization to "gather their forces and decide in a more protected space in what way or whether to continue the battle for equality or just outcomes."[7] For our purposes, the enclave public spheres involved black ministers, clubwomen, doctors, teachers, veterans, and sharecroppers who resisted racial subjugation by operating from their homes and communities in the North and South in the 1910s. Though these people are less well known than public figures, their efforts to end violence by testifying about it to federal officials illuminate the mobilization of ordinary people in African Americans' efforts to end violence.[8]

Experiencing the consolidation of white supremacy, seeing its re-presentation in the print culture, exchanging their stories of victimization, and witnessing the indifference of white citizens and elected officials prompted several dozen blacks to reach out of their enclaves for relief from violence in the 1910s. The sense of labyrinthine peril that white supremacy engendered throughout African America made these activists shift from having furtive intraracial discussions of violence to offering testimonies to federal officials about the challenges that black people faced. Indeed, the written testimonies analyzed here reveal the ways that local people formed an enclave public sphere that rallied to make federal officials understand the vernacular history of racial violence.

The pulse of African America beat strongest in local communities. Thus, written testimonies from black folk who witnessed violence secondhand help cut a swath through the morass of impersonal newspaper reports on violence as well as the dominant public sphere's and public figures' dominion over national discussions of racial violence that form the basis of many histories of white violence and black resistance. These letters make manifest some covert but defiant ways that black people tapped into what Brundage has called "underground streams of resistance from the past." Black folk used the security of their relative anonymity in their enclaves to resist local whites and to communicate to federal officials the "hidden transcript" of racial violence.[9]

The letters African Americans wrote to federal officials about the violence they endured and witnessed by listening to victims or by reading newspapers reveal the effectiveness of public figures' efforts to publicize the vernacular history of violence, to re-present violence, to create intersubjectivity regarding the consolidation, and to mobilize black people. At the same time, these letters illuminate local people's surreptitious political work to circumvent surveillance and repression in their communities. Blacks who wrote letters to federal officials in which they testified about racial violence embodied the broad social strata of America. They were educated and newly literate, poor and rich, northern and southern, female and male, and deferential and defiant. These testifiers might have participated in local clubs and community institutions; however, they were less likely to hold positions of national leadership, so they enjoyed a much smaller audience than public figures did.

Writing from the privacy of their homes and offices, black folk testified to federal officials about what it was like to be victims of and witnesses to racial violence. Guided by their duty to relate the suffering of their people, testifiers' letters overflow with knowledge of white people's violations of black people's rights and the violent devastation of their lives and crackle with anger over the federal government's failure to respond to state officials' apathetic responses to African Americans' complaints about violence. Testifiers aimed to write black people's experiences of violence and their thoughts on it into the conscience of federal officials during the Taft and Wilson administrations. Letter writers described the vernacular history of violence, they explained their interpretations of citizenship, and they voiced their expectations that federal officials uphold the Constitution by providing black people with equal protection under the law.[10]

When federal officials dismissed these complaints as a matter for the states, testifiers responded by shifting from testifying about violence to condemning federal officials for their lack of concern for the plight of black citizens. African Americans forming the enclave public sphere joined public figures to argue that black people's support for the Great War buttressed their entitlement to relief from racial violence. After the war, blacks emitted what Brundage has called a collective "roar on the other side of silence." This roar over racial violence became audible when black people's concealed hurt, anger, desperation, and percolating indignation burst onto the national scene, first in the renewed procession of migrants from the South to the Northeast and Midwest, then in the form of riots, and finally in fueling the institutionalization of the antilynching crusades.[11]

"Appeal to the Government as a Negro and Citizen"

The crimson tide of the lynching of African Americans that swept through the 1890s ebbed somewhat after the century's turn, but violence persisted as whites worked to subjugate black southerners, who continued to cope in ways that made sense to them. Public figures' creation of the black counterpublic sphere and their re-presentation of consolidated white supremacy as a hydra-headed problem that African Americans needed to attack did not slow the "great mass of hatred" that hit blacks in the southern states. However, public figures' discursive intervention did diffuse knowledge about the implication of the consolidation for blacks. Experiencing this violence directly, reading about it in print culture, or hearing about it from family and friends strengthened black people's intersubjectivity. In the 1910s, blacks who were attempting to reclaim their citizenship vocalized their rage over racial violence in letters to presidents William Howard Taft and Woodrow Wilson and to their attorneys general, George Wickersham and A. Mitchell Palmer.[12]

The consolidation of white supremacy and the greater likelihood that whites would use violence prevented many African Americans from airing their grievances publicly. Some black people responded by sidestepping whites at the local and state level. Rejecting disfranchisement as an effort to silence their political voices, black people chanted their anger over white supremacists' violent subjection of southern blacks in their letters to federal officials. African Americans contacted federal officials because they were mindful of the ways that the federal government had exercised its authority by abolishing slavery, by extending citizenship rights to black people, by suppressing the first Ku Klux Klan, and by providing public forums for victims and witnesses to testify about violence. This action anchored black people's belief that federal officials were the ultimate guarantors of their rights as citizens. In spite of the federal government's failure to intercede on behalf of blacks whom white southern legislators had banished from political and public life in the 1890s, black people's letters and public demonstrations show their continued faith in an active state and their efforts to invoke the Constitution as grounds for the federal government to protect their civil and political rights.[13]

Although many blacks had faith in federal officials' ability to act, they had also witnessed officials' failure to intervene during the consolidation. African Americans knew that they could not rely on officials to initiate reform regarding violence, so they started to apply pressure to make officials act. For example, black activists met in December 1911 to stage a protest pilgrimage to the White House to censure federal officials for their failure to address the lynchings of more than sixty black people that year. "When President Taft sees that black cloud hanging around his White House, . . . he will sit up and take notice," organizer Reverend A. Mark Harris declared. Activists in the enclave public sphere—familiar with the white-supremacist power structure that sought to provoke feelings of social and political impotence among blacks—defied apathetic local and state authorities by taking their protests to federal officials.[14]

African Americans wrote frank and fervent letters to federal officials in which they explained the sense of helplessness the violence engendered. Their letters contain a sense of their collective and experiential knowledge of the diluting of freedom's promise by racial violence. Unlike the testimonies that black people gave at congressional hearings, which they provided months or years after experiencing or witnessing violent attacks, letter writers picked up their writing instruments or sat down at typewriters days after they had experienced or witnessed violence. In writing letters to federal officials, blacks averted the reprisals that might have resulted from public protests within their communities. Indeed, in the privacy of personal letters that they addressed to the White House, to the president, to attorneys generals, and to the DOJ, a choir of black women and men tried to educate federal officials on the harm of racial violence, and they demanded a response of legal or restorative justice.[15]

Most testifiers wrote as petitioners but with a sense of deliberate citizenship that contradicted white citizens', elected officials', and the dominant public spheres' depictions of black people as being ignorant, uncivilized, and unworthy of citizenship rights. Federal officials were not always African Americans' first resort. Indeed, some black southerners first wrote their governors, testifying about violence and requesting investigations into lynching, pardons for wrongful convictions, and financial reparations for the loss of life and property. Officials' responses to these requests for redress yielded no results, which prompted victims and witnesses to direct their letters to agents of the federal government.[16] For example, on December 11, 1911, E. T. Washington, of Hubbard City, Texas, wrote the DOJ. Washington testified, "These [white] people he[re] don't care . . . that I work hard to take [c]are of my family and to pay my debt and how ever it don't matter." Law enforcement officers, according to Washington, "will [ar]rest a [black] man for nothing [and make] him pay a fin[e]" while allowing whites to abuse and kill blacks with impunity. Washington explained that two white men invaded his home in the middle of the night and terrorized his family. Washington informed local authorities of the home invasion, but they took no action. Afterward, Washington wrote a letter to Texas governor Oscar B. Colquitt asking for redress, to which he received either no response or an unsatisfactory one. Thus, when he wrote the DOJ, Washington asked these officials to read his letter and "[speak] a good word [to Governor Colquitt] if you cant do no more." There is no indication that the DOJ acted on Washington's request.[17]

Other testifiers—despondent over the apathy that local and state authorities had showed toward protecting blacks from white mobs and toward punishing known perpetrators of violence—wrote letters in which they appealed directly to the federal government. For example, Aaron P. Johnson of Muskogee, Oklahoma, wrote Attorney General Wickersham, testifying on the behalf of fifty black families that were driven from their homes and their lands in 1912. According to Johnson, whites ordered the families to leave Bryant County and threatened to kill them if they failed to comply. The black families responded by appealing to local authorities for protection, but when authorities took no action, they attempted to harvest their crops and sell their land. Before the deportees exited Bryant County, some managed to receive a third of the value of their stock and crops, but according to Johnson, most families received nothing. Johnson asked Wickersham about any legal grounds the families had for suing the county for damages to help them get some compensation for the losses they sustained in the ordered exodus. The letter itself suggests that blacks hoped that officials might offer relief. Yet the tone of Johnson's letter indicates that these families, displaced by violence, worried that, until agents of the state and federal governments deigned to treat them as citizens, no such protection or compensation would be coming.[18]

Regardless of how African Americans came to write federal officials, the tenor of their letters reflects their frustration with violence and with the failure of local and state authorities to treat them as citizens. These epistles also reveal the letter writers' full appreciation for the conditions caused by the consolidation and their belief that federal officials should intervene. Black southerners had lived with the consequences of the Supreme Court's decisions that southern states had full authority over determining and upholding black people's citizenship rights and that southern business owners and local and state officials could provide racially segregated public accommodations. They coped with Congress's and the White House's failure to stop southern states from disfranchising black men and thereby denying them not only the right to hold elected office and to elect officials who would protect their interests but also the right to sit on juries and to fair treatment in the legal system. These people also saw African Americans whom whites accused of crimes being abducted and killed by posses and mobs and denied their basic constitutional and human rights, without a word from many federal officials. Some of these people wrote to federal officials assuming that these men were ignorant of the violence that southern blacks endured at the hands of white citizens and of the indifference of state and local authorities. On the whole, African Americans' letters portray their belief that federal officials were open to reason and that if they explained what was happening in the South and aligned black people's concerns with the nation's principles of freedom, citizenship, self-determination, and respect for the rule of law, then officials would intervene on their behalf.[19]

Some black writers enclosed newspaper clippings with their letters. As Ida Wells-Barnett had done two decades earlier, these testifiers thought that reports of racial violence from the nation's mainstream papers might give their requests for redress more credibility.[20] E. D. Rosewood of Asheville, North Carolina, probably thought this when he wrote President Taft on January 24, 1912. He cited the rarity of picking up the newspaper without "having to see where some poor Negro has been strung up and brutally murdered by a mob as [though] he were a dog." Moreover, Rosewood included clippings from the Asheville *Citizen* that covered the lynching of four blacks in Hamilton, Georgia. The mob overpowered the jailor, dragged three men and one woman to the outskirts of town, tied them to trees, and riddled their bodies with bullets. According to Rosewood, the white men lynched these people "because suspicion pointed to one of them for the killing of a white man." Noting the traditional legal procedures for handling such matters, Rosewood explained, "They all died without even a preliminary hearing." Assistant Attorney General W. R. Harr replied on the president's behalf, declaring that federal authorities were "without power to intervene" under the Supreme Court decision in *Hodges v. United States* (1906).[21]

The tenor of the letters from Washington, Johnson, and Rosewood reflect the writers' sense of their marginalized position in American society with respect to class, geography, and race. These testifiers knew that many whites, including state and federal officials, saw African Americans as second-class citizens. Nonetheless, these letters also symbolize black people's cognizance of their rights and the consequences of the federal government's failure to protect them and honor their rights. The epistlers' comprehension of their place in the nation and their belief in the need for federal action to combat racial violence often informed the tone of the letters they wrote. Thus, like the Mississippi veterans, many testifiers wrote using deferential language, hoping to convey the gravity of their situations and to advance their claims.

Letter writers' subjectivity and their geographic location in the country shaped the tone of their letters. Most southerners addressed federal officials as "Your Honor," "His Excellency," and "Sir." These people used phrases such as "wishing not take up too much of your time," "not wishing to offend," and "hoping that I have not trespassed my rights," as they asked federal officials for relief from violence. Southerners often tried to assure federal officials that all African Americans wanted was a "fair deal" and a real chance to transcend their enslaved heritage. Some writers even signed their letters, "your faithful servant." Southern testifiers appealed for the federal government's acknowledgment of and respect for their rights at a time when disfranchisement at the state level had compromised African Americans' ability to claim their rights as citizens at the national level.

In writing letters to officials in the Taft and Wilson administrations, these people hoped to inform federal officials of the circumstances under which southern whites forced blacks to live. These letter writers also testified about how violence affected them as victims and witnesses. In testifying about violence, they attempted to close the gaps of race and sociopolitical status between themselves and officials of a seemingly remote government. Black southerners tried to connect with the president or members of his administration on a personal level because they hoped that a personal connection with marginalized citizens might make federal officials respond positively to black people's appeals for assistance. Although African Americans living in the Northeast and Midwest faced intense racial discrimination in employment, in housing, in the criminal justice system, and in education, these people enjoyed greater access to these opportunities than did the southerners on whose behalf they wrote. Indeed, this might explain why letters from northerners often began with "Dear Mr. President" or "Dear President Wilson" and emitted a tone that was more confrontational than that of their southern counterparts.[22]

A close examination of the letters shows how class and educational distinctions also informed the style and substance of African Americans' written testimonies. Many poor and newly lettered people handwrote their letters, sometimes in barely legible scripts, while those people who had received more formal education and enjoyed a higher social status in the South and the North typed their letters or wrote them in very elegant scripts and did so using institutional letterhead. Some newly lettered writers and those who appear to have been striving wrote in more deferential tones, while their more educated, "aspiring class" counterparts penned the most blistering critiques. Further, while men constituted the bulk of the writers, the tone with which some women wrote make their letters stand out.[23]

The letter of a clubwoman named Mrs. M. Cravath Simpson of Boston exemplifies the extent to which geography, social position, and gender shaped the tone of some letters. Simpson, president of the Anti-Lynching Society of Afro-American Women, wrote without restraint. In her 1912 letter to President Taft, she conveyed that she thought the New Year a "fitting time" to address him, while "thresh-hold flames for the mistakes of the past can best be remembered." Citing the president's silence on lynchings in Decaturville, Tennessee—where two white men killed a farmer and his children—as the inspiration for her letter, Simpson reminded Taft of his inaugural address. In that speech the president called on black people to "base their hope on the results of their own industry, self-restraint, and business success, as well as upon the aid and comfort and sympathy of their white neighbors in the South." By Simpson's account, the farmer, his children, and other blacks had aspired to achieve the models Taft suggested, but when the president remained mute after whites murdered them, she felt compelled to act.[24]

The Anti-Lynching Society adopted the motto "Organized to Publicly Protest Man's Inhumanity to Man," and protest Mrs. Simpson did. The clubwoman upbraided the president for what she characterized as his "one-sided" respect for the law and his failure to protect black people's rights. Noting that he planned to run for a second term, Simpson wrote, "I cannot help but smile for I do not think this year, you will take any colored man into your home," as Taft had done during his first campaign. "No," the clubwoman promised, "there is no colored man this year who will be duped by your persuasive talk." Simpson even ventured to say, "few, if any, [colored men] will cast their ballot for you. They will remember your silence on lynching, . . . how you suffered colored soldiers to be Jim-Crowed, . . . and every thing else despicable you have done against them." Even if black men did not remember, Simpson assured Taft that "the women of the race will help them remember."[25]

Simpson cited the authority and influence that African American women wielded in the black enclave and counterpublic spheres, despite their being denied the franchise. Indeed, black women were dynamic and outspoken participants in black conventions, where they affected votes by offering their perspective on matters facing black people during Reconstruction. These women remained actively involved in black political culture; however, as Elsa Barkley Brown revealed, during the 1880s and 1890s, they lost much of the ability to participate in the black public sphere that they enjoyed during Reconstruction. They responded to these changes by working within their homes and existing institutions to retain some of their "lost authority." These women also formed groups such as the women's movement in the National Baptist Convention and the NACW. They created "their own pulpits from which to speak." Wherever possible, black clubwomen asserted their authority over conditions affecting black people in their homes, in churches, and in workplaces, as well as in other civic spaces. Clubs, literary societies, and labor networks became the new sororities in which black women retained their voices and expressed their opinions to people in the dominant, enclave, and counterpublic spheres.[26]

Some writers, such as Simpson, appear to have never endured racial violence. Yet the tone of nonvictims' letters conveys how bearing witness to this violence, knowing the vernacular history of violence, and understanding its effect on African Americans kindled intersubjectivity and a sense of responsibility for taking action. Indeed, Simpson's organization was one of many that formed to help black people overcome the challenges they faced. Simpson's reference to making colored men recall the president's silence on lynching and on the treatment of black soldiers also shows the political capital that black women wielded in their homes and in their home spheres. In addressing the president directly, Simpson and other women demonstrated their awareness and subversion of black women's exclusion from formal politics. This black sisterhood exhibited their deliberate citizenship rights when they appealed to the president and other federal officials for relief for black southerners.[27]

Black letter writers joined public figures in striving to juxtapose black people's upstanding demonstrations of their character and behavior with those of the whites trying to subjugate them. These letter writers worked to affirm black people's humanity and their suitability for civil and political rights. Testifiers used the brutality of racial violence to question southern whites' fitness for citizenship and to interrogate the nation's claim to being a model democracy. Southern blacks who were familiar with racial violence and officials' apathy felt that they had an accurate read on the character of whites and the need for an active state. Their northern counterparts had only to read about the violence or to remember their own or their kin's southern experiences to reach similar conclusions about violent whites.[28]

One unique feature of these activists' letters is their candor about white people and their behavior. Because of the new posture that whites exhibited during the consolidation of racism, black southerners could be reticent in speaking about whites to whites. Richard Wright, in "The Ethics of Living Jim Crow," explained how his "Jim Crow education" involved learning an extensive list of subjects that blacks could not discuss safely with whites or in the presence of whites. Near the top of this list was any criticism of whites or any challenge to the logic of white people's superiority and black people's inferiority. Indeed, many African Americans strategically deployed the politics of deference to white people's authority. Thus, blacks avoided open confrontation with whites, they remained silent about violence, and they even utilized a "double-voiced discourse," or what W. Fitzhugh Brundage has called a "discursive insubordination," when they discussed whites in the presence of other whites or topics that might be offensive to whites. Black southerners rarely discounted the injustices they faced, but white supremacy made them rely on the security of the enclave to fume or to be honest about their beliefs and opinions. When black folk discussed whites and violent resubjugation publicly, they resisted in what Brundage has characterized as "oblique" ways.

In all, black southerners resisted white supremacy and averted violence by mastering the ability to tell white southerners what they wanted to hear.[29]

Some of the African Americans who wrote federal officials did not use a "double-voiced discourse" or speak obliquely about racial violence. In fact, many testifiers' observations of racial violence and the apathy of state officials in letters to federal officials were especially candid. The letters of Jason M. Smith, E. D. Rosewood, and E. T. Washington exemplify African Americans' complaints about the apathy of local and state authorities to whom victims of violence took their concerns. Smith, who was driven from his home for helping his neighbor escape from a Georgia lynch mob, explained, "The state local administrators of the law will not protect Negroes in their rights." Black North Carolinian E. D. Rosewood wanted Taft to read the clipping of the Georgia lynchings and then imagine "a poor helpless woman being marched thru the streets to a post and amidst her piteous cries and protesting her innocence, . . . she is strung up and lynched like a brute, without even a m—— [illegible] or an officer, save the janitor, doubtless he approved—, seemed to care." Rosewood strategically used the imagery of a lynching of an isolated and "helpless woman" to embody the plight of blacks. E. T. Washington explained that local authorities had told him that "th[e]re are no laws for Negroes" in the Constitution except those which whites chose to recognize.[30]

In writing Taft and relating reports of racial violence and black people's limited defenses against it, testifiers hoped to draw out of the president a sense of responsibility to aid marginalized citizens. At the same time, these letters signify organic intellectuals' attempts to circumvent racial subjugation at the local level. What is more, the tenor of the letters, indeed their existence, symbolizes African Americans' belief in and assertion of their citizenship rights even at a time when popular culture, science, and public policy claimed they were inferior and that they had no rights that white people needed to respect. The Mississippi veterans' letter about military service, Washington's statement about wanting to take care of his family, Simpson's observations about the industrious Tennesseans, and Rosewood's depiction of the woman marched to her death by a Georgia mob show letter writers' portrayal of blacks as people who were exemplars of American citizenship and who needed the protection of federal officials. These upstanding Americans, testifiers proclaimed, were worthy of receiving due process and equal protection under the law. Letter writers believed that when local and state authorities failed to protect black people's rights, the responsibility fell to the men who swore to uphold the Constitution and to protect the nation and all of its citizens.

At the core of most letters was African Americans' desire that federal officials recognize black people's suffering and uphold their constitutional rights and that white citizens and elected officials treat them fairly. When white citizens failed to treat blacks equally and authorities failed to protect them from lynch mobs, black people's letters show that they expected state and federal authorities to uphold the law. For example, C. P. Covington of Louisiana, Missouri, wrote Taft's Attorney General Wickersham, "As citizens the federal constitution guarant[ees] us life li[b]er[t]y and the pursuit of happiness. . . . The guarantees of the constitution certainly is as sacred and binding in that pledge to citizens at home as is treaty agreements to protect naturalized citizens where they return to their native countries." Likewise, J. B. Harper, of the Colored Industrial High School in Rocky Mountain, North Carolina, wrote Taft as a citizen: "I feel it worth while to appeal to the government as a Negro and citizen of this dear country of ours." Hastings Howard, writing from Chihuahua, Mexico, listed laws that prohibited racial intermarriage, labor conditions resembling slavery, disfranchisement, and lynching as "violations of the united states constitution." Covington reminded Taft that the responsibility to uphold the Constitution "and see that all American citizens are equally protected" was his. Indeed, the invocation of citizenship within these letters shows black people's comprehension of the ideals of American democracy. African Americans' letters claiming citizenship and demanding protection under the Constitution typify their strategic use of the extralegal violence that southern blacks endured to challenge federal officials to honor the Constitution by ensuring equal participation in American life and protection for all of its citizens.[31]

However much segregation, disfranchisement, and extraordinary violence limited many black folks' formal access to the nation's political arena, they engaged the political sphere through their letters. These activists attempted to show their understanding of and fitness for citizenship despite policies and attitudes that imbued a sense of racial exclusion. Black letter writers never knew what the federal government would do in response to receiving their letters about violent resubjugation. Some may not have even cared, but others requested specific responses that ranged from making a public statement denouncing violence to helping enact legislation that would make lynching a federal crime. E. D. Rosewood expressed his feelings of desperation and his belief in the need for federal officials to act by opening his letter to Taft with, "there is none other to appeal for justice save you."[32]

Black folks' epistles also show their grasp of the concept of dual federalism and the multidimensional aspects of the Fourteenth Amendment. Indeed, letter writers knew that the Constitution granted African Americans citizenship and thereby entitled them to due process and equal protection under the nation's laws. They also understood that popular constitutionalism and disfranchisement at the state level hindered their authority in local and state governance, which enabled white citizens and elected officials to violate their civil and political rights. Thus, the state governments' failure to provide blacks with due process and equal protection under the law fortified many letter writers' belief in black people's entitlement to a federal audience for their grievances. Commenting on the swiftness with which Americans had seen Taft move on international affairs, Simpson scolded, "Why not enforce the laws of our government for all its citizens? Why not protect the nation's honor at home as well as abroad, or suggest new federal laws that will do it, if those in our constitution are not adequate?" Seeing the president as the final executor of the nation's laws, many black folks wanted federal officials to compel state officials to comply with existing laws on due process and murder and to punish whites who broke the law. In taking this approach, blacks tried to "write themselves into the moral and political conscience" of the executive branch. In other words, they used private letters to appointed and elected officials to comment on the public matter of extralegal violence and to drive home the point that federal officials needed to intervene. Indeed, Rosewood ended his letter by boldly telling Taft, "It's up to you to put a hand out" to stop racial violence.[33]

Federal officials—citing a constitutional inability to act under *Hodges v. U.S.* (1906) and its predecessors the *Slaughter-House Cases* and the *Civil Rights Cases*—failed to act on black people's appeals for federal protection and restorative justice. It is important to recognize that African Americans' requests for federal protection were not unreasonable or even without precedent. The nation's chief executives might have committed themselves to ending violence. For example, officials could have expanded federal authority over the states by encouraging Congress to enact legislation, ordering a DOJ investigation and giving it prosecutorial power, threatening southern governors with federal investigators, and expressing their intent to follow through on such threats. None of these actions might have ended lynching or other forms of violent resubjugation. However, letter writers believed that any action would send a message of the federal government's contempt for violent whites and indifferent local and state authorities.

African Americans had seen federal officials assert the federal government's authority over the states during the late nineteenth century when they chose to do so and were, in fact, going to see officials expand federal power during the twentieth century. For example, federal officials deployed Secret

Service agents to investigate and help suppress the Klan during Reconstruction. Likewise, all components of the federal government, concerned with maintaining positive diplomatic relations, had intervened when white mobs lynched foreign nationals. Indeed, presidents, members of their administrations, and members of Congress worked in tandem by publicly disparaging the states and the citizens of states whenever these killings occurred. Moreover, in some instances, officials compelled the states to pay monetary damages and introduced legislation in 1902 to federalize punishment for the lynching of foreign nationals, which drove down the number of mob attacks on immigrants from China, Italy, and Mexico. Yet, regarding racial violence against black citizens, many federal officials shrugged off the government's responsibility for ensuring that blacks enjoyed due process and equal protection under the law by deferring to the states.[34]

The federal government's response to letter writers' complaints about violence suggests that national authorities' lack of concern for African Americans' rights echoed the indifference of local and state officials. Indeed, when public figures wrote letters and requested formal meetings with federal officials, these officials responded because they needed to, to keep up the appearance of addressing citizens' concerns. Although meetings with tepid or indifferent presidents or members of Congress was not what black public figures wanted, they probably felt their voices were heard. Black folks' social stature, however, reduced federal officials' need to listen to their appeals for relief from violence or take action. Indeed, there was no political consequence for federal inaction, given many African Americans' subjugated position throughout the nation. Black people's sociopolitical status—with the majority of the African American population in the South segregated, disfranchised, and terrorized and those in the Northeast and the Midwest just beginning the process of coordinating their initiatives—left the people who were forming the enclave public spheres barely capable of creating the political tempest necessary to elicit government action. Thus, rather than take seriously the origins, nature, and consequences of racial violence and African Americans' embrace of their citizenship rights to get redress for their grievances, presidents such as Taft offered platitudes lamenting the violence. Instead of taking action by expanding federal protection over black people's civil rights, federal officials claimed to be powerless to act and lectured blacks, telling them that if they were industrious and comported themselves appropriately, the violence would end.

Letters that black folk wrote to the president regarding violence were forwarded to the DOJ. The forwarding of African Americans' letters to the DOJ seems a logical response to letters that decried violations of the law. The use of mail-sorting apparatus, the number of DOJ replies, and the number citing the *Hodges* decision make it hard to believe that the Taft administration was oblivious to the black citizenry's concerns about racial violence. The administration's deference to judicial precedent and to states' rights while blacks were subjected to violent resubjugation amid indifferent state officials indicates a tacit endorsement, if not of the violence, then of the failure of states to enforce specific laws on murder and mob violence. For example, in 1912, W. A. Briggs of Wetumpka, Alabama, wrote Taft asking him to investigate the violent conditions suffered by an aged black convict imprisoned at the Alabama State Penitentiary. Assistant Attorney General Harr forwarded the letter to Governor Charles Henderson, citing the lack of federal jurisdiction over the matter.[35]

Black southerners' banishment from public and political life created an absence of risk for federal inaction, suggesting that letter writers believed that the presidential administrations of Taft and Wilson lacked not the constitutional ability but the political will to intervene when state officials refused to ensure that African Americans received their constitutionally granted rights to due process and equal protection under the law. Federal officials might have presumed that black folk did not have the political acumen to understand their civil and political rights and to appreciate the complexities of dual federalism, under which they were considered citizens of both the federal government and the states in which they lived. Black folks' letters, when combined with public figures' speeches and writings, suggest that they did understand. Elizabeth McHenry has shown that many African Americans learned to read using key American political documents as reading primers and that these texts circulated among blacks in the postbellum South. Public figures also made a point to educate black folk on their citizenship rights and any changes in their civil and political rights. All of this suggests that many African Americans knew their constitutional rights. As Christopher Waldrep reveals, many blacks, especially such public figures as T. Thomas Fortune and John Mitchell, Jr., rejected the argument that racial violence was a matter for the states, especially when these states were not fulfilling their constitutional obligation to their black citizens and when officials exercised federal control over citizenship when they saw fit. Nonetheless, African Americans did not yet have the political capital to create social and political penalties for federal indifference to racial violence. Rebuffed but undeterred, black people would have to take advantage of northern and racially based progressive reforms and the First World War to demand a federal response to violence.[36]

The plague of defeat that Simpson cast down on Taft's reelection bid appeared to come to a head in the fall of 1912. When deciding to vote, black men seemed to recall the failure of Republican administrations to address racial violence. Meanwhile, to be elected, Woodrow Wilson had beguiled many African Americans with promises of progressive reform. The Democrats' sound defeat of divided Republicans in the election led some blacks to believe that they would no longer have to endure a president who remained silent on the outrages that white citizens and state officials perpetrated against them. At the same time, other blacks divined in Wilson's southern and Democratic roots a racial conservative in progressive clothing. These observant blacks were closer to the mark in their predictions about Wilson. Indeed, what black people got in their new commander in chief was a southerner who endorsed white supremacy through his policies and practices. Wilson supported laws banning interracial marriage and issued an executive order allowing segregation within federal employment, with the explanation that doing so reduced interracial friction. To add insult to injury, Wilson screened D. W. Griffith's *Birth of a Nation* in the White House and reportedly hailed the film's depiction of U.S. history.[37]

African Americans' prewar letters to Wilson indicate their hope that the progressive reforms that candidate Wilson promoted to assume the office of the presidency would include them. For example, in 1913, Francis H. Warren, a black attorney, journalist, and chairman of the Detroit branch of the NAACP, wrote Wilson regarding a white mob's killing of S. W. Green, the Supreme Chancellor of the Colored Knights of Pythias. Warren asked Wilson to use his clout as a southerner to appeal to white southerners to reject such violence. Warren believed that public support for mob violence—which was reflected in the size of lynch mobs and the failure of local authorities to bring even known perpetrators to justice—facilitated lynching's existence. Warren also invoked the political philosophies of Thomas Jefferson and Theodore Roosevelt to compel the president to renew black people's "hope [for] fair and equal treatment" under the law. Warren noted that the United States was supposed to be the "land of the free." For the Negro, he reported, the American dream was "yet to be." Indeed, Warren's discussions of African Americans' hopes and dreams of freedom and civil and political rights signify that he and other blacks believed in the nation's founding principles despite state and federal officials' failure to honor those pledges in ways that were meaningful for black people. These promises could be realities for both blacks and the nation if federal officials saw fit to make them so, letter writers believed. On the whole, blacks saw quickly that Wilson continued the federal government's failure to act on racial violence.[38]

Writers such as Chicagoan J. B. Winston hoped to stir Wilson to condemn violence and to make lynching a capital crime by humanizing the victims of racial violence in their letters. Citing four lynchings reported in the *Daily Press* in 1915, Winston wrote, "These persons are of flesh and blood like yourself. . . . They were American women like your wife and daughters. These [women] have been outraged. To them their homes were like your home is to you, hallowed with the same dear association. These have been pillaged and burned." Winston thought this violence was an "indictment of a government for criminal neglect" in its failure to condemn this violence and to ensure that authorities protected black prisoners from lynch mobs and brought perpetrators to justice. Winston also noted that while Europe had "sunken deep in war" and the world "bristles with guns," it was time for "intelligent listening and clear thinking" about the conditions plaguing African Americans in the United States.[39] The volume and intensity of black political letters grew during the war, and the tone exhibited in black people's wartime correspondence, in newspapers, and in the nation's towns and streets shifted toward confronting federal officials as the Great War politicized and mobilized African Americans.

The Great War through the Prism of Racial Violence

The First World War helped propel forward black people's collective resistance to racial violence. The war's potential promise for African Americans to advance their civil and political rights was not apparent immediately, however. At the commencement of the war, many blacks were too preoccupied with domestic affairs to fret extensively about the tensions percolating across the Atlantic. In fact, Woodrow Wilson's executive order sanctioning the segregation of federal employment, the widespread and enthusiastic release of *Birth of a Nation*, and the highly publicized lynchings of Texan Jesse Washington and affluent South Carolinian Anthony Crawford in 1916 consumed black people's priorities at the local and national levels.[40]

As the situation in Europe deteriorated and federal officials and the American press cast worrisome gazes across the Atlantic, black letter writers tried to remind members of the Wilson administration and the mainstream press of their responsibility for addressing problems at home. For example, John Monroe wrote a letter to Wilson in December 1916 observing that only "when there will be no more lynching of American citizens at home, America will be more justifiable in her foreign mission." Responding to calls for "soldiers of democracy," Monroe reminded the president that black men's military service in previous wars had illustrated black people's worthiness of enjoying citizenship rights. However, according to Monroe, "until [black people are] protected as citizen[s] of these United States, [appealing to black people's sense of their] Americanism means nothing and America is unsafe" for black men and their families. Along with sending best wishes for the holiday season, Monroe asked the president to speak about protecting black people's rights in the United States in his inaugural address to Congress, but no statements about racial violence appeared in Wilson's speech. Four months later, the United States declared war on Germany and entered the global conflict, which temporarily suspended African Americans' fight to command federal officials to address racial violence.[41]

Most blacks responded enthusiastically to the prowar propaganda of the Committee on Public Information, which used posters, newspapers, and movies to explain why the nation needed to enter the war after Wilson's initial declaration of neutrality. When Wilson swore to make the world "safe for democracy" and the United States mobilized to enter the Great War, some black public figures demanded unequivocal support from black folk. They believed that backing the war would give credence to black people's insistence on federal officials' need to address violent resubjugation. In fact, W. E. B. Du Bois asked fellow blacks to "put aside our special grievances and close ranks" with the nation to preserve democracy. A lot of blacks responded positively to Du Bois's "Closed Ranks" editorial that was published in the *Crisis*, the NAACP's periodical.[42]

Like the Civil War and Spanish-American War before it, the First World War embodied an opportune moment for African Americans to advance their civil rights agenda. While black men served overseas, many black folk at home saw the conflict and the nationwide call for "soldiers of democracy" as the means to escape or end racial violence. Some people living in enclave communities needed little convincing to support the war. They purchased Liberty Bonds, rationed goods, satisfied the labor shortage, and registered for the draft. They endorsed the war, hoping that their demonstrations of patriotism and loyalty would result in an elevation of black people's status and an acknowledgment of their demands for civil and political rights. Other blacks knew better. The violent realities of the South as well as federal authorities' failure to address racial violence engendered some skepticism among black people about the nation's willingness to make good on the promise of democracy at home.

At the start of the American intervention in the war, thousands of black men were already serving in the army and the National Guard. The 1917 passage of the Selective Service Act sent in thousands more, whom the military activated into service.[43] The number of black registrants reflected some of the longing of people in some southern communities for black men to escape racial violence, even if that meant serving in a segregated army and being relegated to subservient roles. The opportunities for advancement that some soldiers and their families gained through service in previous wars set the precedent for the potential rewards of military service even under these conditions. The discrimination that black soldiers endured within the military and in places where the army stationed black units illustrated to African Americans the extent to which black men needed to support the war for freedom and democracy at home as much as abroad. In southern towns and cities, black soldiers endured abuse and insults from the white civilians and soldiers angered at the sight of uniformed black men bearing arms. Outraged whites were determined to make black men—who had come from across the country—conform to white southerners' expectations for deference to white supremacy. In August 1917, tensions between soldiers and the Houston police force culminated in a riot after a soldier tried to stop a police officer from beating a black woman. In the aftermath, twenty civilians and soldiers lay dead; the military charged sixty black soldiers with mutiny and prosecuted and hanged thirteen of them for participating in the riot. The hanging of the soldiers tested African Americans' patriotism, and it became clear to many blacks that white America's full recognition of their citizenship rights might be too much to expect after the war.[44]

The violence in Houston was not an isolated incident. Violent assaults on black civilians and soldiers were recurring episodes throughout the war. One month before the Houston riot, racial tensions welling up over housing and labor in East St. Louis, Illinois, burst in a riot. When it was over, several dozen black people had died, and thousands fled the city in a terror-driven exodus that made some Americans call the riot the nation's first pogrom. Violence on the home front punctuated the repression that African Americans felt. Some blacks argued that these crimes were worse than the European pogroms, which black soldiers had gone to war to help oppose.[45]

Reading about these violent assaults on black soldiers and civilians engendered feelings of rage and vulnerability in black people. As they juxtaposed reports on local violence with accounts of the fighting abroad, African Americans knew that no alliance of nations or even a strong contingent of domestic civilians, agencies, and governments was prepared to go to war to end racial violence. With white southerners exhibiting no signs that they would stop attacking black people, blacks fled the region. Despondent over southern socioeconomic conditions, blacks who had endured and borne witness to violence discussed migration with family members and friends. They communicated their anger over the conditions of southern life in a more public manner by flocking toward northern urban centers in pursuit of a better livelihood. Through written testimonies among family and friends and from southerners to northern newspapers such as the Pittsburgh *Courier* and the Chicago *Defender*, some migrants explained the cumulative weight of violent resubjugation as one reason they left the South.

Enjoying a nationwide circulation, black northern newspapers provided black southerners with public forums to testify about racial violence. These papers publicized concerns black people expressed about violence that were articulated only in private places throughout the South or in letters to federal officials. Some letters to the *Defender* cited the violence blacks endured and witnessed in the South as a reason for their need to relocate. For example, in a letter dated April 1, 1917, from Macon, Georgia, one southerner noted, "We are being shot down here like rabbits for every little [offense]." On May 13, a writer from Birmingham, Alabama, declared that he was trapped "in the darkness of the South." This writer was "trying [his] best to get out" as he was "counted no more th[a]n a dog." This Alabaman used the language of "darkness" and feeling "trapped" to convey the bleak and depressing conditions of southern life for many blacks.[46]

Migrants promised prospective patrons and employers that they were good, industrious citizens who needed assistance with relocating and were hoping to find steady employment. These people wanted to assure northerners and midwesterners that they would do well once they were "away from the Lynchman's noose and torchman's fire." Like the letters to presidents and to DOJ officials, these epistles to black newspapers, in conjunction with the migration itself, underscore the existence of an enclave public sphere. They also signify some African Americans' collective belief that if they could just escape the "darkness" of the South, then their lives would improve considerably. Neither these complaints nor the renewed migrations stopped the violence.[47]

Some migrants who testified about violence noted that during assaults on black communities, especially in cases in which black people fought back, whites ordered an exodus of black residents. Faced with heavily armed white men, some testifiers reported that they or their neighbors were driven from their homes, plantations, and towns under the threat of continued or heightened violence. Wartime migration allowed thousands of blacks to escape violent oppression in the South. It also triggered a demographic shift, with cultural and sociopolitical implications for African Americans' efforts to mobilize against violence. Many migrants took advantage of northern and midwestern opportunities for achieving individual advancement by attaining employment and education and by participating in the political arena, in ways that southern disfranchisement prohibited. These people voted and joined unions and new reform organizations such as the NAACP, the Urban League, and Marcus Garvey's Universal Negro Improvement Association (UNIA). They also shared their experiences of violent resubjugation, further diffusing knowledge of this violence and inspiring others to action.

The Great Migration of African Americans out of the South and into the Northeast and Midwest had political implications for African Americans' efforts to enact social and political reform. Northerners and these transplanted southerners were able to work on behalf of their southern counterparts by preserving kinship ties across space. Having responded to localized violence, southern transplants—with the aid of letters and the support of earlier migrants and activists operating in urban areas and the North—aired their frustration with violent resubjugation. Public figures relayed black people's indignation on a national level, as discussed in the preceding chapter. The desire to share their experiences of violence and to communicate their anger over white supremacy galvanized black folk.[48]

Letter writers inundated the Wilson administration with testimonies of experiencing and witnessing violence as well as petitions for relief from violence. A pastor from Tulsa, Oklahoma, named E. Johnson wrote the DOJ, protesting the "negro slave system," in which blacks were forced to work for little to no earnings and under the threat of violence. Johnson accused the government of failing to make good on Abraham Lincoln's promise of freedom to black people. Johnson censured the DOJ for permitting the "evil" of violent white supremacy to "corrupt the whole nation" and to bring the country down. Equating African Americans' plight to that of the Israelites described in the Old Testament, Johnson declared, "Now your only hope is to let the Negro go and restore to him all that you have robbed him of and make him a citizen without legal distinction." Chords of salvation and redemption sound throughout black people's letters, as do their efforts to demonstrate and strengthen black people's covenant with the nation.[49]

Some letter writers seemed to envision American presidents as gracious, God-like men who were capable of liberating blacks from their insecure position in the South. These testifiers believed that knowledge of the vileness of racial violence and the ways it handicapped black people's citizenship and contradicted the nation's principles would compel federal officials to provide federal protection for black people's civil and political rights. As Johnson's letter reveals, certain writers represented African Americans as a chosen people, whom Lincoln delivered from slavery. These activists saw black people's efforts to provide for their families and to work hard for their employers and their decision to fight in the country's wars as honoring their end of their covenant with the nation that emerged from Reconstruction. They saw their support for Wilson during his presidential campaign and during the war in similar terms. Indeed, a few letters even point toward black people's deep conviction that Wilson's ingratitude and indifference and the repeated breaching of African American citizens' binding contract with the nation was deserving of their withholding their faithful and loyal service.

On July 28, 1918, Wilson issued a public statement on racial violence. The tone and the timing of the president's statement reflect how little impact black people's testimonies about racial violence had on him. The pressure to condemn violence exerted by public figures and privately in letters written by black folk appeared to carry little weight in the president's speech. What carried greater weight and what induced action was German propaganda, threatening to saturate the South, that employed lynching and the violence in East St. Louis to foment black people's opposition to U.S. involvement in the war. The president decried lynching as a "disgraceful evil" that emulated Germany's "disgraceful example" of lawlessness and discredited the nation's claim as the "champion of democracy." Wilson called on "all who revere America and wish to keep her name without stain or reproach [to] cooperate" to end lynching. On the issue of federal officials intervening to ensure that African Americans enjoyed due process and equal protection under the law, the president explained that there was no need for federal action.[50]

Wilson's denunciation of lynching in the same breath as he pandered to white southern conservatives by dismissing the need for federal intervention into African Americans' complaints about violations of their civil and political rights should not have surprised black people, given his administration's stance on the matter. Nonetheless, while blacks probably appreciated the president's statement, Wilson's failure to pursue a more aggressive course of action to end violence flaunted the administration's indifference toward ensuring that black people enjoyed the promise of democracy at home. Statements by black folk and public figures suggest a shift in tone that disclosed black people's growing fury over violent resubjugation. This frustration became the catalyst for the zealous action needed to put racial violence into the nation's consciousness and to create a mandate for change. Progress did not come easily for African Americans. Indeed, the sentiment expressed by the federal officials and the white citizenry favored the return to prewar race relations.

The First World War intensified preexisting social, economic, and political misfortune on the home front. Some whites, unsettled by the war, black migration, and New Negro consciousness, turned again to white supremacy to impose order on African Americans, who had been rejuvenated by the rhetoric and reality of supporting the war. Many whites flocked toward the Ku Klux Klan, whose resurgence in 1915 had an effect on racialized interpretations of who was and who was not entitled to enjoy the promise of American democracy in the postwar era. Government fears of a replication of the 1917 Russian Revolution instigated a campaign—in cooperation with employers, citizens, and private groups—to suppress dissent. Through the Espionage and Sedition Acts, federal officials expanded the government's size and reach, which empowered authorities to monitor the mail, to censor the press, to restrict speech, and to imprison black radicals. The fear of dissent generated the unfolding of a blanket of federal intelligence agencies and intolerance that culminated in the First Red Scare and eventually delivered Warren G. Harding to the White House. Disturbed by the social dislocation of the war and mindful of African Americans' growing demands for equality, whites supported Harding's declaration that the nation needed "not heroics, but healing; not nostrums, but normalcy; not revolution, but restoration; not agitation, but adjustment." The federal government and the white American citizenry longed for a return to prewar conditions that supported the racial status quo. However, African Americans' behavior suggests they had other plans for postwar America.[51]

"A Sterner, Longer, More Unbending Battle"

White Americans' expressions of their desire for a "return to normalcy" portended their continued use and acceptance of racial violence. This sent a shiver throughout African America. The migrations, the letters from black folk about violent resubjugation, the speeches of public figures, and the publications of black print culture illustrate black people's increasing refusal to accept "normalcy," "restoration," and "adjustment" if that meant continued violence. Black people's private letters, their participation in public celebrations, and their establishment of civil rights organizations signaled a renewed intent to implement practices and reforms to end racial violence.

Through the black press and the migrations, New Negroes announced their new identity and their determination to reject a return to normalcy that allowed for continued violent resubjugation, and they did so with increasing fanfare. In February 1919, members of the army's all-black Fifteenth Regiment marched up Fifth Avenue in New York City. The sight of black soldiers returning home in full military garb and parading through the nation's streets was probably a breathtaking spectacle. The sight of black soldiers stoked anxiety in whites who had participated in, supported, or read about violence against black people during the war. Whites who sought to dominate black people had reason to be fearful. The parade, reports of which were reproduced widely throughout black print culture, evoked great pride in blacks. This and other homecoming events kindled an expectation that soldiers would help black people bring home the promise of democracy and equal citizenship.

In an April 1919 address before the Men's Progressive Club welcoming black soldiers home, the Reverend Frances J. Grimké expressed his desire for veterans to join the fight against racial subjugation. Grimké explained that he hoped the troops would "play a man's part in the longer and more arduous struggle that is before us in battling for our rights at home." Similar rhetoric of a campaign against white supremacy ran throughout black print culture, which black folk consumed. The treatment that black soldiers and civilians received at the hands of whites during the war left many black activists bitter. They knew that the majority of white people remained unfazed in their hatred despite black men's service in the war and black people's support for the war at home. Wartime violence as well as calls for the return to prewar race relations reflected white people's fears of black people's militancy. However, the war, the continued violence, and the new discourse surrounding a desire to return to normalcy drove home to many activists a clear and unequivocal need to ensure blacks enjoyed due process and equal protection under the law.[52]

In May 1919, Du Bois's "Returning Soldiers" editorial appeared in the *Crisis*. Du Bois had represented the NAACP at the Paris Peace Conference and investigated black soldiers' reports of racist treatment in the military. Returning to a nation where African Americans were beset by the conditions of violent resubjugation, Du Bois penned the famous editorial. Declaring "we are cowards and jackasses if now that the war is over, we do not marshal every ounce of our brain and brawn to fight a sterner, longer, more unbending battle against the forces of hell in our own land," Du Bois articulated the rallying cry that characterized African Americans' priorities for the postwar era: "*We return. We return from fighting. We return fighting.*" He ended the essay with the assertion that black soldiers had helped to preserve democracy in France and that they would do it at home "or know the reason why." Du Bois's treatise enunciated African Americans' amplified disillusionment with the failure of their support for the war to help end racial subjugation. The 1919 editorial captured black people's apparent preparation to compel the nation to make real the promise of democracy, which Americans posited as a national ideal and which the Wilson administration used as the reason for entering the war. Blacks reading the editorial from their enclave communities likely warmed to the essay's powerful rhetoric.[53]

It was shortly after the *Crisis* published "Returning Soldiers" that the first of twenty-five racial disturbances that rocked the nation throughout the summer occurred. The riots of Red Summer point to black people's mobilization against violence. After the war, fewer black people expressed the fear of violent reprisal that may have prompted blacks to be more conciliatory two decades earlier. They might have believed that conditions had progressed from the days when Ida Wells fled Memphis with a bounty on her head and when threats of lynching prompted journalist Jesse Chisholm Duke to flee Montgomery. Alternatively, they might have thought that the "lynching culture" that emerged in the 1890s and white citizens' and elected officials' continued disregard for black people's lives had reached a point that the fear of reprisal was less intense than the fear of not confronting violence. Black southerners' refusal to surrender their rights inspired white southerners to up the ante on their campaign of resubjugation. African Americans' private and public demands for protection were not enough to persuade the federal government and the greater national citizenry to intervene. Black people's behavior in the riots signals their embrace of Du Bois's declaration that they "return fighting."[54]

African Americans' resistance to the riots showed that for three generations, blacks had endured violence, listened to and written the vernacular history of violence, and heard the cant about being good, industrious people and the need for them to defer to whites to avert violence. But in the postwar period, public figures' calls for "fighting back" and "battling for our rights" became the anthem of a people who reached a consensus that racial violence would not continue to go unchecked. Experiencing and witnessing lynching, the discrimination against black soldiers, and the calls for self-defense running throughout the black print culture inspired more black people to practice the politics of defiance in their encounters with whites. Indeed, discerning observers of black folk and public figures might have seen the signs that the most significant grievance blacks had, what they would not tolerate in the postwar era, was mob violence.

As shown in the preceding chapter, the fear of political radicalism in the United States prompted federal officials to enact laws that circumscribed

Americans' rights and their ability to agitate for social and political reforms. The postwar Red Scare's transformation of the nation's political climate constrained African Americans' ability to challenge the status quo on racial violence. With the force and violence that white citizens, state officials, and federal troops used against black people during the riots of Red Summer, it became clear that while black self-defense captured the nation's attention, that attention was not always favorable. The federal government's surveillance of Americans ensnared defiant blacks as white citizens and politicians conjured explanations for African Americans' unprecedented engagement in and advocacy of self-defense during the riots. After the war, the DOJ and its Bureau of Investigation spied on black activists. The bureau classified as "subversive" many black people's complaints about the nation, forcing more activists to rely on the security and anonymity of their enclave communities to resist violence. The action blacks needed to compel federal intervention into violence in an environment of coercive surveillance could be politically precarious. This reality forced some of the most prominent public figures to proceed with caution. However, some black people's letters to federal officials during this period reveal the shift in their attitudes toward the federal government. In the postwar period, letter writers switched from asking federal officials to help African Americans to attacking them for failing to protect black people from racial violence.[55]

Many African Americans, who were weary from enduring and reading about violent resubjugation and who were perhaps unaware of or indifferent to the surveillance program, refused to stand down in the face of the Red Scare's climate of political repression. This perhaps explains why letters that black people wrote to the Wilson administration took on a more caustic and livid tone after the war. A man named B. Emmanuels of Washington, D.C., wrote the DOJ a letter denouncing President Wilson in June 1919. Emmanuels asked whether racial violence was worse than the anarchism and terrorism that the president declared himself against during the Red Scare or the recent mail bombs sent by extremists to business and political officials in several cities. "How many Negroes have the savages of your race killed?" he inquired. Emmanuels believed that the president neither knew nor cared but was certain that he could relay the number of German casualties "quicker than the blinking of an eye." Emmanuels argued that the government's default to the states'-rights doctrine was "a feeble excuse for remaining silent" about racial violence. If the president had the power to protect the lives of those who were threatened by anarchists, this letter writer wondered, "why is it you have not the same power to protect Negroes" who "fought for universal democracy" and who were denied their basic civil and human rights? "How long, O Department of Justice," Emmanuels ended his letter, "will such injustices prevail? Justice, demands of the powers that be, protection for the millions of Afro-American citizens."[56] The DOJ records show no written response from the administration.

Black people who endured and witnessed racial violence continued to reach out to federal officials for restitution. They used specific examples of violence to voice their outrage over the plight of southern blacks as well as the federal government's apparent apathy toward their suffering. The treatment that black service members received at the hands of violent whites struck particular anger in letter writers. Theodore Hawkins, an ex-soldier of Williamsport, Pennsylvania, wrote a letter in which he argued, if democracy "cannot control lawlessness, then democracy must be pronounced a failure." Some African Americans believed that extralegal violence compromised democracy, while others believed that democracy, when interpreted, executed, legislated, and adjudicated indiscriminately, was the key to ending this violence. If the federal government would not protect black civilians from lynching, then many letter writers believed that officials should play a more active role in at least protecting black service members and prosecuting crimes against them.[57]

Attorney William L. Jones of Buffalo, New York, wrote several letters to the DOJ requesting an investigation into the murder of a soldier who had been lynched while still in uniform in Blakely, Georgia. If Private William Little's murder went unpunished, Jones feared that black people would begin to think of all "such wrongs and outrages [committed] upon their race." He predicted that, "sooner or later, . . . the white race, if not our nation, will have to pay the penalty for . . . all unlawful acts . . . against the colored race, where our country does nothing about it." The penalty, Jones implied, was violence similar to that of the riots. Jones also noted that racial violence could jeopardize the nation's reputation with other countries. "How can the U.S. set an example for the rest of the world," he asked, "when it allows the colored race to be treated in our own country, in this way, by the white race with impunity?" Jones was probably more concerned with the quandary in which black people found themselves than he was with the nation's falling into disrepute. However, like other blacks, Jones recognized that the violence that black people had already endured was not enough to persuade federal officials to intervene. These letter writers saw in the nation's investment in its standing in the world an opportunity to compel government officials to action.[58]

In October 1919, C. J. Johnson, from Pensacola, Florida, wrote President Woodrow Wilson to call his attention to the September 29 lynching of three male prisoners in Montgomery, Alabama. Johnson asked that such violence "be put to an end." Acknowledging the procedures for "trial by jury" and "not by mob," Johnson prevailed on Wilson to offer African Americans refuge under the nation's laws. He explained that black people believed in "abiding by the laws as they are laid down." Johnson informed the administration that blacks were only asking for due process and equal protection when authorities charged African Americans with crimes and for the prosecution of whites who committed crimes against them. Citing black people's respect for the law and their cooperation during the war, Johnson wrote, "It is hard to know that our wives bear sons to go on the firing line and fight like heroes for this country and then return home and be burned, shot, lynched unjustly." This language signifies black people's strong belief that military service should yield enough national gratitude to inspire change. Johnson spoke to Wilson man to man and claimed for black women the wartime rhetoric about the sacrifices that white mothers had made to the war effort. Black mothers deserved equal veneration, Johnson wrote, and not to have their sons slaughtered by some of the very people whose interests black men's military service had helped to protect. As was typical of letters sent to American presidents appealing for redress against violence, Wilson's office forwarded Johnson's letter to the DOJ. Assistant Attorney General R. P. Stewart wrote back explaining, "The federal government has no jurisdiction over the offense of lynching, the matter being one in the control of the several states. If you will examine the decision of the Supreme Court in *Hodges v. United States*, you will find the matter fully discussed."[59]

Mr. T. R. Hart, a resident of Little Rock, Arkansas, responded to a form letter he received from the DOJ by explaining that blacks were asking for "nothing" but a "fair deal." Hart asked if there was "no cure for lynching." Hart thought that after using black soldiers to fight the war in France, the least the federal government could do was not to "allow them to be mob[bed] and also lynched." If, as explained by the form letters sent to letter writers requesting relief from violent resubjugation, personnel at the DOJ could not act, then Hart wanted the attorney general to give governors and county judges a "stric[t] warning" about lynching and to be more aggressive about ending extralegal violence "then and there." Hart even offered to help end the violence himself. He asked for an appointment as a U.S. marshal and promised to break the practice in twelve to eighteen months.[60]

Hart's letter is instructive of many African Americans' belief that it was the responsibility of federal officials to check violations of their civil and political rights. Enough southern whites had tolerated violence against blacks that activists had little faith in their changing their opinions of and support for lynching. Indeed, southern state officials showed little inclination toward protecting black people from this violence or punishing whites in its aftermath. Thus, blacks felt compelled to call on the federal government to direct local executives and judiciaries to uphold existing laws on murder and crime and to administer justice fairly. Hart's offer to play a more active role in ending extralegal violence himself may have been an effort at self-promotion. However, his offer might also have sprung from the belief that if the personnel or will to suppress racial violence were deficient, then he was ready to serve. The DOJ did not take Hart up on his offer.

The DOJ did not dismiss all complaints about mob violence. When the Mississippi veterans wrote the War Department and asked for an investigation of the lynching of Will Moore on the grounds that he was a soldier, the War Department sent the request to the DOJ. The DOJ investigated Moore's lynching but dropped the case when it discovered that Moore had not served in the military.[61] This incident notwithstanding, blacks found reaching out to the federal government and testifying about violence to be a futile exercise.

Some frustrated and reform-minded black people joined reform endeavors sponsored by northern-based organizations such as the African Blood Brotherhood, the Communist Party, the NAACP, and the UNIA. Black people's defiant self-defense in the riots, the radicalized language of public figures, and the tone of letters from black folk helped convince Attorney General A. Mitchell Palmer that blacks were "seeing red." Although federal officials rarely took action to uphold black people's civil and political rights, they did pay attention to their letters, their publications, and their behavior in everyday life. Black men's advocacy of and engagement in self-defense during the riots elicited red baiting and hysterical suggestions that black people's resistance to subjugation threatened the country, rather than an acknowledgment that they were trying to alleviate black people's suffering from violence and to advance their desire for equal rights. African Americans decided that they needed to communicate their frustrations with racial violence and to demand reform in formal and institutionalized ways to gain the attention of white citizens and state and federal officals.[62]

Despite indications that the nation might not make good on the promise of democracy regarding African Americans, the actions of some local people illustrate the extent to which the war galvanized blacks who were still in pursuit of civil and political rights. Epistolary practices from people living in enclave communities, public figures' re-presentations of racial violence, and black people's ongoing responses to it dramatize the extent to which the New Negro consciousness—that which advocated and legitimated the kind of defensive action seen in the riots—was not merely the "wishful prophesies" of public figures. Southern blacks' engagement in self-defensive action against racial violence since emancipation and the anger expressed in many letters suggest that this defiance was their reality communicated on a more public level and in a more political way. Letters from black writers in the North and South to presidential administrations from Taft through Harding provide insight into black people's enthusiasm to ensure democracy at home for African Americans or, as Du Bois put it, to "know the reason why." This language suggests that some African Americans believed that black people could or would revolt if the nation did not live up to its democratic principles.[63]

Some black people's behavior during the riots of Red Summer, the most noteworthy of which occurred in Chicago; Elaine, Arkansas; and Washington, D.C., demonstrated to the nation some African Americans' decision to reject a return to prewar race relations. Although black people bore the brunt of the casualties—largely because of attacks by agents of the state sent to preserve order—white people were counted in the several dozen fatalities and the several hundred injuries. Whereas the injury and death of black people at the hands of whites in riots was a regular occurrence, white people suffering similar injuries at the hands of blacks was another matter.[64]

Some African Americans took great pleasure in black men's participation in the riots. In a letter published in the *Crisis*, an unidentified southern woman communicated her delight over reports of black men defending their communities in the Washington riot. She wrote, "The Washington riot gave me the thrill that comes once in a life time. I was alone when I read between the lines of the morning paper that at least our men had stood up like men, and struck back. . . . The pent-up humiliation, grief and horror of a life time—half a century—was being stripped from me." In the riot, black men had returned violence with violence. Their defense of their communities increased the damage to white people's lives and property and prompted President Wilson to send federal troops to restore order. For this writer, the riots reflected black people's demonstration of their frustration with violent resubjugation and black men's power to protect black women and their homes. In this writer's opinion, black women of the South knew well "the extreme suffering and humiliation" that southern blacks endured. According to her,

> Only colored women know how many insults we have borne silently, for we have hidden many of them from our men because we did not want them to die needlessly in our defense; we know the sorrow of seeing our boys and girls grow up, the swift stab of the heart at night to the sound of a

strange footstep, the feel of a tigress to spring and claw the white man with his lustful look at our comely daughters, the deep humiliation of sitting in the Jim Crow part of a street car and hear the white men laugh and discuss us, point out the good and bad points of our bodies. God alone knows the many things colored women have borne here in the South in silence.

Few of the Red Summer riots involved reported instances of sexual violence or sexual harassment directed at black women. However, this letter is another articulation of the gender-based nature of racial violence and its consequences for African Americans. That the writer, as a politically marginalized woman, felt comfortable articulating this in a letter to the *Crisis* merits consideration.[65]

As shown earlier in this chapter, clubwomen such as those from the NACW argued that it was black women's responsibility to speak on behalf of their sex and race. They spoke and wrote about the ways that violence affected black women disproportionately. Some women also helped develop a "politics of silence" on sexual violence, adhering collectively to what Darlene Clark Hine calls a "cult of secrecy, a culture of dissemblance" to protect the inner sanctum of black women's lives, where they remained the most vulnerable. But it was people from enclave communities who testified about physical and sexual abuse to the Freedmen's Bureau and to Congress. After Reconstruction, many of these rape survivors testified about their suffering to their families and reported attacks to civil authorities. These defiant women and their male supporters put on the public record sexual violations of black women and provided activists in the counterpublic sphere with their ammunition.[66]

This woman's letter, in relating her sex's specific victimization and frustration, embodied the efforts of black females to break the silence on their sexual suffering and humiliation at the hands of whites. The letter suggests that some women's dissemblance about rape and sexual exploitation were conscious decisions not only to facilitate their own survival but also to protect their families and communities from assured white reprisal. This testifier related a torturous paradox facing black females: survivors who testified about sexual harassment and rape often put their families at risk for violence, death, and displacement if black men retaliated against the perpetrators. That the letter writer saw any likely casualties from this action as "needlessly" in black women's defense contradicted the proclamations of some public figures who argued that black men should risk their lives to protect their families and to avenge attacks on them. In this writer's estimation, the harassment and even the sexual assaults that black females endured were not deserving of the loss of their fathers', sons', husbands', or brothers' lives. This writer's letter signifies many black women's awareness of the patterns of violence that could emerge from incidents of rape. Black men, to spare their loved ones further victimization, would take on efforts to avenge female honor individually or in small numbers. This brand of vengeance put these men and their families at risk of almost certain harm.

More than two hundred years of devaluing black womanhood had allowed white men to develop stock responses to black females' complaints about rape and being propositioned for sex; these responses included bragging about raping black females and denying rape while simultaneously questioning the woman's or girl's honor. Black men often responded to these insults with force, continuing the cycle of violence and increasing the likelihood of black injury or death as a result of direct violence or collateral damage. Some black women, to spare their loved ones and themselves additional trauma, engaged the politics of deference to allow the men in their lives to avoid violence. The tone of this writer's letter suggests that she understood that some of the *Crisis*'s readers might not have appreciated the sacrifices southern black women and girls made for their families. Whereas gender-based deference to whites to protect loved ones robbed some black females of their voice, a sense of self and a need to relate what only black women knew about this violence on a more public scale inspired this writer's letter.[67]

The letter also captures the elevated pulse of African Americans' reactions to the riots. Black people's decisions to defend themselves during Red Summer were born out of an atmosphere of violence in black women's and men's everyday lives that became impossible to endure. Pushed to the breaking point by continued violence and by the strains of the war, some males "stood up like men, and struck back." To many African Americans, black men's participation in the riots was a "thrilling" demonstration of their manliness and masculinity that was tantamount to what Franz Fanon called a "cleansing force." This force freed oppressed people from their "inferiority complex and from [their] despair and inaction; it [made them] fearless and [restored their] self-respect."[68] Explaining how the "pent-up humiliation, grief and horror of a life time . . . was being stripped" from her, the writer interpreted the riots as the symbolic releasing of compressed steam that had been building since Redemption.

Black men's collective action in the riots distinguished their responses from the largely individualistic opposition to extraordinary violence. The riots exacted casualties, but the occurrence of bloodletting and destruction of property on both sides of the racial divide caught the nation off guard. The riots ultimately forced white citizens as well as local, state, and federal officials, who might have previously dismissed black women's and men's complaints about the conditions of life for African Americans, to take note, if not action. Expressing the plight of women, seeing the riot in gendered terms, and relating both the helplessness and power of black men, this epistler provides an intimate analysis of black women's and men's interpretation of the sea change that the war and its repercussions caused in African America. This writer's letter to the *Crisis* also signals the relevance of black print culture and of the NAACP in the lives and minds of black southerners.

Conclusion

Federal officials shrugged off African Americans' complaints of racial subjugation and refused to extend the federal government's authority to help them combat racial violence, but black people took even greater advantage of a new way of thinking about resisting subjugation that was converging at the national level. Public figures' re-presentation of the hydra of white supremacy diffused knowledge about the impact of resubjugation on black people's lives. However, it was black folks' letters, their role in the migrations, and their action in the riots that elucidate the depth of African Americans' frustrations with racial violence.

Black people's letters coincided with formal measures taking shape to use political action and the Fourteenth Amendment's protections to ensure that African Americans received due process and equal protection under the law. The groundswell of opinion and action resisting the violence of resubjugation came from African Americans' sense of urgency and from their cognizance that collective action was the most effective means of confronting lynching. To produce even limited changes in a social and legal structure that tacitly supported lynching as one form of resubjugation, black activists understood that they would have to challenge white citizens' and officials' desire for a return to normalcy and to change the nation's institutional arenas to enact reform. African Americans' contribution to the war, the endurance of violence throughout the South, its spread to the North, and the advancement of progressive reform created a political climate that was ripe for action.

African Americans located in the Northeast and Midwest played a crucial role in the congealment of collective reform. These people extended a hand to black southerners who were struggling to fight white supremacy. These northern-based activists—motivated by black southerners' ultimately futile efforts to arrest this violence, victims' and witnesses' audacious decisions to resist violence by reporting it, and their understanding of the vernacular history of racial violence—used lynching to embody black people's oppression, to advocate collaboration, and to try to reform the nation's social and legal structure. From the collective sense of the impact of lynching on black people, a reform movement to confront racial subjugation was born. Individuals and organizations agreed that they needed to amass the political capital to transform white people's dismissal of black people's citizenship. However, there was no consensus on the process needed to end lynching and to advance civil rights reform until the 1900s.

The antilynching movement of the 1910s was not inevitable. Indeed, earlier efforts to mobilize black people against violence had failed to enact reforms. The crusade that emerged from African Americans' sense of the need for collective action had to accomplish a lot before it could help blacks advance beyond slavery. To wage the battle against racial violence, and what Du Bois called the "forces of hell," victims and witnesses needed to relate their experiences of violence. Organizations serving the interests of African Americans needed to tap into preexisting networks to recruit and sustain support from diverse constituencies. Together these activists had to foster a shared understanding of the impact of violence and use this knowledge to mobilize politically. Progressive organizations with shared objectives and similar constituencies often worked in tandem, but they diverged on ideologies and tactics and often competed with each other for status. To ensure that black people enjoyed the civil and political rights guaranteed in the Constitution, these individuals and organizations had to cast aside those differences, to mobilize grassroots operations, and to use Americans' reverence for the existing judicial and legal system.

5

"It Is Not for Us to Run Away from Violence"

Fueling the NAACP's Antilynching Crusade

Caddo Parish, Louisiana, was abuzz with discussion of reports streaming in from a town near Blanchard in December 1913. A posse of twenty white Louisianans lynched brothers Frank and Ernest Williams for allegedly murdering a white man named Calvin Ballard. The national press reported that the Williams brothers had confessed to killing Ballard in retaliation for his shooting of a relative of theirs. The NAACP, under the authorization of W. E. B. Du Bois and through the direct action of white attorney Chapin Brinsmade, reacted to these reports by firing off inquiries to members in Louisiana and in Texas.[1]

Because the national headquarters of the NAACP was located in Manhattan, the organization's leadership had to rely on black folk and members of branches dispersed throughout the South for information on local matters involving racial violence. For the particulars on what happened in Caddo Parish, Brinsmade wrote community-based activists including member Reverend G. W. Stringfellow, of Cameron, Texas: "Whenever a lynching occurs we try to obtain the facts from someone who knows them personally. We never use the names of our informants unless they want us to. Our object in getting these facts is to keep a record of all lynchings that occur. . . . Can you tell me about this matter or ask someone who can?"[2] Caddo Parish had recently become a "hot bed for lynching," so progressive residents were eager to supply the NAACP with details about the killings. From local reports came news that the Williamses made no confessions and that the mob executed them because the brothers knew the identities of the white men who killed Ballard.[3]

Some respondents did more than respond to the NAACP's requests for information; they also offered recommendations for action. P. L. Blackman suggested, "If the Association would spend a few dollars in this vicinity [to collect] evidence sufficient to arrest and convict, it would go far in diminishing these crimes." Brinsmade responded that although he would consult others, the NAACP leadership did not "expect to make any extended investigations of lynchings at places so far South." Brinsmade followed up by writing Kathryn M. Johnson, a member stationed in New Orleans, to ask about the worthiness of such an investigation. The NAACP had "always felt that money spent in investigating lynching so far south would be a throw away," Brinsmade explained. Citing the advancement among the black population there, the community's receptiveness to restorative justice, and the successful prosecution and conviction of whites who murdered blacks, Johnson replied that investigating and exposing lynching in Caddo Parish was a sensible endeavor for the association.[4]

Chapin Brinsmade's belief that investigations in the Deep South were "throw away[s]" exposes the NAACP for what it was in 1913: a fledgling organization with limited resources that was struggling to enact social and legal reforms in an environment that was receptive for progressive reform but still hostile to issues of social justice for black people. Although the NAACP eventually became a great civil rights organization, its ascendancy was slow. It achieved this status by building interracial coalitions, by participating in progressive reforms, and by nurturing a relationship with victims of racial violence. In this chapter, I use NAACP publications as well as correspondence among the organization's leadership, its local members, governors, and victims and witnesses to chart the development of the association's antilynching campaign. Many people know about the NAACP's crusade against lynching and the link between the antilynching crusade and the civil rights campaigns of the 1950s and 1960s. However, few know that the association's antilynching crusade was the result of several decades of African Americans' individual and collective efforts to mobilize against racial violence and that victims' and witnesses' testimonies were one driving force behind it.[5]

The architects of the NAACP's civil rights agenda in the 1910s certainly wanted a revolutionary movement on the scale of the one that emerged in the 1950s and 1960s. However, transformative social movements do not simply happen because oppressed people want them to. Sociologists argue that social movements are complex phenomena whose emergence and successes are contingent on sociopolitical factors—political opportunities, mobilized social structures, and cultural frames—coming together at the right time and in the right way. In the case of African Americans' fight for civil and political rights, activists had to take advantage of and create the right conditions in which to advance reform. They had to develop social movement organizations to coordinate political action and to mobilize Americans to work together to apply concerted political pressure to produce social change. They also had to develop discursive frames about violence to get the support of moderate white citizens and of elected state and federal officials for their efforts to pass federal antilynching legislation.[6]

The NAACP achieved its reputation as a civil rights juggernaut by building on earlier reform efforts and by taking advantage of political opportunities for advancing reform initiatives. To combat the hydra-headed problem of racial subjugation, the association developed separate reform movements with limited goals until the environment changed and presented activists with the opportunities they needed for advancing transformative reform. These smaller initiatives included campaigns to challenge disfranchisement and segregation and to end lynching. Like other institutions serving African Americans during the Progressive Era, the NAACP's founders and members had many reasons for joining the crusades against lynching. The horrific nature of mob violence as well as its extralegal dimensions and its acceptance among many white Americans made lynching unbearable to African Americans and helped them unite with white progressives to develop a solution to end the violence by punishing the perpetrators and their abettors. Some of the NAACP's black founders and members had experienced or witnessed racial violence and were therefore committed to ending it and advancing broader civil rights reforms. Many of the association's white founders were ideological descendants of the abolitionist movement and were committed to using the Constitution as a legal basis for defeating racial discrimination and violence.[7]

The conditions that African Americans and their white allies needed to launch a formal crusade against lynching did not start to crystallize until 1909, when the NAACP joined the chorus of activists and organizations attempting to beat back the hydra of white supremacy. The association's founders carried forth and refined T. Thomas Fortune's work by reaching into the South and extending a hand to black people who were caught between the hammer of violence and the anvil of indifference of white citizens and elected officials. The NAACP did this by taking advantage of the nation's receptiveness to reform that Progressivism created. Its leadership acquired money to investigate racial violence and to publish their critiques of it. The association also established the *Crisis*, a periodical that editor W. E. B. Du Bois used to publicize issues affecting black people and to make the case for mobilizing politically against violence. The organization built its reputation by presenting a professional leadership, by listening empathetically to victims' and witnesses' testimonies, and by mobilizing local social networks. Over time, the NAACP developed a persuasive argument for enacting legislation against lynching that resonated not only with victims and witnesses but also with progressive and moderate whites across the nation. Consequently, it was the NAACP's strategies and institutionalized campaign to end lynching that helped African Americans lay the foundation for what became the modern civil rights platform.[8]

Examinations of the NAACP's press statements, its pamphlets, its catalogs of lynching, and the *Crisis* reveal a passionate but seemingly remote organization that spoke of and on behalf of victims and witnesses of racial violence. Yet analysis of the back-and-forth correspondence between local people and the national office presents a different picture. The association—with its interracial composition, its massive bureaucratic infrastructure, its magnanimous leadership, and its location in a northern metropolis—could have been an organization that was out of touch with and indifferent to the wants and needs of black folk. However, unpublished records of the NAACP reveal the relations between victims and witnesses and the national office. The association's leadership certainly learned of violence from mainstream and black print culture. Indeed, the speeches and writings of NAACP officials point to their outrage over witnessing this violence through reading newspapers, which fueled their determination to play a role in ending it. NAACP officials also bore witness to black people's suffering by listening to or reading their testimonies about it. The unpublished dialogue about violence, which occurred between victims and witnesses, local leaders, and the national leadership, was one factor in the NAACP's eventual ability to surmount the hesitancy reflected in Brinsmade's letter and to launch a nationwide campaign to end violence.[9]

Victims and witnesses who had learned of the association's antilynching activity through conversations and through the organization's outreach programs, pamphlets, newspaper reports, and the *Crisis* began contacting the NAACP with testimonies about the violent horrors they had endured and witnessed. Most of the testifiers writing federal officials in the Taft and Wilson administrations were *secondhand witnesses* to the violence, who often wrote on behalf of victims. However, many people contacting the NAACP after the First World War were *victims* and *eyewitnesses*, people who were on the front lines of the wars of white supremacy.[10] These were the people who saw loved ones and neighbors slain or dragged from their homes to be slaughtered at another location and who prepared victims' funerals. They were mothers such as Mattie Glover, who wrote the NAACP inquiring about her son Eddie, who disappeared in 1925, and they were fathers such as Gainer Atkins, who wrote the NAACP about getting justice after a mob lynched his son Charlie. In their determination to get justice for themselves, their loved ones, and their neighbors these indomitable women and men managed to put into words the unthinkable and unspeakable things that happened to them and to people in their communities. Unlike indifferent federal officials, the NAACP provided empathetic responses to victims' and witnesses' testimonies of violence and to their entreaties for assistance.[11]

The amount of correspondence between the NAACP and victims, the sensitivity with which the NAACP responded to people's letters, and the unyielding determination some activists had in attempting to get justice for lynching victims' family members suggests that there is a direct link, if one that was not explicitly articulated by the NAACP, between testifiers' accounts of violence and the association's antilynching crusade. The association dispatched members of its fleet to collect and verify data from victims and witnesses. NAACP leaders wrote empathetic letters to survivors and kept their correspondence confidential. Letter writers turned NAACP leaders and members into witnesses, people who experienced the horrors of racial violence vicariously through their interchanges with victims. The association also directed letter writers to local resources, penned letters to state and federal officials on victims' behalf, and published accounts of violence for the world to know what was happening to African Americans. Without the testimonies of victims and witnesses, the NAACP would not have known as much as it did about violence and its impact on black people as they did and probably would not have been as motivated to pursue reform. The NAACP leadership, local members, and black folk through their correspondence "wrote themselves into consciousness" about violence and the need to develop and maintain institutionalized campaigns to end it.[12] The NAACP channeled victims' testimonies into a discursive frame—specifically, an argument about honoring the Constitution—to manipulate the levers of American thought and power to end lynching.

"Take Hold of This Problem Ourselves"

The development of a reform movement to end violence only occurred after the NAACP emerged like a phoenix from the ashes of defunct civil rights campaigns. Indeed, to understand the rise of the NAACP and the challenges the organization overcame to launch its crusade against racial violence requires revisiting earlier campaigns. Attentive to deteriorating conditions throughout the South, T. Thomas Fortune, through his newspaper, the New York *Freeman*, and his organization, the Afro-American League, asked African Americans to mobilize to challenge white supremacy in 1887. Fortune, who was at the vanguard of political mobilization against white supremacy, wrote that black people needed to "take hold of this problem" themselves: "make so much noise that all the world shall know the wrongs we suffer and our determination to right these wrongs." The league's list of grievances included the already-existing threats to black suffrage, segregation, and "the universal and lamentable reign of lynch and mob law."[13]

Fortune, like his peers John Bruce and John Mitchell, initially advocated a platform that promoted self-defense. Fortune believed that the league should carry out its functions diplomatically by publishing accounts of violence and demanding a more forceful federal intervention into southern affairs when local and state officials failed to protect black people's constitutional rights. However, Fortune promised, if white supremacists responded to black people's peaceful campaigns for social justice with violence, then "it is not for us to run away from violence."[14]

As chapter 2 illustrates, the league did not run from violence, but the organization never managed to mobilize enough people to advance meaningful civil rights reform. The organization suffered from financial problems; a lack of support from besieged black folk and from black public figures, whose reliance on white people's patronage constrained their activism; and ideological differences on the best way to address violations of black people's rights. By 1893, Fortune declared the league defunct. The timing of the league's emergence and withdrawal marked the initial phases of the consolidation of racism, which might explain why black activists were not able to establish an organization to mobilize local people to apply political pressure to end violence. Additionally, the political climate of the consolidation was not conducive to Fortune's efforts to promote what Christopher Waldrep calls "black constitutionalism," the idea that if local and state governments failed to protect black people's rights when whites operated outside the confines of the laws, the Fourteenth and Fifteenth Amendments enabled federal officials to intervene. It was only when disfranchisement, segregation, and more spectacular violence began laying waste to black people's rights that other activists picked up the Fortune's mantle and revived his work.[15]

Each of the league's successors tried to build on Fortune's platform of uniting nationally and taking advantage of and creating new political opportunities to advance reform. The Afro-American Council, which was established in 1898, duplicated the league's platform of "taking hold" of white supremacy. The council, which was invigorated by Booker T. Washington's endorsement, received national press attention and greater participation by and support from black public figures and folk than the league had. Yet with this support came new debates over leadership and the course of action needed to slay the hydra of white supremacy. The Tuskegean's influence necessitated the council's alignment with his advocacy of the politics of strategic deference to white supremacy. This generated tensions with such members as W. E. B. Du Bois and Ida B. Wells-Barnett, who argued for a more aggressive strategy to combat racial discrimination. Amplifying internal divisions was the gnawing lack of support from black folk, who prioritized survival and who still harbored feelings of distrust for public figures. The council survived initially, but the organization later succumbed to the loss of its leader and competition from other organizations.[16]

Reformers continued to mobilize and to work on developing new ways to frame their arguments for reform. Waldrep has identified a coterie of white progressives who in 1903 established the Constitution League, a group whose mission was to confront legalized discrimination using the Fourteenth Amendment. What is more, in 1905, Du Bois, Mary Talbert, William Monroe Trotter, and some progressive whites launched the Niagara Movement. The founders created this organization hoping to establish a civil rights program that involved embracing the politics of defiance in an aggressive pursuit of social justice that was disdained by many Washingtonians. With leaders who were more militant and who had a more aggressive stance on civil rights, the Niagara Movement presented a direct threat to the authority over the black public spheres that was enjoyed by the Afro-American Council. Therefore, Washington and Fortune attempted to revive the almost-defunct organization to smash the Niagara activists. Within three years of the Niagara Movement's establishment, it languished because of financial hardship and the council's successful campaign to vanquish its competition. The council survived until Booker T. Washington's 1915 death, when remaining members joined forces with other civil rights groups. When the Niagara Movement disbanded, many members joined white progressives such as those from the Constitution League to form the NAACP after the Springfield, Illinois, race riot of 1908.[17]

The NAACP's emergence during the Progressive Era marked a clear distinction from the earlier efforts to mobilize African Americans and to confront the hydra-headed problem of white supremacy. The NAACP was committed to developing legal strategies to secure full citizenship rights for blacks. The founders had the benefit of earlier organizations' efforts to mobilize. They enjoyed a political environment that was more conducive to reform, a stronger sociopolitical network, and a better appreciation for the impact of the consolidation of racism and the best ways to confront it. These activists also embraced the style and ideology of progressivism. Rather than simply report violence and call for its end, the NAACP pursued interracial cooperation and developed a progressive framing mechanism that involved using the existing legal and judicial system to advance a comprehensive plan of civil rights reform. This plan of legal gradualism included fighting racial subjugation through the courts and through Congress, using the Constitution's due process and equal protection clauses to attack disfranchisement, segregation, and lynching. Massachusetts attorney general and NAACP member Arthur E. Pillsbury played a critical role in developing the NAACP's argument for federal antilynching legislation. Pillsbury argued that "forbidding a State to deny equal protection [was] equivalent to requiring the State to provide it." The states infringe on black people's rights when local and state officials fail to protect blacks from lynching or fail to prosecute known perpetrators. When they fail to do this, "there is a denial of equal protection," to which Congress may respond by passing legislation to prevent or punish this violation of citizenship rights. This became the NAACP's key argument for convincing members of Congress to pass federal antilynching legislation.[18]

The ways that violence had pulled apart black people's lives helped some of the NAACP's leadership shift from its initially broad goal of dealing segregation, disfranchisement, and violence one fatal blow toward a very specific campaign of confronting racial violence. Activists made this choice because they understood from victims' and witnesses' testimonies that violence represented the worst of white supremacy. Moreover, many of the black members of the NAACP had experienced violence themselves; and if they had not, they learned of it through kin and from print culture. They appreciated that violence made other violations of African Americans' social, economic, and political rights possible. The conditions that led to the killing of black people and its acceptance among white citizens and elected officials informed the NAACP's decision to establish a multifaceted program designed to stamp out racial violence.[19]

The NAACP collected data on lynching from newspapers and victims and witnesses and projected its findings into the dominant public spheres and the black enclave and counterpublic spheres to help mobilize Americans to support its efforts to pass federal antilynching legislation. The organization replicated Ida Wells-Barnett's work by mining southern newspapers for information needed to report violence and to restyle white public opinion on lynching. At the same time, the association published results from its investigations of violence in such publications as *Notes on Lynching* (1912), *Thirty Years of Lynching* (1919), and *Burning at the Stake in the United States* (1919). These pamphlets, in addition to the *Crisis*, newspaper editorials, reports, and literary writings facilitated the association's efforts to hammer away at the deceptive excuses for lynching and to highlight the contexts of violence, the characteristics of lynchers, and the effects this violence had on African Americans. The NAACP published this information to educate Americans and to recruit members to the organization. The organization also replicated the work of abolitionists and inundated members of Congress, white public figures, governors, and members of the press with its investigative reports on lynching. On the whole, the association embraced the progressive strategy of using sociological research to educate whites because it believed that reshaping Americans' knowledge about this violence was an important arrow in the quiver of its campaign to make a case for federal antilynching legislation.[20]

To compel elected officials to support its crusade against lynching, the NAACP needed to prime the pump and begin with officials' white constituents. The association's campaign to change white public opinion about lynching involved joining fellow activists in taking away from lynchers and their apologists the distorted representation of mob violence as the best device for subjugating what they characterized as a criminal black population. For example, responding to one southern white woman's widely published essay arguing that lynching would end if blacks stopped committing crimes, NAACP field secretary James Weldon Johnson struck back in a letter to the New York *Globe*. Lynching, Johnson explained, "is not so much due to the criminal tendency of the Negro as it is to the criminal tendency of the southern whites" who thwarted African Americans' rights to due process and who shielded lynchers from prosecution. By creating antilynching propaganda and confronting lynchers and their defenders in the press, the association reframed the discourse about lynching. The NAACP hoped that its discursive intervention would elicit the support it needed to lobby members of Congress and to secure the passage of antilynching legislation. Re-presenting extralegal violence as a malignant tumor threatening the nation, the NAACP thus capitalized on the existing momentum for progressive reform to secure its place among progressives and in the hearts and minds of African Americans.[21]

To generate support for its antilynching campaign, the NAACP exercised extreme caution in the cases it used to argue for federal antilynching legislation. The NAACP's handling of Marie Scott's lynching underscores the organization's selectivity on the cases it used to recruit allies and to "make the world know" about lynching and racial violence. On a March night in 1914, two intoxicated white men skulked into the black residential section of Wagoner, Oklahoma, looking for female sexual prey. The men snuck into a home occupied by a seventeen-year-old woman named Marie Scott and tried to assault her. Scott's screams brought her twenty-one-year-old brother to her rescue. In the fight that ensued, one of the Scott siblings killed Lemuel Pease. Both the Scotts fled.[22] Marie hid in a chicken coop while waiting for a man, named Sam Hendricks, to arrange her escape from Wagoner. Hendricks—perhaps in an attempt to curry favor with whites, to avoid being killed, or to avert a massacre—revealed Scott's location to local authorities. Authorities arrested Marie believing that if she did not kill Pease, then she was responsible for his death. Before authorities could prosecute her, a mob overpowered the jail and seized her. The men threw a noose around her neck and dragged the teenager kicking and screaming to her death atop a telephone pole near the jail. Scott's lynching intensified efforts to escort her brother from town. When whites could not locate her brother, they ordered blacks living in Wagoner to leave the town or die.[23]

Reports that a white mob had lynched a young black woman spread across African America. NAACP leaders, after reading reports of this incident and receiving letters demanding that it conduct an investigation into Scott's killing, dispatched inquiries to collect local intelligence. The association received numerous rejoinders, but the question of Scott's character ran throughout the reports. The particulars of her life were so "revolting and so shocking" that attorney W. Scott Brown, Jr., of nearby Muskogee, Oklahoma, declined to discuss them in his letter to NAACP secretary May Childs Nerney. The questions regarding Marie Scott's character stymied the NAACP's investigation into her death.[24]

Print culture spread the news about Scott's lynching far beyond Oklahoma and New York City. Mrs. E. W. Anderson, secretary of the Friday Club of San Diego, California, read about the lynching in her local newspaper. The murder of the young woman cut Anderson personally and inspired her to write the NAACP. The Friday Club's motto was "Deeds Not Words," which underscored the clubwomen's commitment to taking specific action to confront white supremacy. Anderson cited this motto as the motive for her request that the NAACP hire a detective to "go into Oklahoma and get evidence to convict the perpetrators of this murder." The clubwoman offered to activate the federated women's network to "notify every State President and she could in turn notify each club" to raise funds and awareness for investigating Scott's murder and bringing her killers to justice. Nerney assured Anderson that the association wanted to do everything in its power to "prevent these frightful atrocities" and was happy to cooperate with the Colored Women's Clubs in "any practical way." Brinsmade's letter to Anderson echoed Nerney's interest in preventing and punishing lynching but ruled out further investigation and the use of the case as an example of lynching's horrors.[25]

To the NAACP, a thorough investigation of Marie Scott's killing and the publication of the seemingly salacious details of Scott's life would not "result in obtaining public sympathy for the victim." The NAACP's intelligence suggested that Scott's character was "as bad as possible" and that her behavior was "revolting and shocking." This language indicates that some local people believed that Scott might have had a history of scandalous behavior. Furthermore, the NAACP did not believe that Oklahoma was a suitable locale for a thorough investigation because reports suggested that lynchings were as much the "general spirit of lawlessness as race hatred."[26] No subsequent report on the Scott lynching came from the association's initial informants. However, a dispatch arriving from the black settlement of Blackdom, New Mexico, contradicted the earlier reports of Marie Scott's character. Jason Harold Coleman, manager of the settlement, relayed information that Marie's brother had supplied to the Pullman porters who helped smuggle him into Mexico. Scott's brother, who escaped to New Mexico with the assistance of friends, reportedly told the porters that he murdered Pease when he found the men trying to rape Marie. With this new information, the association tried vainly to verify not the facts of Marie Scott's lynching but the matter of her character.[27]

Marie Scott's lynching could have presented the NAACP with a unique opportunity to further debunk the rape-myth theory that filled white southerners' justifications and apologies for lynching. Publishing an exposé on the lynching of a teenage woman would have also allowed the association to drive home the horrors of southern violence and to generate more support for federal legislation. The association's correspondence suggests that Scott's character stopped the organization from "making the world know" about her lynching. To Scott's family, friends, and neighbors, and to other victims of violence, the respectability of her character was probably irrelevant. However, to the fledgling interracial organization, the character of the organization and the people it represented could not be impugned. If the NAACP undertook a public campaign for a victim and her or his character could not withstand the scrutiny of the dominant public spheres, then it risked losing the compassion it needed to change public sentiment about racial violence and the need for federal legislation to end it. The association's leadership continued to canvass the South for reports on violence, to write editorials and pamphlets, and even to give stirring speeches, but the character of victims and what Evelyn Brooks Higginbetham calls the "politics of respectability" remained a determining factor in whether it simply cataloged the deaths or used them as a driving force for reform.[28] To secure support for federal antilynching legislation, the association could not allow anything or anyone to distort the public face of its brand. The association's internal correspondence suggests that the organization routinely found itself in the cross hairs between whites whose endorsement they needed to enact progressive reform and blacks who were marred and horrified by violence.

"Make So Much Noise"

In the 1910s, the NAACP plodded ahead in its scheme to carry out Fortune's plan to "take hold" of racial violence by invoking violations of the Constitution. As a product of Progressive Era reform, the NAACP's strategy for ending lynching mandated relating violence and framing its demands for reform in ways that attracted progressive whites to the cause. The association's social justice mission ranged from changing public sentiment about lynching to lobbying Congress to pass legislation to make lynching a capital crime. Asking white southerners to stop lynching, massacring, and raping black people or driving them off their land was futile. Instead, the NAACP joined activists in the counterpublic sphere by using print culture to relate violence and to publicize local and state authorities' failure to prosecute these gross violations of laws on murder and mobs. As mentioned earlier, the association published a widely circulated pamphlet titled *Thirty Years of Lynching*, in which it provided readers with maps, tables, and chronological lists of lynch sufferers. The NAACP added to this with dozens of exposés, editorials, and reports condemning lynching. The association relied heavily on funds procured by such affiliates as Mary Talbert's Anti-Lynching Crusaders to spread information about its investigations into lynching.[29] It was through this antilynching propaganda that the NAACP leadership marshaled print media to shame some whites and dared them to deny or defend mob violence. In fact, aware that most whites still believed that lynching was a local and state matter and not a federal one, the NAACP also assailed local and state executives for failing to punish perpetrators and to protect known lynching targets from mobs. When governors complained that they were helpless to suppress the will of white citizens, the association offered a solution in the form of a federal antilynching bill.

Although the NAACP found Marie Scott's lynching to be an unsuitable case study for "making the world know," the organization's investigations into lynching produced other cases that were appropriate for re-presenting this violence for the dominant public spheres. The *Crisis* published an exposé on the hanging of a mother and son. A mob hanged Laura Nelson, an African American woman, and her teenage son, L. W., for Laura's alleged murder of deputy sheriff George Loney on May 25, 1911. Loney approached the Nelson home in Bolney, Oklahoma, in pursuit of a man named A. Nelson for alleged larceny. According to newspaper reports, L. W. shot the deputy, but Laura claimed to have done so, possibly hoping that authorities would be more lenient with her than with her son. Still, the mob took Laura and L. W. Nelson from police custody. The men dragged the mother and son six miles to the Canadian River, where they hanged them from the steel bridge spanning the river. Adding to the horrors inflicted on the Nelson family, several members of the mob reportedly sexually assaulted Laura before they killed her and her son. Moreover, photographers captured the aftermath of the killings on film and turned the images into postcards.[30] Afterward, authorities took the bodies to relatives in Okemah for burial, but the family and neighbors refused to assume responsibility, forcing Okfuskee County to arrange and pay for the burials.[31] The lynching of a mother who tried to protect her son, the belief that the Nelsons' background could withstand public scrutiny, and the macabre photographs resulted in the NAACP's publishing an exposé on the killing. Key to the NAACP's publications on the Nelson killings was the photographic images. The association used such examples as this one to build its case for commanding state and federal officials to intervene on black people's behalf.[32]

NAACP Executive Chairman Oscar Garrison Villard penned a letter to Oklahoma governor Lee Cruce in which he questioned the civilization of white Oklahomans and demanded the governor uphold his state's laws on murder by insisting that the perpetrators be brought to justice. Villard's letter elicited a response from Cruce in which the governor defended the reputation of his state and its white citizens. Cruce used lynch supporters' claim that the killing of a police officer incited uncontrollable passions of white residents to lynch the Nelsons. Cruce argued that Oklahoma's laws were "adequate" and its "juries competent, and except in cases of extreme passion, which no law and no civilization can control." "The administration of justice is attended [to] in this State," the governor assured Villard. Cruce suggested that the NAACP play as much of a role in preventing black people's "outrages" against white people as it did protesting the lynchings of black people. Cruce promised to see that "those who are guilty [of killing the Nelsons] are brought to punishment." The association argued that no action had been taken to bring the perpetrators to justice and that black people knew that they could never secure social justice as long as they simply relied on such southern governors as Cruce to uphold the law when they defended lynching by citing the uncontrollable passions of white citizens for personal justice.[33]

The NAACP, by reading newspaper reports, by conducting its own investigations, and by receiving reports from local people, found more cases around which to build a counternarrative on lynching. In December 1918, the association reported that two black youths' attempts to have intimate relationships with two black girls and perhaps to protect the girls from their white employer's sexual exploitation ended with a quadruple lynching in Shubuta, Mississippi. According to a NAACP special investigator's report, local people had described a white dentist named D. E. L. Johnston as a "no-count" alcoholic who lived on his father's farm. Upon meeting and entering into a sexual relationship with twenty-year-old African American Maggie Howze, Johnston induced Maggie and her sixteen-year-old sister, Alma, to live and work on the farm where he lived with his wife and children. Sometime after allegedly impregnating both girls, Johnston hired brothers Andrew and Major Clark, aged fifteen and twenty, respectively. Major Clark and Maggie Howze dated, and the two eventually became engaged to marry. When Johnston learned of their affair, he reportedly ordered Major to leave Maggie alone and threatened to kill him. Residents in town reported that a quarrel ensued and morphed into a physical confrontation when Clark learned that Johnston had probably impregnated both sisters—Maggie was six months along, and Alma was due within weeks.[34]

Johnston died under mysterious circumstances, and authorities arrested the young people. On December 20, when reports surfaced that Major Clark had confessed, white men stormed the Shubuta jail, where authorities had brought the four youths for a preliminary trial. Convincing the deputy sheriff to grant them access to the prisoners, the mob seized and drove the Howze girls and the Clark boys to the bridge that spanned the Chicakasawha River. Members of the mob fastened nooses of joining ropes to the bridge's girders and around the victims' necks, ignoring their protestations of innocence and pleas for mercy. Witnesses testified that Maggie Howze put up the biggest fight. Declaring, "I ain't guilty of killing the doctor and you oughtn't to kill me," Maggie fought and caught herself on the bridge twice. The men beat the young woman, before they threw her over the bridge to her death. The lynchers left the youths' bodies on the bridge as a reminder to local blacks of the penalty for killing white men, no matter their standing in the community.[35]

The NAACP related the Shubuta killings to the public by contradicting the dominant public spheres' representation of Johnston as an upstanding white man. Readers of the New York *Times* would have read an account that reported that authorities had arrested the youths for killing the dentist, that Major confessed, and that a mob killed them. Readers of "The Shubuta Lynchings," in the May 1919 edition of the *Crisis* would have read a different story. Walter White, who went south to investigate the killings, wanted the NAACP's audience to know that black and white people in the community believed Johnston had probably impregnated the Howze sisters and that he attempted to drive away the boys who had sought the girls' affection. His investigation revealed that authorities had arrested the young people and that a white jury would have probably tried and convicted them before sentencing them to death. Instead, white folk in the community rallied to exact "rough justice." Witnesses also testified to White that authorities forced a confession from Clark only after they stripped and placed him astride a vise and applied the device to his testicles. White's interviews with witnesses revealed that some whites, who were outraged at seeing the victims' remains hanging from the bridge, asked black residents to take the victims' bodies down and to make arrangements for their burials. These black Mississippians refused, asserting, "The white folks lynched them and they can cut them down." In refusing to retrieve the victims' bodies, these people showed the limitations of the indignities they would suffer at the hands of whites trying to subjugate them. Their defiance forced authorities to retrieve the bodies for the coroner to examine. The association wanted readers to know the full extent of the white-supremacist depravity in Shubuta and throughout the region. It consulted victims and witnesses and reported its findings to the public as it made its case for federal antilynching legislation when local and state authorities failed to bring lynchers to justice.[36]

The White House and the DOJ retained their position that ending lynching and prosecuting perpetrators was a state matter according to the limits the Constitution placed on the federal government's powers, which the Supreme Court had reinforced. The NAACP's strategy for using the existing legal and judicial system to advance civil rights reforms meant that the leadership appreciated the implications of the state-sovereignty argument against federal antilynching legislation. However, the leadership also recognized the ways that governors, by their refusal to condemn lynching and to demand that law enforcement officers protect prisoners in their custody and that prosecutors indict and convict perpetrators, were complicit in the communal sanctioning of lynching. The association decided to hold accountable state executives for the persistence of lynching within their states' borders. NAACP leaders launched discursive attacks at governors by writing public and private letters asking them to explain the countermeasures they deployed to prevent lynching or the action they took to bring perpetrators to justice.

The association used every weapon in its arsenal to make its point about the states' responsibility for addressing lynching, including the First World War and white Americans' outrage over European atrocities. On March 6, 1918, the NAACP executive secretary, a white progressive named John R. Shillady, characterized the lynching of Jim Lewis, Jim Jones, and William Powell by white farmers for allegedly stealing hogs in Delhi, Louisiana, as "an indefensible attack upon the morale of the nation at a time when justice and law enforcement at home are essential to national prestige abroad." In a published letter to Governor R. G. Pleasant, Shillady remarked that the failure of state officials to check violence put the country "in a most embarrassing and difficult position." The hypocrisy of the nation was exposed, Shillady posited, when the president sought to protest "outrages committed in Belgium or Armenia" but not in America. In a letter to Texas governor W. P. Hobby, published on June 3, 1918, the association wrote that, in a time of war, "it behooves Texas to do everything through its officials to stamp out mob violence." Lynching, Shillady observed, was "a cancerous growth upon the body politic and unless checked will spread as it has done during the orgy of bloodshed" in Texas. The letter ended by asking, "Is Texas going to uphold her laws in this present crisis?" In writing southern governors, the association acknowledged its understanding of the federal stance on extraordinary violence—that handling this violence was a matter for the states. In publishing the letters and even underscoring governors' failure to respond, the NAACP attempted to pressure state executives to uphold existing laws on murder and crime.[37]

The association's response to what it characterized as a lynching spree in Louisiana was representative of its campaign to hold governors responsible for ending lynching by bringing lynchers to justice. In August 1919, the leadership wrote an open letter to Governor Luther E. Hall. Five of the state's twelve lynchings in 1919 occurred between August 5 and 9, with four occurring in Ouachita Parish. Authorities charged Henry Holmes with robbing and murdering S. H. Madden, a white grocer. Before a mob lynched Holmes on August 6, he allegedly implicated Preston Griffon and Charles Hall in the murder. Local authorities tried to protect the prisoners by moving them from the jail to the city hall tower, but the mob found them, snatched the men from the tower, and hanged them in the yard. Two days later, a posse lynched an unidentified man just outside the parish for the alleged murder of a white man. The governor's apparent indifference to the violence and local authorities' failure to arrest and prosecute known perpetrators prompted an NAACP intervention.[38]

Joel E. Spingarn, the white chairman of the NAACP board of directors, tried to reason with Governor Hall by using the state's image as a motivation for action. The association knew, Spingarn assured Hall, that these crimes did not have the approval of the "best of the South" and that the "good name of the State of Louisiana will suffer on account of them." The chairman invoked tensions across the Atlantic, hoping to point out the ways that white Americans' condemnation of violence abroad rang hollow when they tolerated within the nation's borders violence that was "equal in barbarism than any that are reported from the theatre of war in Europe." Spingarn beckoned the governor to show his commitment to ending violence by condemning mob violence publicly and by helping bring to justice the killers of Holmes and the unidentified man. The letter suggested that Hall's commitment to eliminating the violence and to punishing known perpetrators would "restore a condition under which the people may count on the orderly administration of justice."[39] Spingarn's letter to Governor Hall had little impact; lynchings continued throughout Louisiana, with five more occurring in December, and the governor took no action. The association responded to this inaction by continuing to write governors, using their state's image to elicit action, and then making a case for federal antilynching legislation.

Walter F. White also joined the fight to confront white Americans' tolerance of lynching during a time when they condemned violence abroad. He used the lynchings in Shubuta to question the United States' participation in the meeting to establish the League of Nations. "Ten thousand Leagues of Nations may be formed," White declared in his confidential report, and "the leaders of thought throughout the world may talk of democracy until the end of time, but as long as lawless mobs can willfully murder in cold blood citizens of whatever race they may be as the Shubuta mob has done, the world is not a place 'made for democracy' nor can America dare even discuss any principles which remotely relate to democracy or any of its allied terms."[40] White cited the indifference of state executives as the reason why "mobs commit such unspeakable outrages with no fear whatever of any punishment." The association wired Mississippi governor Theodore Bilbo asking him what steps he would take to ensure authorities punished the lynchers of the four black youths. When a reporter from the New Orleans *Picayune* asked the governor for a reply to the NAACP's inquiry, Bilbo retorted, "No, not tonight, but I might give you a little advance information to the effect that I will tell them to go to H——." White inquired, "Can there be any wonder that lynching mobs kill Negroes as they would wild beasts in the most barbaric manner possible, when the governor of the state thus answers the inquiry of other American citizens concerning the punishment of those who are guilty of having perpetrated one of, if not the most damnably barbaric outrages in the history of America?" Having witnessed the violence of the Atlanta riot and interviewed lynchers, victims, and witnesses, White felt especially righteous in condemning governors who executed only the state laws and policies that preserved white supremacy.[41]

Bilbo's response was typical of many reconciliationist governors of the South. Bilbo complained that civil authorities and state officials were "helpless" to suppress the "inevitable" will of white citizens who were determined to lynch. After the burning at the stake of John Hartfield of Ellisville, Mississippi, Bilbo asserted,

> The State has no troops, and if the civil authorities at Ellisville are helpless, the state is equally so. Furthermore, excitement is at such a high pitch throughout south Mississippi that any armed attempt to interfere with the mob would doubtless result in the death of hundreds of persons. The Negro has confessed, says he is ready to die, and nobody can keep the inevitable from happening.[42]

Southern governors clung firmly to the state-sovereignty argument regarding ending mob violence. Southern members of Congress often joined governors in working to prevent the passage of federal antilynching legislation. The NAACP argued that southern state authorities could not have it both ways. If civil authorities were "helpless" and incapable of suppressing white citizens' passion to step outside the law to exact rough justice, then association leadership reasoned that governors would surely welcome federal assistance in upholding the law and in maintaining order. Some governors would not bite, but the NAACP took its argument to the next logical step. It made the case for the need for federal antilynching legislation by crunching the numbers on lynching and by publishing reports in which it underscored the state officials' complicity in allowing the violence to occur and the perpetrators to go unpunished.

In such press releases as "63 Lynched in U.S. in 10 Months," the association published annual report cards that tallied the "red records" of lynching. In 1920, the national office sent telegrams to governors in states where lynchings occurred and asked governors to explain to the American people the steps they had taken to prevent lynching or to "arrest and punish" the perpetrators. The cumulative weight of this strategy put more governors on the defensive.[43] Most state executives responded to these telegrams, which the NAACP released to the wire services, with statements indicating that the good white citizens of their states "deplored" lynching. North Carolina governor Thomas Bickett explained that he was "horror stricken" by the lynching of Ed Roach and offered a $400 reward to bring lynchers to justice and that after every event he called on the solicitor general to investigate. In response to a telegram asking for explanation of the lynching of two black men, Governor Hobby told the press that Texas was "amply able to take care of the situation without suggestions from the outside."[44]

With the Civil War's wounds still festering, white conservatives responded with recalcitrance to even the idea of federal intervention into southern affairs to protect black people from racial violence. Hysteria over the prospect of renewed sectional strife had restrained some white progressives from insisting that the southern officials uphold the letter and spirit of the Constitution. Many of these people understood that lynching, segregation, and disfranchisement contradicted the first principles of the nation's founding and the second principles that emerged from progressive Reconstruction. However, many northerners continued deferring to the white southerners' management of what they called their "Negro problem." When white northern progressives strayed from this agreement, white southern conservatives raised the specter of renewed conflict to put them in check. Civil rights activists had seen conservative whites suppress white progressives' inclinations to intervene on racial violence since Reconstruction. The NAACP understood the veiled threat in both Bilbo's and Hobby's stance, but its leadership felt that such recommendations "from the outside" and questions about the states' capacity to execute their laws were merited. If the southern states were not going to honor black citizens' rights to due process and equal protection, then the association was prepared to call on Congress to uphold its responsibility to enforce the provisions of the Fourteenth Amendment.[45]

The NAACP used information from its investigations and its correspondence with victims and witnesses to drive home the need for federal legislation. It sent members of Congress its reports on lynching, and it petitioned them for meetings to discuss antilynching legislation. Congress responded to this pressure by holding hearings in the summer of 1920. As the NAACP leadership assailed state and federal officials for their failure to address lynching, it continued to collect intelligence on violence, to publish counternarratives to violence, and to lobby for federal legislation. In a document titled "Why a Congressional Investigation of Lynching in the United States?," the association laid out the number of people killed, the general failure of authorities to arrest or prosecute known perpetrators, and the sociopolitical consequences of violence for the nation.[46] To collect and re-present this information, the NAACP had to rely on activists in the enclaves. In May 1919, when the NAACP office received reports of the lynching of James Waters for allegedly assaulting the twelve-year-old daughter of his employer in Dublin, Georgia, Shillady wrote Dr. H. T. Jones and Dublin Branch president G. W. Williams asking for additional information. Local members reported that Waters's actual transgression was serving notice of his departure from the farm. Like other black people who were subjected to violence when they completed labor agreements and were ready to move on, Waters decided to defy white supremacy by advancing his own socioeconomic interests over the interests of his employer. On the day of his departure, Waters's employer had the sheriff arrest him, presumably because Waters owed the white man money. Incited by allegations of the rape, a posse of white men abducted Waters from custody and lynched him, with little protest from the sheriff. In response to this violence, hundreds of blacks prepared to leave Dublin and surrounding areas, joining blacks displaced by violence who settled in urban areas of the South or who decamped to northern cities.[47]

Violence of this nature continued and remained an impetus for black victims and witnesses to depart the South. After a mob of a thousand whites marched twenty-three-year-old Lloyd Clay down a public highway in Vicksburg, Mississippi, and lynched him on May 14, 1919, a similar exodus of black residents occurred. Someone had implicated Clay as the black man who had entered the room of a white woman named Hattie Hudson. As the sheriff watched, "puffing vigorously on a cigar," the mob fell upon Clay; white women and children poured kerosene on the man before someone set him on fire. Bystanders evidently saw women aiming guns at the dying man, and one even accidentally shot and fatally wounded a white onlooker.[48] Afterward, witnesses reported that blacks fled the city "by the scores." When some white planters, merchants, and landlords sought to stop the exodus of the primary source of cheap labor, some defiant blacks were so determined to leave that they walked miles to nearby railroad stations to board trains leaving the region. By the summer's end and in partial response to Red Summer violence, the congealment of African Americans' consciousness about the need for collective reform had occurred. These reformers were poised to make even greater strides toward bringing justice to black mothers such as Mrs. Clay.[49]

The NAACP understood that racial violence embodied the oppressive conditions under which too many blacks lived. Indeed, violence was the issue that struck at the hearts and minds of African Americans and merited the most vigorous effort to eliminate. The leadership was confident that their commitment to social justice for black people would translate into the support of black folk. Within a short period after its establishment, the NAACP had reached into the South's deepest spaces through leaflet campaigns, recruitment meetings, and speaking tours conducted by Mary Talbert, William Pickens, and Addie Hunton. The association expanded its membership base by capitalizing on the spirit of progressive reform. It used the existing sociopolitical networks of local activists to mobilize black folk in their communities. The strategy worked, resulting in a slow increase in membership. As the NAACP rose in stature, it also faced stiff competition from other reformist organizations.[50]

In 1919, the NAACP responded to this pressure by asserting itself among civil rights groups in confronting racial violence and by convening its first national conference on lynching. Conferees wrote and signed what became "An Address to the Nation on Lynching," which called for a congressional investigation into mob violence and for passage of federal antilynching legislation. More than one hundred people signed the address. The association—in accordance with the belief among many white citizens and numerous state and federal officials that lynching was a matter for the states—had initially attempted to persuade state officials to take active steps toward suppressing the violence. But now, under the executive authority of James Weldon Johnson and his assistant, Walter White, the association inaugurated its campaign for a federal remedy for lynching through the Dyer Anti-Lynching Bill. The existence of the legislation suggests that the NAACP had recruited a sufficient number of white opponents of lynching to its efforts to enact federal antilynching legislation. The bill's proponents intended to use the states' apparent disinclination or inability to protect blacks from lynching or to punish known lynchers. The NAACP decided to set in motion its plan to use the due process and equal protection clauses of the Constitution to make mob violence punishable in federal courts. To secure legislation, it needed to convince more whites that lynching embodied a problem for black people and a constitutional problem for the nation that required a federal solution.[51]

NAACP founders sustained Fortune's belief that "the Constitution implied federal policing powers" that were not stated explicitly. The Constitution limited the federal government's power and protected the powers of local and state governments regarding the treatment of their citizens. But the NAACP insisted that federal officials could assert federal authority over the states when local and state officials disregarded the law or failed to fulfill their responsibilities for prosecuting crimes such as murder and mob violence. The association's leadership believed that respect for the rule of these laws could propel Congress into passing antilynching legislation. Activists believed that southern governors' failure to ensure that African Americans who were sought and captured by law enforcement received due process and protection equal to that of white citizens and their failure to bring known lynchers to justice merited federal action.[52]

The NAACP's antilynching pamphlets and reports on violence, its campaign of targeting southern governors, and the threat of federal antilynching legislation elicited better responses from state officials. For example, more state executives responded to reformers' demands that they uphold state laws on lynching and mob violence by trying to prevent lynchings or by playing a more active role in bringing perpetrators to justice. Governor Bickett authorized National Guardsmen from Durham to "shoot straight" into the mob attempting to storm the jail to lynch three black men held for identification in the assault of a white woman. The machine gunners killed one and injured two of the white men who were crowded outside the jail near Graham. Alabama governor Thomas Kilby intervened after the lynching of three black men in late 1919. Although this effort stopped the would-be lynchers in North Carolina and gave pause to those in Alabama, white folk across the region would not have their desire for "rough justice" thwarted so easily.[53]

Indifferent white citizens, law enforcement officers, and state executives were not the association's only challenge during this period. Unlike the Niagara Movement, the NAACP survived the Tuskegee machine's efforts to jettison threats to Washington's campaign of strategic deference to white supremacy. Washington's 1915 death facilitated the association's efforts to solidify its position in the progressive power structure and in the heart of African Americans. At the same time, concerned about the NAACP's seemingly conservative approach of using the existing legal system and crossing the color line by working with whites, A. Phillip Randolph, Cyril Briggs of the African Blood Brotherhood, and William Monroe Trotter and Ida B. Wells-Barnett of the National Equal Rights League (NERL) demanded more aggressive action to counter violence. These ideological tensions had undermined the efforts of earlier organizations to end lynching. The question of whether the same problems would befall the NAACP remained to be seen.[54]

Some interorganizational cooperation existed. This was not difficult because many blacks had memberships in multiple organizations. The NAACP drew heavily from the NACW, the Tuskegee Institute, the Commission of Interracial Cooperation (CIC), and the Federal Council of Churches to weave a nationwide web of blacks and whites who were committed to ending lynching. These organizations established their own branches to protest against lynching. The NACW created a Department for the Suppression of Lynching and Mob Violence, led by Nannie H. Burroughs. Ida B. Wells-Barnett formed the NERL's Antilynching Bureau. These other organizations had the potential to cut in on the NAACP's target constituency and to challenge the association's strategy, which triggered interorganizational strife. For example, the International Uplift League petitioned President Wilson for an executive remedy for lynching. Its campaign and a letter from executive secretary David N. W. Campbell to the NAACP exemplify some of the intraracial strife amid the crusade against racial violence. Campbell assailed the association's annual collection of funds from "an already over-burdened colored race with the same old promise of What we are going to do to stop LYNCHING." In essence, Campbell was accusing the association of taking money from black folk without delivering the reforms it promised. Many activists questioned the slow pace of the association's campaign of legal gradualism. His accusation was one of the least offensive ones hurled at the NAACP by potential competitors, but the association's leaders gave as good as they got to protect their interests.[55]

The NAACP leadership weathered the storm of competition and tried to sidestep the Afro-American League's and the Afro-American Council's problems by cooperating with other organizations in calculated ways. Always scanning the wire services for press coverage of reports of lynching, Brinsmade wrote J. A. D. Lawson of Galveston, Texas, for confirmation when he learned through the Galveston *News* that a group of people had met at the Wesley Tabernacle Methodist Episcopal Church to establish the first antilynching society in the South. Brinsmade's letter suggests that the association's idea of cooperation meant folding the fledgling society into the NAACP's existing efforts. Lawson was unable to locate further information on this meeting and the intended organization; however, Brinsmade's letter indicates the association's fear of allowing another organization to usurp its authority on challenging lynching. When the NAACP could not "cooperate" with other organizations, W. E. B. Du Bois wielded his power as editor of the *Crisis* to attack and to neutralize any threats to the association.[56]

In 1920, the NAACP faced a challenge that was more difficult to address than local antilynching campaigns. Intraracial tensions about the overwhelmingly white executive leadership of the association began to dissipate after the board of directors appointed James W. Johnson to the position of executive secretary. However, the NAACP's new black leadership found itself competing with other civil rights organizations for status as the organization that best served black people's needs. The biggest threat to the association was Marcus Garvey and his Universal Negro Improvement Association. The Booker T. Washington–inspired Jamaican immigrant founded the UNIA in 1914 to create a working-class movement to advance the interests of black people. The UNIA boasted a large membership in comparison to the NAACP. With an emphasis on cultural heritage, racial uplift, and black entrepreneurial endeavors, the UNIA reached into rural and urban spaces, drawing a membership in the millions. Garvey and the UNIA captured the one thing that had eluded the Afro-American League, the Afro-American Council, and even the NAACP: the support of the black folk.[57]

Garvey appealed to black southerners' aspirations for self-determination, their feeling of racial pride, and their belief in the African continent as the place where blacks would secure their racial destiny in ways that the NAACP did not. The UNIA waged nasty public debates with the NAACP leadership over the best strategies and goals for the race. Garveyites' blistering critiques of the NAACP leadership and the antilynching campaign notwithstanding, neither Garvey nor the UNIA offered any real solutions to mob violence, despite the UNIA's large southern membership. Indeed, when Garvey was asked about lynching at the 1922 International Convention, a federal spy that had infiltrated the UNIA reported that Garvey declared that lynching will be stopped only through "industrialism and acquiring high standing in the realms of finance by the Negro on his own initiative, thereby arresting the respect and serious consideration of the world." Garvey may or may not have recognized that he was putting the responsibility for ending lynching on black people rather than on the whites who attacked them or that his statements echoed sentiments expressed by lynchers and their apologists.[58]

Not all of Garvey's supporters agreed with his solution to ending racial violence. Southern delegates and recent transplants to the Northeast and Midwest disagreed with Garvey, according to a Bureau of Investigation (BOI) informant. A black Oklahoman depicted lynching as a form of "temporary insanity," which there was only one way of stopping: the "meeting of a destructive force with an organized force, by fighting fire with fire." One South Carolina delegate, citing black people's prolonged begging, preaching, and praying for legal justice, echoed this sentiment by proclaiming, "If the law cannot protect a man's family and his home, [it] is for Negroes to organize and protect themselves." Concerned with the apparent ignorance of some UNIA leaders of black people's experiences of mob violence, an East St. Louis riot survivor asserted, "Laws against lynching will not save you when an infuriated gang of roughs gets after you. The only way to protect yourself is to keep them off by force."[59] Later this same year, the BOI used the evidence collected by spies to ensnare Garvey for fraudulent use of the mail service to sell stock for his steamship company, the Black Star Line. The dragnet resulted in Garvey's indictment and his 1927 deportation. His arrest, however, did not stop Garvey from continuing his verbal assaults on the NAACP, but the association moved forward.[60]

Once the NAACP survived the challenge of Marcus Garvey and the UNIA, the association went on to work in tandem, but not without conflict, with other civil rights organizations including Randolph's Brotherhood of Sleeping Car Porters and the National Urban League. With many artistically inclined members in the NAACP's ranks, its leaders participated in the congregation of black writers, artists, and performers in what became the New Negro Renaissance. The NAACP incorporated these organizations and individuals into its antilynching campaign. With the bitterness of the debate between the association and the UNIA behind it, the organization could turn its attention to black southerners who were terrorized by violent whites and increasingly receptive to an institutional campaign to end racial violence.[61]

Racial violence persisted despite the association's emerging campaign to enact federal antilynching legislation. The campaign for the Dyer bill and the Red Summer riots, however, put extraordinary violence in the spotlight like never before. The NAACP's 1919 conference jump-started a national discussion on mob violence. At the same time, black and progressive white newspapers, the Tuskegee Institute, and the NAACP plastered the nation with antilynching propaganda. The NAACP also resurrected its annual report cards in which it broadcast the number of lynchings each state had and called on governors and their white citizens to account for the violence. Activists acknowledged the attempts that some governors and law enforcement officials had made to abort lynching and to punish perpetrators, but they argued that the inconsistent state-level opposition to lynching necessitated federal intervention.[62]

Writing Themselves into Consciousness

As the NAACP gained national recognition and more support for its antilynching work at its 1919 conference, black folk reached out directly to the organization. The wartime expansion of the association's membership and its attainment of representative status among civil rights organizations probably made it more appealing to southern blacks who were ready to join it in confronting extraordinary violence. The conference propelled the association's intervention into the antilynching crusades, but 1919 was significant for other reasons. James Weldon Johnson's appointment as the executive secretary of the NAACP changed the demographic profile of the organization's leadership. Quite a few of the white trustees remained, but Johnson's appointment sped the transition of the public face of the association's leadership from white to black.

This transition of leadership coincided with an increase in correspondence to the association from victims and witnesses of racial violence. What sparked the rise in black southerners' letters to the NAACP about lynching is not clear. Population shifts from south to north and from farm to town and city as well as the spread of New Negro consciousness might have given more people the confidence to write the association. Lynching had continued to decline after the century's turn; however, there were still several dozen of reports of lynching each year. Black people's support for making the world "safe for democracy" during the First World War did not make them safe from violent white supremacists at home. Indeed, the violence meted out to black civilians and soldiers during the riots of 1919 intensified African Americans' commitment to combat democracy's violations at home. Whether the demographics of the association's leadership really mattered to black folk is difficult to know. However, Johnson's appointment might have made more black people see the NAACP leadership as more receptive to black folks' concerns about violence.[63]

What is clear from the NAACP's records is that after 1919, more black folk started writing the national office, reporting the violence they endured and witnessed, and asking for guidance and assistance. Correspondence between the association and its local members fill the archival records for before 1919. However, many letters discussing lynching after 1919 came from victims, witnesses, and sometimes members writing on victims' behalf. These letter writers probably learned of the association's efforts to end lynching via the work of local branches, newspaper reports, speaking engagements, and church, lodge, and literary-society meetings. The tone of black folks' letters to the association and the language testifiers used indicate their belief that they might have not only sympathetic supporters in the NAACP but also black people who understood the vernacular history of racial violence and therefore shared their determination to end it. Similar to the women and men who sought out Freedmen's Bureau agents and who testified before Congress, the black people writing the NAACP managed to put into words the violence they experienced and witnessed. And similar to the letters that activists wrote to Presidents Taft and Wilson, many people writing the NAACP after 1919 were attempting to circumvent white supremacists in their local communities.

Letters from black folk reflect a mix of optimism and anxiety about writing the NAACP. These people were struggling to survive white supremacy, and they wanted justice. As people read about the association's campaigns in the *Crisis* or other print culture and heard sermons and speeches about the need for black people to "fight back," the NAACP offered hope to people whom white supremacy shut out of American life and whose lives and interests state and federal officials had failed to protect. However, if the wrong person intercepted a letter to or from the NAACP, then the writer would likely face the worst of local white people's anger. Many letter writers articulated their awareness of the risk of writing to the association. For example, in November 1919, a black resident of Hawkinsville, Georgia, typed a letter to the NAACP on stationery belonging to the Standard Life Insurance Company of Atlanta. Claiming to be a member of the Hawkinsville chapter, the author had probably witnessed the violence and learned of the NAACP through print culture reporting the association's activities and its efforts to lobby for federal legislation. He or she wanted to report the lynching of a black minister named Henry Pickett in Dodge County. The writer explained that on the morning of November 12, two white men went to the home of Pickett, "under the disguise of an officer claiming to have a warrant for him." The white men took Pickett a quarter of a mile from his home and shot him. Explaining, "[I] will not give my name for reasons," the author reported that people in the community knew the killers and could identify one of Pickett's white neighbors as one of the perpetrators. The letter writer offered to furnish additional information so long as the association promised not to publicize information that could direct vengeful whites to her or him.[64]

Though some letter writers wrote promising more information, others supplied all the information needed in their first correspondence. An anonymous letter writer from Eufaula, Alabama, wrote Johnson to let the

NAACP know "that another color[e]d man has been a victim of a mob." The writer supplied Johnson with information on the lynching of Will Freeman. Freeman reportedly owed money to a white man whom the letter writer described as "this old cracker." The white man took Freeman to court; the court ruled in Freeman's favor, drawing the white community's ire. As Will Freeman exited town by train, a posse of "bloodthirsty hoodlums" piled into cars and beat the train to its destination. The men seized "the poor fellow" from the train and drove to a spot five miles outside Eufaula, where they shot him to death and threw his body in the river before the police arrived. The white men claimed that black people had killed Freeman and threw him in the river. Describing the subsequent conditions in Eufaula for black people as "almost hopeless," the letter writer explained that he wanted Johnson to "look into the matter" and to make contact with Governor Thomas E. Kilby. Kilby had spoken publicly against lynching, offered rewards for information leading to the prosecution of lynchers, and even authorized the National Guard to protect prisoners. Still, the writer probably believed that a letter from the NAACP would carry more weight than one from a black citizen. He also might have worried that state and local officials might be able to use the information he supplied about Freeman's lynching to trace the letter back to him. These letters signal black people's readiness to strike back against white supremacy and their awareness of the local and federal surveillance programs that involved monitoring the mail for seditious material or anything that overtly challenged the white power structure. Black radicals had already fallen into the DOJ's dragnet to suppress dissent, and some southern states had initiated campaigns to ban the NAACP. Because of the Red Scare and the nation's reaction to the riots of Red Summer, many African Americans proceeded with caution.[65]

The people writing letters to the NAACP wanted to do their part to end white supremacy, but they also wanted to make sure that the association understood the peril in which they placed their lives for even being associated with the organization. Indeed, letter writers reported violence, as the letter writer from Alabama showed, and some used their letters to testify about other aspects of race relations. Although this writer started his letter with a report on Will Freeman's lynching, he ended the letter by asking Johnson to look into the fact that "the very men who run a round and l[y]nch Negroes are sleeping with color[e]d women." One white man in his neighborhood "makes it by the whole sale" of having sex with black women. No one says a word while "the old crackers just crowds to Negro women's house here." The writer was afraid to intervene on black women's behalf because he was afraid that he and his family "would be burned out and probably killed." He declined to sign his name, citing concerns about reprisal, but he asked Johnson to look into this matter, to report it, and to send the findings to the Montgomery *Advertiser*.[66]

In writing to the NAACP, this man expressed a conviction, common among letter writers, that the civil rights organization could and would honor his request and provide assistance by publicizing the motives behind Freeman's killing and some white men's hypocritical behavior regarding interracial sex. It is not clear whether this Alabaman saw himself communicating with Johnson, black man to black man, about white men's sexual activity with black women or whether he would have written the same type of letter to the NAACP's executive secretary if he had been white. Nonetheless, in writing Johnson and discussing what he did, the letter writer perhaps felt that local newspaper editors and Governor Kilby would dismiss the complaint of a citizen and would-be constituent but that ignoring a full-blown report on the violence from the association might be more difficult.

Other black people penned letters to the NAACP asking it to intercede with state officials. Letter writers' familiarity with the power dynamics in their towns and states often led them to instruct the association on the course of action needed. A writer claiming to be a member from Proctor, Arkansas, wrote Joel Spingarn regarding the discovery of the body of a lynched man near the Brown Plantation. The man's body was so decomposed upon discovery that no one could identify him. According to this letter writer, the kidnapping of people from one locale and the disposal of their bodies in another was "the way they are doing [things] now," so "no one can tell who you are and claim that a [u]nknown party did the act." Further, the body appeared near the location of a recent political meeting. This person wanted Spingarn to know that "time is growing [worse] inst[ea]d of better." If Governor Thomas C. McCrae could not stop violence and the conditions it caused in black life, then the writer urged Spingarn to plead with him to "arm the Negro of the South and tell them any where they find one [lynching] to . . . kill ever[y] thing that look white." Then "[lynching] will be don[e] a way" with, and he could claim responsibility for its end. The author closed the letter with the hope that Spingarn would persuade the governor to protect black people's rights, to enforce the state's existing laws on crime, and, if he would not, then to empower southern blacks to "strai[ght]en out the [white] South" by sanctioning black people's self-defense in the face of lynching.[67]

In the 1920s, shortly after the NAACP's campaign for federal antilynching legislation gained momentum, reports of the practice declined. Much of the mainstream press hailed what many saw as white people's understanding that lynching was wrong. Johnson and other public figures associated the reduction in mob attacks with several factors. First was the national discussion of lynching fed by the Dyer bill, which the House of Representatives passed before it ran up against the southern Democratic phalanx in the Senate. Second was the northward migration of blacks, testing the South's rural and urban industries. Southern planters and industrialists understood, Johnson posited, that lynching must stop "if the best labor the South can get for its plantations and industries is to be retained." Third, with the world beginning to grow smaller, with U.S. ascendancy to superpower status, and Britain's and Germany's admonitions against lynching, this violence compromised Americans' claims of their moral superiority. Despite the apparent decrease in incidents of lynching, whites' continued use of violence to subjugate black southerners motivated the NAACP to continue its push for federal legislation to ensure that black people enjoyed due process and equal protection under the law.[68]

Southern blacks continued to write to the national NAACP in the 1920s, but their refusal to attach their names to any correspondence is revealing of their concerns. These people were comfortable with expressing their deeply held frustrations about racial violence to the association, but they remained suspicious of the organization and its willingness and ability to keep their correspondence confidential. Some of this might have been because postwar letters came more from black folk rather than from those who were already affiliated with the NAACP. For example, a writer from Birmingham, Alabama, wrote the NAACP regarding the lynching of a "race man." According to the author, the black man's death would have gone unknown had it not been for the man's family and neighbors, who saw the man "snatched from his bed by a mob of cruel red necks who infest this part of the land." The letter writer reported that the sixty-year-old Will McBride was walking along the road when he encountered a group of white girls on their way to school. After the encounter, the girls told their teacher that McBride had threatened them. The teacher reported the girls' story to authorities, who took McBride into custody. At the preliminary hearing, the girls confessed that McBride merely frightened them, and the judge released him. The court's ruling of McBride's innocence was not enough to dissuade whites of their need to administer their own style of justice. On July 12, 1923, white men grabbed McBride from bed and drove him up and down the streets, "blowing their horns and yelling, trying to drown the poor man's voice crying for help."[69]

When the letter writer wrote the NAACP, he had the very specific objective of making sure the world knew what happened to Will McBride. The testifier had reason to be worried. The southern white press offered conflicting reports on the episode. One paper reportedly described the man as someone likely hit by an automobile and left for dead, while another cited the coroner's report in describing the incident as "a beating by unknown parties." According to the author, eyewitnesses to the kidnapping were "given orders to leave town." The writer wanted to make sure that the nation learned of McBride's death. He hoped to see it reported "in large letters in some papers right here in Birmingham where they have tried to keep it a secret."[70]

Like some other southern writers, this person wanted to remain anonymous. "I am for my race," the author promised, "but [I] can't publish my name just now." The writer asked the association to pass information on this killing to the Chicago *Defender*. The *Defender* was one of the largest and most popular black newspapers; it took such an aggressive stance on racial violence that many southern cities and towns banned it. Cognizant of the likelihood that a letter addressed to the *Defender* might trigger a local inquiry, this writer asked the association to serve as a go-between; he or she believed that the paper would publish a story on the killing, and "some of the Ku Klux Klan at Adamsville will know that their deeds are known." The NAACP responded by writing Alabama governor W. Edward Brandon and asking him to investigate McBride's death and to punish the murderers; the organization also issued its own press release to inform the nation about McBride's murder and the intimidation of black residents.[71]

The NAACP continued to correspond with black southerners to learn about violence and to help violent whites "know that their deeds are known." The leadership used the basic information it acquired from these testimonies to collect data, to learn of any changes on the ground, and to develop propaganda to make the case for reform. For example, in 1924, assistant secretary Walter White wrote Bert Roddy of Memphis, Tennessee, asking him to confirm a report in the New York *World* of the murder of Walter Bell by a white posse in Tunica, Mississippi. White felt that even though the number of reported lynchings had declined, newspaper accounts of blacks "killed by posses" had become the new euphemism for lynching and asked Roddy for confirmation. When Reverend S. M. Gibbs wrote White of the lynching of a black man at Wildwood, Florida, White sent an inquiry to Bishop John Hurst of the Baltimore chapter of the African Methodist Episcopal Church. Hurst explained that he knew few people in the backwoods town between Ocala and Leesburg, which he described as having few "signs of civilization." Although Hurst knew "reliable" black folk in Ocala, he did not feel comfortable approaching them with questions about the lynching, "for they would take the scare at once and perhaps do us more harm than good." Hurst felt that the only way to investigate the matter was "to have some white detective to undertake it, or some colored man who could easily pass for white." In cases in which no white detective was wanted or needed and family members of victims wanted justice, the NAACP's national office dispatched members to investigate.[72]

The back-and-forth correspondence between the Manhattan office of the NAACP and Blondelle Whaley about the assassination of her brother V. H. "Pink" Whaley illuminates the association's efforts to get justice for the families of lynching victims. Blondelle Whaley testified to a South Carolina NAACP member named H. O. Walker about Pink's killing. Walker relayed to James Weldon Johnson the details leading up to Whaley's killing. Walter White wrote Blondelle, explaining that the national office was "terribly shocked" to hear of Pink's killing and that they were "very eager" to help "in securing the punishment of the murderers" of Blondelle's brother. White promised, "We are giving no publicity whatsoever . . . as we want to do nothing which might in any way jeopardize the situation." White invited Miss Whaley, who was a teacher at Claflin University, to write him "freely and frankly," letting him know "what the exact facts are" and advising the organization if it "can be of any help."[73]

White learned from Blondelle that Pink Whaley was a prominent real estate and cotton broker in St. Matthews. In 1924, he began receiving threats from white men in the community. Whaley's alleged transgression was being wealthy enough to outbid white cotton brokers. Frustrated with Whaley's success, local whites would ignore his bids on their cotton. Pink also held the mortgages on a number of white people's homes. Whaley's financial success and the power it gave him over poor whites engendered great frustration among residents. White men ordered him to leave St. Matthews or die. Whaley owned a lot of real estate and did not want to leave his family and his property, so Whaley and Blondelle traveled to Governor Thomas McLeod's office in Columbia, where they were met by Sheriff Hill. The Whaleys asked for protection, and Hill reportedly asserted that Pink needed it.[74]

According to Blondelle, McLeod told Pink that he could not send the militia to protect him. The governor advised Whaley to "stop what he was doing . . . and look out for himself." The Whaley siblings returned to St. Matthews, but subsequent threats prompted Pink to relocate to Orangeburg. When Whaley returned to St. Matthews to manage his personal and professional obligations, white men lured him from his home and killed him at a railroad station. Blondelle Whaley was anxious to see her brother's murderers brought to justice, so she contacted Walker, who contacted the NAACP. Upon receiving Walker's letter, the association wrote Governor McLeod to confirm his role in the events leading up to Whaley's death in 1925. When Blondelle responded to White's letter, she explained, "I have been extremely nervous and up-set following my brother's . . . murder and have been unable to concentrate my mind on anything." The Whaley family had been busy attempting to deal with Pink's murder and to settle the affairs of his estate. Blondelle explained that her sister-in-law would offer a reward for capturing the killers "when it is felt she can do so with safety." She promised to write again when the family had "reached more definite plans," but no further record of the case exists.[75]

The correspondence between black folk and the NAACP leadership reveals the intersubjectivity that racial violence kindled between testifiers and their NAACP listeners and their shared commitment to ending violence. On July 21, 1926, a local activist named Thomas Jordan, of Philadelphia, Mississippi, wrote a letter to NAACP headquarters. Jordan asked the NAACP leadership to initiate communication with Dave Gaines, a recent survivor of violence in Waynesboro. Jordan, who described himself as a friend of Gaines's, explained that he had been directing his complaints to the DOJ, but with the conditions in the South "growing against us," he felt the NAACP would be more receptive. Jordan included Gaines's letter to him, which explained that when some white men attempted to attack his son, he defended him. Rather than arrest the white men for assault, the sheriff arrested Gaines. Gaines never made it to the jail because law enforcement officials carried him into the woods and handed him over to a white gang. Gaines did not describe what the white men did to him in the woods, but he did explain that he wrote a complaint to Governor Henry Whitfield, who responded that he could do nothing to assist him. Gaines asked Jordan, "Please help me to get [what happened to him] up North." Although the records do not detail what eventually happened, on August 6, 1926, White wrote to Gaines, asking him to write more about his experience with the gang, so the NAACP could judge whether it could offer assistance.[76]

As a testament to the association's growing reputation among black folk, more southerners wrote the NAACP directly to ask for advice and assistance. On June 20, 1926, Gainer Atkins, formerly of Georgia, wrote to ask for assistance in seeking damages for the violence committed against his family in 1922. Atkins explained that a crowd of whites from Washington and Jefferson Counties descended on the family's home on May 22, 1922. Someone accused thirteen-year-old Charlie Atkins of killing a white female postal worker.

According to Gainer, the white man who killed the woman gave Charlie the woman's car afterward to detract attention from his role in the murder. A crowd of whites lynched Charlie, tied Gainer and his wife to a stump, and beat them. Afterward, authorities arrested Atkins and his wife, imprisoning him for twenty-one months and her for seven. When he wrote in 1926, Atkins had relocated to Camden, New Jersey. He requested a recommendation of a lawyer for his suit. "I am getting old," Atkins explained to Walter White, and "miss the sup[p]ort of my family and fe[e]l that the state should help me to b[u]ry this burden." White initially replied that he was "taking the matter up with well informed people in Georgia" and promised to keep Atkins apprised of any developments.[77]

Shortly thereafter, White wrote Atkins directing him to Will Alexander of the CIC. Atkins followed White's advice. However, because Atkins "did not get very much satisfaction," he wrote another letter to White in September 1926. Having secured a lawyer, Atkins begged White to do what he could to investigate the matter. Atkins explained to White, "The loss of my child is worse than all." He wanted to contact federal officials about bringing charges against the state of Georgia for its failure to prosecute members of the mob that killed Charlie and for the loss of his earnings and his home while he and his wife were imprisoned. Atkins asked White to explain to him "just how to get at it, and just who and how to get at the matter" of securing justice for his family. Acknowledging that his lawyer had cleared him and his wife of the crimes for which they were imprisoned, Atkins asked White to "answer soon" because, he said, "my child is gone, he suffered death, my wife suffered for a long time and also myself." Regarding the outcomes for survivors such as Blondelle Whaley, David Gaines, and Gainer Atkins, the trail goes cold.[78]

By the mid-1920s, the NAACP had achieved its status as the representative civil rights organization for African Americans. The correspondence between the NAACP and black southerners continued, which reveals their shared commitment to ending extraordinary violence. This cooperation transcended region and social status and was essential for the antilynching crusade. The association could accomplish little without the direct participation of black folk. This cooperation was essential to sustaining the momentum for civil rights reform when lynching began to wane and the NAACP failed to push Dyer, and subsequent antilynching bills, through both chambers of Congress.

Reports of lynching continued to decline in the 1920s. In 1923, the New York *Times* responded to reports of approximately thirty lynchings with the headline "Last Year Lowest in Lynching." Roughly sixteen lynchings were documented in 1924. The Foreign Press Service, which was distributed throughout Europe, Asia, and Latin America, released a review of American news titled "Lynching on the Decline." With reports of the drop in the number of lynchings occurring, the leadership of the NAACP took full credit. In a speech before the Conference on Inter-Racial Justice, James Weldon Johnson acknowledged that in the past, there had been "sporadic assaults" on lynching, but the first fully orchestrated and financed effort to end violence was conducted by the NAACP. Johnson credited the association's propaganda campaign for cutting at the "main root" of lynching evil, the lie that the "Negro was by nature a rapist and that lynching was meted out solely as punishment for that crime." Although Johnson spoke truthfully about the "systematic" nature of the association's campaign, his statement shows how effective the association had become in assuming credit for the work of its predecessors and the distance the organization had traveled in its campaign against lynching. To claim and maintain its role as the representative organization for black people, such tactics were essential. The means by which it achieved this status reflects the long road to the NAACP's rise through the ranks to become the premier civil rights organization.[79]

The NAACP lobbied Congress for legislation and expended much energy neutralizing its detractors among southern demagogues, state authorities, and federal opponents of legislation. This included publishing annual supplements to its "Thirty Years of Lynching," originally published in 1919. It also included NAACP leaders publishing such new reports and exposés on violence as James Weldon Johnson's *Lynching: A National Disgrace* and "The Practice of Lynching." Antilynching bills and the association's tactics of publicizing its work kept lynching in the public spheres. The association continued its previous efforts to appeal to federal officials to condemn lynching and other forms of extraordinary violence, to publicize violence, and to help victims get justice. For example, when white Tulsans rioted in 1921, killed several hundred blacks, wounded thousands, and sacked the black Greenwood district, the NAACP, which had a local branch, was on hand. The national leadership made sure that Americans learned the contexts and costs of this violence for black Tulsans, most of whom were dispossessed by the destruction. In January 1923, white Floridians responded to reports of a black escaped convict and a white woman's charge of rape by descending on the black enclave in Rosewood. Over several days of terror, the mob killed at least five black people, destroyed black people's homes and businesses, and forced black people to hide in the swamps and flee the town. The association worked directly with victims and spoke on their behalf to make sure the public knew what transpired in Rosewood and how local authorities were already trying to cover it up. In addition to publicizing incidents of violence, the NAACP filed lawsuits on behalf of victims.[80]

The NAACP continued to reach out to federal officials for relief from violence. After whites beat and burned at the stake a black man named G. H. Donaldson near Rocky Ford, Georgia, on March 6, 1925, James Weldon Johnson penned a letter to President Coolidge. Along with his request for Coolidge to urge Congress to pass the Dyer bill, Johnson enclosed a newspaper clipping of the incident as evidence of "the continued inability of the States to apprehend and punish lynchers." The Macon *Telegraph* reported that everyone in the community knew the identity of the lynchers. Governor Cliff Walker even offered a $500 reward for the apprehension of the guilty men, yet Johnson asked Walker to put the resources of his office to greater use by actively investigating the lynching rather than waiting passively for a citizen to come forward. The NAACP used incidents of lynching and riots to insist that the nation's chief executive formally endorse antilynching legislation. Coolidge, like his predecessors, merely offered platitudes on the violence and stood fast to his belief that lynching was a matter for the states. Reacting to this enduring ambivalence, the association linked any increase in the number of lynchings that were reported in newspapers to white southerners' realization that Congress had "no intention" of passing federal antilynching legislation.[81]

Responding to pressure from the NAACP and from other antilynching activists, state executives began to take a more active role in reducing the number of lynchings and identifying and punishing perpetrators, and the mainstream press began condemning lynchers and their apologists among white folk, state officials, and law enforcement officials. The association republished an editorial from the *St. Luke Herald* that observed that a "complete change of sentiment is gradually taking place." "Under the menace of the lifted hammer of a Federal law," the editorial explained, "public sentiment directed from the press and pulpit, and in the rank and file of the masses has changed so completely that one is dumbfounded."[82]

Reports that lynching was dying out, which flowed across the public spheres in the 1920s, did not persuade William Pickens that activists needed to stop their campaign for legislation. Pickens had reason to be concerned. A long-term member of the NAACP, Pickens became director of branches in 1918. This position put him in direct contact with people from enclaves experiencing violence. Pickens's interchange with black folk gave him a different perspective on the violence than what he read in print culture, so he decided to set the record straight. The publication of reports documenting more than a dozen lynchings in 1925 signaled to many Americans that "Judge Lynch," after a lengthy term on the bench of American life, was on his deathbed. State executives, mainstream newspapers, progressive reformers, and even some black newspaper editors began congratulating southern states for the drop in lynching. In December that year, Will Alexander, the white director of the CIC announced that despite Mississippi's high ranking among that year's lynching statistics, he thought the governor and the state were "aroused as never before" to end lynching.[83]

Pickens wanted to make sure that Americans were not being hoodwinked with the print media's hyperbole on the white South's commitment to punishing lynchers and to driving out the violence. He decided to stop what he saw as the victory lap of those who suggested that the campaigns for ending lynching had completed their mission. Pickens saluted public figures for their antilynching work, but he expressed his concern that those who were in less contact with black folk might be buying the "camouflaging propaganda" about the white South's opposition to lynching. Black folk "would not be fooled," Pickens reasoned, because they knew how insincere white southerners were in their statements about punishing perpetrators of violence. Like other reformers, Pickens called attention to the problems still faced by black men and women. Citing a North Carolina case in which a jury gave a six-month sentence to a white man for raping a fourteen-year-old African American girl—a sentence that would have surely been death by mob if the perpetrator had been black and the victim white—Pickens derisively referred to the white southerners' claims of opposing all violence as "a lie."[84]

White southerners were not opposed to rape, Pickens railed: "they are opposed to equality, even legal, political and industrial equality for black people." For every alleged rape of a white woman that ended in a lynching or a formal death sentence for a black man, he argued there were twenty-five cases of "actual rape of colored women [and girls] by white men" that went unpunished. According to Pickens, "The hypocrites know it,—and they know that not one time out of a thousand will any white man there be punished for either lynching a Negro man or raping a Negro woman or girl." Pickens asked black public figures to continue pressing for federal legislation and not to give credit to white southerners, governors, or newspapers until "something is actually done" about lynching and rape. If white southerners were truly committed to ending violence, they "would have supported [the passage] of this bill." The reality for Pickens and other opponents of racial violence was that the public attention to lynching and the campaign for federal legislation was not enough to arrest it.[85]

Conclusion

The lack of enough political support for the Dyer bill to pass both houses of Congress did not stop African Americans' campaigns against racial violence. Black folk, with the assistance of the NAACP, other organizations, and public figures, continued to testify about lynching and to inject their suffering into the public spheres. Victims' and witnesses' insistence on relating and publishing the vernacular history of racial violence; their willingness to proclaim their suffering and to testify about violence; their skillful use of the rhetoric of citizenship, civilization, and constitutionalism in their endeavors to enact federal legislation; and their decision to conjure international criticism and to broadcast the widespread consequences of the nation's toleration of this violence put lynchers and their apologists on the defensive. Crusaders never secured the federal antilynching bill that they wanted. However, the brazen "lynching culture" that rushed to the fore in the 1890s had receded. Newspaper reports indicate that after the 1920s southern whites continued to use violence, but their behavior was appreciably less deadly and certainly less public than that of their predecessors. The continuation of ordinary violence and intermittent reports of an upsurge in lynching kept blacks and their white allies on the alert.[86]

The Great Depression brought a slight increase in reports of lynching, but activists noticed that lynching practically disappeared from the headlines of American newspapers. This did not stop them from crusading to end other forms of racial violence. Readers of black and progressive white print culture in the 1930s would have been much more familiar with fatal beatings, stabbings, and shootings by white posses and gangs than with public hangings and burnings by mobs. In spite of the apparent reduction in extraordinary violence, the campaign to legislate against mob violence and to bring lynchers to justice continued. For example, the Association of Southern Women for the Prevention of Lynching published such bulletins as "Are the Courts to Blame?" After a 1933 lynching in Tuscaloosa, the Southern Commission on the Study of Lynching published a comprehensive investigation titled "The Plight of Tuscaloosa." The CIC produced a pamphlet titled "The Mob Still Rides: A View of the Lynching Record, 1931–1935," to call attention to the persistence of lynching in spite of the dramatic decline.[87]

The continuing violence motivated Walter White to press the NAACP to mount annual campaigns for federal antilynching legislation. Similar to William Pickens, White remained unconvinced that southern whites had abandoned their desire to subjugate blacks violently. Indeed, black folk continued to write White and other members of the association with their testimonies about violence. In 1932, when White succeeded Johnson as the executive secretary of the NAACP, he could finally press his agenda for enacting federal antilynching legislation unhindered. The new secretary saw in the liberal-reformist atmosphere of Franklin Roosevelt's administration, changes in black America, a southern white liberal determination to help end violent resubjugation, and his own successful lobbying for the Dyer bill signs of a potential sea change.[88]

Advocates of federal legislation persevered because, while some hoped that changing white Americans' opinions on lynching was enough to end the practice, many recognized how capricious the opinions of white folks could be. The history and character of white supremacy had revealed that while different levels of intensity existed, racial violence showed no indication of ending of its own accord. Indeed, correspondence from black folk suggested that although the headlines reporting lynching in the 1890s were virtually silent by the mid-1930s, violence continued on a much quieter level. With the Costigan-Wagner bill, Walter White mounted his most comprehensive piece of antilynching legislation to date. The bill made a crack at holding southern states responsible for enforcing their own laws on murder by assuring that citizens enjoyed due process and equal protection under the law. If a state, or its agents, failed or refused to protect prisoners against a mob, then that state would have violated the due process clause, activating federal action. The bill passed the House, and it also bore the distinction among antilynching bills of earning a favorable report from the Senate Judiciary Committee. However, the legislation failed when the Senate refused to pass it. According to "Lynching Goes Underground: A Report on a New Technique," a report used to galvanize support for the bill, black people were still being killed, but their disappearance was "shrouded in mystery, for they are dispatched quietly and without general knowledge."[89]

The NAACP failed to secure federal antilynching legislation, but the association garnered significant public support for its work. Through the antilynching crusade, black activists gained formal experience in mobilizing local people, accessing and working with the political and public spheres, and making politically acceptable arguments for federal action—skills needed for their efforts to transform the nation's social and legal structure regarding black people. Walter White, as a result of his work, established cordial relations with the Harry Truman administration and pressed for civil rights legislation, including an expansion of the federal government's power to protect black people's rights and one last antilynching drive. White's tenacity paid off. In 1947, Truman's President's Committee on Civil Rights (PCCR) gave the association a forum to argue for reforms on segregation, disfranchisement, and lynching. *To Secure These Rights*, the PCCR's report, contained an appreciable number of the NAACP's civil rights initiatives for asserting federal power over the states to protect black people's rights, including a statement urging Congress to make lynching a capital crime. Racist opposition, combined with the pressure from the Cold War, scuttled congressional efforts to implement *To Secure These Rights*.[90]

Years of resisting white supremacy individually converged in the 1910s as black people left the South and reached out of the region for assistance from federal officials and civil rights activists in the Northeast and Midwest. Institution building from the 1880s through the 1920s yielded an extensive organizational base to mobilize black people to press for reform. African Americans, regardless of their geographic location, ideology, and social status, used the national and international context to frame their arguments for ending or prosecuting lynching and securing social justice. These people fulfilled Fortune's goal of "taking hold" of the problem of lynching and "making the world know" the wrongs black people suffered at the hands of whites. By the 1930s, the NAACP's efforts to reach back into the South and its mobilizing strategies broadened its membership and nurtured relationships with local people who experienced or witnessed racial violence.

The reform movement to end lynching did not produce a federal antilynching bill. However, lynching and other forms of extraordinary violence continued to decline for a variety of economic, political, and social reasons, including pressure supplied by the NAACP's antilynching crusade. With lynching on the wane, White still pressed for legislation as a guaranteed protection of black people's lives and rights. Internal records reveal that other leaders, such as NAACP legal counsel Charles Hamilton Houston, resisted White's efforts and argued for using the knowledge they had gained through their campaign of legal gradualism to pursue reform in public policies affecting education, labor, and criminal justice. White continued to push the association to support federal antilynching legislation until he retired. The continuing threat of federal legislation and the nation's growing role on the geopolitical scene put pressure on southern whites and drove down the number of incidents of lynching.

Epilogue

Closer to the Promised Land

In 1954, Walter White sat down to finish writing *How Far the Promised Land?* The antilynching crusader observed how much the United States had changed since his birth during the zenith of lynching, his initiation to extraordinary violence via the Atlanta race riot, and when James Weldon Johnson's recommendation of him to the NAACP's executive board of directors allowed him to serve the antilynching crusade in 1918. Surveying American culture at the dawning of a more coordinated civil rights campaign, White wrote,

> Perhaps the most valuable of all of the evidences of progress can be seen in the fact that now, as I am finishing this book, something seems to have been left out. It would have been impossible a quarter of a century ago . . . to write a book on the status of the American Negro without devoting at least one voluminous chapter to lynching. That such a chapter no longer needs to be included reflects the changing pattern of race relations in the United States.[1]

When White died in 1955, blacks were closer to living without community-sanctioned racial violence and closer to enjoying the full benefits of citizenship. Antilynching crusaders never achieved their goal of passing federal antilynching legislation. However, the recession of lynching made it possible for experienced civil rights activists to build on previous efforts and to develop a broad plan of legal challenges to other forms of extralegal violence and to legal segregation and disfranchisement.[2]

That activists' campaigns against Jim Crow and disfranchisement started to achieve legislatively and judicially measurable success in the 1950s is no accident. They started to gain traction precisely because of the combined efforts of black folk, public figures, and progressive organizations such as the

NAACP to fight the hydra-headed problem of white supremacy. As reformers' efforts began to pay off and the civil rights revolution gained momentum, whites looking to maintain power rose in resistance. In fact, one of the last gasps of the white power structure in the South was to attack blacks who resisted subjugation and who initiated or joined the civil rights campaigns. Whites attacked black veterans who attempted to mobilize their communities. A white mob in Walton County, Georgia, killed two black couples in 1946, performing one of the nation's last mass lynchings. Whites also continued to rape, assault, and murder black people and to firebomb African Americans' churches, homes, and meeting places. In some cases, public sentiment had changed enough to result in some local and state level prosecutions for attacks on black people.[3]

Victims' and witnesses' testimonies, newspaper reports, and speeches of the late nineteenth century had sounded the alarm of the tsunami-like wave of white supremacy. Similarly, the killing of Emmett Till or the four school girls in Birmingham's Sixteenth Street Baptist Church, the torturing of student activists jailed in Nashville, the cutting down of George Lee, Medgar Evers, and Martin Luther King, Jr., and the everyday attacks on other activists were reminders of past violence and harbingers of future violence if racial subjugation went unchallenged. Victims of and witnesses to the violence of the modern civil rights era developed a new vernacular history that they used to make their case for civil rights reform. The nation's increasing receptivity to reform made many Americans react differently to black people's testimonies of violence. Indeed, white conservative southerners' resistance to reform nurtured a belief among more white progressive and moderate citizens and elected officials about the need for a complete transformation in the legal and social structure and for some federal intervention when local and state authorities failed to uphold black people's civil rights. Reading and watching reports of violence or listening to victims' and witnesses' testimonies kindled intersubjectivity among African Americans and their allies and reinforced activists' determination to vanquish violent white supremacy once and for all.[4]

Activists in the civil rights movement tapped into African Americans' tradition of resistance, and they borrowed heavily from the tactics of the earlier campaigns. Veterans of the antilynching crusades intensified their pursuit of legal remedies for civil rights abuses. At the same time, they fortified their efforts to use racial violence to make their case for civil rights reform. Likewise, activists who had inherited the intergenerational costs of violence fought whites by regaining their authority in local governance. They also bore arms to secure their homes and communities and to defend their right to full citizenship. Some local activists pursued tactics of nonviolent direct action, but survivors of violence and people fearful of enduring violence supported the civil rights movement's strategy of nonviolence in theory but in practice rejected nonviolent action in favor of what some called "armed self-reliance."[5]

Another strategy that victims and witnesses employed was continuing the development and sharing of the vernacular history of racial violence. Activists created and participated in new public forums where they testified about and against racial violence and demanded justice and civil rights reform. Survivors of violent attacks and the family members and friends of those killed in campaigns of resistance to the civil rights movement testified about their suffering to public audiences and gave interviews to journalists. Musicians infused protest songs with references to violence they endured or witnessed. Testifiers shared their suffering at mass meetings and protest meetings across the nation. In 1964, the indomitable Fannie Lou Hamer testified before the Credentials Committee at the televised Democratic National Convention about the intimate details of the violence she and fellow activists endured in response to their efforts to vote and to organize people in their community. She concluded her testimony by asking, "Is this America, the land of the free and the home of the brave, where we have to sleep with our telephones off the hooks because our lives be threatened daily, because we want to live as decent human being, in America?" What Hamer and other testifiers shared was a continuing tradition of a "duty to relate" what only black people victimized by racial violence knew and felt about it and to make the nation and world bear witness. For perhaps the first time since Reconstruction, more Americans were willing to listen, and their resounding answer to questions that activists such as Hamer posed was "no."[6]

As the civil rights movement gained momentum, African Americans intensified their efforts to use racial violence to make their case for reform. Activists used the media to re-present racial violence and the ethos tolerating it as fundamentally un-American. The nation and the world were watching, and its citizens could not help but hear, see, and know the wrongs African Americans suffered. The miasma of white supremacy that had hung over the United States continued to linger, but it began to dissipate as more Americans joined civil rights activists in insisting that the nation uphold its moral and legal principles.

Pieces of congressional legislation, presidential executive orders, and judicial decisions are the barometers that sociologists and political scientists often use for judging the success or failure of a social movement.[7] Indeed, the depth and breath of legislation, executive orders, and judicial decisions achieved during the 1950s and 1960s are what make the civil rights movement the quintessential social movement, the one against which other social movements are measured. The African Americans who resisted white supremacy by testifying about and against racial violence and who mobilized to use lynching to embody the horrors of white supremacy and to secure federal action did not achieve any of these standards for success. In fact, a strict adherence to social movement theory might result in some arguments that the antilynching crusade was an unsuccessful reform movement. However, this book has argued that in the process of testifying about racial violence, victims and witnesses created their own history of who they were as a people, and this history is what helped black people mobilize to confront racial violence in the 1910s. While the antilynching crusaders did not achieve their objective of securing federal antilynching legislation, it was through this campaign to end violence that African Americans and their allies learned the skills and strategies they needed for success in future civil rights campaigns. Thus, in the process of mobilizing against violence, these women and men who testified about violence and organized campaigns to resist it laid much of the groundwork that helped African Americans and the nation edge closer to the Promised Land of full citizenship rights and participation in American life.

Notes

NOTES TO THE INTRODUCTION

1. Testimony of James Hicks, November 14, 1871, in *Testimony Taken by the Joint Select Committee to Inquire into the Condition of Affairs in the Late Insurrectionary States: Mississippi*, 891–895 (hereafter Mississippi Klan Testimony). I do not edit or use "*sic*" in my subjects' representations of what they experienced or witnessed, unless modifying the quotation clarifies its meaning.

2. Ibid., 893.

3. Ibid.

4. When I use the term "witnesses" alongside "victims" I mean primary witnesses, people who actually saw violence occur but were not victims, as well as secondary witnesses, people who learned of the violence through conversations with kin or who learned about it from newspapers, public speeches, sermons, and other elements of print culture.

5. Testimony of James Hicks, 893.

6. Christopher R. Waldrep, *African Americans Confront Lynching*, 1, 3.

7. My exploration of black people's testimonies of violence and their efforts to disseminate knowledge about violence as a method for advancing civil rights reform builds on very important scholarship on racial violence after slavery and African Americans' resistance to it. For analysis of this violence, identification of victims, and efforts to unmask perpetrators and understand their motives and actions, see Elsa Barkley Brown, "Imaging Lynching"; W. Fitzhugh Brundage, *Lynching in the New South*; Stewart Tolnay and E. M. Beck, *Festival of Violence*; Gilles Vandal, *Rethinking Southern Violence*; Christopher R. Waldrep, *Many Faces of Judge Lynch*; George C. Wright, *Racial Violence in Kentucky*. For efforts to illuminate the imprint of this violence on American culture and collective memory, see Dora Apel and Shawn Michelle Smith, *Lynching Photographs*; Jacqueline Goldsby, *Spectacular Secret*; James H. Madison, *Lynching in the Heartland*; Jonathan Markovitz, *Legacies of Lynching*; Amy L. Wood, *Lynching and Spectacle*; Shawn Michelle Smith, *Photography on the Color Line*; and Koritha A. Mitchell, *Living with Lynching*. This listing is not comprehensive, but it highlights the scope of this literature.

8. See Allen W. Trelease, *White Terror*; V. P. Franklin, *Black Self-Determination*; Gladys-Marie Fry, *Night Riders in Black Folk History*.

9. See Nell Irvin Painter, "Soul Murder and Slavery"; Robin D. G. Kelley, "We Are Not What We Seem"; Charles M. Payne, *I've Got the Light of Freedom*.

10. Judith Lewis Herman, *Trauma and Recovery*, 1.

11. Mary Prince, *History of Mary Prince*, 200. Dwight McBride also discusses Prince's narrative and what he calls abolitionists' "rhetorical use of experience" to relate their

histories and to educate their audiences about the realities of slavery. See "I Know What a Slave Knows," in Dwight A. McBride, *Impossible Witnesses*, 85–102.

12. Shoshana Felman and Dori Laub, *Testimony*, 5. For analysis of African Americans' "discursive intervention" against lynching, see W. Fitzhugh Brundage, "Roar on the Other Side of Silence."

13. I take the idea of testimony as a form of direct action from Temma Kaplan. See Kaplan, "Reversing the Shame and Gendering the Memory," 180; see also Aldon D. Morris, *Origins of the Civil Rights Movement*. I am also instructed by Walter Johnson's analysis of different types of agency. See "On Agency."

14. Felman and Laub, *Testimony*, 16, 57–58.

15. Testimony of Mary Brown, October 21, 1871, in *Testimony Taken by the Joint Select Committee to Inquire into the Condition of Affairs in the Late Insurrectionary States: Georgia, Volume I*, 375 (hereafter Georgia Klan Testimony).

16. Michael T. Taussig, "Culture of Terror—Space of Death"; Sasanka Perera, "Spirit Possessions and Avenging Ghosts," 164, 159.

17. Edward E. Baptist, "Stol' and Fetched Here," 245. My analysis of the vernacular history is also guided by Michel-Rolph Trouillot's work on the power and the production of history and on who gets to tell their own histories. See Michel-Rolph Trouillot, *Silencing the Past*.

18. See James C. Scott, *Domination and the Arts of Resistance*.

19. See Anne P. Rice, ed., *Witnessing Lynching*.

20. African Americans' collective memory of racial violence suggests that the violence they endured and witnessed existed on a continuum that ranged from the ordinary to the extraordinary. Ordinary violence occurred on a daily basis and became a normalized feature of southern life. White people doled out ordinary violence that was individual and spontaneous and took the form of threats and intimidation, such nonfatal assaults as whipping and beating, and some assaults that ended in death but were not necessarily the perpetrator's intent. This violence rarely made newspaper headlines, but it was an important feature of white people's efforts to resubjugate blacks. When ordinary violence did not yield a submissive black person or a larger black population, these whites shifted to extraordinary violence. Extraordinary violence was often premeditated, but it could be spontaneous. White posses, gangs, and mobs administered extraordinary violence collectively and were more likely to torture, to rape, and to kill their targets. Extraordinary violence included acts of nightriding, lynching, and rioting.

21. Robert B. Stepto, "Narration, Authentication, and Authorial Control," 146–147.

22. For discussion of the impact of violence, beyond its physicality, see Nancy Scheper-Hughes and Philippe Bourgois, "Introduction: Making Sense of Violence," 1–2; McBride, *Impossible Witnesses*, 10–11.

23. Lisa Gring-Pemble has characterized the "pre-genesis" stage of social movements as the individual and collective development of a consciousness that there is an urgent crisis that requires action, that others share that assessment, and that collectively they can enact change. See Gring-Pemble, "Writing Themselves into Consciousness," 42.

24. NAACP, "NAACP Anti-lynching Campaign Chief Cause of Lynching Decline, Says J. W. Johnson," press release, October 25, 1924, Papers of the NAACP, Reel 3, frames 0060, 0075–0076 (hereafter Papers of the NAACP).

25. Trauma theory and social movement theory have been critical to my thinking about African Americans' experiences of and responses to racial violence and to my develop-

ment of this book. Trauma theory is an interdisciplinary field that has its roots in psychology and anthropology, and it involves the examination of the human consequences of violence, namely, the physical and psychological injuries or wounds that humans endure as a result of experiences that range from emotional abuse and physical attacks to war and genocide. See Herman, *Trauma and Recovery*; Arthur Kleinman, Veena Das, Mamphela Ramphele, and Pamela Reynolds, eds., *Violence and Subjectivity*; Arthur Kleinman, Veena Das, and Margaret Lock, eds., *Social Suffering*; Veena Das, Arthur Kleinman, Margaret Lock, Mamphela Ramphele, and Pamela Reynolds, eds., *Remaking a World*; Cathy Caruth, *Unclaimed Experience*. This scholarship has helped me think about how people experience violence, how they make sense of the violence and a world shaped by violence, and if and how they give voice to what happened to them. It was critical to my ability to examine not only the act of testifying about violence but also the language that victims used. Social movement theory is another interdisciplinary field, rooted in sociology and political science, that studies social mobilization, specifically, why, how, where, and when people create or take advantage of political opportunities to advance reform initiatives, to develop mobilizing strategies, and to develop framing mechanisms to justify reform. The literature from this field has informed my understanding of the political contexts in which mobilization occurs or is hindered, how people mobilize resources and sustain that mobilization over time and across space, and how activists strategically use language to frame their calls for different types of social mobilization. Social movement theorists argue there are two types of social movements; reform movements and revolutionary movements. Reform movements have specific but limited goals of reforming one dimension of a larger legal and social structure. Revolutionary movements seek to transform the entire legal and social structure. African Americans living through Redemption and the consolidation of white supremacy in the turn-of-the-century decades wanted a revolutionary movement that transformed the nation. However, social, economic, and political realities constrained their ability to end racial violence. African American activists and their white allies set in motion several related but separate reform movements with limited goals that included ending lynching and legal segregation. The NAACP's antilynching crusade was one such reform movement. Over time, the lessons learned in these reform movements and their successes converged into revolutionary reform. See Doug McAdam, John McCarthy, and Mayer Zald, *Comparative Perspectives on Social Movements*; and Doug McAdam and David A. Snow, eds., *Social Movements*.

26. W. E. B. Du Bois, "The Souls of White Folk," 18.

27. See George Lipsitz, *Life in the Struggle*, 9–1 and 117–144.

28. Painter, "Soul Murder and Slavery."

29. See Jacquelyn Dowd Hall, *Revolt against Chivalry*; Herbert Shapiro, *White Violence and Black Response*; Robert L. Zangrando, *NAACP Crusade against Lynching*; Sandra Gunning, *Race, Rape and Lynching*; Nan Elizabeth Woodruff, *American Congo*; Patricia A. Schechter, *Ida B. Wells-Barnett and American Reform*; Simon Wendt, *Spirit and the Shotgun*; Hannah Rosen, *Terror in the Heart of Freedom*; Danielle L. McGuire, *At the Dark End of the Street*; Waldrep, *African Americans Confront Lynching*.

30. See Jonathan Markovitz, "Antilynching and the Struggle for Meaning," in *Legacies of Lynching*, 1–31; August Meier and John H. Bracey, "The NAACP as a Reform Movement, 1909–1965"; Mary Jane Brown, *Eradicating This Evil*; Crystal N. Feimster, *Southern Horrors*; Patricia A. Sullivan, *Lift Every Voice*; Waldrep, *Many Faces of Judge Lynch*.

31. I refer readers to the biographies, monographs, and narrative accounts of individual activists such as Ida B. Wells-Barnett, Walter F. White, and Jesse Daniel Ames and of major episodes of race riots such as in Memphis, New Orleans, Wilmington, Chicago, Rosewood, and Tulsa.

32. See Bruce E. Baker, *This Mob Will Surely Take My Life*; William D. Carrigan, *Making of a Lynching Culture*; Grace Elizabeth Hale, *Making Whiteness*; Joel Williamson, *Crucible of Race*; C. Vann Woodward, *Strange Career of Jim Crow*.

NOTES TO CHAPTER 1

1. "Resolutions of Petersburg Negroes," produced June 9, 1865, published in New York *Daily Tribune*, June 15, 1865, and republished in Herbert Aptheker, *Documentary History of the Negro People*, 538.

2. W. E. B. Du Bois, *Black Reconstruction in America*; Eric Foner, *Reconstruction*; Donald Nieman, *To Set the Law in Motion*.

3. I use "testimonial interviews" to describe instances when victims and witnesses testified about violence in settings in which officials swore them to tell the truth about what they experienced or witnessed. I take this phrase from Thomas Trezise, "Between History and Psychoanalysis," 23.

4. See Paul A. Cimbala and Randall M. Miller, eds., *Freedmen's Bureau and Reconstruction*.

5. Veena Das and Arthur Kleinman, introduction to *Remaking a World*, 20, 23.

6. Baptist, "Stol' and Fetched Here," 245.

7. Restorative justice is based on the belief that instead of punishing known perpetrators, authorities and communities should focus on trying to heal from past violence. For discussion, see Sherrilyn A. Ifill, *On the Courthouse Lawn*, 120–124.

8. For recent analysis of the riots, see Rosen, *Terror in the Heart of Freedom*.

9. bell hooks, "Homeplace," in *Yearning*, 42, 46–47.

10. Earl Lewis, *In Their Own Interests*, 5. African Americans established their gender roles through "rhetoric, organizational activities, literature, and daily public rituals." For analysis of the models African Americans used to organize their families, their gender roles and conventions, and their homes, see Martin Summers, *Manliness and Its Discontents*, 19–21; and Orlando Patterson, "Broken Bloodlines," in *Rituals of Blood*, 1–168.

11. See Herbert G. Gutman, *Black Family in Slavery and Freedom*; Wilma King, *Stolen Childhood*; Leon Litwack, *Been in the Storm Too Long*.

12. See Gerald David Jaynes, *Branches without Roots*; Peter J. Rachleff, *Black Labor in the South*; Julie Saville, *Work of Reconstruction*; testimony of Richard Pousser, November 14, 1871, *Testimony Taken by the Joint Select Committee to Inquire into the Condition of Affairs in the Late Insurrectionary States: Miscellaneous and Florida*, 277 (hereafter Florida Klan Testimony).

13. See Donald G. Nieman, *Black Freedom/White Violence*.

14. "Miscellaneous Reports and Lists Relating to Murders and Outrages," Bureau of Refugees, Freedmen, and Abandoned Lands, Records of the Assistant Commissioner for the State of Louisiana, National Archives Microfilm Publication M1027, Reel 34, frames 0267–0268 (hereafter Louisiana BRF&AL). For analysis of sexual coercion during slavery and after slavery, see Saidiya V. Hartman, *Scenes of Subjection*; and Merril D. Smith, *Sex without Consent*.

15. "Reports of Outrages and Arrests, June 1866–January 1867," Records of the Assistant Commissioner for the State of North Carolina, National Archives Microfilm Publication M843, Reel 33 (hereafter North Carolina BRF&AL). Please note that this microfilmed set contains no frame numbers. For additional information on violence against freedwomen, see Catherine Clinton, "Bloody Terrain"; and Thavolia Glymph, *Out of the House of Bondage.*

16. Louisiana BRF&AL, frames 0267–0268.

17. William N. Sanders, Galveston, Texas, to Office Sub Asst Comr &c at Sherman, Texas, October 6, 1866, and Albert Bevans to Office Sub Asst Comr at Sherman, October 6, 1866, Records of the Assistant Commissioner for the State of Texas, Bureau of Refugees, Freedmen, and Abandoned Lands, National Archives Microfilm Publication M821, Reel 32 (hereafter Texas BRF&AL), frames 0424, 0422; "Miscellaneous Reports . . . Louisiana, March 9, 1867," Louisiana BRF&AL, frame 0280.

18. See Waldrep, *Many Faces of Judge Lynch*, 67–84.

19. Foner, *Reconstruction*, 228–280. For a recent reexamination of Andrew Johnson's tenure as president, see Annette Gordon-Reed, *Andrew Johnson.*

20. "Address from State Convention of North Carolina Negroes," published in New York *Daily Tribune*, October 7, 1865, and republished in Aptheker, *Documentary History of Negro People*, 542.

21. See Edward C. Royce, *Origins of Southern Sharecropping.*

22. See Thomas Holt, *Black over White*; Elsa Barkley Brown, "To Catch the Vision of Freedom"; Steven Hahn, *Nation under Our Feet.*

23. See George C. Rable, *But There Was No Peace.*

24. Ibid.

25. Trelease, *White Terror.*

26. B. G. Shields to Governor Pease, June 14, 1868, Texas BRF&AL, frames 0816–0818; B. G. Shields to Capt. William E. Oakes, July 11, 1868, Texas BRF&AL, frames 0800–0802.

27. Shields to Oakes.

28. Joe Easley to Hon. M. L. Armstrong, newsprint, "Letter from Hopkins County, Sulphur Springs, July 17, 1868," Texas BRF&AL, frames 0823–0824.

29. "Report of Assaults with the Intent to Murder, Committed upon Freed People in the Division of Albany from January 1st to October 31st 1868," Bureau of Refugees, Freedmen, and Abandoned Lands, Records of the Assistant Commissioner for the State of Georgia, National Archives Microfilm Publication M798, Reel 32 (hereafter Georgia BRF&AL). Please note that the microfilmed files for this record set contain no frame numbers.

30. "Lists of Murders and Other Outrages Reported to Headquarters Bu. R. F. and A. Lands, District of Louisiana during the Month of November 1868," Louisiana BRF&AL, frames 0234–0242.

31. "Report of Murders and Assaults in Thomasville Sub District from January 1st to October 1st 1868" and "Report of the Names of Freed People Who Have Been Murdered or Assaulted with Intent to Kill, within the Sub District of Rome, Georgia, from January 1, 1868 to October 1868," Georgia BRF&AL; "Target 1 Reports of Outrages and Arrests, June 1866–January 1867," North Carolina BRF&AL. For discussion of enslaved women's resistance and some of the violence they faced in the transition from slavery to freedwomen, see Stephanie M. H. Camp, *Closer to Freedom*; Laura F. Edwards, *Gendered Strife and Confusion*; and Glymph, *Out of the House of Bondage.*

32. "Lists of Murders and Other Outrages Reported to Headquarters Bu. R. F. and A. Lands, Fifth Sub-District of Louisiana during the Months of August, September, and October 1868," Louisiana BRF&AL, frames 0330–0331.

33. "Lists of Murders and Other Outrages Reported to Headquarters Bu. R. F. and A. Lands, District of Louisiana during the Month of November 1868," Louisiana BRF&AL, frames 0236, 0239.

34. "Synopsis of Murder &c. Committed in Parishes of Caddo and Bossier September and October 1868," Louisiana BRF&AL, frame 0336; "Lists of Murders and Other Outrages Reported to Headquarters Bu. R. F. and A. Lands, District of Louisiana during the Month of November 1868," Louisiana BRF&AL, frames 0237; "Synopsis of Murder," frame 0336. It mattered little that some whites were working at cross-purposes with planters and farmers who depended on black people's labor.

35. Louisiana BRF&AL, frame 0239.

36. Testimony of Alexander K. Davis, November 6, 1871, Mississippi Klan Testimony, 470–472.

37. For a history of American intelligence, see Rhodri Jeffreys-Jones, *Cloak and Dollar*; Lou Faulkner Williams, *Great South Carolina Ku Klux Klan Trials.*

38. Robert B. Stepto, "Narration, Authentication, and Authorial Control," 147.

39. McBride, *Impossible Witness*, 89.

40. Das and Kleinman, introduction to *Remaking a World*, 4; Stepto, "Narration, Authentication, and Authorial Control," 147.

41. Testimony of Robert Meacham, November 10, 1871, Florida Klan Testimony, 107.

42. Testimony of Emanuel Fortune, November 10, 1871, Florida Klan Testimony, 96. See Michael L. Lanza, *Agrarianism and Reconstruction Politics*; Dylan C. Penningroth, *Claims of Kinfolk.*

43. Testimony of Emanuel Fortune, 100.

44. Testimony of Robert Meacham, 106.

45. Testimony of Abram Colby, October 28, 1871, Georgia Klan Testimony, 702.

46. Testimony of Doc Rountree, November 14, 1871, Florida Klan Testimony, 280, 281. It is possible that some witnesses exaggerated the amount of land they owned because they hoped for restitution. However, many men brought to the hearings paperwork that proved how much land they had acquired.

47. Testimony of Alfred R. Blount, January 7, 1879, *Inquiry into the Alleged Frauds and Violence*, Senate Report 855, in *Senate Reports*, vol. 2, 45th Cong., 3d sess. (1878–1879). A black man with the surname Blount testified at the congressional hearings on the investigations into the 1878 election and into the Exoduster movement. In the first hearings, the man's name is listed as Alfred R. Blount, but in the second hearings, the man's name is listed as A. R. Blount. I believe that this is the same man, so I refer to him throughout the book as Alfred Blount.

48. Fry, *Night Riders in Black Folk History.*

49. See Foner, *Reconstruction*, XVII and 110–118.

50. Testimony of William Coleman, November 6, 1871, Mississippi Klan Testimony, 483.

51. Ibid., 490, 489.

52. Ibid., 486, 484. Nightriders donned disguises, presumably to conceal their identities.

53. For discussion of the slaveholding apparatus's efforts to contain black people on plantations and to police their movements, see Camp, *Closer to Freedom.*

54. Testimony of Emanuel Fortune, November 10, 1871, Florida Klan Testimony, 94; testimony of Joseph Turner, November 11, 1871, Mississippi Klan Testimony, 770–771, 772; testimony of William Coleman, 488.

55. Testimony of Joshua Hairston, November 11, 1871, Mississippi Klan Testimony, 798; testimony of Henry Reed, November 11, 1871, Florida Klan Testimony, 109; testimony of Daniel Lane, October 27, 1871, Georgia Klan Testimony, 653; testimony of Alexander K. Davis, 472.

56. For discussions of domestic captivity and of the awesome power that perpetrators hold over victims during these episodes, see Herman, *Trauma and Recovery*, 74.

57. Testimony of William Coleman, 488.

58. Testimony of Edward Carter, November 8, 1871, Mississippi Klan Testimony, 1085. It is not clear from Carter's testimony whether the assault on his family occurred in 1870 or 1871. Most witnesses testified to violence that happened in 1870 and 1871.

59. Testimony of Mary Brown, October 21, 1871, Georgia Klan Testimony, 375.

60. Testimony of Caroline Benson, October 21, 1871, Georgia Klan Testimony, 387. Several possibilities explain victims' and witnesses' testimonies of multiple explanations for the assaults on them. This might reflect some individuals' inability of to piece together the events of traumatic attacks. However, the different explanations also suggest that all or none of the reasons offered by the white men might have informed their assaults on black people. Some white perpetrators explained their behavior mostly in response to black people's inquiries. The reasons that white men gave for attacking black families might have been legitimate, but as Benson's testimony suggests, some explanations seemed illogical in the face of more pressing evidence such as black people refusing sex, arguing about wages, refusing to vacate land, or competing with white people for land or wages.

61. Testimony of Caroline Smith, October 21, 1871, Georgia Klan Testimony, 402; testimony of Sarah Ann Sturtevant, October 23, 1871, Georgia Klan Testimony, 462–465; testimony of Tilda Walthall, October 21, 1871, Georgia Klan Testimony, 407–408; testimony of Hester Goggin, October 21, 1871, Georgia Klan Testimony, 408–409; testimony of Rena Little, October 21, 1871, Georgia Klan Testimony, 410; testimony of Letitia Little, October 21, 1871, Georgia Klan Testimony, 410–411; the reference to the character of the white woman with whom John Walthall was accused of associating is in testimony of Maria Carter, October 21, 1871, Georgia Klan Testimony, 413.

62. Rosen, *Terror in the Heart of Freedom.*

63. Testimony of Samuel Tutson, November 10, 1871, Florida Klan Testimony, 54–59; testimony of Hannah Tutson, November 10, 1871, Florida Klan Testimony, 59–64, quotations from 60. Rosen offers a detailed description of the ritualized nature of McCrea's assault of Tutson in *Terror in the Heart of Freedom.*

64. Testimony of Hannah Tutson; testimony of Samuel Tutson.

65. Testimony of Hannah Tutson, 61.

66. Testimony of Samuel Tutson.

67. Ibid; testimony of Thomas Allen, October 26, 1871, Georgia Klan Testimony, 607–618.

68. Testimony of Alfred Richardson, July 7, 1871, Georgia Klan Testimony, 2.

69. Testimony of Edward Carter, 1085.

70. In 2004, the United Nations High Commissioner for Refugees established the Inter-Agency Internal Displacement Division in the Office for the Coordination of Humanitarian Affairs to demonstrate the significance of internally displaced people. Amnesty International, "Sudan: Darfur: 'Too Many People Killed for No Reason.'"

71. Because witnesses had little reason to expect financial restitution for their losses and the transcripts of their testimonies do not express any requests for compensation, I believe that we can accept their estimations of the material losses they endured. Local documents such as census records and city/town directories would confirm property ownership among African Americans. Testimony of Alfred Richardson, 9.

72. Testimony of Mary Brown, 375; testimony of Henry Lowther, October 20, 1871, Georgia Klan Testimony, 356–357.

73. Testimony of Joseph Beckwith, November 14, 1871, Mississippi Klan Testimony, 889.

74. See David W. Blight, *Race and Reunion.*

75. Marcelo M. Suarez-Orozco, "The Treatment of Children in the 'Dirty War,'" 384. See Rosen, *Terror in the Heart of Freedom*, for an examination of African Americans' testimony during the Memphis Riot. See also James G. Hollandsworth, *Absolute Massacre.* Analysis of recent incidents of collective violence and war crimes offers additional insight into the meaning, expectation, and importance of testifying for individual and communal healing after violence. See Marcelo M. Suarez-Orozco, "Speaking of the Unspeakable"; Ross, "Speech and Silence," 272.

76. Discoveries in the realm of psychology and violence have illuminated the immediate and delayed symptoms of trauma. See Herman, *From Trauma to Recovery.*

77. Testimony of Alexander K. Davis, 474, 478.

78. Petition from Kentucky Negroes, in Aptheker, *Documentary History of Negro People*, 594.

79. Philip Joseph, "Memorial from Alabama Negroes" to President Grant, circa December 1874, in Aptheker, *Documentary History of the Negro People*, 600–604.

80. Michael Perman, *Road to Redemption*, 78. For discussions on postbellum racial ideology, see Blight, *Race and Reunion*; George M. Fredrickson, *Black Image in the White Minds*; Williamson, *Crucible of Race.*

81. See William Gillette, *Retreat from Reconstruction*; and Heather Cox Richardson, *Death of Reconstruction.*

82. The Court's record of retracting the civil protections developed by progressive Republicans started with the *Slaughter-House Cases* (1873). In this case, the Court decided that the protection of African Americans' civil rights was the responsibility of the individual states and not of the federal government. The Court continued its record of constraining the federal government's ability to protect African Americans' civil rights by individuals and states through the *Civil Rights Cases* (1883) decision, which put the citizenship rights of black southerners in the hands of white southerners, the very people from whom progressive Republicans believed they needed protection. See Robert J. Kaczorowski, *Politics of Judicial Interpretation.*

NOTES TO CHAPTER 2

1. See *Inquiry into the Alleged Frauds in the Late Elections*, Senate Report 855, in *Senate Reports*, vol. 2, 45th Cong., 3d sess. (1878–1879), xiii (hereafter cited as *IALE*, Senate Report 855). Of the 159 witnesses who testified before the committee, 30 were black. It is not always clear which witnesses Congress subpoenaed, which answered a general call, or which appeared because of communication about the committee. Witnesses who held elected office and were featured most prominently in both the attacks and press cover-

age of them and complained to Congress or President Hayes were subpoenaed. Others may have answered a general call or were summoned to testify subsequent to previous testimony. See "Home Rule under Nichols," NY *Times*, January 20, 1879.

2. Letter to Rutherford B. Hayes from Shreveport, Caddo Parish, Louisiana, dated March 10, 1879, read into evidence by Henry Blair during the testimony of Henry Adams, March 13, 1880, Senate Report 693, *Report and Testimony of the Senate Committee of the United States Senate to Investigate the Causes of the Removal of Negroes from the Southern States to the Northern States*, 46th Cong., 2d sess. (1880), 157–158, emphasis in original (hereafter *ICRNSN*, Senate Report 693). There does not appear to be a formal response to this letter. We can learn the social stations and ages of the witnesses from the specific questions asked by the committee related to age, occupation, length of residence in the parishes, and political affiliation.

3. Blight, *Race and Reunion*.

4. For a typed transcript of the original speech, see "The Honorable Frederick Douglass, His Speech on the Color Question," July 5, 1875, Papers of Frederick Douglass in the Library of Congress, Speech, Article and Book File, Manuscript Division, Library of Congress, http://memory.loc.gov/cgi-bin/ampage (accessed July 18, 2011), quotation on p. 4. David W. Blight discusses this speech at length. See Blight, *Race and Reunion*, 2, 98–139; and David W. Blight, "What Will Peace among the Whites Bring?," 396.

5. Blight, *Race and Reunion*, 4, 14.

6. Du Bois, "Souls of White Folk," 24; See Michael Rogin, "The Sword Became a Flashing Vision."

7. See Blight, *Race and Reunion*. Many historians are more familiar with the reconciliation between the North and the South for the period of the early 1900s, when white northerners converted to white southerners' views on Reconstruction and equal rights for African Americans. Scholars can see evidence of a widespread commitment to reconciliation in print culture, public policy, and popular culture. However, I use the term "reconciliation" as it appears in President Hayes's rhetoric during his whistle-stop tour throughout the South. I do so because I believe that the reconciliation between the North and South began during Reconstruction and intensified after its end, a fact with which many blacks were familiar. For additional information on southern life after Reconstruction, see Edward L. Ayers, *Promise of the New South*.

8. I am not suggesting here that the antagonism between whites from the two regions over the war and Reconstruction had dissipated, because it did not. Most historians agree that white northerners might have believed that white southerners were wrong in their efforts to subjugate African Americans by circumventing Reconstruction policies. By 1877, however, white northerners were less invested in intervening in the South's political affairs than they had been during progressive Reconstruction. For discussion of Hayes's policy see, Rayford W. Logan, "The 'Let Alone' Policy of Hayes," in *Negro in American Life and Thought*, 12–36.

9. For a detailed description of the tour, see Logan, *Negro in American Life and Thought*, 21–30, quotations from page 24. See also "The President's Southern Trip," NY *Times*, September 27, 1877, and "An English View of the President's Southern Tour," NY *Times*, September 21, 1877. Dual federalism is the concept that the state governments and the federal governments are equal but sovereign. Under this interpretation, the federal government enjoys the jurisdiction and power expressed explicitly in the Constitution.

10. John Mercer Langston, "The Other Phase of Reconstruction," delivered at Congregational Tabernacle, Jersey City, New Jersey, April 17, 1877 (Washington, DC: Gibson Brothers, 1877), Daniel A. P. Murray Pamphlet Collection, Rare Book and Special Collections Division, Library of Congress, digital ID: lcrbmrp t2203, http://hdl.loc.gov/loc.rbc/lcrbmrp.t2203.

11. Logan, *Negro in American Life and Thought*, 24, 26.

12. Foner, *Reconstruction*; Rable, *But There Was No Peace.*

13. According to reports in the New York *Times*, political violence occurred in Arkansas, Mississippi, and South Carolina. See, for example, "Arkansas Bourbons," NY *Times*, January 4, 1879; and NY *Times*, December 12, 17, 30, 1878. The Teller Committee contemplated trips to all locales but limited their inquiry to South Carolina, Louisiana, and Mississippi, publishing the results for the first two. William Windom and Henry W. Blair, "Report of the Minority," *ICRNSN*, Senate Report 693, xix.

14. Testimony of Alfred Blount, January 7, 1879, *IALE*, Senate Report 855. En route to New Orleans, Blount learned, from people who had learned of his plight and aided his flight, of several plots to assassinate him. Blount warned the committee, "No two or 3, or fifty, can contend with an organization in northern Louisiana who are in opposition to the Republican Party. I will tell you that it will require the U.S. Army." Ibid., 139–140. In both the records for the *IALE* and the *ICRNSN*, a black man with the last name of Blount testifies.

15. See Gail Bederman, *Manliness and Civilization*; and Summers, *Manliness and Its Discontents*; testimony of Alfred Blount.

16. Testimony of Randall McGowan, January 11, 1879, *IALE*, Senate Report 855, 412–413.

17. Ibid. For more of McGowan's account, see "Louisiana under Nichols," NY *Times*, January 27, 1879. The white men's fear indicates that some white men's recognition of the possibilities of restitution so close to the end of Reconstruction. The men could have chosen to kill everyone involved, but they decided that punishing McGowan for his recalcitrance would suffice.

18. Testimony of Duncan C. Smith, January 8, 1879, *IALE*, Senate Report 855, 237; testimony of Alice Blount, January 9, 1879, *IALE*, Senate Report 855, 160; testimony of Duncan C. Smith, 237.

19. Knowing the racial identity or political ideology of either plantation owner is impossible without further research, but both plantations housed enough blacks to maintain a "quarter" from which those fleeing the violence gathered. Testimony of Washington Williams, January 8, 1879, *IALE*, Senate Report 855, 234; Caddo Parish Report and Caledonia Parish Report, *IALE*, Senate Report 855; testimony of Washington Williams.

20. Testimony of Rebecca Ross, January 8, 1879, *IALE*, Senate Report 855, 188–191; testimony of Arthur Fairfax, January 8, 1879, *IALE*, Senate Report 855, 174–177.

21. Testimony of Claiborne Cammon, January 11, 1879, *IALE*, Senate Report 855, 419–422; testimony of Alfred Blount, 132-133.

22. See Franklin, *Black Self-Determination.*

23. Testimony of Claiborne Cammon, January 11, 1879, *IALE*, Senate Report 885, 419–421. For discussions of dulled sensibilities regarding the threat of violence in a culture of terror, see Green, *Fear as a Way of Life*; and Michael T. Taussig, *Nervous System.*

24. Testimony of Alfred Blount; testimony of Robert J. Walker, January 8, 1879, *IALE*, Senate Report 855, 239.

25. Testimony of Washington Williams, *IALE*, Senate Report 885, 230.

26. Testimony of Fleming Branch, January 8, 1879, *IALE*, Senate Report 855, 184–186; testimony of A. J. Bryant, January 16, 1879, *IALE*, Senate Report 855, 335. David Young's white neighbors urged him to leave and cross the river to Mississippi when they learned of impending violence. Randall McGowan went to a Democratic judge for protection and assistance in bringing the men who kidnapped him to justice. Testimony of Henry Adams, March 12, 1880, *ICRNSN*, Senate Report 693, part 2, 111.

27. Testimony of David Young, January 18, 1879, *IALE* Senate Report 855, 371; testimony of Alfred Blount, January 7, 1879, *IALE*, Senate Report 855, 131.

28. White Democrats in South Carolina resorted to poll taxing, ticket rigging, and other means to discourage black voting. Report Summary, *IALE*, Senate Report 855, xlvi.

29. For a comprehensive examination of the Fairfax case, see Nell Irvin Painter's "The Campaign of 1878 in Louisiana," in *Exodusters*, 160–174. The NY *Times* ran reports titled "Home Rule under Nicholls" and "Louisiana under Nicholls" that probed "home rule" under his watch and how Democrats used violence to carry several parishes. See NY *Times*, January 20, 1879, and January 27, 1879.

30. "Letters of Mr. William E. Chandler, Relative to the So-Called Southern Policy of President Hayes, Together with a Letter to Mr. Chandler of Mr. William Lloyd Garrison" (Concord, NH: Monitor and Statesman Office; Washington, DC: Gibson Brothers, 1878), Daniel A. P. Murray Pamphlet Collection, Rare Book and Special Collections Division, Library of Congress, digital ID: lcrbmrp t2001, http://hdl.loc.gov/loc.rbc/lcrbmrp.t2001.

31. Williamson, *Crucible of Race*; W. E. B. Du Bois, "Souls of White Folk," 18.

32. Du Bois, "Souls of White Folk," 24.

33. See Douglas A. Blackmon, *Slavery by Another Name.*

34. See Waldrep, *African Americans Confront Lynching.*

35. Henry Adams, during his testimony, submitted to the committee the newspaper clippings, letters, circulars, and testimonies of violence that he collected over the years, which Republican senators read for the record. Testimony of Henry Adams, 175–213.

36. For discussion of Lincoln's colonization plans, see Eric Foner, *Fiery Trial*; and Philip W. Magness and Sebastian N. Page, *Colonization after Emancipation.*

37. See Michele Mitchell, *Righteous Propagation*; Claude A. Clegg, *Price of Liberty*; Painter, *Exodusters.* Some 153 black and white men testified before the five-man Senate committee established to investigate the exodus. Black women testified in both the 1870–1871 Klan inquiry and the 1878 South Carolina inquiry, and their absence from these investigations is curious but probably explained by the fact that few migrants testified. *ICRNSN*, Senate Report 693, iii. See also Darlene Clark Hine, "Rape and the Inner Lives of Black Women in the Midwest."

38. Suarez-Orozco and scholars of terror recognize collective denial, or "knowing what not to know," as a coping response to violence. For discussion of "the importance of knowing what not to know," see Suarez-Orozco, "Speaking of the Unspeakable," 367. Suarez-Orozco quotes Juan Corradi's phrase "passion for ignorance" on page 368. See testimony of Isaac Bell, April 10, 1880, *ICRNSN*, Senate Report 693, part 3, 193–195. Some migrants such as Philip Brookings testified, but these witnesses appear to have been a group of returnees. See testimony of Philip Brookings, April 8, 1880, *ICRNSN*, Senate Report 693, part 3, 107–111.

39. Painter, *Exodusters.*

40. Testimony of John H. Johnson, *ICRNSN*, Senate Report 693, part 2, 290–291. Johnson's testimony does not identify the woman's name, her homeplace, or the precise location of her killing and that of her child.

41. Ibid., 292–293; testimony of J. W. Wheeler, April 5, 1880, *ICRNSN*, Senate Report 693, part 3, 7.

42. Testimony of H. Ruby, April 22, 1880, *ICRNSN*, Senate Report 693, part 3, 413–433.

43. See testimony of Henry Adams, 101–214. For the catalog of violence that Adams documented as being inflicted primarily on black Louisianans from 1866 through 1876, see pages 192–211, and for affidavits collected, see pages 211–214. Adams's listing of the attack on Washington Douglas, in testimony of Henry Adams, 195.

44. Testimony of Benjamin Singleton, April 17, 1880, *ICRNSN*, Senate Report 693, part 3, 381.

45. Testimony of John H. Johnson, 294; testimony of Benjamin Singleton, 383–384.

46. Testimony of Henry Adams, 105, 141.

47. "A Colored Man," Nashville *Weekly American*, April 3, 1879, and New Orleans *Times*, April 18 and 19, 1879, both quoted in Painter, *Exodusters*, 28–29, 214. Painter discusses African Americans' political debates surrounding the Exoduster movement at length and quotes Pinchback's "small-fry" remarks. See Painter, "Meetings and Conventions in the Wake of the Exodus," in *Exodusters*, 212–224; Pinchback quoted on page 213.

48. The politics of defiance involved black people who were insolent. They questioned white people's claims to authority over their lives, asserted their dignity, and fought back. The defiant bore arms and abetted loved ones targeted by posses, but they also assaulted, robbed, and murdered whites in self-defense or in retaliation. These African Americans demanded justice and redrew the contours of the mainstream press's depictions of racial violence and its causes. Defiant black people also migrated and initiated the campaigns to end violence. These blacks—or those people whose responses brought shame, injury, or embarrassment to whites or impugned a white person's character—were the most likely to experience the violent wrath of whites. At the other end of the spectrum is the politics of deference, which involved black people's strategic decisions to submit to the established white-supremacist racial decorum as a means of self-preservation. This strategic deference involved dissembling, eschewing unnecessary interracial contact, engaging in obsequious behavior in the company of whites, pleading for mercy, and surrendering to law enforcement or a mob. The politics of deference and the politics of defiance reflect my belief that African Americans' agency in the contexts of violence and oppression was more complex than a lot of scholarship acknowledges. African Americans had agency, or a sense of their power to act, but they chose to act on it in ways that were informed by their assessment of the circumstances in which they found themselves being attacked or oppressed. My analysis of what I consider to be the gray zone of African American agency in the contexts of violence and oppression is informed by reading such works as Walter Johnson's "On Agency" and W. Fitzhugh Brundage's "Roar on the Other Side of Silence."

49. Windom and Blair, "Report of the Minority," *ICRNSN*, Senate Report 693, iii–vi, x, xvii, xxv.

50. See Jerry H. Bryant, *"Born in a Mighty Bad Land."*

51. For discussion of some changes in white Americans' thoughts and behaviors regarding African Americans' civil and political rights, see Hale, *Making Whiteness*; and Matthew Frye Jacobson, *Whiteness of a Different Color*.

52. See Rosen, *Terror in the Heart of Freedom*; LeeAnna Keith, *Colfax Massacre*; Charles Lane, *Day Freedom Died.*

53. The New York *Times* and the Chicago *Tribune* covered lynching throughout its existence. The *Tribune* was one of the first news organizations to start compiling lynching statistics and publishing annual reports. Early in the *Times*'s coverage of lynching, it frequently assumed the guilt of lynching victims and only questioned the lawlessness of their deaths. Some of this may be the result of recycling of stories from the Associated Press, which some African American newspaper editors declared the enemy of the Negro. It was not until after the turn of the century, when lynching came under more widespread assault by black and white progressive, that the *Times* changed the tone of its coverage. New York *Age*, August 31, 1889, and September 14, 1889. For some analysis of the newspaper coverage of lynching, including presumptions of innocence or guilt and the compilation of statistics, see Christopher R. Waldrep, "Raw, Quivering Flesh"; and Waldrep, *Many Faces of Judge Lynch.*

54. Chicago *Tribune*, January 14, 1882.

55. See Tera W. Hunter, *"To 'Joy My Freedom."*

56. Arkansas *Weekly Mansion*, August 18, 1883, and July 28, 1883.

57. Arkansas *Weekly Mansion*, October 2, 1883.

58. The five cases composing the decision were the result of incidents occurring in states from New York to California where blacks had been denied access or equal accommodations in spaces such as inns, theaters, and railway cards. "The National Convention," Arkansas *Weekly Mansion*, September 15, 1883.

59. Reprinted from the St. Louis *Globe Democrat* in the *Weekly Mansion*, October 27, 1883; "Our Civil Rights Held Inviolate," and "Civil Rights: Opinions of the Press," *Weekly Mansion*, November 3, 1883. See also Waldrep, *African Americans Confront Lynching.*

60. "Civil Rights: Opinions of the Press," *Weekly Mansion*, November 3, 1883.

61. "Address to the Colored People of Louisville," *Weekly Mansion*, October 27, 1883.

62. Timothy Thomas Fortune, *Black and White*, 29. The Court's decision was the culmination of a series of cases, beginning with the *Slaughter-House Cases* (1873), in which the Court created the precedent that the Fourteenth Amendment did not put all areas of racial discrimination under federal jurisdiction, meaning that only states' violations of nationally recognized privileges merited federal intervention. Those national privileges were limited to the national franchise and travel in the nation's capital. For extended discussion of African Americans' efforts to use the Constitution to defend against white supremacy, see Waldrep, *African Americans Confront Lynching.*

63. See Woodward, *Strange Career of Jim Crow.*

64. Du Bois, "Souls of White Folk," 23.

65. Ibid., 19.

66. See Waldrep, *Many Faces of Judge Lynch.*

67. See David Grimsted, *American Mobbing*; and Michael J. Pfeifer, *Rough Justice.*

68. See "A Negro Hanged to a Tree," NY *Times*, February 5, 1884; "A Lynching Party Balked," NY *Times*, May 21, 1884; "Negroes Leaving Kentucky," NY *Times*, May 26, 1884; "Serious Questions in Georgia," NY *Times*, September 7, 1884. During this period, approximately four people were reportedly lynched for arson, four for assault, two for robbery, seven for burglary, two for quarrels with whites, one for miscegenation, and one for conspiracy against whites.

69. When news coverage of papers such as the New York *Times* or the Chicago *Tribune* specified the race or ethnicity of the victim and alleged perpetrators, with headlines such as "Lynched by Negroes" or "Lynched by His Own Race," they signaled lynching's racialized connotations. I believe that for papers to comment on the race of victims or perpetrators is to say—implicitly or not—that lynching was becoming a form of extralegal violence used exclusively by white men against black people. For examples, see NY *Times*, March 21, 1885, and September 19, 1885. See Pfeifer, *Rough Justice*. For analysis of rape and lynching, see Bruce E. Baker, "Lynch Law Reversed."

70. See Apel and Smith, *Lynching Photographs*; Grace Elizabeth Hale, "Deadly Amusements," in *Making Whiteness*, 199–239; Shawn Michelle Smith, "Spectacles of Whiteness," in *Photography on the Color Line*, 113–145; Amy L. Wood, *Lynching and Spectacle*; and Amy L. Wood, "Lynching Photography and the Visual Production of White Supremacy."

71. For ideas about "good death," specifically, a death that is peaceful and natural, see Drew Gilpin Faust, *This Republic of Suffering*. For information on rise of lynching, see Carrigan, *Making of a Lynching Culture*, 132–161; Patterson, "Feast of Blood," in *Rituals of Blood*, 169–232; "*Free Speech Throttled* in the South," New York *Freeman*, May 29, 1886.

72. "Free Speech Throttled in the South," New York *Freeman*, May 29, 1886.

73. "Eleven Men Slaughtered," NY *Times*, March 19, 1886; New York *Freeman*, January 22, 1887.

74. "Lynching in Maryland," New York *Freeman*, December 3, 1887, and December 10, 1887. Scholars have explored rape in the context of mob violence at length. See Lisa Lindquist Dorr, *White Women, Rape, and the Power of Race in Virginia*; Rosen, *Terror in the Heart of Freedom*; and Diane Miller Sommerville, *Rape and Race in the Nineteenth-Century South*.

75. New York *Freeman*, August 20, 1887; "A Negro Hanged to a Tree," NY *Times*, February 5, 1884; "A Lynching Party Balked," NY *Times*, May 21, 1884; "Negroes Leaving Kentucky," NY *Times*, May 26, 1884; "Serious Questions in Georgia," NY *Times*, September 7, 1884.

76. Reprinted in the "The Lawless South," New York *Age*, June 23, 1888.

77. New York *Freeman*, May 29, 1886, and April 30, 1887.

78. "M. Edward Bryant of Alabama, 1887," *Christian Recorder*, January 19, 1888, in Aptheker, *Documentary History of the Negro People, Volume* 2, 673–674.

79. See Leon Litwack, *Trouble in Mind*.

80. New York *Freeman*, June 4, 1887. See Waldrep, *African Americans Confront Lynching*.

81. New York *Freeman*, June 4, 1887.

82. Ibid.

83. All reprinted in New York *Freeman*, June 25, 1887.

84. Ibid.

85. For African Americans' inward-looking campaigns to address the problems plaguing the race, see Mitchell, *Righteous Propagation*.

86. New York *Freeman*, August 6, 1887.

87. All reprinted in "The New Exodus Project," New York *Age*, February 11, 1888. Not all black papers opposed migration. While questioning the destination of Arkansas, the New York *Age* saw migration as evidence that "the people are becoming more intelligent and manly, and less disposed in consequence to endure injustice of any sort." *Age*, March 30, 1889.

88. Signed by a group of one hundred "uneducated and hardworking" black Montgomerians. Reprinted in Allen W. Jones, "Black Press in the 'New South,'" 220.

89. New York *Freeman*, January 22, 1887.

90. Birmingham *Negro-American*, reprinted in the New York *Age*, June 23, 1888.

91. *Age*, August 18, 1888.

92. *Age*, January 5, 1889.

93. "New Orleans Memorial to the People of the United States," *Louisiana Standard*, August 25, 1888, in *Congressional Record*, 50th Cong., 1st sess. (1887–1888), appendix, 8993–8994, reprinted in Aptheker, *Documentary History of Negro People*, 741–743.

NOTES TO CHAPTER 3

1. "Colored Men Shot," Richmond *Planet*, January 4, 1890.

2. "Eight Negroes Lynched," NY *Times*, December 29, 1889.

3. "Colored Men to Retaliate," "Colored Men Shot," and "Colored Men Aroused," *Planet*, January 4, 1890, and "Barnwell: Detailed List of the Suffering Survivors at the Scene of the Tragedy," *Planet*, March 22, 1890.

4. "Colored Men to Retaliate"; "Colored Men Aroused."

5. Logan developed this concept to describe what he considered to be the lowest point in race relations since the Civil War. See Logan, *Negro in American Life and Thought*; Du Bois, "Souls of White Folk," 18–19.

6. Michele Mitchell's work on black racial destiny after Reconstruction spotlights the ways in which African Americans "turned inward" to alleviate their plight. Black activists politicized features of African Americans' private lives to advance the race. See Mitchell, *Righteous Propagation*. Turning inward was not a passive response to the consolidation; it was a strategic one that helped black people mobilize against white supremacy. See Komatra Chuengsatiansup, "Marginality, Suffering, and Community," 34.

7. Catherine R. Squires expands notions of the multiple public spheres to include African Americans in a way that reflects their unique history, diverse social status, and relationship to the dominant public sphere. See Squires, "Rethinking the Black Public Sphere," 460. I thank Shannon King for recommending this text to help me make better sense of African Americans' different approaches to challenging racial subjugation.

8. See Jane Mansbridge and Aldon D. Morris, eds., *Oppositional Consciousness*.

9. Christopher Waldrep raises compelling questions about whether lynching actually increased or whether newspapers just became more attentive to reporting on the practice. See Waldrep, *Many Faces of Judge Lynch*. The idea of a "lynching culture" is supported by William Carrigan's analysis of the emergence of both lynching and a broad tolerance of the practice by ordinary residents of Central Texas. See Carrigan, *Making of a Lynching Culture*. See also Woodward, *Strange Career of Jim Crow*, for developments of legal segregation, and J. Morgan Kousser, *Shaping of Southern Politics*, for analysis of disfranchisement. For the criminalization of black people's behavior, see Khalil G. Muhammad, *Condemnation of Blackness*.

10. Gail Bederman has noted the ways that gender ideology evolved in the late nineteenth century. See Bederman, *Manliness and Civilization*; and for discussions about evolving ideologies of black manhood, manliness, and masculinity, see Marlon B. Ross, *Manning the Race*; Summers, *Manliness and Its Discontents*.

11. "Raped," Washington *Bee*, January 11, 1890.

12. See Evelyn Brooks Higginbotham, *Righteous Discontent*; Stephanie J. Shaw, *What a Woman Ought to Be and Do.*

13. Rebecca Latimer Felton, "Needs of Farmers' Wives and Daughters," 143–144. For analysis of the impact of media reporting on lynching and rape, see Jacquelyn Dowd Hall, "The Mind That Burns in Each Body"; and Martha Hodes, "Sexualization of Reconstruction Politics."

14. See Deborah Gray White, *Too Heavy a Load.*

15. Although I have no specific evidence that the Vanter party acted in response to the victims' requests for retribution, the rhetoric of rape, defense, and retribution by black people suggests that even if women did not ask for retribution, there was a communal expectation of it. "White Men's Crimes," Richmond *Planet*, March 4, 1893. Bruce E. Baker documents a case of black men's revenge for the rape of a young girl in "Lynch Law Reversed." Darlene Clark Hine has written on the elusiveness of sources on white men's rape of black women. Black women rarely reported these assaults to authorities and did not often use the language of rape to describe sexual violence. See Hine, "Rape and the Inner Lives of Black Women in the Midwest"; and Rosen, *Terror in the Heart of Freedom.* For analysis of correspondence between black folk and state executives, see Wright, *Racial Violence in Kentucky.*

16. For a discussion of the reporting of black women's rape in late-nineteenth-century newspapers, see Gunning, *Rape, Race, and Lynching*; bell hooks, "Continued Devaluation of Black Womanhood"; Gerda Lerner, ed., *Black Women in White America*, 172–193; Markovitz, "Antilynching and the Struggle for Meaning," in *Legacies of Lynching.*

17. Gunning, *Race, Rape, and Lynching.*

18. "A Call for a Southern Conference," Richmond *Planet*, April 5, 1890. The attending delegates' social positions are not clear, but given the culture of uplift existing among the black aspiring class, a significant number of them were likely middle class. Mitchell argues that "aspiring class" more accurately describes the aspirations of black people and their economic realities vis-à-vis the white population than does "middle class." See Mitchell, *Righteous Propagation*, 9.

19. Christopher Waldrep makes a compelling argument for scholarly attentiveness to the dynamic nature of newspaper coverage of lynching. Lynching accounts in the NY *Times* from the late nineteenth century suggest that editors accepted local white communities' interpretation of violent resubjugation, but by the 1910s the *Times*'s editors, along with those of many mainstream papers, began taking a somewhat more critical position on lynching. See Waldrep, *Many Faces of Judge Lynch.*

20. "John E. Bruce's Speech, 1889," in Aptheker, *Documentary History of Negro People*, 656–657. Aptheker notes that the occasion and the location of the speech are not indicated in Bruce's papers at the Schomburg Center for Research on Black Culture.

21. Ibid.

22. "Race Troubles: Reported That All Negroes in Alvin Have Been Ordered to Leave," *Planet*, May 25, 1895.

23. Ibid.

24. "Horrible Butchery," *Planet*, August 15, 1896.

25. The "regulation" of the boy referred to the way southern white opponents to Reconstruction resisted Union military authority and tried to restore prewar social relations.

"Regulations" involved beating and perhaps killing those who violated southern mores. "A Brave Defender," *Planet*, May 23, 1896; "Jack Trice Resists Lynchers," Cleveland *Gazette*, May 30, 1896, in Aptheker, *Documentary History of Negro People*, 795; "White Superiority in Florida," editorial from the Springfield (Massachusetts) *Weekly Republican*, January 19, 1896, in Ralph Ginzburg, ed., *100 Years of Lynching*, 9–10.

26. "White Superiority in Florida," 10.

27. For the concept of "co-ownership" of trauma, see Dori Laub, "Bearing Witness or the Vicissitudes of Listening," in Shoshana Felman and Dori Laub, *Testimony*, 57–58.

28. "Can't Lynching Be Stopped?," Omaha *Afro-American Sentinel*, July 3, 1897, in Aptheker, *Documentary History of Negro People*, 796.

29. Joseph L. Wiley, "Mob Violence: Its Remedy and Its Cures," *Planet*, March 27, 1897.

30. "Horrible Treatment," *Planet*, September 12, 1896.

31. There is no indication that the posse sexually assaulted Mrs. Beavers. Ibid.

32. Ibid.

33. Editorial page, *Planet*, May 25, 1895. For discussions of people being overwhelmed in a crisis, see John Leach, "Why People 'Freeze' in an Emergency"; and John Leach "Cognitive Paralysis in an Emergency."

34. Anna Julia Cooper, *Voice from the South*, 26, 27.

35. See Henry Louis Gates, Jr., and Gene A. Jarrett, eds., *New Negro*. For additional analysis of resistance to white supremacy, see J. Douglas Smith, *Managing White Supremacy*.

36. See Bederman, *Manliness and Civilization*; Ross, *Manning the Race*; Summers, *Manliness and Its Discontents*.

37. "Meant Business," *Planet*, June 1, 1895.

38. Charles A. Lofgren, *Plessy Case*.

39. "The Fast of Protest," NY *Tribune*, May 4, 1899, in Aptheker, *Documentary History of Negro People*, 799–800; "A Few of the Many-Negroes to Save Themselves," Indianapolis *Freeman*, September 30, 1899. For African Americans' fears of race suicide and extermination, see Mitchell, *Righteous Propagation*. "Lynching," Indianapolis *Freeman*, January 20, 1900.

40. "A New Slavery," Indianapolis *Freeman*, September 22, 1900.

41. "What of the Twentieth Century?," Indianapolis *Freeman*, December 29, 1900.

42. See Robert J. Norrell, *Up from History*; Manning Marable, *Black Leadership*; Kevin K. Gaines, *Uplifting the Race*; Mitchell, *Righteous Propagation*.

43. Ida B. Wells-Barnett, "Booker T. Washington and His Critics"; W. E. B. Du Bois, *Souls of Black Folk*; John Edward Bruce, "Blood Red Record: A Review of the Horrible Lynchings and Burning of Negroes, by Civilized White Men in the United States: As Taken from the Records" (Albany, NY: Argus, 1901), Daniel A. P. Murray Pamphlet Collection, Rare Book and Special Collections Division, Library of Congress, digital ID: lcrbmrp t1718, http://hdl.loc.gov/loc.rbc/lcrbmrp.t1718 (accessed July 18, 2011).

44. See Edward L. Ayers, *Vengeance and Justice*; Lawrence M. Friedman, *Crime and Punishment in American History*; Margaret Vandiver, *Lethal Punishment*; Brundage, *Lynching in the New South*.

45. "As Told by an Eyewitness," *Planet*, March 4, 1893.

46. See Gaines, *Uplifting the Race*; White, *Too Heavy a Load*; Waldrep, *African Americans Confront Lynching*; Bederman, *Manliness and Civilization*; Gunning, *Race, Rape, and Lynching*.

47. "With a Rifle in His Hand," *Planet*, August 4, 1900.

48. "Two Pictures," Indianapolis *Freeman*, March 3, 1916. See also Blackmon, *Slavery by Another Name.*

49. "Murdered Them: A Frivolous Excuse for Taking Human Life," *Planet*, September 4, 1897.

50. "The Butchery at New Orleans" and "With a Rifle in His Hand," *Planet*, August 4, 1900. For the most detailed account of the life and death of Robert Charles and the New Orleans riot, see Ida B. Wells, "Mob Rule in New Orleans," in *On Lynchings*; Jacqueline Jones Royster, ed., *Southern Horrors and Other Writings*; and William Ivy Hair, *Carnival of Fury*.

51. "With a Rifle in His Hand"; Brundage, *Lynching in the New South*, 77.

52. Southern whites did work regionally to prevent arms shipments to black southerners, as they did in the days before the 1898 Wilmington massacre and in other locales where the potential for interracial rioting existed. Collaborating whites also policed the cargoes of freight trains to preempt shipment. See H. Leon Prather, Jr., "We Have Taken a City."

53. The governor put the St. Augustine Guard, Gainesville Guard, and the Halifax Rifles of Daytona on guard to go to Jacksonville on immediate notice. "Colored Men Aroused," *Planet*, July 30, 1892.

54. "A 'Remedy' for Lynching," Indianapolis *Freeman*, September 1, 1900.

55. Ibid.; Cooper, *Voice from the South.*

56. "The Colored Women's Convention," Indianapolis *Freeman*, July 27, 1901; Hazel V. Carby, *Reconstructing Womanhood.* For other representations of women's efforts to shape the understanding of or discourse related to violence against women, see Ida B. Wells-Barnett, "Red Record" and "Southern Horrors," in *On Lynchings*; Angelina Weld Grimké, "Rachel"; Mitchell, *Living with Lynching*; Koritha A. Mitchell, "Antilynching Plays"; White, *Too Heavy a Load.*

57. See "The Anti-lynching Crusaders: A Million Women United to Suppress Lynching," Schomburg Center Clipping File, Part I: 1925–1974, Micro-F FSN 002 895-2. Lauren Berlant conceived of the notion of "diva citizenship." Berlant argues that diva citizenship is a type of political activism in which women enter the public spheres from which men historically excluded them. These diva citizens assert themselves and insert their voices into such traditionally male-dominated public spheres as the media, higher education, or electoral politics. They spell out the problems they face as women or problems that have a disproportionate impact on women to educe male sympathy and support for allowing them to play an active role in finding solutions to their problems. See Berlant, *Queen of America Goes to Washington City*, 223–224.

58. "Aged Negro Dies Defending His Race," Indianapolis *Freeman*, August 2, 1919. The mob killed Washington in May 1919, but newspapers were slow to report the killing and only did so after the NAACP published its own account in a pamphlet titled "A Lynching Uncovered by the NAACP" (August 1919), 3–4. The NAACP noted that the Atlanta *Journal-Constitution* did not report the lynching until July 25, 1919, and other newspapers followed suit. The *NY Times* reported "Lynching Kept Secret," scooping the *Journal-Constitution*'s publication by one day and presenting to readers the community's efforts to contain reports of the killing.

59. "The Trouble in Florida," *Planet*, July 3, 1897; "Can't Lynching Be Stopped?," Omaha *Afro-American Sentinel*, July 3, 1897, in Aptheker, *Documentary History of the Negro People*, 796; "Colored Men Aroused," *Planet*, July 30, 1892.

60. For analysis of women's defense of their communities, see Brown, "To Catch a Vision of Freedom"; and Timothy B. Tyson, *Radio Free Dixie*.

61. See David A. Cecelski and Timothy B. Tyson, eds., *Democracy Betrayed*; David Fort Godshalk, *Veiled Visions*; Lane, *Day Freedom Died*; Gregory L. Mixon, *Atlanta Race Riot*; John H. Moore, *Carnival of Blood*; Prather, "We Have Taken a City"; John C. Rodrigue, *Reconstruction in the Cane Fields*.

62. See Charles L. Lumpkins, *American Pogrom*.

63. Squires, "Rethinking the Black Public Sphere," 460; Charles W. Chesnutt to W. E. B. Du Bois, July 27, 1903, in Aptheker, *Documentary History of Negro People*, 848–849.

64. Waldrep makes this case in *African Americans Confront Lynching*, xvi.

65. "Rape, Lynch Negro Mother," Chicago *Defender*, December 18, 1915.

66. See John Edgar Wideman, "Charles Chesnutt and the WPA Narratives."

67. Robert Adger Bowen, "Radicalism and Sedition among the Negroes as Reflected in Their Publications," New York City, July 2, 1919, Federal Surveillance of Afro-Americans, 1917–1925: The First World War, the Red Scare, and Garvey Movement, microfilm collection (hereafter FSAA), Reel 12, frame 0030; "Slaps Woman, Race Riots Takes Place," Indianapolis *Freeman*, November 16, 1918.

68. "How the Negro Feels," Hannibal *Record*, July 18, 1918. See also Mark Ellis, *Race, War, and Surveillance*.

69. *Crisis*, May 1919.

70. The federal government monitored these local reports concerning black people's acquisition of weapons and munitions and found them to be false. See reports on firearm acquisition in FSAA.

71. "White South Fears Colored Uprising," Indianapolis *Freeman*, December 21, 1918; "Mississippi Dreads Negro Uprising," Indianapolis *Freeman*, July 5, 1919. See Steven A. Reich, "Soldiers of Democracy."

72. See Richard C. Cortner, *Mob Intent on Death*; Grif Stockley, *Blood in Their Eye*; Arthur I. Waskow, *From Race Riot to Sit-In*; Lee E. Williams, *Anatomy of Four Race Riots*.

73. Claude McKay, "If We Must Die," 70. See also Winston James, *Holding Aloft the Banner of Ethiopia*.

74. Indianapolis *Freeman*, July 26, 1919. See Waskow, *From Race Riot to Sit-In*. See also William L. Tuttle, "Violence in a 'Heathen' Land."

75. Waskow, *From Race Riot to Sit-In*, 28.

76. Quoted in ibid., 34. As a result of the four days of rioting, there were nine immediate casualties, thirty subsequent ones, and more than 150 injuries from both black and white mob action.

77. "Home Guard Out While Negroes Hold Ground," Indianapolis *Freeman*, July 26, 1919. See FSAA, 1917–1925 reports on chambers of commerce activities; Indianapolis *Freeman*, October 25, 1919.

78. "Reward Offered for Church Burnings," Indianapolis *Freeman*, October 25, 1919. For reports on the Cooper killing and church fires, see "Fatally Wound Wrong Negro," Dublin *Herald*, July 2, 1919; "Lynch Negro, Burn Church," New York *Sun*, August 29, 1919; and "Church Burnings Follow Negro Agitator's Lynching," Chicago *Defender*, September 6, 1919, all reprinted in Ginzburg, *100 Years of Lynching*, 122, 123, 134.

79. For analysis of the shift in newspaper sentiment, see Waldrep, "Raw, Quivering Flesh"; and Waldrep, *Many Faces of Judge Lynch*.

80. James E. Gregg, "Race Riots: Preventive Measures," Hampton Institute Press Service, reprinted in *The Southern Workman*, Papers of the NAACP, Reel 2, frames 0524–0525.

NOTES TO CHAPTER 4

1. "Letter from Some Soldiers to the Finance, War Department," June 2, 1919, FSAA, Reel 14, frame 0429. The Justice Department cataloged letters such as these under subversive activities, but the Bureau of Investigation did not seem to investigate every letter writer; thus, it is difficult to know the specific identities of letter writers.

2. Ibid.

3. Dr. James S. Lennon to President William Howard Taft, December 12, 1911, FSAA, Reel 14, frame 0250, emphasis in original.

4. John F. Monroe to President Woodrow Wilson, December 1916, FSAA, Reel 14, frame 0151.

5. Assistant Attorney General W. R. Harr to James Lennon, December 14, 1911, FSAA, Reel 14, frame 0249.

6. See Mitchell, *Righteous Propagation*; Litwack, *Trouble in Mind*.

7. Squires, "Rethinking the Black Public Sphere, 458; Jane Mansbridge, "Using Power/ Fighting Power," quoted in ibid., 457.

8. African Americans had a long history of initiating contact with federal officials that preceded the 1910s. I limit my focus to letters written during this period to illuminate the institutionalization of reform.

9. Squires, "Rethinking the Black Public Sphere," 458. Earl Lewis discusses the ways that black southerners used segregation to congregate, to vent about violent resubjugation, and over time, to plot their strategies of resistance. See Lewis, *In Their Own Interests*. See also Lipsitz, *Life in the Struggle*, 229; Kelley, "We Are Not What We Seem"; and Scott, *Domination and the Arts of Resistance*.

10. For the efforts of some public figures to do this, see Waldrep, *African Americans Confront Lynching*, 13–38.

11. For analysis of the rhetorical bridges that can emerge from epistolary practices, see Gring-Pemble, "Writing Themselves into Consciousness." W. Fitzhugh Brundage shows the myriad ways that black people resisted racial violence. He notes that they did not always make loud and grand gestures because doing so could endanger their lives. Many of them practiced what Russian philosopher Mikhail Bakhtin called a "double voiced discourse." See Brundage, "Roar on the Other Side of Silence"; and Mikhail M. Bakhtin, *Dialogic Imagination*. Walter Johnson provided a needed corrective for scholarly examinations of the different types of agency African Americans exhibited in the face of the oppression of slavery and, by extension, the subjugation of the Jim Crow era. See Johnson, "On Agency." Ida B. Wells led the first wave of antilynching crusades in the 1890s. See also Mia Bay, *To Tell the Truth Freely*; Paula Giddings, *Sword among Lions*; Schechter, *Ida B. Wells-Barnett and American Reform*.

12. "Lynching Statistics by Year and Race," Tuskegee Institute, presented in Zangrando, *NAACP Crusade against Lynching*, 6–7.

13. Christopher Waldrep addresses African Americans' systematic approaches to racial violence. He argues that after Reconstruction, blacks invoked the Constitution and the law as a source for demanding civil rights and protection from violence. See Waldrep, *African Americans Confront Lynching*.

14. Organized political letter-writing campaigns do not appear in black newspapers during this time. However, it is not difficult to imagine how or why African Americans came to write federal officials for relief from violent resubjugation. Black churches, organizations, newspapers, political clubs, and literary societies had engaged in activities that politicized their communities since emancipation. Formal and informal letter-writing campaigns might have been part of their strategy, but the length, content, and tone of the letters and the authors' failure to cite campaigns (or other writers) as prompting their letters suggests a more individualized than institutionalized initiative at work in the prewar years. The addressing of letters to the "White House," "The President of the United States," and the "Federal Government" instead of directly to the Department of Justice—the arbiter of legal matters—affirms the absence of a formally organized campaign. Some letters written directly to the DOJ appear to be subsequent to having received a response from the DOJ as opposed to the president. "Negro Pilgrimage to Stop Lynching," NY *Times*, December 13, 1911. Newspaper reports do not confirm that the planned procession occurred.

15. The practice of letter writing has a long history in the United States. See William Merrill Decker, *Epistolary Practices*; and Leila A. Sussman, *Dear FDR*.

16. Through formal education, literary societies, itinerant booksellers, newspapers, church activities, and public readings, black southerners gained varying degrees of literacy. The 1880 U.S. Census reported 70 percent of the black population as illiterate; the illiteracy rate dropped to 30 percent by the 1910 Census. Elizabeth McHenry, *Forgotten Readers*, 4.

17. E. T. Washington to the Department of Justice, December 11, 1911, FSAA, Reel 14, frame 0241.

18. Aaron Johnson to Attorney General George Wickersham, January 8, 1912, FSAA, Reel 14, frames 0288–0289. Tracing the outcomes of letter writers' requests for restitution is difficult unless the DOJ took the formal action of investigating the concerns brought to them. The DOJ took action in one case involving the alleged lynching of a returned soldier. The investigation proved that the lynched man was not a veteran, prompting the DOJ to drop the case.

19. Correspondence between black southerners and their governors is likely found within the personal papers of governors. The massive work that this research would entail and the fact that most correspondence with state authorities left African Americans' search for justice unfulfilled led to my decision to exclude these from my analysis.

20. Royster, *Southern Horrors*; Bay, *To Tell the Truth Freely*; Schechter, *Ida B. Wells-Barnett and American Reform*.

21. E. D. Rosewood to President William Howard Taft, January 24, 1912, FSAA, Reel 14, frames 0221–0222; "Lynch Four Negroes," NY *Times*, January 23, 1912; Assistant Attorney General W. R. Harr to E. D. Rosewood, February 3, 1912, FSAA, Reel 14, frame 0221.

In *Hodges v. United States*—a peonage case from Arkansas that involved eight black workers' complaints about working under white intimidation—the Court held that the white plaintiffs, James A. Davis and James O. Hodges, likely used armed intimidation to coerce labor out of their employees. Yet based on the precedent of Fourteenth Amendment cases, the Court determined that the violation of citizens' rights by *other citizens* was a state matter—rather than a federal one—despite the "due process" clause. In cases in which private individuals violated the rights of other citizens, the state's authority prevailed.

22. See Decker, *Epistolary Practices*; and Sussman, *Dear FDR*.

23. Mitchell, *Righteous Propagation*, 9.

24. Mrs. M. Cravath Simpson to President William Taft, January 1, 1912, FSAA, Reel 14, frame 0230. See also William Howard Taft, "President Taft denounces lynching."

25. I have looked for additional information supporting the existence of the Anti-Lynching Society of Afro-American Women but to date I have found no specific reference to the organization and its activities. Thus, I am unable to provide information on its origins and demise. I suspect that the society was a faction of the Northeastern Federation of Women's Clubs, as Simpson was a prominent member from at least 1903 to 1918. What I do know from a report in the Cleveland *Gazette* is that as early as 1903, she excited crowds with passionate speeches as a member of the Women's Era Club of Boston. In one speech, Simpson argued that the "barbarism of these so-called civilized lynchers is analogous to the atrocities of their forefathers who had ships plying the African Oceans laden with thousands of human souls to sell into bondage. Their revolting heinousness, and the crimes of today might give to the devil wonder and cause hell to reconsider its likeliness." Moreover, a subsequent letter from Simpson to the Bureau of Information reveals that by 1918 she had become chairwoman of the Northeastern Federation of Women's Clubs. "Crime of Mobs," Cleveland *Gazette*, August 23, 1903. "Mrs. M. Cravath Simpson, President of the Anti-Lynching Society of Afro-American Women: Organized to Publicly Protest against Man's Inhumanity to Man," January 1, 1912, FSAA, Reel 14, frame 0230; inaugural address of William Howard Taft, March 4, 1909, available online at the Yale Avalon Project, http://avalon.law.yale.edu/20th_century/taft.asp (accessed May 5, 2011). For more on women's activism, see Feimster, *Southern Horrors*.

26. Brown argues that after slavery ended, African Americans saw suffrage as belonging to the entire community. Thus, although only black men gained the franchise during Reconstruction, black women participated in the black public sphere by attending political rallies and sharing their opinions with delegates and legislators. After Reconstruction, black men started to limit black women's participation in the black public sphere. See Brown, "To Catch the Vision of Freedom"; Elsa Barkley Brown, "Negotiating and Transforming the Public Sphere," 107–111; Higginbotham, *Righteous Discontent*; Shaw, *What a Woman Ought to Be and Do*; White, *Too Heavy a Load*; Glenda E. Gilmore, *Gender and Jim Crow*; Paula Giddings, *When and Where I Enter*.

27. See Mitchell, *Righteous Propagation*; Gaines, *Uplifting the Race*; Hall, *Revolt against Chivalry*; Feimster, *Southern Horrors*.

28. See Bederman, *Manliness and Civilization*.

29. Richard Wright, "Ethics of Living Jim Crow"; Brundage, "Roar on the Other Side of Silence," 274. For additional discussion of black people's representations of Jim Crow and of white people's attitudes and behaviors, see Mia Bay, *White Image in the Black Mind*; and Neil R. McMillen, *Dark Journey*.

30. Rosewood to Taft; Jason M. Smith (Atlanta, Georgia) to U.S. Attorney General George Wickersham, February 22, 1912, FSAA, Reel 14, frames 0216–0218; Washington to Department of Justice. The literary scholar Lauren Berlant argues that the use of an innocent child or woman to embody a model citizen is a widespread strategy. Even though this individual is recognized as a citizen who lacks a certain degree of political rights, his or her helplessness is intended to educe a protective impulse from the audiences. See Berlant, "Theory of Infantile Citizenship," in *Queen of America Goes to Washington City*.

31. C. P. Covington to Attorney General Wickersham, December 21, 1911, FSAA, Reel 14, frame 0235; J. B. Harper to President William Howard Taft, October 25, 1911, FSAA, Reel 14, frame 0257; Hastings Howard to President William Howard Taft, October 5, 1911, FSAA, Reel 14, frame 0258.

32. Rosewood to Taft.

33. Simpson to Taft; Gring-Pemble, "Writing Themselves into Consciousness"; Rosewood to Taft.

34. To promote order and moralism at home, the nation's leaders could not afford to incur international criticism by allowing the lynching of foreign nationals to go unpunished. Fear of international commentary on lynching occupied the minds of many American presidents. It was concern for the appearance of domestic disorder that motivated Wilson to speak publicly. See United States, Department of State, "Correspondence in Relation to the Killing of Prisoners in New Orleans on March 14, 1891" (Washington, DC: Government Printing Office, 1891); Clive Webb, "Lynching of Sicilian Immigrants in the American South"; William D. Carrigan and Clive Webb, "Lynching of Persons of Mexican Origin or Descent."

35. W. A. Briggs to President William Howard Taft, June 2, 1912, FSAA, Reel 14, frame 0147; Assistant Attorney General W. R. Harr to Governor Charles Henderson, June 12, 1912, FSAA, Reel 14, frame 0173. One might rightfully ask whether a presidential admonition against white terror would have had any effect. We know from the continuance of violence after public denouncements of presidents such as William McKinley, Theodore Roosevelt, Taft, and Woodrow Wilson that they did not. Yet this likely has more to do with the fact that none of them made these statements with the force of a credible threat of intervention, which as we saw during the 1950s and 1960s, made all the difference. See Schechter, *Ida B. Wells-Barnett and American Reform*, 122.

36. African Americans devoured political writing in the form of treaties, appeals, and journalistic materials that would have given some black readers access to nationally espoused political ideas and to the function of black citizenship. This access undoubtedly equipped them with a general understanding of the meaning of democracy and what it meant to act like citizens. Their access to diverse texts and the immediate circumstances many black southerners lived would have illuminated the contradiction more than any formal gestures of the black intelligentsia could have. McHenry, *Forgotten Readers*. See also Waldrep, *African Americans Confront Lynching*.

37. See Litwack, *Trouble in Mind*; Wood, *Lynching and Spectacle*.

38. Francis H. Warren to President Woodrow Wilson, June 18, 1913, FSAA, Reel 14, frame 0160.

39. J. B. Winston to President Woodrow Wilson, March 13, 1915, FSAA, Reel 14, frame 0154. Winston cited a Byhalla, Mississippi, lynching on November 25, 1914, when a mob lynched Mr. and Mrs. Fred Sullivan for alleged arson. He reported the mob of Shreveport, Louisiana, that lynched seventeen-year-old Lewis Watkins by tying him to a stake, throwing gasoline on him, and setting him afire on December 18, 1914. Winston also cited the January 1915 episodes in Monticello, Georgia, where a mob snatched from jail a father, a son, and two daughters who had been imprisoned for moonshining and then lynched them, and in Gulfport, Mississippi, where Edward Johnson was taken from authorities and shot to death. Assistant Attorney General Ernest Knowles responded, "By reference from the President, the Department is in receipt of your letter . . . in which

you direct attention to various lynchings of colored people. In reply you are advised that these crimes are punishable in the State courts, and so far as appears Federal authorities are without jurisdiction in these premises." Assistant Attorney General Ernest Knowles to J. B. Winston, March 18, 1915, FSAA, Reel 14, frame 0153. For press coverage of the Monticello lynchings, see "Southern Chivalry Rebuked by Lynching," Indianapolis *Freeman*, January 23, 1915; and "Judge Park Raps Lynching," Indianapolis *Freeman*, February 27, 1915. See also "Dan Barber Lynching at Monticello, Georgia," Papers of the NAACP, Reel 1, frames 0473–0474.

40. The lynchings of Washington and Crawford were two of the most public expressions of violent resubjugation in the years before the war. Jesse Washington was charged with the assault and murder of the wife of his white employer and received a sham of a trial in a courthouse crammed with fifteen hundred angry whites. The white jury convicted Washington swiftly and issued a support of his execution before the mob dragged him from the courtroom to a tree and erected a splendid pyre over which they burned him before mutilating his body before a crowd of ten thousand that swarmed to collect the victim's body parts. Photographers were on the scene to capture the event; the photos were displayed in newspapers nationwide and turned into postcards sold in stores and by itinerant sellers throughout the South. By 1916, Anthony P. Crawford had managed to overcome his enslaved heritage by becoming a prominent landowner in Abbeville, South Carolina. This type of black success infuriated whites. When enterprising blacks dared argue with white men, as Crawford did, it initiated the ritual of violence that plagued the South. The white clerk with whom Crawford argued wielded an ax at Crawford, who tried to defend himself but was arrested. Upon his bail release, a white mob assaulted him at home before turning him over to authorities. The mob remobilized and took Crawford from the jail, strung him up to a tree, and riddled his body with bullets. See Carrigan, *Making of a Lynching Culture*; and Philip Dray, *At the Hands of Persons Unknown*.

41. Monroe to Wilson, December 1916.

42. W. E. B. Du Bois, "Closed Ranks," *Crisis* 16 (July 1918): 111.

43. To the chagrin of black soldiers and their supporters, the black intelligentsia (the NAACP and many newspaper editors) accepted segregated military service, believing that adamant challenges would derail the larger struggle for civil rights. They settled for resounding the call that leaders first issued to the War Department during the Spanish-American War for the commissioning of black officers to lead black troops. The army complied, but most black officers performed menial tasks alongside soldiers as laborers and stevedores.

44. See Robert V. Haynes, *Night of Violence*.

45. For a recent investigation into the East St. Louis riot and representations of the riot as a pogrom, see Lumpkins, *American Pogrom*.

46. For primary accounts of southern conditions, migrants' requests for information, and correspondence between the North and the South, see Emmett J. Scott, "Letters of Negro Migrants of 1916–1918" and "More Letters of Negro Migrants of 1916–1918." Quotations from Scott, "More Letters of Negro Migrants," 438, 440. Researchers who have investigated the causes of the Great Migration have debated the role that violence played in black southerners' decisions to migrate from the region. Most African Americans left the South for the employment opportunities created by the First and Second World Wars, but some migrants' testimonies, oral histories, and local newspaper accounts of migra-

tions after lynchings or riots suggest that some of the several million black people who participated in the Great Migration left because of violence they endured, witnessed, or feared. For analysis of the migrations, see Peter Gottlieb, *Making Their Own Way*; James R. Grossman, *Land of Hope*; Darlene Clark Hine, "Black Migration to the Urban Midwest"; Isabel Wilkerson, *Warmth of Other Suns*; James N. Gregory, *Southern Diaspora*; and Eric Arnesen, *Black Protest and the Great Migration*.

47. Scott, "More Letters of Negro Migrants," 450.

48. See Gottlieb, *Making Their Own Way*; Grossman, *Land of Hope*.

49. E. Johnson to the Department of Justice, September 4, 1918, FSAA, Reel 14, frames 0043–0044.

50. "Statement by President Woodrow Wilson, July 26, 1918 regarding Lynching and Its Effect at Home and Abroad," Papers of the NAACP, Reel 1, frame 1069.

51. Theodore Kornweibel, Jr., *"Seeing Red,"* xiv–xv.

52. Francis J. Grimké, "Address of Welcome to the Men Who Have Returned from the Battlefront," New York City, April 24, 1919, Papers of the NAACP, Reel 2, frames 0318–0319. To understand Grimké's earlier efforts to confront lynching, see Grimké, *Lynching of Negroes in the South*.

53. W. E. B. Du Bois, "Returning Soldiers," *Crisis* 18 (May 1919): 13–14. For additional analysis of African Americans' fight for civil rights during and after the war, see Reich, "Soldiers of Democracy"; and Mark Robert Schneider, *"We Return Fighting."*

54. See Schechter, *Ida B. Wells-Barnett and American Reform*; Carrigan, *Making of a Lynching Culture*.

55. Kornweibel, *"Seeing Red."*

56. One event prompting the expansion of federal surveillance of Americans was the bombing of several residences, including one belonging to Attorney General A. Mitchell Palmer. It is to this event that Emmanuels refers. Emmanuels to the Department of Justice, June 5, 1919, FSAA, Reel 14, frame 0434.

57. Theodore Hawkins to President Woodrow Wilson, December 20, 1919, FSAA, Reel 14, frame 0339.

58. "Negro Veteran Lynched for Refusing to Doff Uniform," *Defender*, April 5, 1919; William L. Jones to Attorney General A. Mitchell Palmer, July 31, 1919, FSAA, Reel 14, frame 0404. Little had refused to remove his uniform, likely feeling a sense of entitlement to wear the uniform in which he fought and not wishing to go home in his underwear. With the assistance of some nearby whites, who prevailed on the toughs to leave him alone, he went on his way, continuing to wear his uniform in spite of anonymous notes ordering him to stop and to leave town. When Little was discovered beaten to death on the city's outskirts after a mob attack, he was wearing his army uniform. Jones, responding to a similar incident that happened weeks earlier than his July 31 letter, declared that as "good soldiers," colored men were as entitled to wear their uniform as their white counterparts were. The Buffalo, New York, attorney noted that this case should not "go unpunished" and suggested that, if guilty, the lynchers be "hung or imprisoned."

59. C. J. Johnson to Woodrow Wilson, October 7, 1919, FSAA, Reel 14, frames 0352–0353; Assistant Attorney General R. P. Stewart to C. J. Johnson, October 13, 1919, FSAA, Reel 14, frame 0351; C. J. Johnson to R. P. Stewart, October 25, 1919, FSAA, Reel 14, frame 0350.

60. T. R. Hart to the Department of Justice, July 13, 1919, FSAA, Reel 14, frame 0413.

61. "Letter from Some Soldiers to the Finance, War Department." Because the soldiers claimed that Will Moore was a veteran, the DOJ approved the investigation into the matter. The assistant U.S. attorney of Biloxi, Mississippi, in a letter to Attorney General Palmer reported that Moore was not a soldier but a "bootlegger plying his trade among the employees of the Ten Mile Lumber Company." Foreman W. C. Rodgers reportedly objected to Moore's whiskey sales and apprehended Moore, but before he could turn Moore over to the deputy sheriff, Moore killed him. Employees of the lumber company and other interested whites allegedly killed Moore before the deputy arrived. Assistant United States Attorney to Attorney General Mitchell Palmer, June 19, 1919, FSAA, Reel 14, frame 0424. Following the lynching, someone took a photograph of Moore's lynched body and turned it into a three-and-a-half-by-five-and-a-half-inch postcard.

62. According to one historian, Palmer and his cohort of government officials themselves "saw red" in their inability to see black people's wartime rhetoric and action as an independent desire to break from the status quo, rather than as their influence by and reliance on radical, "red" doctrine. See Kornweibel, *"Seeing Red."*

63. August Meier and Elliott Rudwick, "Black Violence in the Twentieth Century," 410.

64. See Waskow, *From Race Riot to Sit-In*.

65. Letter to the editor, *Crisis* 19 (November 1919): 339.

66. See Cooper, *Voice from the South*; Alexander Crummell, "The Black Woman of the South: Her Neglects and Her Needs" (Cincinnati, Woman's Home Missionary Society of the Methodist Episcopal Church, circa 1880), Daniel A. P. Murray Pamphlet Collection, Rare Book and Special Collections Division, Library of Congress, digital ID: lcrbmrp t0c20, http://hdl.loc.gov/loc.rbc/lcrbmrp.t0c20 (accessed September 10, 2010); W. E. B. Du Bois, "Damnation of Women"; and Addie Hunton, "Negro Womanhood Defended," *Voice of the Negro* 1, no. 7 (July 1904); Hine, "Rape and the Inner Lives of Black Women in the Midwest."

67. I have no evidence that this letter is not authentic, but extensive research on the NAACP merits critical examination of this letter. Even if an actual black southern woman who had endured or witnessed racial violence did not write the letter herself, then the person claiming to write it on her behalf wanted to insert black women's perspectives on the violence into the public sphere.

68. Franz Fanon, "Concerning Violence," in *Wretched of the Earth*, 94.

NOTES TO CHAPTER 5

1. "Louisiana Mob Hangs Two Negro Murderers," December 13, 1913, Tuskegee Institute News Clipping File, Series II, Reel 221, frame 0200.

2. Chapin Brinsmade to Reverend G. W. Stringfellow, July 11, 1914, Papers of the NAACP, Reel 1, frame 0407.

3. J. D. Williams to Chapin Brinsmade, December 27, 1913, and Reverend W. M. Weal (Marshall, Texas) to NAACP, December 29, 1913, Papers of the NAACP, Reel 1, frames 0330, 0340.

4. P. L. Blackman to Chapin Brinsmade, January 5, 1914; Chapin Brinsmade to P. L. Blackman, January 9, 1914; Chapin Brinsmade to Kathryn M. Johnson, January 13, 1914; Kathryn M. Johnson to Chapin Brinsmade, around January 24, 1914, Papers of the NAACP, Reel 1, frames 0336, 0349, 0351, 0352. The racial identities of local people are not always expressed in their letters.

5. For comprehensive analysis of the NAACP's antilynching crusades, see Markovitz, *Legacies of Lynching*, 1–31; Meier and Bracey, "NAACP as a Reform Movement"; Wood, *Lynching and Spectacle*; Zangrando, *NAACP Crusade against Lynching*, 6–7. See also Morton Keller, *Regulating a New Society*.

6. McAdam and Snow, *Social Movements*.

7. Waldrep, *African Americans Confront Lynching*; Sullivan, *Lift Every Voice*.

8. See Zangrando's *NAACP Crusade against Lynching* for details on fundraising initiatives, the establishment of the Anti-Lynching Committee, and the NAACP's relationship with that committee's sponsor, Philip G. Peabody.

9. See "Notes on Lynching in the U.S. Compiled from *The Crisis*, 1912," in "Lynching: Chronology, 1892–1919," Schomburg Center Clipping File, Part I: 1925–1974, Micro-F-1 FSN SC 002, 893-1.

10. When I use the phrase "wars of white supremacy," I do so invoking Nancy Scheper-Hughes's concept of "small wars and invisible genocide." Historically we can see major wars and governmental genocides. However, the systemic and systematic violence of everyday life in some cultures obscures our appreciation for the depth and breadth of the destruction of life and livelihood. See Nancy Scheper-Hughes, "Small Wars and Invisible Genocides." See also Linda Green, *Fear as a Way of Life*.

11. Mattie Glover to NAACP, August 31, 1928, Papers of the NAACP, Reel 4, frames 0753–0754; Gainer Atkins to Walter White, Papers of the NAACP, Reel 3, frames 0317–0318.

12. Gring-Pemble, "Writing Themselves into Consciousness."

13. New York *Freeman*, June 4, 1887. For detailed analysis of the origins, purpose, and demise of the Afro-American League and the Afro-American Council, see Emma Lou Thornbrough, "The National Afro-American League," 495.

14. Thornbrough, "National Afro-American League," 496. Fortune later demurred in his position on self-defense, eventually adopting a more conciliatory approach when he aligned himself with Booker T. Washington as a member of the Afro-American Council.

15. Waldrep, *African Americans Confront Lynching*, 23.

16. See Benjamin R. Justesen, *Broken Brotherhood*.

17. Waldrep, *African Americans Confront Lynching*, 64; Paul Finkelman, *Lynching, Racial Violence, and Law*; Roberta Senechal, *Sociogenesis of a Race Riot*; Sullivan, *Lift Every Voice*.

18. Albert E. Pillsbury, "A Federal Remedy for Lynching," *Crisis*, March 1912, 205–208.

19. Walter White witnessed his father defend his family's home during the Atlanta riot. A white gang assaulted James W. Johnson, leaving him with physical and emotional scars. Ida B. Wells endured the lynching of three friends, and an angry mob destroyed her newspaper and threatened her life. W. E. B. Du Bois experienced the lynching of Sam Hose, learning that the man's body parts were on display in a nearby store. See Walter F. White, *Man Called White*; Kenneth Janken, *Walter White*; James Weldon Johnson, *Autobiography of an Ex-colored Man*; Goldsby, *Spectacular Secret*; Ida B. Wells-Barnett, *Crusade for Justice*; David Levering Lewis, *W. E. B. Du Bois*.

20. See Zangrando, *NAACP Crusade against Lynching*; Sullivan, *Lift Every Voice*; Waldrep, *African Americans Confront Lynching*. Writers applied their creative talent to re-present lynching during the period of its existence and produced a very large body of work. See, for example, Kathy A. Perkins and Judith L. Stephens, eds., *Strange Fruit*, and Rice, *Witnessing Lynching*.

21. James Weldon Johnson to the *Globe*, letter to the editor, August 25, 1919, Papers of the NAACP, Reel 2, frames 0407–0408.

22. "Making Wagoner a White Town," Indianapolis *Freeman*, June 6, 1914; "Colored Woman Is Hanged," Seattle *Times*, March 31, 1914; and "Was Powerless to Aid Sister Who Was Raped and Lynched," New York *Age*, April 30, 1914, all in Ginzburg, *100 Years of Lynching*, 90–91; and *Crisis* (June 1914), in NAACP, *Thirty Years of Lynching*, 23.

23. "Making Wagoner a White Town"; "Was Powerless to Aid Sister Who Was Raped and Lynched." Neither the press coverage of Marie Scott's lynching nor the correspondence to and from the NAACP conveys the larger social networks of the Scott family. This makes speaking definitely about the Scott family difficult.

24. Chapin Brinsmade to Reverend H. T. S. Johnson, April 14, 1914; Chapin Brinsmade to J. R. Coffey; J. R. Coffey to Chapin Brinsmade, April 2, 1914; W. Scott Brown, Jr., to May Childs Nerney, April 16, 1914, Papers of the NAACP, Reel 1, frames 0369, 0374, 0371, 0375.

25. May Childs Nerney to Mrs. E. W. Anderson, April 22, 1914; Mrs. E. W. Anderson of the Friday Club to NAACP, April 13, 1914; Chapin Brinsmade to Mrs. E. W. Anderson, April 22, 1914, Papers of the NAACP, Reel 1, frames 0381, 0384, 0382.

26. Brinsmade to Anderson. The correspondence does not reveal any specific details about Scott's reputed indiscretions.

27. Jason Harold Coleman to MaBelle A. White of the NAACP, May 15, 1914, Papers of the NAACP, Reel 1, frame 0388. The records I examined are inconclusive as to whether external pressure regarding the report from Marie Scott's brother changed the NAACP leadership's perspective on publicizing her death.

28. Higginbotham, *Righteous Discontent*, 14 and 185–220.

29. NAACP, *Thirty Years of Lynching*. See also Zangrando, *NAACP Crusade against Lynching*; and Feimster, *Southern Horrors*.

30. *Crisis*, July 1911, in NAACP, *Thirty Years of Lynching*, 18. Before the lynching, authorities had deemed Laura Nelson innocent of the shooting. Her husband pled guilty of cattle theft and was imprisoned, which probably saved his life. A grand jury did investigate the incident. Two three-and-a-half-by-five-and-a-half-inch postcards were made of Laura Nelson's lynched body, copyrighted by a G. H. Farnum. One is a close-up of Laura alone barefoot (on the opposite side, the postcard is stamped "unmailable"), and the other is of Laura and L. W., hanging from the bridge crossing the Canadian River in Okemah. See also Hazel Ruby McMahan, *Stories of Early Oklahoma—A Collection of Interesting Facts, Biographical Sketches and Stories Relating to the History of Oklahoma*, Oklahoma Society Daughters of American Revolution, 1945, Oklahoma City: Oklahoma Historical Society Library; "Notes on Lynching in the U.S. Compiled from *The Crisis*, 1912."

31. For some African Americans, participation in burial ceremonies for lynched family members might have allowed families to give sufferers dignity in death that they did not enjoy in the last stages of their lives. It might have also been cathartic and facilitated the healing process. For others, burial services for lynching victims might have been too costly, too hard to bear, and likely to stoke existing antiwhite hatred that might make families and communities vulnerable to violence. The perpetrators and their apologists, fearing reprisal but looking to confirm their superiority, would have likely stalked the burial services and monitored the statements and behavior of attendees for signs that they might try to avenge the killings of their loved ones.

32. See Wood, "Lynching Photography and the Visual Production of White Supremacy."

33. *Crisis*, August 1911, 153.

34. Walter F. White, "Extract from Confidential Report of Shubuta Lynchings by Special Investigator of the NAACP," January 29, 1919, Papers of the NAACP, Reel 1, frames 1302–1303, 1353–1358.

35. Ibid.

36. Ibid; "Lynch Four Negroes; Two of Them Women," NY *Times*, December 21, 1918; "The Shubuta," *Crisis* 18 (May 1919): 24–25. It is difficult to know for certain whether those who refused to take down the bodies were the victims' relatives. Although some African Americans had some choice of whether they witnessed an actual lynching or its aftermath, others did not. Some mobs forced—at gunpoint and with the threat of violence—the family members and neighbors of lynch sufferers to attend the event. Family members of the Howze sisters did see the bodies after some group took down the bodies. Walter F. White to C. P. Dam (Washington, DC), March 19, 1920, Papers of the NAACP, Reel 2, frame 0682. See Pfeifer, *Rough Justice*.

37. NAACP press releases, March 6, 1918, and June 3, 1918, Papers of the NAACP, Reel 1, frames 0846–0847, 1019–1020.

38. "Mob Lynches Two Negroes at Monroe," "Two Negroes Lynched," and "Two Negroes Lynched at Monroe, Louisiana," Tuskegee Institute News Clipping File, Series II, Reel 221, frame 0217. These black men might have been innocents, co-conspirators, or the actual perpetrators.

39. Joel E. Spingarn to Governor Luther E. Hall, Louisiana, September 3, 1914, Papers of the NAACP, Reel 1, frame 0415.

40. Undated draft of confidential report on Shubuta, Mississippi, lynchings, Papers of the NAACP, Reel 1, frames 1353–1358. The NAACP published parts of White's report in the *Crisis*.

41. Ibid., frame 1358.

42. Quoted in NAACP, "Why a Congressional Investigation of Lynching in the United States?," report, circa June 1919, Papers of the NAACP, Reel 2, frames 0466–0468.

43. NAACP, "63 Lynched in the U.S. in 10 Months, 11 Burned, 20 Shot, 19 Hanged," press release, November 8, 1919, Papers of the NAACP, Reel 2, frame 0480.

44. "Burn 2 Negroes at Stake," NY *Times*, July 7, 1920; NAACP, "Two Southern Governors Reply to Advancement Association's Telegram," press release, July 20, 1920, Papers of the NAACP, Reel 2, frame 0751.

45. See Waldrep, *African Americans Confront Lynching*.

46. "Why a Congressional Investigation of Lynching in the United States?," frames 0466–0476.

47. James Weldon Johnson to Dr. H. T. Jones (Dublin, Georgia), May 28, 1919, and newspaper clipping titled "Wanted to Leave Farm is Lynched," Papers of the NAACP, Reel 2, frames 0118, 0124.

48. News clipping without date or title, Papers of the NAACP, Reel 2, frame 0125.

49. Ibid.

50. See NAACP press release May 28, 1919, Papers of the NAACP, Reel 2, frame 0119.

51. See Zangrando, *NAACP Crusade against Lynching*, 51–53.

52. Waldrep, *African Americans Confront Lynching*, 21–23.

53. "Shoot into Mob Surrounding Jail," NY *Times*, July 20, 1920; "Kilby Aroused," NY *Times*, October 1, 1919; Pfeifer, *Rough Justice*.

54. See Asa Philip Randolph with Chandler Owen, *Truth about Lynching*. The African Blood Brotherhood was a short-lived underground organization of black radicals founded by Cyril Briggs in 1918 with the agenda of black self-determination. The ABB routinely advocated self-defensive action and retaliation as a legitimate response to racial violence, through the pages of its periodical, the *Crusader*.

55. David N. W. Campbell of the International Uplift League to the NAACP, June 4, 1919, Papers of the NAACP, Reel 2, frames 0144, 0145. See also Brown, *Eradicating This Evil*; Feimster, *Southern Horrors*; Waldrep, *Many Faces of Judge Lynch*; and Waldrep, *African Americans Confront Lynching*.

56. Chapin Brinsmade to J. A. D. Lawson, August 11, 1914, Papers of the NAACP, Reel 1, frame 0414.

57. See Judith Stein, *World of Marcus Garvey*.

58. The silence on the UNIA's failure to develop a strategy for ending lynching echoes that of Garvey himself on the matter except when castigating the NAACP's antilynching platform. FSAA, Reel 1, frame 0165. See Stein, *World of Marcus Garvey*.

59. FSAA, Reel 1, frame 0112.

60. See Jeffreys-Jones, *Cloak and Dollar*; and Rhodry Jeffreys-Jones, *FBI*.

61. See "The Anti-Lynching Crusaders: A Million Women United to Suppress Lynching," Schomburg Center Clipping File, Part I: 1925–1974, Micro-F FSN 002 895-2; Feimster, *Southern Horrors*.

62. With no fixed definition of lynching, the civil rights organizations debated the actual number of lynchings reported. See Waldrep, *Many Faces of Judge Lynch*, 127–150.

63. Zangrando, *NAACP Crusade against Lynching*; Sullivan, *Lift Every Voice*.

64. Anonymous letter from Hawkinsville, Georgia, November 19, 1919, Papers of the NAACP, Reel 2, frame 0493. It is difficult to know whether this letter writer was actually a member of the NAACP or thought the letter might carry more weight if he or she identified as such. Many of the association's local members used their names, and the tone of their letters suggests a familiarity with the organization and knowledge of the leadership. This letter writer addressed the letter to the NAACP and offers a salutation of "Greetings."

65. Anonymous letter from Eufaula, Alabama, January 14, 1922, to James Weldon Johnson, Papers of the NAACP, Reel 2, frame 0994.

66. Ibid.

67. Anonymous letter from Arkansas to Joel Spingarn, November 21, 1922, Papers of the NAACP, Reel 2, frame 1101.

68. NAACP, "26 Lynchings in 1923 as against 61 during 1922/Decline in Mob Murders Laid to Agitation for Federal Law & Migration/Mississippi and Florida Lead with 5 Each," press release, December 21, 1923, Papers of the NAACP, Reel 2, frame 1109.

69. Anonymous letter from Birmingham, Alabama, to the NAACP, July 30, 1923, Papers of the NAACP, Reel 2, frames 1197–1198.

70. Ibid.

71. Ibid.; Walter F. White to Governor W. Edward Brandon, August 16, 1923; and NAACP, "Report Unpunished Lynching of 60 Year Old Negro at Adamsville, Alabama," press release, August 17, 1923, Papers of the NAACP, Reel 2, frames 1197–1198, 1199, 1201.

72. Walter White to Bert Roddy, September 16, 1924; John Hurst to Walter White, June 24, 1924, Papers of the NAACP, Reel 3, frames 0062, 0047.

73. Walter White to Governor Thomas G. McLeod, September 10, 1925; James W. Johnson, press release regarding assassination of V. H. Whaley, September 12, 1925; H. O. Walker to James W. Johnson, October 1, 1925; Walter White to Miss Blondelle Whaley, October 10, 1925, Papers of the NAACP, Reel 3, frames 0212, 0213, 0226.

74. Blondelle A. Whaley to Walter White, February 17, 1926, Papers of the NAACP, Reel 3, frame 0291.

75. Ibid.

76. Thomas Jordan to NAACP, July 21, 1926; Dave Gaines to Thomas Jordan, July 19, 1926; Walter White to Dave Gaines, August 6, 1926, Papers of the NAACP, Reel 3, frames 0307–0313.

77. Gainer Atkins to Walter White, June 20, 1926; Gainer Atkins to Walter White, July 16, 1926; Walter White to Gainer Atkins, July 26, 1926, Papers of the NAACP, Reel 3, frames 0317–0318, 0319–0320, 0321.

78. Walter White to Gainer Atkins, August 9, 1926; Gainer Atkins to Walter White, September 6, 1926; Walter White to Gainer Atkins, July 26, 1926, Papers of the NAACP, Reel 3, frames 0305, 0317–0318, 0321–0323.

79. "Last Year Lowest in Lynching Cases," NY *Times*, March 16, 1924; "Lynching on the Decline," Foreign Press Service *Weekly Bulletin*; NAACP, "NAACP Anti-Lynching Campaign Chief Cause of Lynching Decline, Says J. W. Johnson," press release, October 25, 1924, Papers of the NAACP, Reel 3, frames 0060, 0075–0076.

80. James Weldon Johnson, *Lynching*; James Weldon Johnson, "Practice of Lynching"; Zangrando, *NAACP Crusade against Lynching*. For comprehensive coverage of what many scholars describe as the "worst race riot" in the nation's history, see Alfred L. Brophy, *Reconstructing the Dreamland*; James S. Hirsch, *Riot and Remembrance*; Scott Ellsworth, *Death in a Promised Land*; Tim Madigan, *Burning*. For details on the massacre in Florida, see Michael D'Orso, *Like Judgment Day*.

81. NAACP, "NAACP Writes President Coolidge on Georgia Burning Alive of Negro," press release, March 6, 1925; NAACP, "Thirteen Lynchings in First Six Months of 1926," press release July 16, 1926, Papers of the NAACP, Reel 3, frames 0158, 0297.

82. NAACP, "This Week's Editorial: Sixteen Lynched in 1924," press release, January 16, 1925, Papers of the NAACP, Reel 3, frame 0113.

83. In 1925, the NAACP documented eighteen lynchings, an increase of two from the year before. All the victims were African American. Of the eighteen, the most occurred in Mississippi, with six, followed by Florida with three. NAACP, "Dr. W. W. Alexander Reports Mississippi Roused over Lynching," press release, December 31, 1925, Papers of the NAACP, Reel 3, frame 0244.

84. William Pickens, "Every Effort to Punish Lynchers," undated [1925], Papers of the NAACP, Reel 3, frame 0229. For additional information on Pickens's research on lynching, see William Pickens, *Lynching and Debt-Slavery*.

85. Ibid.

86. Carrigan, *Making of a Lynching Culture*.

87. See Association of Southern Women for the Prevention of Lynching, "Are the Courts to Blame?," February 1934, Claude A Barnett Papers, Series I, Reel 5, frames 0356–0364; Southern Commission on the Study of Lynching, "The Plight of Tuscaloosa," 1933, Claude A. Barnett Papers, Series I, Reel 5, frames 0368–0385; Commission on Interracial

Cooperation, "*The Mob Still Rides: A Review of the Lynching Record, 1931–1935*" (Atlanta, n.d.), Schomburg Center Clipping File, Part I: 1925–1974, Micro-F FSN Sc 002 893-7.

88. See Zangrando, *NAACP Crusade against Lynching*; and Walter F. White, *How Far the Promised Land?*

89. See Zangrando, *NAACP Crusade against Lynching*; and White, *Man Called White*; "Lynching Goes Underground: A Report on a New Technique," Schomburg Center Clipping File, Part I: 1925–1974, Micro-F FSN Sc 002 893-8.

90. Steven F. Lawson, ed., *To Secure These Rights.*

NOTES TO THE EPILOGUE

1. White, *How Far the Promised Land?*, 229; White, *Man Called White.*

2. For the relationship between civil rights campaigns, see Jacquelyn Dowd Hall, "Long Civil Rights Movement."

3. See Laura Wexler, *Fire in a Canebrake*; Allison Berg, "Trauma and Testimony in Black Women's Civil Rights Memoirs"; Steve Estes, *I Am a Man!*; Payne, *I've Got the Light of Freedom*; John Dittmer, *Local People*; McGuire, *At the Dark End of the Street.*

4. See Elliot Jaspin, *Buried in the Bitter Waters.*

5. See Tyson, *Radio Free Dixie*; Wendt, *Spirit and the Shotgun*; Hasan Kwame Jeffries, *Bloody Lowndes.*

6. Testimony before the Credentials Committee, Democratic National Convention, Atlantic City, New Jersey, August 22, 1964, in Catherine Ellis and Stephen Drury Smith, eds., *Say It Plain*, 51–53.

7. See McAdam and Snow, *Social Movements*, xviii–xxvi; and McAdam, McCarthy, and Zald, *Comparative Perspectives on Social Movements.*

Works Cited

MANUSCRIPT AND MICROFILM COLLECTIONS

Barnett, Claude A., Papers/Associated Negro Press, 1918–1967. Chicago Historical Society, Archives and Manuscripts Department. Chicago, IL.

Federal Surveillance of Afro-Americans, 1917–1925: The First World War, the Red Scare, and Garvey Movement. Frederick, MD: University Publications of America, 1985.

Library of Congress, Washington, DC
  Daniel A. P. Murray Pamphlet Collection

National Archives and Records Administration
  Bureau of Refugees, Freedmen, and Abandoned Lands Papers

Oklahoma Society Daughters of American Revolution, 1945. Oklahoma City: Oklahoma Historical Society Library.

Papers of the National Association for the Advancement of Colored People. Part 7: The Anti-lynching Campaign, 1912–1955. Series A: Anti-lynching Investigative Files, 1912–1953.

Schomburg Center Clipping File. Part I: 1925–1974. New York: New York Public Library, 1974.

Tuskegee Institute News Clipping File. Tuskegee, AL: Tuskegee Institute, 1978.

PUBLISHED SOURCES

Amnesty International. "Sudan: Darfur: 'Too Many People Killed for No Reason.'" *Africa* 54, no. 8 (February 2004): 1–45.

Apel, Dora, and Shawn Michelle Smith. *Lynching Photographs*. Berkeley: University of California Press, 2008.

Aptheker, Herbert, ed. *A Documentary History of the Negro People in the United Slates, Volume 2: From the Recosntruction to the Founding of the NAACP*. 3d ed. New York: Citadel, 1992.

Arnesen, Eric. *Black Protest and the Great Migration: A Brief History with Documents*. Boston: Bedford/St. Martin's, 2002.

Ayers, Edward L. *The Promise of the New South: Life after Reconstruction*. New York: Oxford University Press, 1992.

———. *Vengeance and Justice: Crime and Punishment in the 19th Century American South*. New York: Oxford University Press, 1986.

Baker, Bruce E. "Lynch Law Reversed: The Rape of Lula Sherman, the Lynching of Manse Waldrop, and the Debate over Lynching in the 1880s." *American Nineteenth Century History* 6, no. 3 (September 2005): 273–293.

———. *This Mob Will Surely Take My Life: Lynchings in the Carolinas, 1871–1947*. London: Hambledon and London, 2008.
Bakhtin, Mikhail M. *The Dialogic Imagination: Four Essays*. Austin: University of Texas Press, 1981.
Baptist, Edward E. "'Stol' and Fetched Here': Enslaved Migrations, Ex-slave Narratives, and Vernacular History." In *New Studies in the History of American Slavery*, edited by Edward E. Baptist and Stephanie M. H. Camp, 243–274. Athens: University of Georgia Press, 2006.
Bay, Mia. *To Tell the Truth Freely: The Life of Ida B. Wells*. New York: Hill and Wang, 2008.
———. *White Image in the Black Mind: African-American Ideas about White People, 1830–1925*. New York: Oxford University Press, 2000.
Bederman, Gail. *Manliness and Civilization: A Cultural History of Gender and Race in the United States, 1880–1917*. Chicago: University of Chicago Press, 1995.
Berg, Allison. "Trauma and Testimony in Black Women's Civil Rights Memoirs." *Journal of Women's History* 21, no. 3 (Fall 2009): 84–107.
Berlant, Lauren. *The Queen of America Goes to Washington City: Essays on Sex and Citizenship*. Durham: Duke University Press, 1997.
Blackmon, Douglas A. *Slavery by Another Name: The Re-enslavement of Black People in America from the Civil War to World War II*. New York: Doubleday, 2008.
Blight, David W. *Race and Reunion: The Civil War in American Memory*. Cambridge: Belknap Press of Harvard University Press, 2001.
———. "'What Will Peace among the Whites Bring?': Reunion and Race in the Struggle over the Memory of the Civil War in American Culture." *Massachusetts Review* 34, no. 3 (Autumn 1993): 393–410.
Brophy, Alfred L. *Reconstructing the Dreamland: The Tulsa Race Riot of 1921*. Oxford: Oxford University Press, 2002.
Brown, Elsa Barkley. "Imaging Lynching: African American Women, Communities of Struggle, and Collective Memory." In *African American Women Speak Out on Anita Hill–Clarence Thomas*, edited by Geneva Smitherman, 100–123. Detroit: Wayne State University Press, 1995.
———. "Negotiating and Transforming the Public Spehre: African American Political Life in the Transition from Slavery to Freedom." *Public Culture* 7 (Fall 1994): 107–111.
———. "To Catch the Vision of Freedom: Reconstructing Southern Black Women's Political History, 1865–1880." In *African-American Women and the Vote, 1837–1965*, edited by Ann D. Gordon et al., 66–99. Amherst: University of Massachusetts Press, 1997.
Brown, Mary Jane. *Eradicating This Evil: Women in the American Anti-lynching Movement, 1892–1940*. New York: Routledge, 2000.
Brundage, W. Fitzhugh. *Lynching in the New South: Georgia and Virginia, 1880–1930*. Urbana: University of Illinois Press, 1993.
———. "The Roar on the Other Side of Silence: Black Resistance and White Violence in the American South, 1880–1940." In *Under Sentence of Death: Lynching in the South*, edited by W. Fitzhugh Brundage, 271–291. Chapel Hill: University of North Carolina Press, 1997.
Bryant, Jerry H. *"Born in a Mighty Bad Land": The Violent Man in African American Folklore*. Bloomington: Indiana University Press, 2003.
Camp, Stephanie M. H. *Closer to Freedom: Enslaved Women and Everyday Resistance in the Plantation South*. Chapel Hill: University of North Carolina Press, 2004.

Carby, Hazel V. *Reconstructing Womanhood: The Emergence of the African American Woman Novelist*. New York: Oxford University Press, 1987.

Carrigan, William D. *The Making of a Lynching Culture: Violence and Vigilantism in Central Texas, 1836–1916*. Urbana: University of Illinois Press, 2004.

Carrigan, William D., and Clive Webb. "The Lynching of Persons of Mexican Origin or Descent in the United States, 1848–1928." *Journal of Social History* 37, no. 2 (2003): 411–438.

Caruth, Cathy. *Unclaimed Experience: Trauma, Narrative, and History*. Baltimore: Johns Hopkins University Press, 1996.

Cecelski, David A., and Timothy B. Tyson, eds. *Democracy Betrayed: The Wilmington Race Riot of 1898 and Its Legacy*. Chapel Hill: University of North Carolina Press, 1998.

Chuengsatiansup, Komatra. "Marginality, Suffering, and Community." In *Remaking a World: Violence, Social Suffering, and Recovery*, edited by Veena Das, Arthur Kleinman, Margaret Lock, Mamphela Ramphele, and Pamela Reynolds, 31–75. Berkeley: University of California Press, 2001.

Cimbala, Paul A., and Randall M. Miller, eds. *The Freedmen's Bureau and Reconstruction*. New York: Fordham University Press, 1999.

Clegg, Claude A. *The Price of Liberty: African Americans and the Making of Liberia*. Chapel Hill: University of North Carolina Press, 2004.

Clinton, Catherine. "Bloody Terrain: Freedwomen, Sexuality, and Violence during Reconstruction." *Georgia Historical Quarterly* 76 (Summer 1992): 313–332.

Cooper, Anna Julia. *A Voice from the South*. Xenia, OH: Aldine, 1892. Reprint, New York: Oxford University Press, 1988.

Cortner, Richard C. *A Mob Intent on Death: The NAACP and the Arkansas Race Riot*. Middletown, CT: Wesleyan University Press, 1988.

Das, Veena, and Arthur Kleinman. Introduction to *Remaking a World: Violence, Social Suffering, and Recovery*, edited by Veena Das, Arthur Kleinman, Margaret Lock, Mamphela Ramphele, and Pamela Reynolds, 1–30. Berkeley: University of California Press, 2001.

Das, Veena, Arthur Kleinman, Margaret Lock, Mamphela Ramphele, and Pamela Reynolds, eds. *Remaking a World: Violence, Social Suffering, and Recovery*. Berkeley: University of California Press, 2001.

Decker, William Merrill. *Epistolary Practices: Letter Writing in America before Telecommunications*. Chapel Hill: University of North Carolina Press, 1998.

Dittmer, John. *Local People: The Struggle for Civil Rights in Mississippi*. Urbana: University of Illinois Press, 1994.

Dorr, Lisa Lindquist. *White Women, Rape, and the Power of Race in Virginia, 1900–1940*. Chapel Hill: University of North Carolina Press, 2004.

D'Orso, Michael. *Like Judgment Day: The Riot and Redemption of a Town Called Rosewood*. New York: Boulevard Books, 1996.

Dray, Philip. *At the Hands of Persons Unknown: The Lynching of Black America*. New York: Modern Library, 2003.

Du Bois, W. E. B. *Black Reconstruction in America: An Essay toward a History of the Part Which Black Folk Played in the Attempt to Reconstruct Democracy in America, 1860–1880*. New York: Russell & Russell, 1935.

———. "Closed Ranks." *Crisis* 16 (July 1918): 111.

———. "The Damnation of Women." In *Darkwater: Voices from within the Veil*, edited by W. E. B. Du Bois, 95–108. New York: Harcourt, Brace and Company, 1920. Reprint, Mineola, NY: Dover, 1999.

———. "Returning Soldiers." *Crisis* 18 (May 1919): 13–14.

———. *The Souls of Black Folk*. Chicago: A. C. McClurg, 1903. Reprint, Boulder, CO: Paradigm, 2005.

———. "The Souls of White Folk." In *Darkwater: Voices from within the Veil*, edited by W. E. B. Du Bois, 17–29. New York: Harcourt, Brace and Company, 1920. Reprint, Mineola, NY: Dover, 1999.

Edwards, Laura F. *Gendered Strife and Confusion: The Political Culture of Reconstruction*. Urbana: University of Illinois Press, 1997.

Ellis, Catherine, and Stephen Drury Smith, eds. *Say It Plain: A Century of African American Speeches*. New York: New Press, 2005.

Ellis, Mark. *Race, War, and Surveillance: African Americans and the United States Government during World War I*. Bloomington: Indiana University Press, 2001.

Ellsworth, Scott. *Death in a Promised Land: The Tulsa Race Riot of 1921*. Baton Rouge: Louisiana State University Press, 1992.

Estes, Steve. *I Am a Man! Race, Manhood, and the Civil Rights Movement*. Chapel Hill: University of North Carolina Press, 2005.

Fanon, Franz. *The Wretched of the Earth*. New York: Grove, 1963.

Faust, Drew Gilpin. *This Republic of Suffering: Death and the American Civil War*. New York: Knopf, 2008.

Feimster, Crystal N. *Southern Horrors: Women and the Politics of Rape and Lynching*. Cambridge: Harvard University Press, 2009.

Felman, Shoshana, and Dori Laub. *Testimony: Crises of Witnessing in Literature, Psychoanalysis and History*. New York: Routledge, 1991.

Felton, Rebecca Latimer. "Needs of Farmers' Wives and Daughters" (1897). In *Lynching in America: A History in Documents*, edited by Christopher Waldrep, 143–144. New York: NYU Press, 2006.

Finkelman, Paul. *Lynching, Racial Violence, and Law*. New York: Garland, 1992.

Foner, Eric. *The Fiery Trial: Abraham Lincoln and American Slavery*. New York: Norton, 2010.

———. *Reconstruction: America's Unfinished Revolution, 1863–1877*. New York: Harper and Row, 1988.

Fortune, Timothy Thomas. *Black and White: Land, Labor and Politics in the South*. New York: Fords, Howard, and Hulbert, 1884. Reprint, New York: Arno and the New York *Times*, 1968.

Franklin, V. P. *Black Self-Determination: A Cultural History of African-American Resistance*. New York: Lawrence Hill Books, 1992.

Frederickson, George M. *The Black Image in the White Mind: The Debate on Afro-American Character and Destiny, 1877–1914*. New York: Harper and Row, 1971.

Friedman, Lawrence M. *Crime and Punishment in American History*. New York: Basic Books, 1993.

Fry, Gladys-Marie. *Night Riders in Black Folk History*. Chapel Hill: University of North Carolina Press, 1975.

Gaines, Kevin K. *Uplifting the Race: Black Leadership, Politics, and Culture in the Twentieth Century*. Chapel Hill: University of North Carolina Press, 1996.

Gates, Henry Louis, Jr., and Gene A. Jarrett, eds. *The New Negro: Readings on Race, Representation, and African American Culture, 1892–1938*. Princeton: Princeton University Press, 2007.

Giddings, Paula. *Sword among Lions: Ida B. Wells and the Campaign against Lynching*. New York: Amistad, 2008.

———. *When and Where I Enter: The Impact of Black Women on Race and Sex in America*. New York: Morrow, 1984.

Gillette, William. *Retreat from Reconstruction, 1869–1879*. Baton Rouge: Louisiana State University Press, 1979.

Gilmore, Glenda E. *Gender and Jim Crow: Women and the Politics of White Supremacy in North Carolina, 1896–1920*. Chapel Hill: University of North Carolina Press, 1996.

Ginzburg, Ralph, ed. *100 Years of Lynching*. Baltimore: Black Classic, 1988.

Glymph, Thavolia. *Out of the House of Bondage: The Transformation of the Plantation Household*. Cambridge: Cambridge University Press, 2008.

Godshalk, David Fort. *Veiled Visions: The 1906 Atlanta Race Riot and the Reshaping of American Race Relations*. Chapel Hill: University of North Carolina Press, 2009.

Goldsby, Jacqueline. *A Spectacular Secret: Lynching in American Life and Literature*. Chicago: University of Chicago Press, 2006.

Gordon-Reed, Annette. *Andrew Johnson*. New York: Times Books/Holt, 2011.

Gottlieb, Peter. *Making Their Own Way: Southern Blacks' Migration to Pittsburgh, 1916–1930*. Urbana: University of Illinois Press, 1987.

Green, Linda. *Fear as a Way of Life: Mayan Widows in Rural Guatemala*. New York: Columbia University Press, 1999.

Gregory, James N. *The Southern Diaspora: How the Great Migrations of Black and White Southerners Transformed America*. Chapel Hill: University of North Carolina Press, 2007.

Grimké, Angelina Weld. "Rachel." In *Strange Fruit: Plays on Lynching by American Women*, edited by Kathy A. Perkins and Judith L. Stephens, 27–78. Bloomington: Indiana University Press, 1988.

Grimké, Francis J. *The Lynching of Negroes in the South: Its Causes and Remedy*. Washington, DC, 1899.

Grimsted, David. *American Mobbing, 1828–1861*. New York: Oxford University Press, 1998.

Gring-Pemble, Lisa M. "Writing Themselves into Consciousness: Creating a Rhetorical Bridge between the Public and Private Sphere." *Quarterly Journal of Speech* 84 (1988): 41–61.

Grossman, James R. *Land of Hope: Chicago, Black Southerners, and the Great Migration*. Chicago: University of Chicago Press, 1989.

Gunning, Sandra. *Race, Rape, and Lynching: The Red Record of American Literature, 1890–1912*. New York: Oxford University Press, 1996.

Gutman, Herbert G. *The Black Family in Slavery and Freedom, 1750–1925*. New York: Oxford University Press, 1976.

Hahn, Steven. *A Nation under Our Feet: Black Political Struggles in the Rural South from Slavery to the Great Migration*. Cambridge: Belknap Press of Harvard University Press, 2003.

Hair, William Ivy. *Carnival of Fury: Robert Charles and the New Orleans Race Riot of 1900*. Baton Rouge: Louisiana State University Press, 1976.

Hale, Grace Elizabeth. *Making Whiteness: The Culture of Segregation in the South, 1880–1940*. New York: Vintage Books, 1998.

Hall, Jacquelyn Dowd. "The Long Civil Rights Movement and the Political Uses of the Past." *Journal of American History* 91, no. 4 (2005): 1233–1263.

———. "'The Mind That Burns in Each Body': Women, Rape, and Racial Violence." In *Powers of Desire: The Politics of Sexuality*, edited by Ann Snitow, Christine Stansell, and Sharon Thompson, 328–349. New York: Monthly Review Press, 1983.

———. *Revolt against Chivalry: Jesse Daniel Ames and the Women's Campaign against Lynching*. New York: Columbia University Press, 1979.

Hartman, Saidiya V. *Scenes of Subjection: Terror, Slavery, and Self-Making in Nineteenth-Century America*. New York: Oxford University Press, 1997.

Haynes, Robert V. *A Night of Violence: The Houston Riot of 1917*. Baton Rouge: Louisiana State University Press, 1976.

Herman, Judith Lewis. *Trauma and Recovery: The Aftermath of Violence—From Domestic Abuse to Political Terror*. New York: Basic Books, 1992.

Higginbotham, Evelyn Brooks. *Righteous Discontent: The Women's Movement in the Black Baptist Church, 1880–1920*. Cambridge: Harvard University Press, 1993.

Hine, Darlene Clark. "Black Migration to the Urban Midwest: The Gender Dimension, 1915–1945." In *Black Migration in Historical Perspective*, edited by Joe W. Trotter, 127–146. Bloomington: Indiana University Press, 1991.

———. "Rape and the Inner Lives of Black Women in the Midwest." *Signs* 14, no. 4 (Summer 1989): 912–920.

Hirsch, James S. *Riot and Remembrance: The Tulsa Race War and Its Legacy*. Boston: Houghton Mifflin, 2002.

Hodes, Martha. "The Sexualization of Reconstruction Politics: White Women and Black Men in the South after the Civil War." *Journal of the History of Sexuality* 3 (1993): 402–417.

Hollandsworth, James G. *An Absolute Massacre: The New Orleans Race Riot of July 30, 1866*. Baton Rouge: Louisiana State University Press, 2001.

Holt, Thomas. *Black over White: Negro Political Leadership in South Carolina*. Urbana: University of Illinois Press, 1979.

hooks, bell. "The Continued Devaluation of Black Womanhood." In *Ain't I a Woman: Black Women and Feminism*, 51–86. Boston: South End, 1981.

———. *Yearning: Race, Gender, and Cultural Politics*. Boston: South End, 1990.

Hunter, Tera W. *"To 'Joy My Freedom": Southern Black Women's Lives and Labors after the Civil War*. Cambridge: Harvard University Press, 1997.

Ifill, Sherrilyn A. *On the Courthouse Lawn: Confronting the Legacy of Lynching in the Twenty-First Century*. Boston: Beacon, 2007.

Jacobson, Matthew Frye. *Whiteness of a Different Color: European Immigrants and the Alchemy of Race*. Cambridge: Harvard University Press, 1998.

James, Winston. *Holding Aloft the Banner of Ethiopia: Caribbean Radicalism in Early Twentieth-Century America*. London: Verso, 1999.

Janken, Kenneth. *Walter White: Mr. NAACP*. Chapel Hill: University of North Carolina Press, 2006.

Jaspin, Elliot. *Buried in the Bitter Waters: The Hidden Hisory of Racial Cleansing in America*. New York: Basic Books, 2007.

Jaynes, Gerald David. *Branches without Roots: Genesis of the Black Working Class in the American South, 1862–1882*. New York: Pantheon, 1986.

Jeffreys-Jones, Rhodry. *Cloak and Dollar: A History of American Secret Intelligence*. New Haven: Yale University Press, 2002.
———. *The FBI: A History*. Lexington: University Press of Kentucky, 2007.
Jeffries, Hasan Kwame. *Bloody Lowndes: Civil Rights and Black Power in Alabama's Black Belt*. New York: NYU Press, 2009.
Johnson, James Weldon. *Autobiography of an Ex-colored Man*. New York: Sherman, French, 1912. Reprint, New York: Dover, 1995.
———. *Lynching: America's National Disgrace*. New York: NAACP, 1924.
———. "The Practice of Lynching: A Picture of the Problem and What Should Be Done about It." *Century Magazine* (November 1927): 65–70.
Johnson, Walter. "On Agency." *Journal of Social History* 37, no. 1 (2003): 113–124.
Jones, Allen W. "The Black Press in the 'New South': Jesse C. Duke's Struggle for Justice and Equality." *Journal of Negro History* 64, no. 3 (1979): 215–228.
Justesen, Benjamin R. *Broken Brotherhood: The Rise and Fall of the National Afro-American Council*. Carbondale: Southern Illinois University Press, 2008.
Kaczorowski, Robert J. *The Politics of Judicial Interpretation: The Federal Courts, Department of Justice, and Civil Rights, 1866–1876*. New York: Oceana, 1985.
Kaplan, Temma. "Reversing the Shame and Gendering the Memory." *Signs* 28, no. 1 (2002): 179–199.
Keith, LeeAnna. *The Colfax Massacre: The Untold Story of Black Power, White Terror, and the Death of Reconstruction*. New York: Oxford University Press, 2008.
Keller, Morton. *Regulating a New Society: Public Policy and Social Change in America, 1900–1930*. Cambridge: Harvard University Press, 1994.
Kelley, Robin D. G. "'We Are Not What We Seem': Rethinking Black Working-Class Opposition in the Jim Crow South." *Journal of American History* 80, no. 1 (1993): 75–112.
King, Wilma. *Stolen Childhood: Slave Youth in Nineteenth-Century America*. Bloomington: Indiana University Press, 1997.
Kleinman, Arthur, Veena Das, and Margaret Lock, eds. *Social Suffering*. Berkeley: University of California Press, 1997.
Kleinman, Arthur, Veena Das, Mamphela Ramphele, and Pamela Reynolds, eds. *Violence and Subjectivity*. Berkeley: University of California Press, 2000.
Kornweibel, Theodore, Jr. *"Seeing Red": Federal Campaigns against Black Militancy, 1919–1925*. Bloomington: Indiana University Press, 1998.
Kousser, J. Morgan. *The Shaping of Southern Politics: Suffrage Restriction and the Establishment of One-Party South, 1880–1910*. New Haven: Yale University Press, 1974.
Lane, Charles. *The Day Freedom Died: The Colfax Massacre, the Supreme Court, and the Betrayal of Reconstruction*. New York: Holt, 2008.
Lanza, Michael L. *Agrarianism and Reconstruction Politics: The Southern Homestead Act*. Baton Rouge: Louisiana State University Press, 1990.
Lawson, Steven F., ed. *To Secure These Rights: The Report of President Harry S. Truman's Committee on Civil Rights*. Boston: Bedford/St. Martin's, 2004.
Leach, John. "Cognitive Paralysis in an Emergency: The Role of the Supervisory Attentional System." *Aviation, Space, and Environmental Medicine* 76, no. 2 (February 2005): 134–136.
———. "Why People 'Freeze' in an Emergency: Temporal and Cognitive Constraints on Survival Responses." *Aviation, Space, and Environmental Medicine* 75, no. 6 (June 2004): 539–542.

Lerner, Gerda, ed. *Black Women in White America: A Documentary History*. New York: Vintage, 1972.
Lewis, David Levering. *W. E. B. Du Bois: Biography of a Race*. New York: Holt, 1994.
Lewis, Earl. *In Their Own Interests: Race, Class, and Power in Twentieth-Century Norfolk, Virginia*. Berkeley: University of California Press, 1991.
Lipsitz, George A. *A Life in the Struggle: Ivory Perry and the Culture of Opposition*. Philadelphia: Temple University Press, 1988.
Litwack, Leon. *Been in the Storm Too Long: The Aftermath of Slavery*. New York: Knopf, 1979.
———. *Trouble in Mind: Black Southerners in the Age of Jim Crow*. New York: Knopf, 1998.
Lofgren, Charles A. *The Plessy Case: A Legal-Historical Interpretation*. New York: Oxford University Press, 1987.
Logan, Rayford W. *The Negro in American Life and Thought: The Nadir, 1877–1901*. New York: Dial, 1954.
Lumpkins, Charles L. *American Pogrom: The East St. Louis Race Riot and Black Politics*. Youngstown: Ohio University Press, 2008.
Madigan, Tim. *The Burning: Massacre, Destruction, and the Tulsa Race Riot of 1921*. New York: St. Martin's, 2001.
Madison, James H. *A Lynching in the Heartland: Race and Memory in America*. New York: Palgrave Macmillan, 2003.
Magness, Phillip W., and Sebastian N. Page. *Colonization after Emancipation: Lincoln and the Movement for Black Resettlement*. Columbia: University of Missouri Press, 2011.
Mansbridge, Jane J. "Using Power/Fighting Power: The Polity." In *Democracy and Difference: Contesting the Boundaries of the Political*, edited by Seyla Benhabib, 46–66. Princeton: Princeton University Press, 1996.
Mansbridge, Jane J., and Aldon D. Morris, eds. *Oppositional Consciousness: The Subjective Roots of Social Protest*. Chicago: University of Chicago Press, 2001.
Marable, Manning. *Black Leadership*. New York: Columbia University Press, 1998.
Markovitz, Jonathan. *Legacies of Lynching: Racial Violence and Memory*. Minneapolis: University of Minnesota Press, 2004.
McAdam, Doug, John McCarthy, and Mayer Zald. *Comparative Perspectives on Social Movements: Political Opportunities, Mobilizing Structures, and Cultural Framings*. Cambridge: Cambridge University Press, 1996.
McAdam, Doug, and David A. Snow, eds. *Social Movements: Readings on Their Emergence, Mobilization, and Dynamics*. Los Angeles: Roxbury, 1997.
McBride, Dwight A. *Impossible Witnesses: Truth, Abolitionism, and Slave Testimony*. New York: NYU Press, 2002.
McGuire, Danielle L. *At the Dark End of the Street: Black Women, Rape, and Resistance—A New History of the Civil Rights Movement from Rosa Parks to the Rise of Black Power*. New York: Knopf, 2010.
McHenry, Elizabeth. *Forgotten Readers: Recovering the Lost History of African American Literary Societies*. Durham: Duke University Press, 2002.
McKay, Claude. "If We Must Die." In *African American Poetry: An Anthology, 1773–1927*, edited by Joan R. Sherman. Mineola, NY: Dover, 1997.
McMillen, Neil R. *Dark Journey: Black Mississippians in the Age of Jim Crow*. Urbana: University of Illinois Press, 1989.

Meier, August, and John H. Bracey. "The NAACP as a Reform Movement, 1909–1965: 'To Reach the Conscience of America.'" *Journal of Southern History* 59, no. 1 (February 1993): 3–30.

Meier, August, and Elliott Rudwick. "Black Violence in the Twentieth Century." In *Violence in America: Protest, Rebellion, and Reform*, edited by Hugh Davis Graham and Ted Robert Gurr, 399–412. New York: Signet, 1969.

Mitchell, Koritha A. "Antilynching Plays." In *Post-bellum, Pre-Harlem: African American Literature and Culture, 1877–1919*, edited by Barbara McCaskill and Caroline Gebard, 210–230. New York: NYU Press, 2006.

———. *Living with Lynching: African American Drama, Performance, and Citizenship, 1890–1930*. Urbana: University of Illinois Press, 2011.

Mitchell, Michele. *Righteous Propagation: African Americans and Politics of Racial Destiny after Reconstruction*. Chapel Hill: University of North Carolina Press, 2004.

Mixon, Gregory L. *The Atlanta Race Riot: Race, Class, and Violence in a New South City*. Gainsville: University Press of Florida, 2004.

Moore, John H. *Carnival of Blood: Dueling, Lynching, and Murder in South Carolina, 1880–1920*. Columbia: University of South Carolina Press, 2006.

Morris, Aldon D. *The Origins of the Civil Rights Movement: Black Communities Organizing for Change*. New York: Free Press, 1984.

Muhammad, Khalil G. *The Condmenation of Blackness: Race, Crime, and the Making of Modern Urban America*. Cambridge: Harvard University Press, 2010.

NAACP. *Burning at Stake in the United States: A Record of the Public Burning by Mobs of Six Men during the first six months of 1919 in the states of Arkansas, Florida, Georgia, Mississippi, and Texas*. New York, 1919.

———. *Thirty Years of Lynching in the Untied States, 1889–1918*. Reprint, New York: Arno, 1969.

Nieman, Donald G. *Black Freedom/White Violence, 1865–1900*. New York: Garland, 1994.

———. *To Set the Law in Motion: The Freedmen's Bureau and the Legal Rights of Blacks, 1865–1868*. Millwood, NY: KTO, 1979.

Norrell, Robert J. *Up from History: The Life of Booker T. Washington*. Cambridge: Belknap Press of Harvard University Press, 2009.

Painter, Nell Irvin. *Exodusters: Black Migration to Kansas after Reconstruction*. New York: Norton, 1976.

———. "'Soul Murder and Slavery': Toward a Fully Loaded Cost Accounting." In *Southern History across the Color Line*, edited by Nell Irvin Painter, 15–39. Chapel Hill: University of North Carolina Press, 2002.

Patterson, Orlando. *Rituals of Blood: Consequences of Slavery in Two American Centuries*. New York: Basic Books, 1998.

Payne, Charles M. *I've Got the Light of Freedom: The Organizing Tradition and the Mississippi Freedom Struggle*. Berkeley: University of California Press, 1995.

Penningroth, Dylan C. *The Claims of Kinfolk: African American Property and Community in the Nineteenth-Century South*. Chapel Hill: University of North Carolina Press, 2002.

Perera, Sasanka. "Spirit Possessions and Avenging Ghosts: Stories of Supernatural Activity as Narratives of Terror and Mechanisms of Coping and Remembering." In *Remaking a World: Violence, Social Suffering, and Recovery*, edited by Veena Das, Arthur Kleinman, Margaret Lock, Mamphela Ramphele, and Pamela Reynolds, 157–200. Berkeley: University of California Press, 2001.

Perkins, Kathy A., and Judith L. Stephens, eds. *Strange Fruit: Plays on Lynching by American Women*. Bloomington: Indiana University Press, 1998.

Perman, Michael. *The Road to Redemption: Southern Politics, 1869–1879*. Chapel Hill: University of Chapel Hill Press, 1984.

Pfeifer, Michael J. *Rough Justice: Lynching and American Society, 1874–1947*. Urbana: University of Illinois Press, 2004.

Pickens, William. *Lynching and Debt-Slavery*. New York: American Civil Liberties Union, 1921.

Pillsbury, Albert E. "A Federal Remedy for Lynching." *Crisis* (March 1912): 205–208.

Prather, H. Leon, Jr. "'We Have Taken a City': A Centennial Essay." In *Democracy Betrayed: The Wilmington Race Riot of 1898 and Its Legacy*, edited by David S. Cecelski and Timothy B. Tyson, 15–42. Chapel Hill: University of North Carolina Press, 1998.

Prince, Mary. *The History of Mary Prince, a West Indian Slave*. In *The Classic Slave Narratives*, edited by Henry Louis Gates, Jr., 183–238. New York: Mentor, 1987.

Rable, George C. *But There Was No Peace: The Role of Violence in the Politics of Reconstruction*. Athens: University of Georgia Press, 1984.

Rachleff, Peter J. *Black Labor in the South: Richmond, Virginia, 1865–1890*. Philadelphia: Temple University Press, 1984.

Randolph, Asa Philip, with Chandler Owen. *The Truth about Lynching: Its Causes and Effects, the Remedy*. New York: Cosmo-Advocate, 1917.

Reich, Steven A. "Soldiers of Democracy: Black Texans and the Fight of Citizenship, 1917–1921." *Journal of American History* 82 (March 1999): 1478–1501.

Rice, Anne P., ed. *Witnessing Lynching: American Writers Respond*. New Brunswick: Rutgers University Press, 2003.

Richardson, Heather Cox. *The Death of Reconstruction: Race, Labor, and Politics in the Civil War North*. Cambridge: Harvard University Press, 2001.

Rodrigue, John C. *Reconstruction in the Cane Fields: From Slavery to Free Labor in Louisiana's Sugar Parishes, 1862–1880*. Baton Rouge: Louisiana State University Press, 2001.

Rogin, Michael. "'The Sword Became a Flashing Vision': D. W. Griffith's *The Birth of a Nation*." In *Ronald Reagan, the Movie, and Other Episodes in Political Demonology*, 190–235. Berkeley: University of California Press, 1987.

Rosen, Hannah. *Terror in the Heart of Freedom: Citizenship, Sexual Violence, and the Meaning of Race in the Postemancipation South*. Chapel Hill: University of North Carolina Press, 2008.

Ross, Fiona C. "Speech and Silence: Women's Testimony in the First Five Weeks of Public Hearings of the South African Truth and Reconciliation Commission." In *Remaking a World: Violence, Social Suffering, and Recovery*, edited by Veena Das, Arthur Kleinman, Margaret Lock, and Mamphela Ramphele, 250–279. Berkeley: University of California Press, 2001.

Ross, Marlon B. *Manning the Race: Reforming Black Men in the Jim Crow Era*. New York: NYU Press, 2004.

Royce, Edward C. *The Origins of Southern Sharecropping*. Philadelphia: Temple University Press, 1993.

Royster, Jacqueline Jones, ed. *Southern Horrors and Other Writings: The Anti-lynching Campaigns of Ida B. Wells, 1892–1900*. Boston: Bedford, 1997.

Saville, Julie. *The Work of Reconstruction: From Slave to Wage Labor in South Carolina, 1860–1870*. New York: Cambridge University Press, 1994.

Schechter, Patricia A. *Ida B. Wells-Barnett and American Reform, 1880–1930*. Chapel Hill: University of North Carolina Press, 2001.

Scheper-Hughes, Nancy. "Small Wars and Invisible Genocides." *Social Science Medicine* 43, no. 5 (1996): 889–900.

Scheper-Hughes, Nancy, and Philippe Bourgois. "Introduction: Making Sense of Violence." In *Violence in War and Peace: An Anthology*, edited by Nancy Scheper-Hughes and Philippe Bourgois, 1–31. Malden, MA: Blackwell, 2004.

Schneider, Mark Robert. *"We Return Fighting": The Civil Rights Movement in the Jazz Age*. Boston: Northeastern University Press, 2002.

Scott, Emmett J. "Letters of Negro Migrants of 1916–1918." *Journal of Negro History* 4, no. 3 (July 1919): 290–340.

———. "More Letters of Negro Migrants of 1916–1918." *Journal of Negro History* 4, no. 4 (October 1919): 412–465.

Scott, James C. *Domination and the Arts of Resistance: Hidden Transcripts*. New Haven: Yale University Press, 1990.

Senechal, Roberta. *The Sociogenesis of a Race Riot: Springfield, Illinois, in 1908*. Urbana: University of Illinois Press, 1990.

Shapiro, Herbert. *White Violence and Black Response: From Reconstruction to Montgomery*. Amherst: University of Massachusetts Press, 1988.

Shaw, Stephanie J. *What a Woman Ought to Be and Do: Black Professional Women Workers during the Jim Crow Era*. Chicago: University of Chicago Press, 1995.

Smith, J. Douglas. *Managing White Supremacy: Race, Politics, and Citizenship in Jim Crow Virginia*. Chapel Hill: University of North Carolina Press, 2002.

Smith, Merril D. *Sex without Consent: Rape and Sexual Coercion in America*. New York: NYU Press, 2002.

Smith, Shawn Michelle. *Photography on the Color Line: W. E. B. Du Bois, Race, and Visual Culture*. Durham: Duke University Press, 2004.

Sommerville, Diane Miller. *Rape and Race in the Nineteenth-Century South*. Chapel Hill: University of North Carolina Press, 2004.

Squires, Catherine R. "Rethinking the Black Public Sphere: An Alternative Vocabulary for Multiple Public Spheres." *Communication Theory* 12, no. 4 (November 2002): 446–468.

Stein, Judith. *The World of Marcus Garvey: Race and Class in Modern Society*. Baton Rouge: Louisiana State University Press, 1991.

Stepto, Robert B. "Narration, Authentication, and Authorial Control in Frederick Douglass' *Narrative* of 1845." In *Narrative of the Life of Frederick Douglass, an American Slave, Written by Himself: A Norton Critical Edition*, edited by William L. Andrews and William S. McFeely, 146–157. New York: Norton, 1997.

Stockley, Grif. *Blood in Their Eye: The Elaine Race Massacres of 1919*. Fayetteville: University of Arkansas Press, 2001.

Suarez-Orozco, Marcelo M. "Speaking of the Unspeakable: Toward a Psycho-Social Understanding of Responses to Terror." *Ethos* 18, no. 3 (1990): 353–383.

———. "The Treatment of Children in the 'Dirty War': Ideology, State Terrorism, and the Abuse of Children in Argentina." In *Violence in War and Peace: An Anthology*, edited by Nancy Scheper-Hughes and Philippe Bourgois, 378–388. Malden, MA: Blackwell, 2004.

Sullivan, Patricia A. *Lift Every Voice: The NAACP and the Making of the Civil Rights Movement*. New York: New Press, 2009.

Summers, Martin. *Manliness and Its Discontents: The Black Middle Class and the Transformation of Masculinity, 1900–1930*. Chapel Hill: University of North Carolina Press, 2004.

Sussman, Leila A. *Dear FDR: A Study of Political Letter-Writing*. Totowa, NJ: Bedminster, 1963.

Taft, William Howard. "President Taft denounces lynching: tells representative Negro gathering it is cowardly mob murder: explains the Constitution as the defender of human liberties, and demands respect for the Courts, that these liberties be maintained: advocates higher education for Negroes, that the race may demonstrate its known high ideals." Microform. Washington, DC: Allied Printing Trades Council, 1912.

Taussig, Michael T. "Culture of Terror—Space of Death: Roger Casement's Putumayo Report and the Explanation of Torture." In *Violence: A Reader*, edited by Catherine Besteman, 211–243. New York: NYU Press, 2002.

———. *The Nervous System*. New York: Routledge, 1992.

Thornbrough, Emma Lou. "The National Afro-American League, 1887–1908." *Journal of Southern History* 27, no. 4 (November 1961): 494–512.

Tolnay, Stewart E., and E. M. Beck. *A Festival of Violence: An Analysis of Southern Lynchings, 1882–1930*. Urbana: University of Illinois Press, 1995.

Trelease, Allen W. *White Terror: The Ku Klux Klan Conspiracy and Southern Reconstruction*. New York: Harper and Row, 1971.

Trezise, Thomas. "Between History and Psychoanalysis: A Case Study in the Reception of Holocaust Testimony." *History and Memory* 20, no. 1 (2008): 7–47.

Trouillot, Michel-Rolph. *Silencing the Past: Power in the Production of History*. Boston: Beacon, 1995.

Tuttle, William L. "Violence in a 'Heathen' Land: The Longview Race Riot of 1919." *Phylon* 33, no. 4 (1972): 324–333.

Tyson, Timothy B. *Radio Free Dixie: Robert F. Williams and the Roots of Black Power*. Chapel Hill: University of North Carolina Press, 1999.

U.S. Circuit Court, Fourth Circuit. *Proceedings of the Ku Klux Trials at Columbia, S.C. in the United States Circuit Court, November Term, 1871*. Columbia, SC: Republican Printing Company, State Printers, 1872.

U.S. Congress. *Joint Select Committee to Inquire into the Condition of Affairs in the Late Insurrectionary States: Georgia, Volumes I and II*. Washington, DC: Government Printing Office, 1872. Reprint, New York: AMS Press, 1969.

———. *Joint Select Committee to Inquire into the Condition of Affairs in the Late Insurrectionary States: Miscellaneous and Florida*. Washington, DC: Government Printing Office, 1872. Reprint, New York: AMS Press, 1969.

———. *Joint Select Committee to Inquire into the Condition of Affairs in the Late Insurrectionary States: Mississippi*. Washington, DC: Government Printing Office, 1872. Reprint, New York: AMS Press, 1969.

U.S. Congress, Senate. *Inquiry into the Alleged Frauds in the Late Elections*. Senate Report 855. In Senate Reports, vol. 2. 45th Cong., 3d sess. Washington, DC, 1878–1879.

———. *Report and Testimony of the Select Committee of the United States Senate to Investigate the Causes of the Removal of the Negroes from the Southern States to the Northern States*. 3 vols. Senate Report 693. 46th Cong., 2d sess. Washington, DC: Government Printing Office, 1880.

———. *Select Committee to Investigate Alleged Outrages in the Southern States by the Select Committee of the Senate*. Washington, DC: Government Printing Office, 1871.
Vandal, Gilles. *Rethinking Southern Violence: Homocides in Post–Civil War Louisiana, 1866–1884*. Columbus: Ohio State University Press, 2000.
Vandiver, Margaret. *Lethal Punishment: Lynchings and Legal Executions in the South*. New Brunswick: Rutgers University Press, 2006.
Waldrep, Christopher R. *African Americans Confront Lynching: Strategies of Resistance from the Civil War to the Civil Rights Era*. Lanham, MD: Rowman and Littlefield, 2009.
———. *The Many Faces of Judge Lynch: Extralegal Violence and Punishment in America*. New York: Palgrave Macmillan, 2002.
———. "'Raw, Quivering Flesh': John G. Cashman's 'Pornographic' Constitutionalism Designed to Produce an 'Aversion and Detestation,' 1883–1904." *American Nineteenth Century History* 6, no. 3 (2005): 295–322.
Waskow, Arthur I. *From Race Riot to Sit-In, 1919 and the 1960s: A Study in the Connections between Conflict and Violence*. Gloucester, MA: Peter Smith, 1975.
Webb, Clive. "Lynching of Sicilian Immigrants in the American South." *American Nineteenth Century History* 3, no. 1 (Spring 2002): 45–76.
Wells-Barnett, Ida B. "Booker T. Washington and His Critics." *World Today* 6 (April 1904): 521.
———. *Crusade for Justice: The Autobiography of Ida B. Wells*. Edited by Alfreda M. Duster. Chicago: University of Chicago Press, 1970.
———. *On Lynchings: "Southern Horrors," "A Red Record," and "Mob Rule in New Orleans."* New York: Arno, 1969. Reprint, Salem NH: Ayer, 1991.
Wendt, Simon. *The Spirit and the Shotgun: Armed Resistance and the Struggle for Civil Rights*. Gainesville: University Press of Florida, 2007.
Wexler, Laura. *Fire in a Canebrake: The Last Mass Lynching in America*. New York: Simon and Schuster, 2004.
White, Deborah Gray. *Too Heavy a Load: Black Women in Defense of Themselves, 1894–1994*. New York: Norton, 1999.
White, Walter F. *How Far the Promised Land?* New York: Viking, 1955.
———. *A Man Called White: The Autobiography of Walter White*. New York: Viking, 1948.
Wideman, John Edgar. "Charles Chesnutt and the WPA Narratives: The Oral and Literate Roots." In *The Slave's Narrative*, edited by Charles T. Davis and Henry Louis Gates, Jr., 59–78. New York: Oxford University Press, 1991.
Wilkerson, Isabel. *The Warmth of Other Suns: The Epic Story of America's Great Migration*. New York: Random House, 2010.
Williams, Lee E. *Anatomy of Four Race Riots: Racial Conflict in Knoxville, Elaine (Arkansas), Tulsa, and Chicago, 1919–1921*. Hattiesburg: University Press of Mississippi, 1972.
Williams, Lou Faulkner. *The Great South Carolina Ku Klux Klan Trials, 1871–1872*. Athens: University of Georgia Press, 1996.
Williamson, Joel. *The Crucible of Race: Black-White Relations in the American South since Emancipation*. New York: Oxford University Press, 1984.
Wood, Amy L. "Lynching Photography and the Visual Reproduction of White Supremacy." *American Nineteenth Century History* 6, no. 3 (September 2005): 373–399.

———. *Lynching and Spectacle: Witnessing Racial Violence in America, 1890–1940*. Chapel Hill: University of North Carolina Press, 2009.

Woodruff, Nan Elizabeth. *American Congo: The African American Freedom Struggle in the Delta*. Cambridge: Harvard University Press, 2003.

Woodward, C. Vann. *The Strange Career of Jim Crow*. New York: Oxford University Press, 1966.

Wright, George C. *Racial Violence in Kentucky, 1865–1940: Lynching, Mob Rule, and "Legal Lynchings."* Baton Rouge: Louisiana State University Press, 1996.

Wright, Richard. "Ethics of Living Jim Crow: An Autobiographical Sketch." In *American Stuff: An Anthology of Prose and Verse by Members of the Federal Writers' Project*, edited by the Federal Writers' Project, 39–52. New York: Viking, 1937.

Zangrando, Robert L. *The NAACP Crusade against Lynching, 1909–1950*. Philadelphia: Temple University Press, 1980.

Index

About the Author

KIDADA E. WILLIAMS is an assistant professor of African American history at Wayne State University.